Thomas Torrance, China and the Qiang:

Life in early 20th century Chengdu and among the Qiang of Western Sichuan

Rachel Meakin

British Library Cataloguing in Publication Data:
a catalogue record for this publication
is available from the British Library

ISBN 978-1-912052-80-6

Typeset in 11pt Minion Pro at Haddington, Scotland

Printed by Short Run Press, Exeter

Front cover photos: Thomas Torrance c.1896; Thomas Torrance
c.1928; his Qiang friend and co-worker, Gou Pinsan, c.1934
Back cover photo: Unlocking a Qiang door
All four photos are from the Thomas F. Torrance Manuscript
Collection, Princeton Theological Seminary Library

Contents

Preface

In 2012 I had the privilege of accompanying David Torrance and his daughter Grace for part of David's first visit to China since his family's hurried departure in 1927, when he was just two. The trip included a rediscovery of places in the city of Chengdu, Thomas Torrance's home for nearly forty years, as well a visit to some of the Qiang villages with which Torrance had been so familiar.

Towards the end of the trip David asked if I would consider writing a biography of his father. At the time I was busy with research into the history of the Qiang people, focusing on Chinese references to the Qiang between the Han and Tang periods (206 BC – AD 907), but the idea of a biography stayed in my mind and David and I kept in touch.

In 2018 I had an opportunity to see the Thomas Torrance Papers at Yale Divinity School Library as well as Torrance's correspondence, photos, and other memorabilia within the Thomas F. Torrance Manuscript Collection at Princeton Theological Seminary Library. Since then this biography has gradually taken shape and I am infinitely grateful that Thomas Torrance overcame the temptation to consign his letters and papers to the furnace before leaving China, having realised that they might one day be of value.

Researching this book has been a fascinating process, not only delving into the tumultuous historical backdrop to Torrance's years in China but also following his journey from junior missionary with the China Inland Mission to managing the work of the American Bible Society in Sichuan Province, and the growth of his research and mission work among the Qiang people of northwestern Sichuan. It has been particularly interesting to observe the development of his thinking with regard to Qiang religious practices and their origins, which culminated in his conclusion that people known by the Chinese as 'Qiang' had reached China from the Middle East some time during the Eastern Zhou period (770-256 BC). Although this view has proved somewhat controversial, Torrance's research on the Qiang people, and more generally on the history and archaeology of Sichuan, is still of value and several of his works have been translated into Chinese.

During my own years of studying Chinese and teaching English in China, interspersed with a season studying Social Anthropology at London's School of Oriental and African Studies, I was fortunate to spend over two years teaching in the Qiang region. This was sadly curtailed by the Wenchuan earthquake of May 2008, which turned a spotlight on the Qiang people and resulted in increased research into their history and culture.

This book weaves a story of many threads, reflecting the diversity of Torrance's own interests and experiences and the rapidly changing political environment in which he lived. His keen interest in politics led to good relations with some of Sichuan's military leaders and his letters provide a rare window on Sichuan in the late Qing and Republican periods.

My hope is that this story will appeal to general lovers of biographies but also to anyone with an interest in early twentieth century Chinese history, in anthropology, in all things Chinese, in the history of Christian mission in China, or in the Qiang as one of China's ethnic groups today but also as a people with an intriguing past.

Rachel Meakin
August 2023

Abbreviations

Missionary Societies

ABS: American Bible Society
B&FBS: British & Foreign Bible Society
CIM: China Inland Mission
CMM: Canadian Methodist Mission
CMS: Church Missionary Society

Publications

BSR: Bible Society Record
JNCBRAS: Journal of the North China Branch of the Royal Asiatic Society
JWCBRS: Journal of the West China Border Research Society
WCMN: West China Missionary News

Universities

WCUU: West China Union University (Chengdu)
SOAS: School of Oriental and African Studies, University of London

Reader's Notes

Illustrations

Unless otherwise indicated, all photos are from the Torrance family photo albums stored in The Thomas F. Torrance Manuscript Collection, Special Collections, Princeton Theological Seminary Library.

Bible versions

Unless otherwise indicated, all Scripture quotations are taken from the (NASB®) New American Standard Bible®, Copyright © 1960, 1971, 1977, 1995, 2020 by The Lockman Foundation. Used by permission. All rights reserved. www.lockman.org.

Pronunciation

'Qi' is pronounced similarly to 'chee' so Qiang sounds similar to 'Chee-ang'. In Torrance's day the term 'Qiang' was usually written 'Ch'iang' or occasionally 'Chiang'.

Many Chinese names contain the syllable 'xi', which is pronounced somewhere between 'shee' and 'see'. For example, the name of Deng Xihou, one of the Sichuan generals, would be pronounced similarly to Deng Shee-hou.

Google Earth

A 3D look at Weizhou or Wenchuan County in Google Earth will give the reader a good overview of the terrain and locations visited by Torrance on his summer trips to the Qiang region.

Geographical name changes

In Torrance's day the spelling of place names varied, for example 'Chentu' and 'Chengtu' for today's city of Chengdu. Modern equivalents have generally been used in the text except in quotations where the old spelling is easily understood, e.g. Szechwan for today's Sichuan.

Footnotes indicate where earlier spellings in quotations have been replaced by modern pinyin.

Some names have changed since Torrance's day. In most cases the modern equivalent has been used in the text. Below is a list of old names followed by their current names.

> Chefoo – Yantai
> Guanxian – Dujiangyan
> Kiating – Leshan
> Lifan Town – Xuecheng
> Maozhou – Maoxian
> Meizhou – Meishan
> Qiongzhou – Qionglai
> Suifu – Yibin
> T'o River - Zagunao River
> Tsayto – Qiangfeng
> Weizhou – still in use but also referred to as Wenchuan
>   County Town or just Wenchuan
> Wenchuan – Miansi
> Yazhou – Ya'an
> Zagunao – Lixian county town

In Torrance's day, Lifan was an administrative district which covered today's Li County (Lixian) but also extended east to the town of Weizhou and northwest into today's Ma'erkang County and the western part of Heishui County. It was administered from Lifan Town, today's Xuecheng. In the text Lifan applies to the district and Xuecheng to the town.

Acknowledgements

I am deeply grateful for the encouragement David Torrance and his family have given me in this process, including their helpful reading of the manuscript.

I am also thankful for the warm assistance I received from Joan Duffy in the Special Collections, Yale Divinity School Library and from Kenneth Henke in the Special Collections, Princeton Theological Seminary Library.

I am grateful to Professor Iain Torrance for permission to photocopy material at Princeton pertaining to his grandfather. SOAS Library staff in London have also been very helpful with requests for off-site and difficult-to-find material.

I am forever indebted to my own family and friends without whose support this book would truly never have seen the light of day: Hilary (for her many insightful comments), Ann, Alan, Alison, Pete and Karen, Kristi, Catherine, Jenny, Helen, and many others along the way.

And finally, heartfelt thanks to Jock Stein and Handsel Press for bringing this project to fruition.

MAP OF SICHUAN
(Dotted line indicates
1997 separation of
Chongqing
from Sichuan)

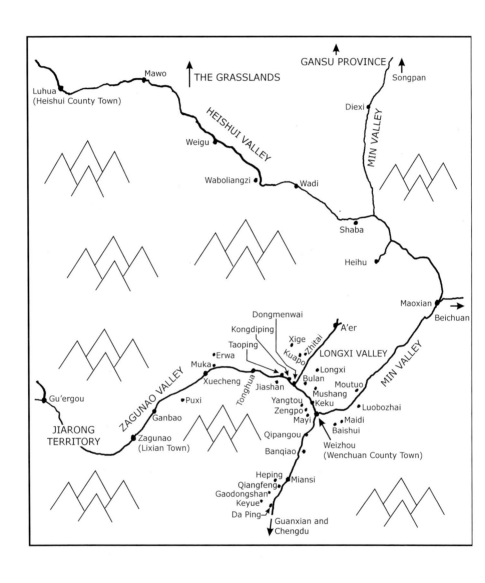

MAP OF PLACES VISITED BY TORRANCE
ON HIS SUMMER TRIPS TO THE QIANG

PART ONE

Chapter 1

Small Beginnings

Thomas Torrance was born on March 12, 1871, five months before the birth of China's Guangxu Emperor, the penultimate ruler of the Qing dynasty. Unlike Guangxu, who died young and in dubious circumstances, Torrance would live to see China change almost beyond recognition as the Qing dynasty collapsed, provincial warlords competed for power, and China struggled to find her post-imperial identity.

Born at Muirhead Farm, Harthill, in the rural, coal mining region of Shotts in the Scottish lowlands, Torrance's childhood was a far cry from the intrigues of the Qing court. His father, Thomas Forsyth Torrance, was a small dairy farmer and a devout Presbyterian, as reflected in the sparsely furnished family home which, nonetheless, housed a collection of theological books. On Sundays young Thomas would don his kilt and walk the four miles with his brother and three sisters to the Kirk of Shotts, famed across Scotland for its seventeenth century Christian revival.

Despite their farming background, neither Thomas nor his younger brother Jimmy followed the family tradition. Jimmy would become a successful joiner and builder whilst Thomas left school at fourteen and moved to the town of Hamilton as an apprentice to a relative by the name of James Paul – 'Draper, Clothier, Milliner and Dressmaker' – at the London House on Quarry Street.

It was a good move for Thomas, who showed a marked flair for business. By the time he was eighteen he had moved into management, entrusted with handling all aspects of the business and rewarded for his integrity and skill with full responsibility for the cash department. In an 1892 reference James Paul was unstinting in his praise for Thomas's achievements: 'I may say in conclusion that he has made a very small business into a very considerable one and that having acted as buyer he has shown very great care and discrimination in this important department.'[1]

---

1   Sept 28, 1892, written by James Paul. The destination of the reference is not given. Paul simply notes that Torrance is leaving him 'for another sphere of work'.

Although Torrance remained committed throughout his life to the Church of Scotland, while still a teenager he had a personal experience of Christian conversion through contact with Revd R. Dykes Shaw, minister of a nearby Free Church, and this opened him up to a wider interdenominational sphere. He was also deeply impacted by stories of Scottish missionary explorer, David Livingstone, who was born in nearby Blantyre and died two years after Torrance was born. At the age of ten, Livingstone had started working long hours in a cotton mill but managed, under the influence of his devout and widely-read father, to educate himself and then support himself through medical, theological, and botanical studies before sailing for Africa with the London Missionary Society.

YOUNG THOMAS TORRANCE

Torrance's own background was less harsh but it is easy to imagine him being inspired by Livingstone as he continued to educate himself alongside his work at the drapery. In 1891, aged twenty, he shared with his parents his desire to go overseas as a missionary but the response was disappointing. Had he wanted to train as a Church of

Back L-R: Thomas, Katie, Jimmy
Front: Maggie, Anne (nee Brownlie), Thomas, Annie

Scotland minister they would gladly have offered their support but the thought of losing him to foreign missions was a step too far. With what the Chinese would applaud as filial piety, he agreed to wait another year and see if the sense of calling was still in his heart. In July 1892, with the calling still strong, he wrote from Hamilton no longer seeking his parents' permission but informing them that he would be starting missionary training in October. The burden on his soul for those with 'no one to tell them of a Saviour' had increased rather than diminished and he was sure this was God's guiding.[2] 'Think not then I want to leave you, or pain you, or harm you in any way,' he wrote. 'It will be a painful wrench, but we will get paid for it an hundredfold more.' From a further comment in the letter it seems that his father was the stronger opponent, having thought him 'daft' for entertaining such notions.

Lacking his parents' financial support but with his savings and the benefit of his own financial acumen, Torrance enrolled at Hulme Cliff College, an evangelical training school in Derbyshire established by Henry Grattan Guinness. His achievements there illustrate how diligently he had studied on his own in Hamilton and how seriously he

2   Thomas Torrance to his parents, July 4, 1892.

then applied himself to his college studies. His results at the end of 1892-1893 show a 77% average score, with his weakest subjects Exegetics (55%) and Greek (66%), and Bible Study (91%) his strongest. By his final exams in May-June 1894 his average had increased to 93% with striking improvement in Exegetics (99%) and Greek (93%) and similarly high achievements in theism, psychology, and logic. Other subjects covered included English grammar, moral science, and theology.

In January 1894 Torrance called on James Paul for a further reference, who once again praised his managerial skills as well as his great abundance of zeal and energy, making it clear that Torrance had 'relinquished a good situation and excellent prospects' to pursue his missionary calling.[3]

That autumn, Torrance moved down to Bow in London for a year of medical studies at Livingstone College, established the previous year by Charles Harford-Battersby and fittingly named after David Livingstone. The training, which was to prove invaluable again and again, was designed to equip missionaries with basic medical knowledge for use on the mission field, both for the locals and in the care of their own families. Some rough notes written by Torrance probably date to this period of study and would be put to good use: 'Opium. Patient falls into heavy sleep. Pupils contracted, breathing stertorous. Wash out stomach with potassium permanganate or emetic. Give hot coffee. Smelling salts cautiously.'[4]

These college years were a rich time for Torrance, meeting people of different backgrounds and listening to inspirational Christian speakers. Men of faith like Charles Spurgeon, George Muller, and D. L. Moody were famous names of the day and people were still talking about six Cambridge graduates who had made headlines in 1885 when they renounced illustrious career prospects and set sail for China with the China Inland Mission (CIM). Both Torrance's college principals – Grattan Guinness and Harford-Battersby – were friends of Hudson Taylor, who had founded the CIM in 1865, and it was to the CIM that Torrance applied for service in China.

From the moors of Shotts and the business in Hamilton, to Derbyshire and then to London, Torrance's world was widening with each step. On November 22, 1895, after some final missionary training with the CIM, the young Scotsman boarded the SS *Australia* and set sail for Shanghai, along with Fawcett Olsen, another new missionary,

3   James Paul, Jan 9, 1894.
4   Written on the back of an 1892 document used as scrap paper.

who would become a faithful and much-needed friend in some of the challenges that lay ahead.

To China, 1895

Some challenges facing Torrance were predictable. He was travelling thousands of miles around the world from one of the most advanced industrialised nations of that era to a culturally alien country in whose language he could not yet converse. Sights and sounds, smells and tastes, dress and etiquette, ways of government, and even modes of transport – all would be completely new.

Less predictable was the volatile political environment. China in the late 1800s was facing troubles on every front. Dissatisfaction with the Manchu rulers of the Qing dynasty was rife among the majority Han people, and the anti-Manchu Taiping rebellion, which had spread out from southern China in the mid-1800s, had seriously challenged the Qing government and left a staggering twenty million Chinese dead.

The encroachment of foreign powers on Chinese territory was also causing widespread anxiety. Chinese opposition to British opium imports from India had sparked the first Opium War of 1839-42 which had concluded with the Treaty of Nanjing, resulting in the cessation of Hong Kong to Britain and the allocation of Xiamen, Fuzhou, Ningbo, and Shanghai as treaty ports on the mainland, where foreigners could reside and trade. The treaty also granted extraterritoriality to British subjects (later granted to other nations, including France, Russia, the US, and Japan), exempting them from China's legal system and giving them trading privileges not accorded to the Chinese themselves, something which incensed many Chinese and created considerable anti-foreign resentment. To add insult to injury, the trade in opium had continued and China was treaty-bound to recompense British financial losses during the war – not only the cost of the war itself but also the cost of the opium confiscated and destroyed by the Chinese.

Torrance's first taste of China was one of these treaty ports. On January 1, 1896, after nearly six weeks at sea, the *SS Australia* docked in the bustling, cosmopolitan city of Shanghai, where the large British-dominated International Settlement had its own self-governing Shanghai Municipal Council and a foreign-run municipal police force. Imposing Western-style buildings, still visible today on the Bund, contrasted with traditional Chinese architecture, and foreign department stores, clubs, and English language newspapers all contributed to a sense of familiarity for many in the foreign community there.

Torrance's destination was the CIM headquarters on Wusong Road, a large compound in the Hongkou area of the International Settlement which included offices, accommodation for missionaries in transit, a small hospital, and a shipping and supplies warehouse. Here he was initiated into the mysteries of Chinese dress: a full-length gown with long wide sleeves, flat shoes with upward-pointing toes (the right indistinguishable from the left), and a cap with a false plait or queue, in keeping with the Manchu custom of the time, which some missionaries replaced by growing their own. Any who found this transition awkward were assured that with 'the exercise of patience and observation these initial difficulties will, however, soon be mastered, and a measure of freedom and grace of movement will in most cases appear in due time.'[5]

By the time Torrance arrived some missionaries had begun to question the necessity of Chinese dress and the issue was under discussion by the CIM Council but in 1896 it was still required. Torrance was also provided with his own Chinese bedding and other travel necessities, as well as Chinese language study books.

The CIM were keen to move missionaries on before they got used to the comforts and cosmopolitanism of Shanghai and after a few days Torrance and Olsen set off on the 300-mile journey inland to the CIM men's training centre at Anqing in Anhui Province for some language study and acculturation. In May they learned that they had been assigned to Chengdu, the capital of the remote, mountain-ringed province of Sichuan in West China, where the CIM had had a presence since 1881. Viewed as a relatively peaceful location, several other missions also had their provincial headquarters there, including the Canadian Methodist Mission, the American Methodist Episcopal Mission, the Church Missionary Society, and the American Baptist Missionary Union.[6] Nonetheless, Torrance's heart may have skipped a beat or two when he learned of his destination, not because of the remoteness but because events in Sichuan the previous year had deeply shaken Chengdu's small foreign community.

On June 1, 1895, the CIM headquarters in Shanghai had received a shocking telegram: 'Riot Ch'en-tu, all Missions destroyed. Friends in yamen.'[7] More detail followed in a letter from Joshua Vale, Torrance's future superintendent in Chengdu, writing from the safety of the

---

5   J. F. Broumton. 'A Busy Centre: Shanghai'. *China's Millions*, 1896, p52.

6   This became the American Baptist Foreign Mission Society in 1910.

7   C. T. Fishe. 'The Riots in Si-ch'uen'. *Millions*, 1895, p125.

governor's yamen. 'A very sad and disastrous riot took place here on 28th and 29th [May], in which all Protestant and R.C. houses, chapels, dispensaries, etc., were destroyed. We all – eighteen missionaries and eleven children – got here safely last night . . . The city is still in a very unsettled state. We all are void of this world's goods.'[8]

Chengdu had been crowded with Chinese celebrating the annual Dragon Boat festival and, for reasons which would become clear, a disturbance had broken out with people throwing stones and driving the Canadian missionaries from their compound. Running to the military barracks nearby, the Canadians found to their dismay that the soldiers were in sympathy with the crowd and the only choice left was to flee up on to the city wall, from where they watched their mission go up in flames. They eventually made it to the CIM premises but over the next couple of days the crowds were out in force again, buildings were ransacked and burned, and by May 30, thanks to the assistance of some friendly Chinese, the foreigners were packed into three small rooms at the yamen, where they spent ten cramped days. Eventually sufficient calm was restored for them to be escorted out of Chengdu and ferried downstream to the treaty port of Chongqing and the reassurance of a British consular presence.

Torrance in local dress

A June 3 account by Adam Grainger revealed some of the reasons for the rioting. At his CIM station in Guanxian, northwest of Chengdu, a threatening crowd had gathered outside. Keeping his composure Grainger had 'invited them to see for themselves if the stories brought from Ch'en-tu about men's bones and children's skulls were true or false, hoping that they would quietly look and go.'[9] Eventually the local mandarin arrived and reassured the crowd that the Graingers 'were

8   Joshua Vale to the CIM office in Shanghai, May 13, 1895. *Millions*, 1895, p126.
9   Ibid.

not Japanese but English, and had come here to do good.'[10] Both the Japanese reference and the rumour about bones were linked to placards which had appeared on the streets of Chengdu, one warning people that foreigners were kidnapping small children (a rumour based to some extent on Chinese suspicion of Western medicine and mistrust of the new Canadian hospital) and another blaming the English, French, and Americans for standing idly by while Japan usurped Chinese territory in the Sino-Japanese war of 1894-95.

The Japanese issue was a fresh, very real wound for the Chinese, in which other nations were seen as complicit. The war had ostensibly been a battle for control of Korea but Japan was set on expansion and had her eye on China's natural resources to aid her rapid industrialisation and modernisation. China's own lack of modernisation was only too evident in the war which, despite her greater human resources, resulted in a humiliating defeat. The Shimonoseki Treaty at the conclusion of the war was negotiated by the British at the request of the Chinese. The British initially suggested two terms for peace: that China pay a war indemnity to Japan and that Korea become a protectorate under the international powers. Japan refused these terms and marched into Liaodong in northeastern China. By April 1895 the Qing government was terrified that Japan would march on Beijing and bring down the dynasty. With no bargaining power left they yielded to Japan's excessive demands: new trading privileges, the handing over of Taiwan, the Pescadores, and the Liaodong Peninsula, and a huge war indemnity of 200 million taels. Although Russia, France, and Germany successfully intervened to block the cessation of Liaodong, their intervention resulted in the addition of 30 million taels to the already excessive Japanese indemnity.[11]

Before the war China had been almost debt free but she was now forced to borrow to pay the indemnity, placing her once again in debt to the West and adding interest to the already crippling burden. In return for the loan the West requested guarantees in the form of further trading concessions including mines, natural resources, import goods, and railways. A Chinese perspective on the pain and humiliation of this period is expressed in Han Suyin's autobiographical work, *The Crippled Tree*, through the words of her uncle, a prosperous Chengdu merchant: 'Then started the terrible years, the years of accelerated wholesale, headlong plunder. China's weakness exposed, the Powers rallied to dismember the foundering land. Britain took control of the

---

10   Ibid.
11   Jung Chang. *Empress Dowager Cixi: The Concubine Who Launched Modern China*. Vintage Publishing. Kindle Edition.

whole of the Great River basin, from Shanghai to Szechuan . . . Russia took Manchuria and Mongolia as her dependencies, building railways there to move her troops into China. France again marshalled her forces for an invasion of Yunnan . . . Germany . . . seized the province of Shandong.'[12] Aware of extensive European colonialism in other nations, there were even those who feared that Westerners would eventually treat the Chinese as African slaves had been treated.[13] This was the China to which Torrance had come and just a few years later the CIM would feel the full force of the Chinese backlash.

In a bid to pour oil on troubled waters, Hudson Taylor strongly advised against any militant compensation demands for CIM losses in the May riots, which had affected several stations in Sichuan. In a letter to the editor of *The Chinese Recorder*, he highlighted the difficult position of missionaries in relation to the policies of their own governments, with which they didn't always agree, and made his position clear regarding the compensation:

> It is a serious question in my mind whether our work suffers most or gains by the interference of our government in such cases as Chengtu . . . It is true that pecuniary compensation may be obtained, and the missionaries reinstated . . . but what of the effect of all this? . . . Is it not that the missionary, if more dreaded, is also more disliked? . . . Must not the effect of appeals necessarily strengthen the belief of the literati that missions are a political agency designed, together with opium, to facilitate the absorption of China by foreign Powers?[14]

Not all foreigners shared Taylor's view but it was welcomed by the Chinese and although it would be November 1895 before Joshua Vale was able to return to Chengdu and begin the CIM restoration, he was well-received by the Chinese officials and found a much less hostile environment.

With the Chengdu property still undergoing reconstruction, Torrance and Olsen were sent to the CIM station at Leshan, a small town eighty miles south of Chengdu, overlooked by a giant Tang dynasty cliff-face Buddha. Although the mission station in Leshan had been looted and damaged, the hostility had come mainly from student

12   Han Suyin. *The Crippled Tree*. Triad/Panther Books. 1984, p82.
13   Ibid., p95.
14   Written Nov 17, 1895. In A. J. Broomhall. *It is not Death to Die!* (Book 7 of *Hudson Taylor & China's Open Century*). Hodder & Stoughton and the Overseas Missionary Fellowship. 1989, p227.

rioters, and after sheltering at the local yamen for several weeks the missionaries there had returned home with an official escort of sedan chairs draped with red silk. As they reached the mission station firecrackers were set off in their honour and their Chinese neighbours, who had helped them flee the rioters, gave them a warm welcome. It was a much better first taste of Sichuan for Torrance and Olsen than Chengdu, where hostilities had been much more widespread.

The rebuilding in Chengdu took time. In April 1896 Vale and his new wife, Annie, had a visit from the English traveller and author, Isabella Bird. She recorded staying with them at a 'palatial residence' where they had been housed by the Viceroy since the 'complete destruction of the mission premises in the riots, a destruction which was also complete in the case of the houses and hospitals of the various other missions, even the bricks of which the buildings were constructed being carried away.'[15]

Despite the destruction, Isabella Bird was impressed with Chengdu and its 14-mile long, 35-foot high wall, topped with a broad promenade. Compared to Beijing she found the city neat and clean, with wide paved streets and a network of rivers and canals crowded with junks and sampans, and she was particularly struck by the shops with their unusually lavish displays by Chinese standards, especially those selling jewellery and rich silk brocades. There were few foreign goods in evidence and she could see no trace of the European influence found in eastern Chinese cities, noting instead the Tibetan musk, furs, and rhubarb in the markets and the 'strange, wild figures of the trading Tibetans in the streets'.[16]

Although Torrance arrived in Chengdu after Isabella's departure and there is no record of him making her acquaintance, there is little doubt that he would have heard of her visit from Vale, and her description of the next stretch of her journey may well have been his earliest indirect encounter with the region inhabited by the Qiang people, with whom he was to become so familiar. Going west from Chengdu across the plain to Guanxian, Isabella and her party followed the Min River up to today's Qiang region of Wenchuan and then turned westwards through Lixian towards Ma'erkang. On the road between the towns of Miansi and Weizhou she began to see evidence of the 'Barbarians' on the hills: 'Singular dwellings made their appearance, crowning hilltops

15   Isabella Bird, *The Yangtze Valley and Beyond*. John Murray. 1899, p352.
16   Ibid., p356.

or poised on ledges – isolated or in clusters. . . . Before long such houses aggregated themselves into villages on great heights, and without any apparent means of access, though that they were inhabited was obvious from the patches of cultivation about them. Among them appear tall towers, sometimes to the number of seven; they are picturesque and fantastic beyond all imagination.'[17]

Once the new CIM premises were ready, Torrance and Olsen moved to live with the Vales in Chengdu, where they continued with language study and got involved with as much mission work as their basic Chinese skills would allow. Learning the language was a joy to some missionaries and a Herculean task to others. In April 1896 the CIM China Council reported that only sixteen of forty-nine probationers had passed the required language examinations. It became such an issue that in 1900 there was a discussion in Council about the difficulties missionaries had 'to keep up the study of the language, because of frequent headaches etc., indicating, apparently, a lack of mental capacity or brain power'. Perhaps this also had something to do with bad lighting or a need for glasses but either way it was decided that language study for future candidates should be started back in Britain to test their 'power of application, memory and articulation'.[18]

Torrance found the language challenging but had the application and ability to do well. In December 1897 he wrote to friends at home with great relief: 'The bulk of the work is over, and I assure you I am glad. You can imagine what it is – the grinding away at a language, 6 months, a year, 18 months and after all, be unable to follow the thread of a conversation. . . . I am far from being proficient even yet, it will be another year at the very least before that stage is reached, but the satisfaction is mine to know that the worst is over.'[19] Writing back then with the optimism of youth, he would continue to have a tutor for some time but eventually achieved a rare degree of fluency. Another missionary, leaving Chengdu after ten years, noted that his failure to attain any real fluency in Chinese had been a hard burden to bear and had left him feeling excluded from Chinese society.[20]

---

17   Ibid., p377.
18   CIM China Council Minutes, Oct 3 and Dec 10, 1900. SOAS Archive and Special Collections, CIM/01/03/2.
19   TT newsletter, Dec 1897.
20   Harold G. Anderson. 'Chengtu – A Retrospect'. *West China Missionary News* (WCMN), Oct 1938, p363.

Travelling with more experienced missionaries to some of the outlying districts around Chengdu provided good language practice. In the cold and damp of February 1897, after just over a year in China, Torrance went south by boat to the town of Meishan where his companion, Mr Cormack, was to conduct the wedding of a Christian Chinese couple. Revealing his keen cultural interest, Torrance spent two precious pages of his December 1897 newsletter digressing from the Christian wedding to tell his readers of traditional Chinese marriage arrangements between a thirteen-year-old boy and a twelve-year-old girl: of the mediator helping to arrange the match; the importance of auspicious days in the process; the good and bad omens which hindered or assisted the actual union five years later; the wedding itself with musicians and drummers; the weeping of the bride as she left her parental home; and the ancestor and idol worship, which was notably absent from the wedding they were attending.

In May 1897 Torrance stayed two weeks in Guanxian with fellow CIM missionary James Hutson while Hutson's co-workers, the Graingers, were away. Guanxian, which would become a place of happy memories for Torrance, lay just at the western edge of the Chengdu plain where the mountains rise up and extend all the way to Tibet. He was glad to leave the bustle of the city for this 'beautiful picturesque country town lying at the foot of the mountains by the side of a mighty rushing tearing river' where, for the first time since arriving in China, he could drink fresh, unboiled water.[21]

Later that year, in the sultry heat of the Chengdu summer, Torrance was laid low with sickness and it was a relief to leave the city again for a month back in the healthier environment of Leshan. Illness was not uncommon among the missionaries. Dysentery, malaria, typhoid, and cholera were some of the threats they faced – and the general stress and strain of life at times added to their susceptibility. A prerequisite to applying to the CIM was that candidates be in agreement with the 'Principles and Practice' of the mission, expressing their willingness to 'count the cost and be prepared to live lives of privation, of toil, of loneliness, of danger' and to 'trust God, as able to meet their need in sickness as well as in health, since it will usually be impossible to have recourse to the aid of qualified physicians.'[22] Torrance's own

---

21   TT newsletter, Dec 1897.
22   *Principles and Practice of the China Inland Mission*, 1903, p2. (First drawn up in 1875.)

situation wasn't quite as extreme as this, especially with the presence of the Canadian hospital in Chengdu, but sickness could still take its toll. While in Leshan news reached Torrance that Joshua Vale had suffered a serious breakdown in health and had been ordered to leave China immediately so Torrance made his way back to Chengdu while Vale, who had not seen England's shores for ten years, left with his wife on furlough.

Torrance's passion for the CIM work was evident in his December 1897 newsletter. The mission had its own church but also rented a shop-front where anyone interested in the 'foreigner's message' or simply curious about things foreign could drop in for a chat and Torrance was in his element conversing with them. This joy extended to his work trips beyond the city. In October he travelled southwest of Chengdu to the town of Qionglai and its surrounding villages with Fawcett Olsen and a Chinese helper. One muddy ten-mile trek brought them to a village which had probably never seen a foreigner before. As Olsen stopped for a brief rest in a tea-shop, he saw Torrance promptly surrounded so tightly by a crowd of locals that he had to move to a more open space in the market place, only to have the crowd press around him again. Having given out all their tracts, the two young missionaries ate some dough strips and bean oil for dinner and trudged back to Qionglai through pouring rain and mud as slippery as ice but, as Torrance wrote, 'A joy filled our hearts that on that night the gospel was in many a home it had never been in before.'[23]

A few days later they encountered two other Chengdu missionaries who were travelling further south to Ya'an. Olsen chose to return to Chengdu as planned but Torrance's curiosity and love of travel got the better of him and he jumped at their invitation to travel on with them. His description of Ya'an reveals his growing interest in things political: 'It is a lovely town nestling among the hills and is on the main road to Thibet. To this country it exports large quantities of tea. Thibet is governed by China and she keeps the monopoly of this trade, shutting off the Indian border and hindering business all she can.'[24] On his return from Ya'an Torrance went down with dysentery, which would plague him on and off for several years to come, but he made a good recovery under the care of Dr Kilborn of the Canadian Methodist mission and Olsen, who proved to be an able nurse.

23   TT newsletter, Dec 1897.
24   Ibid.

Chapter 2

Yu the Wild One and the Boxers
1898–1900

There is no evidence in Torrance's December 1897 letter that he had encountered any serious hostility on his travels but when Hudson Taylor arrived in Shanghai in January 1898 after eight months away from China he could sense a change of atmosphere, one of restlessness among the Chinese and anxiety amongst the foreigners. The spark that had exacerbated tensions was an incident in late 1897 which provided Germany, a late arrival on the scene and another nation hungry for influence, with an opportunity to gain ground in China. On November 1, two German Roman Catholic missionaries had been murdered in Shandong Province by perpetrators thought to be members of the secret Big Swords Society or *Dadaohui*. Germany, which already had a naval squadron in the region, had had its eye on Shandong's Jiaozhou Bay as a potential naval base and the murders immediately offered the prospect of leverage in negotiations with China. On November 7 the admiral of the squadron wired the German admiralty to ask, 'May incidents be exploited in pursuit of further goals?' and promptly received the Kaiser's approval.[1] On November 14 the Germans seized Jiaozhou and in the ensuing negotiations with China, Germany was granted a 99-year lease on more than two hundred square miles of territory administered from Qingdao, as well as exclusive commercial concessions in Shandong, including railway and mining rights.

In response to Germany's acquisition, Russia, which had already obtained the right to build a railway across northern Manchuria, put pressure on the Chinese to hand over control of Port Arthur and Dalian on the Liaodong peninsula and was granted a twenty-five-year lease. Under a most-favoured nation clause in previous Anglo-Chinese treaties, Britain was now in a position to negotiate for more territory but was torn between not wanting to lose ground to competing nations

---

1   Terrell D. Gottschall. *By Order of the Kaiser: Otto Von Diederichs and the Rise of the Imperial German Navy, 1865-1902*. Naval Institute Press. 2003, p156.

and not wanting to see Chinese territory actually carved into colonial sections as opposed to trading spheres. As the push for territory gained momentum, exploiting China's weakness, China agreed in February 1898 not to lease territory along the Yangtze River to any foreign power other than Britain, and in March France was granted a lease on Guangzhou Bay, adjacent to northern Vietnam. By June Britain had expanded its Hong Kong jurisdiction with the lease of an extra 306 square miles on the mainland opposite Hong Kong Island, known as the New Territories. On July 1, as a balance to Russia's occupation of Port Arthur and Dalian and Germany's presence in the Qingdao region, Britain was also granted the lease of an area of 525 square miles in Weihaiwei, Shandong.

A cartoon created in this period by Xie Zuantai reflected the fears of the Chinese at this time. It showed the Russian bear encroaching on China from the north, the British bulldog-headed lion prowling along the Yangtze with its tail curled around the Shandong peninsula, the hand of the French frog extending north across Yunnan into Sichuan, the Japanese sun with its eye on northern China and its foot on Taiwan, and the American eagle approaching from its newly-acquired territory of the Philippines.[2]

In late 1898 Lord Charles Beresford, a British naval admiral and member of parliament, returned from a fact-finding mission on behalf of the Associated Chambers of Commerce. He was highly critical of Britain's recent actions: 'The Diplomatic and Commercial prestige of Great Britain has been affected by the events in Northern China, but only in a slight degree when compared with the loss of good name involved by forcing concessions from China when she is prostrated by involuntary surrenders to Powers stronger than herself . . . We have taken advantage of the impotence and distress of the authorities and people of China to advance our own interests.'[3]

Beresford had talked not only with British officials and businessmen in China but also with representatives of the other foreign nations and with senior Chinese government officials, including the great Chinese statesman Li Hongzhang. In Shanghai, British merchants voiced their concern over China's own lack of security, with neither China's police

2   Xie Zuantai (谢缵泰). 'A Map of the Current Situation' (时局图). Various versions were issued between 1899 and 1903. See for example: https://commons.wikimedia.org/w/index.php?curid=2417509
3   Charles Beresford. *The Break-Up of China*. Harper and Brothers Publishers. 1899, p iv.

nor military being effective enough to control any serious anti-foreigner disturbances that might result from Chinese resentment. Of all China's provinces, they made specific reference to rebellion being already active in Sichuan.[4]

The leader of this unrest in Sichuan was Yu Dongchen, also nicknamed Yu Manzi or Yu the Wild One, who was a member of Sichuan's Elder Brothers Society or *Gelaohui* and a native of Dazu, between Chengdu and Chongqing. A year or so earlier, he and a friend had been involved in a lawsuit with a Chinese Catholic and lost the case owing to the suspected intervention of a foreign priest. Yu was incensed and refused to let the matter rest.

Back in the spring of 1898, the annual spring fair at the Qingyang or Green Ram Temple, just west of Chengdu, had drawn thousands of Chinese from miles around in celebration of the birth of the Chinese philosopher Laozi.[5] Missionaries often used this occasion to distribute literature and talk with the crowds and Yu the Wild One had likewise taken the opportunity to put up posters, accusing the foreigners and the Qing government of collusion against the oppressed and disempowered Han Chinese, many of whom – especially the secret societies – had never accepted their Manchu overlords. Before long, Yu had several thousand followers on the rampage in Sichuan, attacking mainly Chinese Catholics, destroying Catholic property, and making many homeless with relative impunity.[6] Knowing how much local support Yu had, and possibly also being secretly supportive themselves, 'Chengdu officials were willing to look the other way despite the large number being murdered.'[7]

Although Yu's initial grievance was against the Catholics, he and his followers soon ceased to make such distinctions. In May 1898 a CIM family, the Pruens, were travelling in Sichuan and stopped in Nanchong, east of Chengdu, to stay the night with a fellow missionary. As Kate Pruen and her two young daughters waited on the boat while her husband went to find the missionary's house, two men came on board and ordered them to come out on deck, where crowds on the

---

4   Ibid., p76.
5   This Daoist temple is located on Chengdu's first ring road and is a popular tourist attraction nowadays.
6   Broomhall. *Not Death to Die!*, p269.
7   James J. Matthews. *The Union Jack on the Upper Yangzi: The Treaty Port of Chongqing, 1891-1943.* Unpublished PhD thesis. York University, Toronto, Ontario. 1999, p175.

bank watched them for over an hour. 'Then the crowd increased,' wrote Kate, 'and began throwing stones, so we retreated into the cabin, but they began to use larger stones until my husband returned, and there was a pause for a few minutes, only, however, for the stone-throwing to recommence.'[8] The aggression was dampened by a downpour and the arrival of their friend, Mr Platt, bringing sedan chairs for them. Amid shouts of 'kill the foreigners' they managed to escape. Two days later Platt fled for refuge to the yamen as crowds destroyed his rented house.

By June Yu Manzi had decided he needed the Qing officials on his side and switched his anti-Qing stance to a new slogan calling on people to 'Support the Qing and wipe out the foreigners.' A new proclamation was issued reminding the Chinese of various injustices inflicted by foreigners, including the destruction of the Summer Palace in 1860, the Japanese indemnity bankrupting China, the trading policies preferential to foreigners, and now the threat of China's partition by the foreign powers. Urging local support for his bands of followers as they launched their attacks, he assured people that they would earn the love of the emperor as they plundered the foreigners and helped to recoup China's losses. He ended with a call to arms: 'These foreigners are dogs and goats, let us sharpen our swords and drive them out.'[9]

In July Yu's boldness took a new turn with the capture of a French priest, Father Fleury, who was held for several months. The anxiety caused by this unchecked rebellion in Sichuan was by now spreading across the whole foreign community, and among the Chinese Christians – both Catholic and Protestant. In Chongqing the situation was so grave that the foreign consuls ordered the evacuation of all foreign women from the city.

Parallel with the unrest in Sichuan, unprecedented events of a completely different nature were unfolding in Beijing under the youthful governance of the Guangxu Emperor.[10] Like other reformers, Guangxu had recognised that the encroachment of foreign powers had been possible largely because of their technological superiority and the general benefits of a modern, scientific education. If China wanted to compete on the world stage then modernisation was imperative.

---

8   Kate Pruen. *The Provinces of Western China*. Alfred Holness, London; R. L. Allan & Son, Glasgow. 1906, p174.

9   Ibid., p179.

10   The emperor's personal name was Zaitian but he is better known by his regnal name, 'the Guangxu Emperor', meaning 'glorious succession'.

In June, galvanised by this recognition, Guangxu appointed the progressive reformer Kang Youwei as his special advisor and together they attempted to implement a radical programme of change. In one of his edicts, the young emperor painted a dismal picture of how far China was lagging behind:

> Our scholars are now without solid and practical education; our artisans are without scientific instructors; when compared with other countries we soon see how weak we are. Does anyone think that our troops are as well drilled or as well led as those of the foreign armies? Or that we can successfully stand against them? Changes must be made to accord with the necessities of the times. . . . Keeping in mind the morals of the sages and wise men, we must make them the basis on which to build newer and better structures. We must substitute modern arms and western organization for our old regime; we must select our military officers according to western methods of military education; we must establish elementary and high schools, colleges and universities, in accordance with those of foreign countries; we must abolish the *wenchang* (literary essay) and obtain a knowledge of ancient and modern world-history, a right conception of the present-day state of affairs, with special reference to the governments and institutions of the countries of the five great continents; and we must understand their arts and sciences.[11]

For those desperate for change, and there were many, particularly among the younger Chinese in the cities, this seemed almost too good to be true, especially with the promise of combining the 'morals of the sages and wise men' with such rapid modernisation. Rumours reached Sichuan that Guangxu had ordered temples to be turned into schools which would promote Western learning above classical Confucian education. The problem, as CIM historian Alfred Broomhall points out, was that it was 'too much too soon' and they were not able to carry the conservatives – many in powerful positions – with them, especially when financial reforms, such as an annual publication of the government's income, expenditure, and overall budget, threatened to upset their corrupt comfort zones.[12]

In September 1898, dashing the hopes of many, Empress Dowager Cixi decided enough was enough and orchestrated the removal of

---

11 Isaac T. Headland. *Court Life In China: The Capital Its Officials And People.* Revell, New York. 1909, p357. Cited in Odd Arne Westad, *Restless Empire: China and the World since 1750.* The Bodley Head. 2012, p105.
12 Broomhall, *Not Death to Die!*, p269.

Guangxu to the Summer Palace and the arrest and even execution of key supporters of reform, although Kang Youwei and others managed to flee to Japan. In October she followed this with an edict censoring the press and calling for the arrest of newspaper editors. In February 1899 the command went out for provincial leaders to destroy all publications associated with reform and punish those who possessed such material.[13] Han Suyin describes the tense atmosphere in Chengdu during this period, telling of subversive anti-Qing ballads being sung, of Qing spies loitering in Chengdu teahouses to listen for scholars discussing the new ideas, and of elders in her family who were afraid that the 'New Learning' of the reformers would bring moral pollution from the West.[14]

Amidst all these troubles the CIM mission work in Chengdu was continuing as normally as possible. A small Bible school had been started and a new chapel established, which was open in the daytime and three nights a week. Undeterred by the anti-foreign turbulence, locals crowded into the chapel to listen to the preaching. At the CIM outstation in Danling, southwest of Chengdu, their first locally-supported Chinese pastor had been ordained, assured by his congregation that they would provide him with rice, fire-wood, and sweet potatoes.

Although none of Torrance's letters seem to have survived from this period there is one letter to him, dated July 12, 1898, from the Standard Life Office in Shanghai, with details of an insurance policy providing 'assurance for residence in Chengtu for a man aged 29 next birthday'. An added hand-written note explained that the premium was higher for those living in the interior of China – no doubt due to the greater risk to life. Whether by coincidence or because both the troubles and the policy had sharpened Torrance's awareness of his own mortality, scribbled on the back of the letter was a long poem about heaven which, judging by the crossings out and amendments, seems to have been Torrance's own. Another lengthy poem written that year to Torrance's mother, perhaps also prompted by the fragility of the times, reveals the closeness Torrance felt to her and was a poignant mix of his emotions, his evangelical faith, and his hope of seeing her again.

In November 1898 CIM missionary William Fleming and a local Miao colleague were murdered in the neighbouring province of

---

13 Joan Judge. *Print and Politics: 'Shibao' and the Culture of Reform in Late Qing China.* Stanford University Press. 1997, p24.
14 Han, *Crippled Tree*, pp93-95.

Guizhou by rebels apparently influenced by Yu Manzi's anti-foreign incitement. Referring to these deaths at a London CIM meeting in May 1899, the chairman, Sir George Williams, said solemnly and with unwitting accuracy, 'It may be, that some here with us to-day may have to suffer death for Christ, and may obtain that crown which will be an honour and a rejoicing to them in days to come.'[15]

For Torrance personally, things were looking brighter as 1898 drew to a close, despite all the unrest. Before leaving Britain in 1895 he had become engaged to a young lady from Paisley called Mary Bryce, who had since been accepted to join the China Inland Mission. Arriving in Shanghai on December 21, 1898, Mary soon moved to the Yangzhou women's training home in Jiangsu Province where she learned that she had been assigned to Leshan for her two-year probationary period, not too far from Torrance in Chengdu but far enough not to be distracted during her initial phase of language study and further training. In accordance with the CIM's 'Principles and Practice', they were deferring their marriage for two years until Mary had been accepted as a Junior Missionary. This was due to 'the importance of pursuing the prescribed course of study with undivided application, and also on account of the frequent failure of health and great mortality which has been found to prevail among ladies who arrive in China newly married, or who marry too soon after arrival.'[16]

In early March, Mary joined a party under the supervision of an experienced missionary, Mrs James, for the thousand-mile journey up the Yangtze River. The journey was horrendous and it was a much shaken party that disembarked in Chongqing. The Shanghai CIM office reported with relief: 'We are thankful to learn from Mrs. James of the arrival of herself and party at Ch'ung-k'ing, after having several accidents on their journey. They spent one night with their boat stuck on a rock, with a large hole knocked in the front of it, and at other times there were accidents which caused the boat to leak badly. Mr. Smith had been ill, but was better; and Miss Noess was very ill, with fever, on arrival at Ch'ung-k'ing.'[17]

Shortly after this, Mary began to show signs that all was not well and on June 3 the Shanghai office issued a sad notice: 'You will be sorry to hear that Miss Mary F. Bryce, who recently left the Training Home for Si-ch'uen, has had a serious break-down, and Dr. Parry, in consultation with Dr. McCartney, decided that it would be better for her to come

---

15 *Millions*, 1899, pp82-83.
16 *Principles and Practice*, p3.
17 *Millions*, 1899, p30.

to the coast for treatment.'[18] It was a terrible prospect for Mary, having survived such a frightening ordeal, to then face the journey back down the Yangtze to Shanghai in her fragile state of mind. A brief entry in the monthly CIM publication, *China's Millions*, noted that Torrance left Shanghai on July 31 for Chengdu, so it seems he had been given leave to meet her in Chongqing and accompany her on the journey.[19]

Initially, Mary seemed to respond well to the care she received in Shanghai but she then took another turn for the worse and by November her health was such that returning to England seemed the only solution. With the hope that she would recover and return to China, she sailed in the company of a missionary family, reaching England on December 16, 1899, a year after her arrival in Shanghai. For Mary, there was a small mercy in that her departure removed her from China on the eve of one of the worst periods in the history of missions in China. For Torrance, instead of having just one more year until his and Mary's wedding day, there was the uncertainty as to whether she would return and how his whole future would unfold.

A happier aspect of Torrance's life at this time was the formation of an organisation which would be an important part of his life for the rest of his time in China. In January 1899, just as Mary had been starting her training in Yangzhou, a missionary conference took place in Chongqing, convened by Hudson Taylor with the aim of improving coordination between the various missions in the southwestern provinces of Sichuan, Guizhou, and Yunnan. Out of this conference a West China Missions Advisory Board was established and the monthly *West China Missionary News* (WCMN) was launched which, over the next four decades, would play a significant role in the mission community, particularly in Sichuan. As a result of this, an unusual degree of unity and cooperation developed among the various missions and Torrance would benefit much from a wide circle of friendships. Apart from news, the WCMN – to which Torrance contributed frequently over the years – contained articles on a variety of topics including agriculture, education, and Chinese culture and history, as well as reports on social events which did much to help build community, especially in the big cities of Chengdu and Chongqing.

The missionary conference happened to coincide with the rescue of Father Fleury and the arrest of Yu the Wild One, action precipitated by Chinese fear that France would use the situation to demand further

---

18 Ibid., p144.
19 Ibid., p157.

concessions, even as Germany had profited from the murder of its missionaries in the northeast. Yu was condemned to death but in a show of public support for him, which revealed the prevailing mood among the Chinese in Chengdu, 'the news brought out thousands of city dwellers to the streets who prostrated themselves outside the city gate, pleading with the magistrate to repeal the order for Yu's execution.'[20] His sentence was commuted to house arrest, although after a failed escape attempt he was subsequently imprisoned in Chengdu and not released until the fall of the Qing dynasty.

Although Yu's arrest seemed like good news, it was with great consternation that word was then received of a new government decree concerning the Catholics which immediately spelled trouble for the missionary communities, not just in Sichuan but across China. In March 1899, under pressure from the French government, the Chinese government issued a decree granting political status to the Roman Catholic hierarchy in China, bestowing on them equivalence by rank with the Chinese official hierarchy. Bishops were to be equal to the highest provincial position of governor, archdeacons to provincial treasurers and judges, and priests to Chinese prefects.

The Protestant missionaries were dismayed. Owing to the most-favoured-nation clause granting certain foreign powers the right to any concessions offered by China to other nations, this preferential treatment would automatically be applied to them too, even though they wanted no part in it. It was obvious to them that such privileged status would lead to greater resentment on the part of the Chinese and be dangerous not just for foreigners but for the Chinese Christians too. Not only was the newly-awarded status provocative but it also formalised things in a way that threatened to obstruct the freedom many of them had as foreign missionaries who, despite a lack of any special status, were often welcomed by Chinese officials of various ranks. This was frequently the case for Torrance, especially during his later years in China.

An indignant and despairing letter from Arnold Foster of the London Missionary Society to the British-run *North China Daily News* pointed to the folly of according the clergy status they didn't even have in their own countries. Foster even wondered if the move was a deliberate attempt to incite anti-foreign sentiment, thereby distracting the people from the dire condition the Qing government was now in. One of the biggest problems attached to this granting of status was, as

---

20 Yan Lu. *Re-understanding Japan: Chinese Perspectives, 1895-1945.* University of Hawaii Press. 2004, p70.

Yu Manzi had experienced, the power it gave to the clergy in relation to legal matters. Foster clearly articulated the dilemma:

> Here is one of the greatest dangers now threatening . . . our very existence as a spiritual body. The knowledge that a mandarin will not dare to give a case against the Church is a perpetual temptation to designing Chinese to get hold of the missionary's card and to take it into the Yamen on behalf of a litigant. Such a card is worth money . . . If we accept the status that is now offered to us, and if it comes to be generally understood that we can at any time 'demand to see' the officials, these and similar abuses will multiply rapidly.[21]

In closing he urged Protestants to make clear their rejection of the proffered status and request only the same justice for Christian and non-Christian alike.

The unrest in Sichuan was by now somewhat curtailed but disturbing news was beginning to emerge from Shandong, where the Germans had pursued their territorial ambitions. Similar in many aspects to the Yu Manzi movement, attacks on Catholic targets by members of Shandong's Big Swords Society had garnered an element of popular support. Although Yu was a thousand miles away in Sichuan, he had publicly expressed his anger over events in Shandong and his own successes had encouraged others to take the law into their own hands.

In 1899 the Shandong rebels adopted the name 'The Righteous and Harmonious Fists', reflecting their use of martial arts, the perceived justice of their cause, and their conviction that a victorious end – the eviction of all foreigners from China – would justify violent means. Their violence had an added spiritual dimension – the belief that they were immune to the bullets and swords of the enemy. The American Bible Society (ABS) agent in Tianjin described the growing threat posed by these 'Boxers', as the foreigners had begun to call them:

> By the first of last July [1899] the Boxers had added vast numbers to their ranks, and all were armed with broad-swords and in some cases with fire-arms. Gymnastic exercises and drills were going on in hundreds of villages. . . . One placard, which was widely circulated by them, reads as follows: 'The Universal Boxer Society: You are personally invited to meet on the seventh day of the ninth moon. Elevate the Manchus. Kill the Foreigners. Unless this summons is obeyed you will lose your heads.'[22]

---

21 *Millions*, 1899, pp181-2.
22 Cited in *The Boxer Rising: History of the Boxer Trouble in China*. Reprinted

From then on, Shandong had seen continuous attacks. Although the CIM only had one small mission station in Shandong, the CIM boarding school was located on the Shandong coast at Yantai and many missionary families, including some in Chengdu, had the anxiety of knowing their children were only a hundred miles or so from the German-controlled part of Shandong where tensions were high. An added worry for all foreigners was their growing suspicion of official collusion in the violence, meaning there would be little protection if things deteriorated. Empress Dowager Cixi's crushing of the Reform Movement had lent tacit approval to anti-foreign sentiment, which was spreading far beyond Shandong.

That autumn, to the horror of the foreign community, Cixi came closer to allying herself with the Boxers as she issued an edict describing the foreign powers as 'the enemy'. Calling on her military leaders and provincial governors to present a united front against the 'foreign aggressor', she warned foreign governments not to assume that China's weakness would stop her going to war against them.[23] The displeasure among some Chinese at her treatment of the emperor and her resistance to change, as well as the pressure she was under from foreign nations, had left Cixi desperately in need of popular support, and who better to provide it than these anti-foreign militias.

After a lull in the unrest in Sichuan a report reached the Shanghai CIM headquarters in October 1899 that the Nanchong CIM station had been attacked by a crowd still believing the rumours of child-stealing by foreigners. A drought in eastern Sichuan was making matters worse. The people were idle and dispirited and saw the lack of rain as an expression of the displeasure of the gods, perhaps incurred by the foreign missionaries with their 'new teaching' and disregard for the ancient Chinese custom of *feng shui,* and by the Chinese Christians, many of whom no longer participated in or contributed financially to temple festivals and ancestral worship ceremonies.

Chengdu seems to have been spared the worst of the unrest during this period, in part perhaps because of Yu's arrest, but also because the Viceroy of Sichuan, Kui Jun, was on good terms with the foreigners. On a visit to the city in the winter of 1899, British diplomat Charles Bigham found Kui Jun very friendly and the people welcoming and open to foreign methods. Officials seemed forward-looking, admitting

---

from the *Shanghai Mercury,* 2nd edition, August 1901, p1. (No author named.)
23 Marshall Broomhall. *The Jubilee Story of the China Inland Mission with Portraits and Map.* London: Marshall, Morgan & Scott Ltd. 1915, p244.

the usefulness of railways and discussing modernisation in Korea, and one foreign affairs official spoke excellent French having spent time in Paris.[24]

In contrast to Kui Jun in Chengdu, Yu Xian, the governor of Shandong, had become increasingly supportive of the Boxers. Under pressure from the foreign powers, Cixi removed him from his post in December 1899 but instead of punishing him, she invited him to Beijing and in April 1900 appointed him as governor of Shanxi Province, an unmistakable statement of her allegiance to the Boxer cause.

Yu Xian's removal from Shandong came too late to fully protect the province from the Boxers. On December 28 about two hundred of them attacked a group of Chinese Christians, destroying their chapel and offering to protect the other villagers in return for all the Christians being handed over. The ABS agent in Tianjin recorded that they were 'forced to flee without food or sufficient clothing, in the midst of an unusually cold winter'.[25] Two days later, British missionary Sidney Brooks, who had dreamt of his death before leaving England, was attacked by Boxers while travelling by donkey through a village in eastern Shandong. He fled to a nearby temple but found no refuge and was tortured and beheaded. Although Brooks was the only foreigner to die in Shandong, more than two hundred Chinese were killed and many thousands lost their homes. In response to this, the new governor of Shandong, Yuan Shikai, sent his forces against the Boxers, who then moved their activities to Hebei and Shanxi provinces.

In Shanxi, emboldened by Cixi's appointment of Yu Xian as governor, the Boxers became confident enough to train in broad daylight and the April 1900 editorial in *China's Millions* declared that things were more extreme than anything the CIM missionaries had experienced in the last forty years.[26] Some still held out hope that things might calm down, particularly if rain were to end the drought, but such hopes were shattered in June when Cixi issued an unequivocal declaration of war on the foreign powers, giving a clear green light to the Boxers to wreak their devastation on foreign and Chinese Christians alike.

Thankfully for Torrance, Viceroy Kui Jun was one of several governors who ignored Cixi's edicts and attempted to keep their provinces out of

24   Clive Bigham. *A Year in China: 1899-1900. With some account of Admiral Sir E. Seymour's expedition.* Macmillan and Co., Ltd. 1901, p128.
25   *The Boxer Rising,* Shanghai Mercury, 1901, p2. See also *Millions*, 1900, p56.
26   Broomhall, *Not Death to Die!*, p307.

the conflict. However, although the foreigners in Sichuan were spared, this was not the case for some of the local Christians, particularly the Catholics. One Chinese Christian in Guanxian reported that in the summer of 1900 'rumours were very wicked indeed. In the country the RC converts suffered heavily; their houses have been robbed and burned and they themselves killed in some cases; and it was within a hair breadth of a riot in the city itself.'[27] In her father's papers, author Han Suyin found a song that was circulating in Chengdu at this time, clearly supportive of the Boxers and hopeful that they would save people from all their woes:

> The spirit soldiers will come,
> With gold helmets and silver shields,
> Riding on grand white horses,
> Wielding swords of righteous deeds,
> They will kill all the invaders,
> Revenge all our wrongs.[28]

In early July, in a move that some viewed as disrespectful of Kui Jun's efforts to protect them, the British Consul in Chongqing ordered the evacuation of all British nationals from Sichuan. The riots of 1895 and the violence of Yu Manzi and his followers were still fresh in people's memories and the risks just seemed too high. The order must have made Torrance's heart sink. Having made the long trip to Shanghai and back in 1899 he had spent the first few months of 1900 coming to terms with Mary's departure and settling back into some itinerating work, glad of encouraging visits to several village markets. To be facing another journey out for an indefinite period of time was the last thing he wanted. But there was no choice. The Viceroy let it be known that the foreigners in Sichuan should gather at Chengdu, Yibin, and Chongqing, from where he would guarantee their safety out of the province.

As Torrance and his companions made their way down the Yangtze to Shanghai the situation was changing rapidly. On August 14 foreign troops entered Beijing to lift a fifty-five day siege of the foreign legations there, and Cixi, seeing the writing on the wall, fled to Xi'an. As word spread of the foreign victories and Cixi's flight, the Boxers scattered, fearing fierce retribution from the foreign powers.

At the CIM headquarters in Shanghai, which Torrance reached on August 25, it took so long for news of various missionaries to get

27   WCMN, Jan-Feb 1901, p25.
28   Han, *Crippled Tree*, p113.

2 YU THE WILD ONE AND THE BOXERS 1898–1900

through that the grim overall picture wasn't known for months. The CIM staff in Shanghai, along with all those evacuated from stations across China, could only wait in dreadful anticipation as news reached them of this one and that one who had been murdered and this or that one who, as yet, were still alive and trying to make their way to the coast. The chaos and the distances both contributed to delays in communication, as shown by this December entry in *China's Millions*:

> In our issue for November we expressed grave doubts about the safety of our missionaries in Datong. We have since heard that . . . at . . . a station of the Swedish Holiness Union, it was reported that all of the Christians had been taken to Datong Fu, and there, with 100 others, natives and foreigners, Protestants and Catholics, had been put to death; also, that all the foreigners at Guihua Cheng had been killed, and so fierce were the Boxers against everything foreign, that even vendors of matches were said to have been killed, and no one was allowed to wear anything of foreign made material. If these mournful tidings are reliable, our worst fears for Mr. and Mrs. McKee, Mr. and Mrs. I'Anson, Miss Aspden and Miss M. E. Smith are now, alas, confirmed.[29]

The ten Swedish CIM associates had actually been killed on June 29 and the other six missionaries and their children were killed on July 12, all in Shanxi.

The last CIM missionary to die was Flora Glover. With their two small children, she and her husband Archibald had tried to flee east from Shanxi to Tianjin but found their way blocked by the Boxers. Turning back, they were stoned and captured and thought death was imminent but eventually managed to reach their mission station on July 3. Here they heard the terrifying news of Cixi's order that all protection be withdrawn from foreigners. Bribing their way out of the city gate, they headed south, finally reaching the safety of Hankou in Hubei Province on August 14 after a gruelling journey during which they had again been captured, stripped almost naked, released, suffered intense heat and thirst, and witnessed the death of another missionary and child in a group that joined them on their journey. The only human glimmers of light on the journey came from the courageous kindness of some Chinese along the way who were deeply distressed by their plight. In Hankou, on August 18, Flora gave birth to Faith, a baby girl

---

29 *Millions*, Dec 1900, p214. (Pinyin updated.) Guihua Cheng is today's city of Hohhot in Inner Mongolia. In 1900 it was within Shanxi Province.

who managed to survive just eleven days. From Hankou they went by steamer to Shanghai but Flora never recovered from all she had gone through and died on October 25.[30]

In July 1901 the full number of foreign deaths was published in *China's Millions*: across all the missions the total number was 188, comprising 135 adults and 53 children. Of that number, 58 adults and 21 children belonged to the CIM, including the ten Swedish associates. Some had been killed outright, some died later of their injuries, and some, like Flora, died of illness and the deprivations experienced as they fled the killing and tried to reach places of refuge. This was a large number in relation to the size of the missionary community in China but small compared to the deaths of Chinese Christians which numbered in their thousands.

In Shanghai it was a strange time for the hundreds of CIM missionaries gathered there, all with different experiences: some grieving loved ones, some deeply traumatised, some marvelling at miraculous escapes, and some – like Torrance – who hadn't suffered personally but had left their stations, knowing that their fellow Chinese Christians were at risk, and made long journeys out in the shadow of potential danger. Many of the missionaries took advantage of the lull to take early furloughs, with some in serious need of a recovery period and others, in the end, never returning.

Sadly for Torrance, news reached him in February 1901 that Mary was not well enough to handle the demands of life in China and she never did fully recover. This was a great heartache for both of them and in a letter to a colleague years later Torrance revealed how lonely these early years had been for him and how deeply Mary's loss had affected him, describing her as 'one of the gentlest, kindest, most Christ-like women that ever walked.'[31] His loneliness would have been accentuated by Fawcett Olsen's marriage to Florence Kirkwood in early 1899, leaving Torrance as the only single missionary at the Chengdu CIM station.

---

30   Archibald Glover. *1000 Miles of Miracle.* Christian Focus. 2001. (First published in 1907.)
31   TT to Hykes, Feb 3, 1919.

Chapter 3

A Degree of Normality

1901-1907

Early in 1901 the CIM leadership decided that some of the men would return to their stations ahead of the women and children. As the only single CIM man in Chengdu, Torrance was the first to return, sailing with other missionaries for Chongqing in February and travelling on alone to Chengdu, where he arrived on March 14. Although the Chinese New Year celebrations were over by then, Torrance preserved three traditional red paper greetings from that period, one from a district magistrate in Chongqing, one from a provincial judge, and one from a mandarin in Shuangliu, just south of Chengdu, all no doubt keen, like Torrance, to express friendliness after all the troubles.

The welcome he received from the Chinese Christians in Chengdu was extremely heartening. They 'did not know of my coming,' he wrote, 'and it was a welcome surprise that morning when I walked in. Each one vied with the other in shewing their joy over my return. The converts had all stood firm and loyal to their profession, and now they are less liable to fall away than before.'[1] It was a great relief to discover that there had been no damage to the CIM property. Having made sure all was in order, Torrance set out with a Chinese colleague to see how the local Christians had fared at the various outstations. In Pengshan they had fared well but in Meishan the chapel had been closed for several weeks to avoid attack. Danling, where the congregation were supporting their own pastor, had had a harder time with about twenty-five families attacked by rioters. To try and minimise the conflict the Danling chapel had been sealed for two months by the local magistrate. The other outstations had all been able to carry on much as normal.

Through the long hot summer of 1901 and for much of the autumn Torrance and a Swedish CIM associate, Johan Johanson, were the only CIM workers in Chengdu. The consular restrictions on women returning were not lifted until the early autumn and the Graingers,

1   Quoted by Joshua Vale in 'Ch'en-tu and District Revisited'. WCMN, Sept 1901, p86.

who were relocating from Guanxian to Chengdu, didn't reach the city until November. Joshua Vale had returned briefly but left again to join his wife who was expecting a baby in December. In the late autumn Torrance and Johanson spent several weeks itinerating in areas beyond Chengdu and encountered a much more positive attitude among the general populace. One missionary, writing about 'The Present Situation in Si-chuen', reported that places previously hostile were now welcoming and the demand for Bibles and hymn books was greater than their availability.[2] The interest was particularly marked amongst the gentry although there was a need for discernment. There were still those who simply sought foreign connections as a source of assistance in legal matters or other benefits that had little to do with anything spiritual.

On a national level the situation was gradually stabilising. In January 1901, from the safety of her refuge in Xi'an, Empress Dowager Cixi had requested that her senior officials examine the changes originally proposed by Guangxu in 1898. This led to a wide variety of reforms: educational, military, economic, and in government administration. More students were sent to study abroad, in recognition that foreign educational institutions could provide the 'new learning' necessary for China's modernisation, and there was considerable reform regarding male-female segregation, with women seen more in public and female education encouraged. Chinese newspapers also flourished in an environment of greater freedom and – a boon for the foreign community – a Post Office was opened in Chengdu in spring 1902 under the supervision of the Imperial Maritime Customs Services and its Irish inspector-general in Shanghai, Sir Robert Hart.[3]

In September 1901 a post-Boxer 'agreement' was reached between the Qing and the foreign powers which Graham Hutchings describes as 'the most vengeful treaty in the history of Sino-Western diplomacy'.[4] Some aspects were perhaps to be expected, such as the death penalty for Yu Xian, governor of Shanxi, and the stationing of foreign troops between Beijing and Tianjin to protect the foreign communities there. However, the huge indemnity demanded by the foreign powers, to be paid over a forty-year period, was crippling to China and out of

2   William Upcraft, *Millions,* Sept 1902, pp123-124.
3   In 1863 Cixi had appointed Ulsterman Robert Hart, aged 28, as Inspector General of Chinese Maritime Customs. He played a remarkable role until his retirement in 1910 and was awarded various honorific titles by Cixi.
4   Graham Hutchings. *Modern China: A Guide to a Century of Change.* Harvard University Press. 2003, p48.

proportion with foreign losses, especially in the light of the reckless damage and looting their forces had inflicted on the Chinese. The burden was somewhat alleviated by the British who, through Sir Robert Hart, worked with the Chinese to raise general import tariffs and introduce new customs tariffs on goods more often purchased by foreigners in China, such as foreign alcohol and cigarettes. In 1908 the USA also agreed that anything beyond direct compensation would be used to fund scholarships for Chinese to study in America and to fund the establishment of Qinghua University in Beijing.[5]

As they had in 1895, the CIM chose to distance themselves as far as possible from the British and other governments with regard to compensation. To begin with, Hudson Taylor suggested they should not initiate any claims but agreed that, if it was offered, they could accept compensation for destroyed Mission property. The acceptance of any personal recompense offered to individual missionaries should be at their own discretion. However, once he had grasped the extent of the atrocities committed by foreign troops in the Beijing area in response to the Boxers, he changed this to a zero-compensation policy:

> Thousands of Chinese as innocent as our missionaries seem to have been ruined and robbed of their all, and large numbers slain, through the action of the allies, for which China will not be compensated. . . . It therefore seems better to me now that we should trust in God to enable us to rehabilitate our stations when the time comes to reopen them.[6]

This approach had far-reaching consequences. In Shanxi, where so many missionaries had died, the executed governor, Yu Xian, had been replaced by Cen Chunxuan, who invited the various missions to come and discuss reparations. When Dixon Hoste, in charge of CIM affairs in China, visited him and said the CIM would not accept any financial compensation, not for the deaths and injuries nor for the destroyed property, Cen could hardly believe it. This paved the way for high level cooperation between Cen and the Shanxi missionaries, a relationship replicated when he later moved to Chengdu as governor of Sichuan.

In January 1902, after six years in China, Torrance received his Senior Missionary Certificate. The granting of it seems to have been delayed by the Boxer upheavals but it confirmed that he had been in China with the CIM for five years and had passed 'the six examinations required by

---

5   Jung Chang, *Cixi*, Kindle Edition.
6   Broomhall, *Not Death to Die!*, pp468-470.

Village street scene

the Course of Study.[7] With or without all the turmoil this was no small achievement. It was still a problem in the CIM that otherwise effective missionaries were not attaining these required levels of language study but Torrance's rural itinerating, usually with Chinese companions, had been a great advantage, especially in acquiring the local dialect. With the Graingers and Vales now back in Chengdu, Torrance had been relieved of responsibilities in the city and his primary sphere of work was once again on the road and in the smaller towns and villages.

That January saw unusually cold weather in Chengdu. Out in Guanxian James Hutson reported the rare sight of six inches of snow. He also noted troops and supplies passing through Guanxian – equipped with good quality Mausers, opium pipes, and umbrellas – on their way to the Min Valley and the town of Songpan where conflict with the Tibetans was anticipated.[8] Although Hutson had observed increased prosperity among the people, he also wrote of riots in response to new and higher taxes as the central government looked to the provinces to help pay off the post-Boxer indemnity. As a large, prosperous province, Sichuan's share of the post-Boxer indemnity was second only to Jiangsu Province, and a fall in the value of silver had increased the overall indemnity by about twenty percent. The corresponding increase in

---

7   CIM Minutes, 49th China Council Session, Jan 14, 1902.
8   WCMN, March 1902, pp39-40.

taxation, augmented as usual by officials pocketing their own share, was a heavy burden for the general populace. In this instance the tax office was destroyed, the tax barriers torn down, shops shut, and the local magistrate was forced to back down and apply the taxes on a fairer basis.

To add to the people's woes, drought conditions prevailed for the third year in a row in parts of Sichuan and people in the countryside were facing destitution. Eva Allibone in northeastern Sichuan wrote of people abandoning their children and eating weeds and leaves to supplement their meagre one meal a day.[9] In April 1902 Thomas James reported from southeastern Sichuan that the drought meant once again that people had nothing to do and were seeking to placate the rain god. Against this backdrop it gradually became clear that some of the foreign hostility had simply gone underground and was now re-emerging. Brigandage was increasing and in spite of the official policy of reform and foreign cooperation, James told of secret societies growing bolder once again: 'It is now an open secret that they practise the Boxer arts in ever changing places.'[10] Another missionary in Nanchong wrote in August of nightly Boxer drills in isolated country temples.[11]

It is hard to imagine the impact of this new threat on the Christians – Chinese and foreign alike – knowing as they now did of the atrocities suffered only two years previously. In October 1902 an urgent call for prayer was sent by cable to the CIM in London with news of an attack on Chengdu as well as several attacks on mission stations in the region, including those often visited by Torrance. The CIM premises at Meishan had now been destroyed and Danling and Leshan were also under threat. At outstations of the American Methodist and Quaker missions some of the Chinese Christians had been killed and reports eventually emerged that more than a thousand Chinese Catholics had died. So severe was the threat, and so apparently beyond the power of Viceroy Kui Jun to control, that the Qing court stepped in and replaced Kui with Cen Chunxuan, the Viceroy of Shanxi who had worked so well with the mission societies in the aftermath of the Boxers. Cen had been due to take up a position in Guangdong but the situation in Chengdu urgently required someone of his stature and ability.

This unexpected turn of events was a relief to the missionaries, who gave Cen a warm welcome. As representatives of the West China

---

9 *Millions*, 1902, p40.
10 Ibid., pp129-130.
11 Ibid., 1903, p25.

Missions Advisory Board, Torrance (CIM), Dr Harry Canright of the American Methodist Episcopal Mission, and Dr Omar Kilborn of the Canadian Methodist Mission were the signatories of a letter presented to Cen:

> His Excellency, Governor General, T'sen, Sir:
>
> We the undersigned Protestant Missionaries of Chentu, wish to offer to you a respectful word of welcome in Sz-Ch'uan.
>
> We have heard with satisfaction of your vigorous and progressive policy in the North. We realize the difficulty of the task that was given you there, and appreciate the thoroughness with which you carried it through. We know how wisdom and justice dominated your policy in dealing with Mr. Timothy Richards in the matter of the Shan-Si [Shanxi] University, and with Mr. D. E. Hoste regarding the missionary question.
>
> China's most urgent need is liberal, broad-minded rulers. You, honored Sir, we believe to be one of these, a Viceroy who will at once bring glory to his Emperor, Kuang Su [Guangxu], and good to his people. Therefore, we regard your coming to Sz-Ch'uan at the present crisis as an event of happy augury for the future of this great province.
>
> Please, then, accept this expression of our hearty and united welcome.[12]

Perhaps in part a reflection of his Chinese language skills, Torrance was chosen to deliver the letter in person and the following day Viceroy Cen sent a gracious response:

> In respectful reply.
>
> The letter bestowed upon me by all the pastors was handed to me yesterday through pastor Torrance. I am not worthy to receive your praises, and I shamefacedly and unceasingly thank you.
>
> The sudden uprising of rebels in Sze Ch'uan Province at this time is entirely owing to the unpreparedness of the local officials. It is much to be regretted that you should have had cause for alarm. I earnestly hope that this insurrection may speedily be suppressed, and that both the people and the Church may enjoy tranquillity.
>
> Regarding my management of affairs in Shan-Si, it was entirely owing to the fact that all the leaders of your Church were truly able to act according to that precept of the Save the world

---

12   WCMN, Nov 1902, pp128-129. The letter is undated.

Religion "Love men as thyself," therefore the honour should be equally divided between us.

Having come to this place I earnestly hope that, as with the leaders of your Church in Shan-Si, so there may be, between us, mutual confidence and sincerity, that thus I may be able to accomplish in Sze Ch'uan what I was able to do in Shan-Si.

This letter of thanks is sent by hand.

May you daily enjoy happiness.

I respectfully present my name.[13]

Although the unrest wasn't fully quelled, conditions improved considerably after Cen's arrival. He reduced the level of official corruption and enforced government regulations more strictly. Dr Kilborn reported that 'under our enlightened Viceroy, we are making progress. Chentu streets are being cleaned. . . . Oil lamps are set up on low posts at short intervals, and are lit every night. . . . Moreover, well-dressed policemen are now stationed at frequent intervals through the city. Each is armed with a light stick, and all seem well disciplined. Without doubt the cause of law and order is advancing.'[14] Change was slower in the countryside but good rainfall in the autumn of 1902 revived the agriculture and contributed to the peace of the region.

Cen stayed only for eight months and was then moved on to his position in Guangdong. In response to farewell good wishes from the missionary community he wrote, 'I have barely suppressed the disaffected and have but roughly pacified the country. Besides this, I have scarcely made a beginning to all the reforms that are necessary.'[15] He also noted that, due to efforts on both sides, 'Chinese and Foreigners are coming more and more into cordial relations' and expressed a positive view of Christianity, seeing it as a force for good among the people. Thankfully, his successor, Xi Liang, who arrived in the autumn of 1903, pursued these reforms even more fully in his four-year term as governor.

By the time Cen left Chengdu Torrance had departed for his first furlough. The combination of various pressures, both personal and as a result of the tumultuous events happening around him, had taken its toll and he had applied to the CIM China council for furlough in 1903 after seven years in China. Not all such applications were granted, especially for married couples who might go ten years without a furlough, but

13 Ibid., p129.
14 WCMN, April 1903, pp75-76.
15 WCMN, July 1903, p99.

Vale urged the council that 'in consideration of the peculiarly trying experience through which he has passed during his residence in China, and of the fact that he is nervously overstrained, the request should be acceded to.'[16] Having had his own furlough brought forward in 1897 for similar reasons, Vale knew what it was like to try and keep going with what today might be called burn-out. The Council agreed and on February 10, 1903, Torrance sailed from Shanghai, arriving in what was now Edwardian Britain on March 15, three days after his thirty-second birthday. It must have felt strange to be back in Western clothing and blend easily into the English-speaking crowd with no-one pointing out 'the foreigner'.

Torrance initially stayed in London and was a speaker at the annual CIM meetings held in May at Exeter Hall on the Strand. He was in Britain for about eighteen months and although little documentation is available regarding his stay, much of it was probably spent in Scotland regaining his health, seeing his friends and family, which by now included his siblings' spouses and their children, as well as speaking at various churches and meetings and connecting with those who received his letters and prayed regularly for him. By this time his parents were in their early sixties and would have been glad of his help on the farm and it seems likely, too, that he visited Mary Bryce. She was still receiving medical care and, either during this time or in some earlier correspondence, she urged him to move on and marry someone who could cope with the demands of life in China.[17]

Back in China

After almost six weeks on the *SS Macedonia*, Torrance arrived back in Shanghai on October 26, 1904. When weather conditions were fair this sea journey was the most relaxing stage of the journey and from Shanghai onwards there were now better quality steamers on the Yangtze, but negotiating the rapids was always potentially hazardous and on arrival in Chongqing Torrance still faced the ten day overland journey to Chengdu. His arrival in Chengdu in January 1905 was announced in the *West China Missionary News* as that of one 'who returns after two years furlough bringing with him health from the heather'.[18] His stay in Scotland had clearly been restorative.

---

16   CIM Minutes, 51st China Council Session, July 1902.
17   TT to Dr John Hykes, January 23, 1921.
18   WCMN, Feb 1905, p40.

In Chengdu life was now relatively peaceful under Viceroy Xi Liang. The city and its suburbs had been divided into clearly defined districts with street name signs erected and the houses numbered. Street hygiene was much improved with less rubbish-dumping and cesspools and large puddles filled in, helping to reduce malarial breeding grounds. In November 1904 a provincial Chinese daily paper had been launched which included imperial decrees, palace news, Sichuan and Chengdu news, and foreign events, as well as special articles, 'all brought to one's breakfast table every morning in the week!'.[19] In late 1905 a rudimentary fire service was also established, with so-called 'water dragons' which 'now go rattling along the streets and after them bands of braves with banners and buckets for drill fortnightly on the East Parade ground.'[20] Fire was a potential nightmare in the densely packed streets of wooden-framed houses.

Relations between Xi Liang and the missionary community were positive and Xi had made donations to the three Protestant mission hospitals now in Chengdu. In keeping with government reforms, the missionaries had established an Anti-Footbinding Society, printing and distributing tracts urging an end to the practice. On the east side of the city a new foreign store had opened and the range of imported items available for purchase was increasing. A December 1903 advertisement in the WCMN for Samuel Toye and Company in Chongqing included Van Houten's Cocoa, jams, salmon, cigars, opera and field glasses, phonographs, tennis rackets, mechanical children's toys, and photographic materials. Bicycles were also listed, still relatively rare among the Chinese in Chengdu but increasingly popular among those foreigners who could afford them.

In a review of his first year back in China, written in February 1906 to friends and family in Britain, Torrance marvelled at the transformation:

A wonderful change has come over the province since I first came to it ten years ago. It has veered clear round from its former conservative anti-foreign attitude. And the Chentu officials are the leaders of the movement. If they could only have their way the place would soon be hardly recognisable. Even now the change is wonderful. Everything European is the rage. Schools are springing up like mushrooms. The scholars are discarding Chinese clothes and going in for garments as near ours in pattern as they can. . . .

19   WCMN, Jan 1905, p11.
20   WCMN, Dec 1905, p257.

Lately they had foreign sports on a large scale on one of the parade grounds. Over two thousand scholars in the new up-to-date schools were present competing. Only a few years ago none of us would have considered such an advance credible. But to-day it is actual fact. Truly a great modern miracle.

This was a remarkable change from the hostility of the Boxer period, and the positive attitude extended to the churches, schools, and hospitals of the Protestant missions, all of which were now well attended.

The growing familiarity with things foreign was accompanied by more Sichuanese going overseas, and Japan was proving popular as a study destination, an acknowledgement that despite Chinese resentment of the Japanese, their rapid modernisation and industrialisation had much to teach China. Other Chinese had gone to Belgium to study railway engineering and mining, and one group had been sent to the US for three years to train as machine shop apprentices with a view to working in Chengdu's arsenal. The growth of interest in railways and mining was to have a long-lasting impact not only on the future of Sichuan but also, detrimentally, on the Qing dynasty.

Although the CIM had evangelistic and training work going on in Chengdu, Torrance was once again tasked with itinerating and not long after his return he set off for a highly popular religious fair about thirty miles from Chengdu in the company of George Franck, another single missionary who had joined the Chengdu station in 1903. Torrance described the lively occasion in his February newsletter:

It was not altogether a safe undertaking for at such times the crowds are easily excited. Still we went. The Mandarin heard of our going and sent strict orders for our safety. The scene was a never-to-be-forgotten one. Thousands and thousands of people surged in and around the temple that gave its name to the fair. Each visitor brought his or her handful of incense sticks and the result was a huge bonfire in the temple court. . . . We moved around at first amongst the vast concourse to see what there was to be seen but soon selected a suitable place to stand and preach and get rid of our books and tracts. We disposed of good quantities of Christian literature. The crowds on the whole were very orderly. I got struck once with a piece of hard soil but it didn't hurt.

In April 1905, three months after returning from Scotland, Torrance moved to the ancient town of Qionglai to join CIM missionary

James Webster while Fawcett and Florence Olsen went on furlough. He was to remain there nearly two years. Qionglai, formerly known as Qiongzhou, was a two-day journey southwest of Chengdu where the plain meets the foothills of the western mountains and Torrance enjoyed the beauty of the surrounding countryside. He and Webster often travelled out to the smaller towns and villages to talk with the locals and hand out literature, surrounded as usual by a large, curious crowd. The proximity to the mountains didn't seem to bring much respite from the heat, which was a trial at times in the summer months. 'I had one walk of twelve miles in a blazing sun', wrote Torrance, 'and it was a long time before I recovered from the effects of it. In July the heat was so stifling and the mosquitoes so abundant I was almost breaking down but recovered back.'[21] The Mandarin in Qionglai was not friendly towards foreigners but this didn't deter some of the local people, who regularly came to the meetings which Torrance and Webster held almost every evening.

In August Torrance was able to go to the hills above Guanxian for a break from the heat. The rambling Lingyan temple complex had become a popular getaway among the missionaries in western Sichuan and would be Torrance's summer retreat for years to come.[22] Its basic accommodation could house quite a few families and there was a good social atmosphere as the missionaries, many with children, spent time together. It also provided an opportunity for single missionaries to socialise together in a more relaxed environment.

Back in Qionglai the work was thriving and by the end of 1905 there were six Chinese-run CIM outstations in the Qionglai region, and thousands of tracts, Scripture portions, and other books had been distributed. Five men from Qionglai had gone to Chengdu to attend the CIM Bible school, now run by Adam Grainger, which offered general classes in geography, Asian history, and astronomy, as well as lessons on preaching and public reading. In the afternoons the men participated in evangelistic work in and around Chengdu.

Torrance's medical knowledge was put to good use in Qionglai. During 1905 he and James Webster and his new wife tended to about seven hundred patients, as well as providing quinine 'morning, noon and night' for many who succumbed to malaria during the long, hot,

---

21 TT, newsletter, Feb 1, 1906.
22 Torrance always wrote of this as Ling'ai Temple but it is known today as Lingyan Temple (灵岩寺).

humid summer. The quinine they sold at cost price in 'Burroughs and Wellcome's Tabloid form'. On one occasion Torrance was called out to treat a man with a fractured femur, which he put in splints. Returning three days later he found the splints removed because the leg was itching. Having re-set the leg he spoke so sternly to the family that they left the splint on and the man made a good recovery.

One of Torrance's great sorrows was being called to treat opium users, a sorrow made worse by Britain's involvement in the trade. Opium cases fell into two main categories: those who attempted suicide with it and those who were addicted and wanted to break their dependency. Unless the suicide cases were treated promptly it was 'a disagreeable business' with the patient's chances of pulling through quite slim. With the addicts there was more hope. 'They have a hard time for a few days but after a week the worst is over. Opium does men more harm by far than drink and they are more the slaves of it, but under the care of a missionary in an opium refuge or hospital they can be entirely cured of the habit. We have lots of cases in proof.'[23]

In early 1906 the Websters moved to another station and after a much enjoyed Christmas break in Chengdu Torrance was soon back in Qionglai running the station on his own. The work was growing and in the spring eleven local Chinese were baptised, having met Torrance's requirement that they show clear evidence of Christian understanding and commitment.[24] In the summer, instead of going to Lingyan Temple, he travelled with fellow missionary James Stewart up to the coolness of the Kham Tibetan region of Kangding, in today's Ganzi Tibetan Autonomous Prefecture. This was the first of many ventures up into the mountains west of the Chengdu plain but not one that would yet take him into the Qiang area.

In October Torrance returned to Chengdu for a five-day CIM conference. Back in May, Vale, in Britain again for the sake of his wife's health, had spoken at the CIM's fortieth anniversary meeting about the progress being made in Sichuan and the need for the local churches eventually to become self-governing and self-supporting, with Chinese Christians taking responsibility for evangelism and teaching. In keeping with this, there were fifty Chinese representatives from Leshan, Qionglai, and Guanxian attending the conference. Torrance, who preached the final sermon, was tasked with writing conference

23   TT, newsletter, Feb 1, 1906.
24   *Millions*, May 1906, p78.

reports for *China's Millions* and the *West China Missionary News* and described the positive atmosphere.[25] One of the main speakers was the Chinese pastor in Danling, who spoke on the need for 'the enduement of the power of the Holy Spirit'.[26] Alongside the general Christian teaching, topical issues were discussed including polygamy, strong drink, and the problem of conflating aspects of Christianity and Confucianism. There was unanimity regarding polygamy but a small minority wanted more discretion with regard to alcohol, which was an important part of official and business entertaining.

Not long after returning to Qionglai from the conference, Torrance was taken seriously ill with what seems to have been pneumonia and Dr Canright had to rush from Chengdu to attend to him. Once he was strong enough to be moved he was brought to Chengdu where he made a slow recovery and was eventually able to return to Qionglai. When the Olsens arrived back in January 1907 they were full of praise for what Torrance had accomplished in his time there:

> He has been doing good work in our absence – added thirty-seven new members to the church, making a total membership of seventy-three throughout the district – and left the church in a flourishing condition. The interest in the country districts is increasing, and open doors on all sides invite us to enter in.[27]

Moving back to Chengdu, Torrance once again became part of a larger team with the Vales, Graingers, and George Franck, and resumed his work among the Chengdu outstations. Although the wider social circle provided by the various missions in Chengdu was a welcome change it was perhaps a challenge, having run the Qionglai station on his own for a year, to be back to his itinerating and not have responsibility for any of the work in Chengdu. His singleness still seemed to be an impediment to permanently running his own station and George Franck was now engaged to be married and not a potential co-worker for pioneering a new work. At a 1907 CIM conference later in the year, attended once again by many Chinese delegates, Torrance gave a report on his districts of Meishan, Pengshan, and Xinjin, all to the south of Chengdu, where there were nearly two hundred church members. The Meishan Christians were raising funds to support their own Chinese pastor.

25   Ibid., March 1907, p39; WCMN, Feb 1907, pp4-6.
26   WCMN, Feb 1907, p4.
27   WCMN, March 1907, p20. Written by Olsen on Feb 11, 1907.

Further improvements had been made in the city during Torrance's absence, with more trees planted and better sanitation. Construction was also in progress on the first carriage road, about one mile long, connecting Chengdu's south gate with the big Qingyang temple where the annual spring fair was held. In the summer of 1907 serious flooding threatened some of this progress. A huge downpour on August 21 resulted in several deaths and the collapse of walls and homes. Before the city had time to recover it was followed by another torrential downpour four days later, leaving some places under four to five feet of water. This resulted in more deaths and destruction of homes as well as the collapse of part of the old Imperial City wall and a section of the main city wall near the south gate.

Away from the floods, Torrance was at Lingyan Temple again that summer. James Stewart, his Kangding companion of the previous year, was travelling with fellow missionary James Neave into the hill country northwest of Chengdu, looking for potential outstation sites for their Canadian Methodist Mission (CMM). Their interest was primarily in Tibetan groups but their route took them through the region of the Qiang people. Following their report of the trip, a discussion was held between the CMM and CIM regarding this border-tribes district and it was suggested that the CMM open a work in the town of Miansi, on the southern edge of the Qiang region. In the end this never materialised but curiosity about the area was increasing and that same summer William Fergusson of the British & Foreign Bible Society also made a trip there, distributing literature in what he described as 'the aboriginal tribes country to the north-west'.[28]

In December 1907 *China's Millions* carried an article summarising some of the advances being made across the nation as the long-awaited reforms gradually began to make a difference:

In China alone 3,746 miles of railway are now in daily use, while 1,622 miles are under construction; 2,096 modern post offices have been recently opened, which last year handled 113 millions of articles; while 346 telegraphic centres, with 34,641 miles of wire, link up the Empire and keep the most distant Yamen in closest touch with Peking. An educational revolution has been outlined, and in some measure entered upon; a constitutional government has been

28   WCMN, August 1907, p16.

promised; anti-opium regulations put in force, and a modern army organised. On all hands strenuous efforts are being made to grapple with national weaknesses and to qualify the country for a worthy place among the Powers. The spectacle of an awakening China cannot but fascinate the world.[29]

As China changed, so some of the missionaries were also pushing for change in their situation. In late 1906 the CIM Council minutes had recorded that Charles Coates, who would later be stationed in the Qiang area, had written to inform them 'that he had removed his queue, alleging that it had caused injury to his health, and intimating that, as the result of much prayer and thought, he had finally decided that he could not consent to grow another natural one, and further that he had found it impracticable, for several reasons, to wear cap and false queue.'[30]

Indicating the gravity of the situation, Council members, including Bishop Cassels from Sichuan, were asked to make the long journey to Shanghai for discussions in the hope that they could persuade Coates to alter his position. This had clearly become a topic of discussion among the CIM missionaries in Western Sichuan and at the same council meeting a letter was read out signed by seventeen of them, including Torrance, in which, as the minutes reported, they

> expressed their feelings and convictions concerning the matter of wearing the Chinese dress. They alleged that times and customs had changed so rapidly and radically in the district referred to during the past few years that a foreigner in native dress is becoming an object of ridicule among the Chinese. This, with one or two exceptions, they felt to be a hindrance to the work. They, therefore, asked that the subject might receive careful and candid consideration with a view to making the matter of dress – especially the wearing of the queue – optional with individual workers in this district at least.[31]

The discussion continued the following day with the reading out of a letter from Dixon Hoste, now CIM director, to Torrance himself, and of letters between George Franck and Dixon Hoste's deputy, John Stevenson. The

---

29   Marshall Broomhall, 'The Renaissance of China', *Millions*, Dec 1907, p183.
30   CIM minutes, 67th China Council Session, Nov 22, 1906.
31   Ibid.

council had concluded that although some Chinese in the cities along the Yangtze valley had discarded the queue and were wearing a more Western style of dress, until the imperial government officially made such things optional the CIM would continue to insist on Chinese dress and the wearing of the queue for their members in all parts of China. Having imposed the queue on the Han Chinese as a sign of submission after it came to power in 1644, the Manchu government had recently issued an order forbidding their removal, so any such action on the part of missionaries risked being seen as supportive of growing anti-Qing activity among the Chinese. The council's decision seems to have been a wise one. Han Suyin recorded that 'as late as 1907 one man was beaten to death at the railway station in Peking because he wore a false queue and inadvertently lifted his hat, exposing his queueless condition.'[32]

---

32   Han, *Crippled Tree*, p158.

Chapter 4

Annie

1907-1911

On September 17, 1907, a young woman who would change Torrance's life forever set sail for China. Annie Elizabeth Sharpe, twelve years Torrance's junior, was born on October 23, 1883, at her grandfather's house in Mortlake, Surrey. Her mother had married aged twenty and against her father's wishes, but was widowed shortly before Annie's birth when her new husband died suddenly of blood poisoning. A move to nearby Richmond, where Annie spent her early years, was followed by another move to Yorkshire with her grandfather and her mother's step-sister. At the time Annie didn't know why her mother hadn't accompanied them but discovered later that she had remarried, once again without her father's blessing, and that Annie had a half-brother about seven years her junior. Her mother eventually joined them in Yorkshire, returning alone with her son.

Although Annie enjoyed school and being out and about in the countryside, life at home was not so happy and she was often alone. Having hoped to continue her studies, her grandfather then fell on hard times and she felt pressure to find a job. After one bad work experience she found a position in Finsbury Park, north London, as a mother's help. The family treated her almost like a daughter but Annie felt unsettled and when her two cousins, Jeannie and Emily, urged her to join them in Bromley, she moved on and unexpectedly entered one of the happiest periods of her young life.[1]

In Bromley she was able to work in the high-class furnishing business where Jeannie managed one of the departments and at home she conversed easily with both cousins. As they chatted Annie discovered that although they had previously been members of the Church of England her cousins had found a more personal Christian faith through the local Young Women's Christian Association. Their

---

1   Annie Torrance. *Memoirs.* Unpublished, c.1977-79, p2. The cousin's name was Jane Cook but she preferred to be known as Jeannie. She and Emily had lived in Yorkshire for a while and Annie knew them well.

conversations stirred her to reflect on her own faith and one day, having been greatly impacted by a tract about eternal life, she was reading some verses about forgiveness of sin in the Old Testament book of Isaiah and experienced a moment of great clarity:

> Somehow as I read these verses in Isaiah I seemed to pass into another world. Spiritually, the scales began to drop from my eyes. I kept thinking about them and going over them. Everything I had thought before seemed dead and lifeless. All the church-going etc seemed to have been a mechanical exercise, without understanding and without life and light. Everything seemed to appear quite changed and I knew I could never go back to the old ways. I had seen the Light, almost suddenly, and it changed everything.[2]

From that time on Annie became increasingly involved in local mission work with her cousins and felt more satisfied and at peace than she had ever been. Living not far from London they were able to hear some of the famous preachers of the day, one of whom was Dr Grattan Guinness, whose father had founded Hulme Cliff College where Torrance had studied and whose sister Geraldine was married to one of Hudson Taylor's sons. It was a book by Geraldine which planted in Annie's heart the desire to work in China and from then on the idea of becoming a missionary was never far from her thoughts. She was eventually accepted for training at Redcliffe College in Chelsea where she was thrown into 'a life of rigid discipline' such as she 'had not hitherto known' and realised how little she knew and how 'unbendable' she was.[3] Despite this she quickly immersed herself in community living and in her studies, not just biblical but also English grammar, mathematics, music, and other general subjects, all of which helped satisfy her earlier desire to continue her education. After a challenging start it became a highly enjoyable period, perhaps the first time she had really known satisfying friendships beyond her cousins, or experienced such intellectual, social, and spiritual stimulation.

After a final year of training with the CIM in Canonbury, north London, on September 17, 1907, Annie set sail for China on the *Prince Ludwig*, celebrating her twenty-fourth birthday somewhere between Singapore and Hong Kong, just before the ship sailed into a typhoon. 'It was terrific and really terrifying. We went up and down

---

2   *Memoirs*, p9. Isaiah 43:26 and 44:22.
3   Ibid., p13.

mountains of water . . . [but] the Presence of the Lord was nearer than the storm.'[4] The storm lasted a few days and was the most violent she would ever encounter. The ship finally docked in Shanghai on November 1 and after the usual outfitting Annie moved to Yangzhou for her orientation, which included learning not to run – ungraceful and improper, so she was told, for a woman in China.

Dixon Hoste decided to place Annie with the Hutson family in Guanxian rather than with other young single women missionaries under the oversight of Bishop William Cassels in eastern Sichuan. As Annie later wrote in her memoirs, 'Mr Hoste said my station lay near the Borderland to Tibet and I would live with a Scottish missionary and his wife who was rather deaf!'[5] It may be that Hoste knew her spiritual experience was not primarily Anglican but he also seems to have recognised that Annie had the character and maturity to handle quite a lonely and challenging situation.

ANNIE (BACK LEFT) WITH NEW MISSIONARIES FOR CHINA

After a rough journey in a small boat from Yangzhou to their Yangtze steamer, Annie's party of new missionaries travelled to Hankou and enjoyed a few days at the CIM station there before taking another steamer up-river, travelling native class with their own bedding. On this stretch they got stuck on a sandbank and had to be ferried in small boats to another steamer which got them safely to Yichang, where Annie was given never-to-be-forgotten words of advice from resident

4   Ibid., p19.
5   Ibid., p23.

CIM missionary Herbert Squire: 'Never stand aloof from the Chinese. You won't be attracted to them nor them to you if you keep them at arm's length.'[6]

Joined by George Franck and his new wife, they set out on the next stretch through the rapids to Chongqing, travelling by Chinese houseboat for almost six weeks. In Chongqing Annie and the Francks then repacked their possessions for the overland journey to Chengdu by sedan chair. Only certain things could go with them, the rest would be transported by boat, a circuitous route which would take another five or six weeks.

Annie found this last part of the journey the most trying. It was June and stiflingly hot. To make matters worse, having been instructed to consume only their own food and boiled water, the Chinese carrier with the provisions lagged behind and they went for hours the first day with no food or drink. He finally caught up with them but from then on they broke the rules and drank Chinese tea at inns along the way, with assurances that the water had been boiled. With great relief they reached Chengdu on June 20, 1908, where Annie was warmly welcomed by the Graingers who showed her some of the city. After a couple of days she continued to Guanxian and the Hutsons. James Hutson and Adam Grainger were cousins, both Scottish, and Mrs Hutson, to Annie's delight, turned out to be from Bromley. The Hutsons had two children at home, a baby on the way, and one son at the Chefoo boarding school on the other side of China. After nearly three months of constant travelling Annie was glad to meet them and finally settle down.

With its ethnic mix Guanxian probably wasn't quite the China Annie had envisaged. Strategically situated as a hub for Muslim, Tibetan, and Qiang traders coming down the Min Valley from the western mountains and beyond, it was an unusual melting pot. Isabella Bird's 1895 description highlighted the contrasts. On one hand it was 'one of the best-placed cities in China, at the north-west corner of the Chengtu plain, immediately below the mountains'. On the other hand, she found it 'an unattractive town, with narrow, dirty streets, small lifeless-looking shops' and 'an outpost air, as if there were little beyond'.[7] Despite this, it was also 'a great emporium of the trade with Northern Tibet, which is at its height during the winter, when as many as five hundred Tibetans,

6   Ibid., p25.
7   Bird, *Yangtze Valley*, p338.

with their yaks, are encamped outside its wall.' Its chief industry was the manufacture of straw sandals, which Torrance would later buy each year for his own trips beyond Guanxian to the mountains.

SEDAN CHAIR CARRIERS

Annie's main luggage arrived about five weeks later but the boat transporting it had been wrecked between Chongqing and Chengdu and her clothes had been ruined by the river water and running dye, leaving just her Chinese wadded winter garments. Adding insult to injury, robbers broke into the mission house that night and made off with these last pieces of clothing although, having been disturbed at the last minute by Annie calling for the Hutsons, they left behind the old sewing machine she had brought from England and one last bundle of things upon which lay her Bible. Thankfully she was able to make a skirt and blouse out of some silk the Hutsons bought for her.

Like any new missionary, Annie's primary occupation in these early days was learning Chinese. Apart from the Hutsons there were no other foreigners for company and in the evening they would retire early, leaving Annie feeling rather isolated. In retrospect she wished that single missionaries had been assigned in twos, although the situation was intermittently alleviated by visitors passing through, not just those going to the Guanxian hills for the summer but also both missionaries and explorers travelling up the Min Valley to the tribal regions.[8]

8   See D. M. Glover et al, *Explorers and Scientists in China's Borderlands, 1880-1950*. University of Washington Press. 2012.

As Annie's language improved she started accompanying a local Christian woman to hold meetings in the homes of some of the church congregation and later to some of the outstations where they would stay for a week or two. Occasionally she was able to visit Chengdu, where she sometimes helped Mrs Grainger with dress-making, and she also went to Qionglai to see Hannah Overland, who had travelled out to China with her. Hannah was living with the Olsens in Qionglai and was engaged to Charles Coates, infamous for his protest against wearing the queue. To Annie's delight another single missionary, Fanny Riley, was eventually sent to Guanxian for a while and she and Annie enjoyed each other's company. James Hutson had a wide selection of books and Annie later recalled reading aloud from works on Jewish history by Josephus while Fanny knitted.[9]

Annie's first summer was one of the hottest the CIM missionaries could remember but having only arrived in late June and with Mrs Hutson soon to give birth, Annie wasn't able to escape the heat and join the other missionaries in the hills. However, Torrance happened to call in at the Guanxian mission station on his way up to the hills and Annie caught sight of him in the courtyard. 'I came out of my room or was near there when we met. He was dressed in Chinese, tall, slim and really quite striking. He always had remarkable eyes. As we met a strange feeling passed through me that I had never experienced before.'[10]

With the busyness of life and with difficult experiences of marriage within her own family, Annie had not given much thought to romantic relationships so the impact of this encounter took her by surprise. She had pictured herself as a devoted single missionary, not as a missionary wife with devotion in two directions. She and Torrance didn't talk but later that summer she was able to make a very brief visit up to the hills and was invited to a meal with the Olsens at which Torrance was present. She had clearly made an equally instantaneous yet deep impression on Torrance, and the Olsens had been enlisted to further their acquaintance. A while later Annie made one of her visits to the Graingers in Chengdu and was invited to a meal by the Ramsays at which Torrance was also present. Clarence Ramsay, a close friend of Torrance, had previously worked with the CIM in Chongqing but since 1904 had been the Chengdu agent of the American Bible Society. After tea in the garden, the Ramsays left Annie and Thomas alone to chat

9   *Memoirs*, p34.
10 Ibid., p33.

for a while. On her next visit to Chengdu she stayed with the Ramsays which made it easier for her friendship with Torrance to deepen.

That autumn was memorable not just for Torrance and Annie, but for the whole of China. On November 14, 1908, Emperor Guangxu died, his death arranged by Empress Dowager Cixi who, knowing her own was imminent and pulling the strings till the bitter end, had already organised the succession.[11] Cixi died the next day. The successor was two-year-old Emperor Puyi, with his father, Prince Chun, acting as regent, and the transition was peaceful, even though it was clear to many that the Qing dynasty's days were numbered. The December editorial in *China's Millions* was brief and cautious in its comments, lauding Emperor Guangxu as a moderniser but ambivalent about Cixi, suggesting time alone would show what part she had really played during her more than fifty years of influence.[12]

Chengdu was plunged into obligatory mourning, with white cotton draped over gateways and the colour red banned, even down to red buttons of rank on the hats of officials being replaced with blue or black buttons.[13] Schools were closed for five days, music was forbidden for twenty-seven days, and heads and faces were not to be shaved for one hundred days – no small thing for the barbers or their customers judging by Isabella Bird's observation that 'Once a week at least, the Chinese, however poor, must have the front and middle of his head smoothly shaven, or he looks like a convict.'[14]

Early in 1909 Annie was left in charge of the Guanxian station while the Hutsons made the several-month round trip to northeast China to take another of their children to school in Chefoo. Fanny Riley had moved on and Annie was now joined temporarily by Ella Bailey, a fairly new missionary who would eventually work with the Olsens in Qionglai. After a slightly rocky start they did well together and were kept busy with language study, local and outstation visits, and hosting various guests. Once the Hutsons returned, Annie and Ella were able to go up to Lingyan Temple for a rest. There was quite a crowd up there that summer, including Torrance and the Olsens and some of Torrance's good Canadian and American friends. Annie recalled how

11 Jung Chang, *Cixi*, Kindle. An autopsy in 2008 indicated that his death had been caused by a lethal dose of arsenic.
12 *Millions*, 1908, p188.
13 WCMN, Dec 1908, p19.
14 Bird, *Yangtze Valley*, pp80-81; WCMN, Dec 1908, p19.

Torrance seemed to accidentally turn up when she went for walks in the surrounding countryside. For both of them it became 'the summer that was' and they realised that they were falling deeply in love.[15]

Torrance was now thirty-eight and after the sorrow of Mary Bryce's ill health and return to Britain and all the years on his own it seemed he had at last found someone with whom to share his life. At the beginning of September Annie wrote to 'Dear Mr Torrance', signing herself as A.E.S. She was clearly finding it hard to settle into her old routine with the Hutsons and wrote poetically of the hills above Guanxian reminding her of 'woodland rambles, moonlight dreams'. Her love for literature was also revealed in some lines quoted from Longfellow's poem, *A Psalm of Life*, in which her underlinings encouraged Torrance to '<u>Be</u> a <u>hero</u> in the strife!' but also showed the uncertainty she was feeling about the future: 'Let <u>us</u> then be up and doing, with a heart for <u>any</u> fate; still achieving, still pursuing, <u>Learn</u> to <u>Labour</u> and to <u>Wait</u>.'[16] On his return to Chengdu after the summer Torrance also wrote to Annie – with less emphasis on waiting and a very definite proposal of marriage. But the letter was never sent.

During their conversations over the summer Torrance had explained to Annie that he was facing some difficulties within the CIM, but he hadn't told her all the details. In the spring tensions had arisen between himself and his senior CIM missionary at that time in Chengdu, tensions no doubt aggravated by them living at such close quarters in the mission station. The underlying reason concerned an ex-Daoist priest named Wang who had studied at Grainger's Bible school and had been recommended by the senior missionary to work as an evangelist with James Hutson in Guanxian.

Wang had expressed a desire to marry and a match was being arranged by one of the church deacons with a Chinese girl from a mission school in Chengdu. However, Hutson had heard a rumour that Wang was already married and had a child. Knowing he had previously lived in a district where Torrance often itinerated, Hutson had asked Torrance to look into the matter and the rumour was discovered to be true. It was also known to Torrance and others that the deacon arranging the marriage and some of the other church members had fallen into the habit of gambling. The senior missionary, who was in charge of the church, was loath to accept the accusations and he and Torrance found themselves seriously at odds

---

15   *Memoirs*, p37.
16   Annie to TT, Sept 2, 1909.

in their approach to the matter, despite both allegations eventually being proven true.

In April 1909 the senior missionary, and then Torrance, both sent letters of grievance to the CIM Council in Shanghai, Torrance unhappy with the senior missionary for taking the part of the church members who, in their anger, had made accusations against him, and the senior missionary charging Torrance with poor conduct towards the Chinese and remissness in his work – in particular, spending too much time in Chengdu between his trips to the outstations. There was some truth to the latter charge but Torrance had suffered from bouts of dysentery and pneumonia and it took time to recover from the demanding periods of itinerating. In response to their letters the Sichuan CIM superintendent, based in Chongqing, was asked to visit Chengdu and discuss the matter. By the end of his enquiry the best solution seemed to be for the two men to work in different spheres, something about which they were both in agreement, and he recommended that Torrance move to work elsewhere in China with the CIM.

That probably would have been the end of the matter had it not been for a rumour passed on to the superintendent during his visit. The rumour was connected to a prank played at the wedding of missionary John Muir and his wife, which had not only been wrongly attributed to Torrance but was then also embellished. Unfortunately this was included in the report to the council and seems to have tipped the balance with regard to the council's decision. Although they asked the superintendent to investigate the matter further, he seems not to have done so and the Muirs, who would have been the best witnesses, were far away in the remote Tibetan region of Batang. On July 29 the Council wrote to Torrance suggesting that it would be for the best if he offered his resignation. Thankfully the letter came overland and wasn't able to spoil the summer but its arrival coincided with Torrance's written but unsent proposal to Annie.

Torrance would later recognise that his departure from the CIM brought much needed change into his life. The health issues he was battling were wearing him down, not helped by the constant round of itinerating which often meant staying in very basic accommodation, and as he got older he was finding the situation in Chengdu quite restrictive, especially after his independence in Qionglai. However, at the time it was an extremely painful situation and, having been expecting a transfer to another part of China, it was a shock to be facing a return to Britain and a separation from Annie. It was also confusing because, ironically, no-one had actually told Torrance the details of the wedding rumour. The Council considered the matter too indelicate to mention in their letter so simply alluded to conduct which was 'most unbecoming'. What Torrance *had* done was secretly to invite a Chinese band to serenade the Muirs so he must have been bemused by this negative assessment of his behaviour. He only heard the other tale from Annie much later. The record wasn't actually set straight until John Muir returned to Chengdu in 1911, heard the story and refuted it in writing to both Torrance and the CIM. In August 1912 the CIM withdrew the charge connected with the rumour and exonerated Torrance, by which time the senior missionary had moved to a more literature-based role elsewhere in China.

It is clear from Broomhall's candid seven-volume history of the CIM that tensions among missionaries were not unusual, with people from all sorts of backgrounds being thrown together, often living at close quarters in quite intense circumstances and with the added pressure of the political ups and downs of the period. A 1906 article in *China's Millions* had addressed the issue to help new missionaries departing for China: 'Where you have but one, or two, or three men or women at the most, you soon come down to the bare bones of their personality, and there is sometimes a poverty, a lack of understanding, not through lack of Christian life, but through lack of those fresh incomings of other interests that sweeten and sustain and bless, in ways we cannot name, the needs of the soul.'[17]

It was a distressing time for Annie too but with hindsight she was able to be more philosophical about things: 'There had been a clash of personalities and ungrounded suspicion and unkind gossip and it had festered and done its work – all so easy in the mission field, where the community is limited. Missionaries get exhausted, tired and discouraged and alas spiritual zeal may run low.'[18] She also mentions in her memoirs that Torrance had been seen by some of the missionaries as a little fiery and he clearly had a strong code of honour, especially concerning perceived injustice or dishonesty, which perhaps led to exacting high standards from others. He must have sometimes rued the day he was asked to investigate the Wang affair and found himself placed in such an awkward position. Several years later an old Chinese deacon from the CIM church, who had been deeply grieved over the

---

17 *Millions*, Oct 1906, p153. Address given by Principal Forbes Jackson of Harley College at the Lower Exeter Hall Valedictory meeting on Sept 11, 1906.
18 *Memoirs*, p38.

situation, came to visit Torrance and acknowledged that Wang and the other deacon had been furious with Torrance and had sought to cause trouble for him.

Although he was given the option to stay for a further six months, Torrance decided to leave almost immediately for Shanghai and Scotland. The Francks were temporarily in charge of the CIM mission house in Chengdu which made it easy for Annie to stay with them and visit Torrance, who by now was staying with the Ramsays. As Annie wrote in her memoirs, they were precious but sad days. 'The future was quite unknown. Dad had no idea of any prospects. We did not discuss it much either though one thing I well remember he said, "If the Lord means you for me He means it in any land or clime!" I replied, "If the Lord means us for each other, He will bring you back to China." I think he was dubious about that. On the other hand, the thought of my leaving the Mission Field and the CIM was a terrifying one and I did feel if the Lord meant us for each other God *would* bring him back to China. Of course neither of us could then visualise how that could possibly be.'[19]

It made life easier for Annie that she and Torrance were not officially engaged at this time. They both knew they were committed to each other and the lack of a formal engagement saved the need for any explanations about their friendship or any immediate decisions about her future with the CIM. For Torrance the future looked bleak with no plans and no idea how friends and family back home would respond to his sudden return. Left behind in Guanxian, Annie threw herself into her work, living from one of Torrance's letters to the next through the dreary winter and oscillating between discouragement and a sense of God sustaining her.

Back in Scotland at the end of 1909, there was one advantage for Torrance – he had time to write. During his years in China he had developed a passion for local history and archaeology and in 1908-1909, as Chengdu correspondent for the *North China Daily News*, he had written two articles about caves in western Sichuan. The caves were thought by some to have been dwelling places for earlier non-Han inhabitants of the area but Torrance's findings showed they had actually been burial sites, with the remoter ones still containing tombs and grave goods. He concluded his second article with a plea for others with more expertise to continue such investigations in Sichuan's 'very

---

19   Ibid.

large and interesting field for archaeological research.[20] He had also continued to develop his own expertise and in 1910, while he was in Scotland, his first academic article, 'Burial Customs in Sz-chuan', was published in the *Journal of the North China Branch of the Royal Asiatic Society* (JNCBRAS) with illustrations including his own cave diagrams as well as photos taken by Adam Grainger of grave goods Torrance had collected.[21]

The article gave a brief overview of contemporary burial customs: the importance of *feng shui* in selecting the grave site, the masses chanted by Buddhist and Daoist priests, the elaborate mourning procession, and the burning of paper models representing all the deceased might need in the next life – everything from houses to their favourite opium pipe or pack of cards. Giving reasons for dating these customs at least back to the Tang dynasty, Torrance then went further back to examine burials of the Han dynasty and Three Kingdoms periods. His sources included his own field work, discussions with Chinese scholars, and his own reading of Chinese classics and contemporary Western scholars, with references to Confucius, Mencius, and Sima Qian, as well as to Professor Samuel Kidd of University College London, the first Professor of Chinese Language and Literature in Britain.

A breakthrough in Torrance's situation came early in 1910 like a 'bolt from the blue' as Annie described it.[22] His good friend Clarence Ramsay wrote to Annie in Guanxian saying he was planning to resign from the American Bible Society in order to have his own Presbyterian church pastorate elsewhere in China. He suggested that Torrance replace him. With a lighter heart than she'd known for months Annie sent this news to Torrance who responded with delight. Ramsay then sent his proposition to the ABS headquarters in New York and the slow wheels were put in motion for his departure and Torrance's appointment.

In June 1910, Dr John Hykes, head of ABS operations in China since 1893, was, opportunely, in Edinburgh for the first ever World Missionary Conference and met up with Torrance to discuss future

---

20   'The "Mantze" Caves of West Szechuan'. From Our Own Correspondent. Chengtu, Sept 12. (Printed in the *North China Daily News* in late 1909. Date not on newspaper clipping.)
21   TT. 'Burial Customs in Sz-chuan'. JNCBRAS, Vol 41, 1910, pp57-75.
22   *Memoirs*, p39.

plans. As they strolled in Princes Street Gardens it was decided that Torrance, as the new ABS superintendent of colportage in Chengdu, would leave Scotland in January 1911 and arrive in Chengdu by the end of April. Torrance wrote to Annie the next day describing the enjoyable encounter. 'At last my return to China is arranged for. I met Dr. Hykes in Edinburgh yesterday. We had a fine time together. His kindness and cheery talk quite carried my heart by storm.'[23] Hykes had assured Torrance that he would be happy with the ABS, free to preserve his individuality in the work and to make many of his own decisions. Their time together concluded with an afternoon tea of strawberries and cream.

In China, Torrance's friend Fawcett Olsen had been much disturbed by all that had happened and an unsigned and undated copy of a letter, which seems to have been from him to the ABS, laid emphasis on Torrance's suitability for the new job. He wanted 'to make it plain that Mr. Torrance is fully worthy of your confidence and esteem' and he had high praise for Annie: 'He is engaged to be married to a most capable missionary lady who will be able to look after him in a way he has never before known in his long years of service in China.'[24] Hykes had no doubts about the appointment and would later write to the ABS headquarters in New York affirming that it had been a good choice: 'He has fully justified the confidence I had in him and no man could have looked after our interests in West China more conscientiously or more efficiently . . . I am glad to have a man of his type and character associated with me in the work and I know we shall never have occasion to regret his appointment.'[25]

Ever practical, and knowing how long correspondence could take from Scotland, Torrance was already thinking ahead and in his June letter to Annie he asked if she could learn from Ramsay about the ABS book-keeping system in case there was little time for a hand-over. That they were getting married and taking over the Ramsay home was already decided and Torrance asked her to check what household items the Ramsays were leaving behind and what he would need to bring out from Scotland. 'Then send me either a brass ring the size of your finger or a piece of strong paper . . . which will be a size for me

23   TT to Annie, June 1910, n.d.

24   The letter is in pencil and unsigned but the content suggests it was written by Fawcett Olsen.

25   Hykes to Rev. John Fox, D.D., L.L.D., ABS Corresponding Secretary. Aug 30, 1912.

to get the plain ring.'[26] He also offered to buy Annie her own copy of Josephus' *The Antiquities of the Jews*.

In Chengdu Ramsay was becoming impatient to move on with his own plans and it was eventually decided that he would leave earlier than originally planned. To bridge the gap before Torrance's return, the Hutsons gave permission for Annie to make visits to Chengdu to learn about the ABS work and begin supervising essentials at the ABS compound, which included the accounts and the itinerations of the ABS colporteurs, who travelled far and wide in Sichuan as evangelists and literature distributors.

In the spring of 1911, just before taking up these responsibilities, Annie had an unexpected opportunity to travel up to the Qiang area with Ella Bailey to visit Charles and Hannah Coates, who were now in charge of a new CIM station in Weizhou, at the confluence of the Min and Zagunao rivers.

It was the only trip Annie would ever make to the region but it proved invaluable once Torrance started his travels among the Qiang and she could picture his journeys up through the mountains to the Qiang villages. Shod with straw sandals and walking or riding in sedan chairs, she and Ella crossed the Niangziling Pass between Guanxian and the Min Valley and then followed the river up to Weizhou, with the mountains towering ever higher around them. It was a refreshing change of scenery:

> The atmosphere was wonderfully clear and pleasant. It was very quiet save for the tinkle of the bells on the mules as the muleteers came and went through the village. The Coates were exceedingly kind and we had a lovely visit. We went for various walks, crossed rope bridges etc.[27]

During morning devotions with the Coates one day there was a thunderous rumbling under their feet as an earthquake suddenly shook the valley.

Charles and Hannah were expecting their first baby not long after Annie and Ella's visit and Annie arranged for them to stay at the empty Ramsay home for several weeks. Charles was able to assist Annie with some of the ABS work and Ella, a trained nurse, came to help Hannah for the final few days. After a safe delivery, Charles and Hannah soon

---

26   TT to Annie, June 1910, n.d. The wedding ring was eventually made in Chengdu, probably at Annie's suggestion.
27   *Memoirs*, p39.

returned to Weizhou and Annie continued to make preparations for Torrance's return. Only one issue was unresolved – her own position regarding the CIM.

WEIZHOU, AT THE CONFLUENCE OF THE ZAGUNAO RIVER (L)
AND MIN RIVER (R)

PART TWO

Chapter 5

A New Start

1911-1912

Resigning from the CIM was the last thing Annie could have imagined when she set sail back in 1907 and even now, in 1911, it was a terrible thought to leave the mission which, as she wrote, 'had filled my horizon and inspired me with so much'.[1] But it was a relief that Torrance was returning and she would have faced harder choices had he been unable to do so. She finally plucked up the courage to write to the CIM and ask them to release her. To her surprise, before they had time to answer she received a telegram from the ABS in Shanghai saying they had arranged everything with the CIM. She and Torrance were both free to start afresh – in a year that would also be a momentous and tumultuous new beginning for China.

Turning her attention to the forthcoming wedding Annie bought some white silk to make her wedding dress and, as the time drew near, she moved to the new West China Union University campus to stay with Dr Joseph Taylor and his wife, who were good friends of Torrance. Mrs Taylor quickly discovered Annie knew little about cooking and gave her a crash course, including the plum jelly and preserves she happened to be making. Mrs Ramsay also gave her a cookbook which stood her in good stead over the years, although Annie clearly had other priorities: 'In the cooking line I had often thought of the text "labour not for the meat that perisheth" and I disliked the thought of spending one's life in cooking.'[2]

Torrance eventually left Scotland towards the end of March and after stops at Malta, Port Said, Aden, Colombo (his favourite), and Singapore, he arrived in Shanghai on April 30 where he was initiated by Dr Hykes and the ABS staff into the workings of the head office and also bought all sorts of odds and ends not available in Chengdu. Five days later he set out by steamer for Yichang where he was delayed two weeks. From there he had to hire his own transport: a flat-bottomed

1 *Memoirs*, p41.
2 Ibid., p44. See John 6:27.

boat fifty feet long and eight feet wide with a crew of thirteen men, eight of whom were rowers who also served as trackers, hauling the boat upstream with ropes once it entered the stretch of gorges and rapids between Yichang and Chongqing.

HAULING A BOAT THROUGH THE RAPIDS

After eight days 'the rains came on and the water rose daily, till the boat was so high that she was sailing over the top of the cornstalks in the farmers' fields. Then we had many a lively time at the different rapids. At one we broke the rope and went back into the throes of the whirlpools and the surge. At another we got stuck on a rock, and at a third got no end of bashing here and there. Twice we broke the mast; once we smashed our rudder; several times we had to stop leaks.' At one particularly dangerous spot the captain 'danced out with a bamboo in his hand, and, flourishing it over the head of the rowers, yelled, "Do you want to go to hell? Row! Row!" And row they did in earnest.' Torrance was full of praise for the boat crew: 'They laughed, they cursed, they thieved, and occasionally fought, but worked desperately hard and often heroically.'[3]

---

3   TT to Hykes July 12, 1911.

Word of Torrance's arrival had preceded him and on July 8 Annie went by sedan chair to meet him as he approached Chengdu. 'It was indeed a precious moment after all that had passed. God had brought him back to China as I had hoped and He did mean us for each other.'[4] Torrance moved immediately into the old Ramsay home while Annie continued as a guest of the Taylors. The legal side of the marriage still had to be arranged with the Consul and Torrance also needed to get straight into the Bible Society work. Four days later he wrote to Hykes in Shanghai: 'Yesterday I began a fortnight's classes with the colporteurs. This will give them a much needed rest . . . it will enable them to know me, and me to know them, as well as tend to raise the tone of their spiritual life. I hope by this means to prepare for a good autumn's work.'[5]

TWO CHRISTIAN COLPORTEURS WITH THEIR TRACTS AND SCRIPTURES

The wedding took place on August 1 at the British Consulate, followed by a reception at the Taylors' house and a honeymoon settling into their new home – a large traditional wooden property on San-dao-guai, a small lane in a densely populated eastern part of the city. Ramsay had made some adaptations: besides the family quarters it had a Bible depot, meeting hall, and rooms for servants and for colporteurs to use when they were in town. The couple had hoped for time up in the Guanxian hills but political unrest in the region made that impossible and being

4   *Memoirs*, p43.
5   TT to Hykes, July 12, 1911.

together at home was still a treasured honeymoon after nearly two years apart. It was the custom among the foreigners to address people by their surname and Torrance and Annie had spent so little time together that even after they were married Annie, who was quite shy, found it difficult at first to address her new husband as Tom. But it was a wonderful new lease of life for them both after the stresses and strains that had overshadowed everything for so long and, as Annie commented, the ABS work was a role for which Torrance 'was most suitable in every way'.[6]

THE WEDDING DAY

The idyll of this new existence was rudely interrupted after only three weeks by sudden political upheaval which was to have far-reaching consequences for the whole of China. Despite its distance from the capital, the first spark was lit in Chengdu as a result of a railway project which had been initiated by Viceroy Xi Liang. Back in 1903 Britain and the USA had requested the right to build a railway line between Chengdu and the port of Hankou on the Yangtze River, something which would establish Western influence in China's interior even more firmly. Viceroy Xi Liang was opposed to this foreign expansionism and also feared it would reignite anti-foreign sentiment. In a petition to the

6   *Memoirs*, p46.

Qing court he argued strongly for the railway project to be operated by the Sichuanese and in January 1904, with permission from the Qing government, he established the Sichuan-Hankou Railway Company, the first wholly Chinese-owned railway project.[7]

However, in 1908, with insufficient funds raised and some of the Sichuanese participants found guilty of embezzlement, the Qing court stepped in and negotiations began the following year with a Western banking consortium for a loan for the Sichuan-Hankou line. In May 1911, with little progress made on the construction and the Qing government wanting more control, nationalisation of the project was approved dependent on the foreign bank loans. In June, compensation was offered to the Chinese investors but whereas investors in another part of the line from Hankou to Guangdong were offered a reasonable amount, those in Sichuan were offered a poor settlement because of the embezzlement. In response the Sichuanese formed a Railway Protection League to safeguard local investment in the railway and resist both the Qing takeover and the foreign involvement. Before long this had turned into a fast-growing political movement and on August 24, 1911, a citywide strike began in Chengdu, bringing almost everything to a standstill. After a few days the lack of water and the accumulation of human waste had taken its toll and basic services were reinstated but a powerful fresh protest was then initiated, this time burning candles and incense across the city in front of hastily erected memorial placards to the deceased Emperor Guangxu, who had given the original permission for the Sichuanese to build their own railway.[8]

On September 6, under pressure from the government to bring things under control and having received information about a planned uprising by the Railway Protection League, Zhao Erfeng, the acting Viceroy of Sichuan, ordered all foreigners to gather at the unopened new Canadian Hospital on Si-sheng-ci Street, partly for their own protection but also to avoid troops being diverted to guard individual

7   He Yimin. 'Sichuan Province Reforms under Governor-General Xiliang, 1903-1907'. *Chinese Studies in History*, 28:3-4, pp136-156. In Douglas R. Reynolds. *China, 1895-1912: State-sponsored Reforms and China's Late-Qing Revolution: Selected Essays from Zhongguo Jindai Shi (Modern Chinese History, 1840-1919)*. M. E. Sharpe. 1995, p151.
8   Immanuel Hsu. *The Rise of Modern China*. Oxford University Press. 1983, p467; Kristin Stapleton. *Civilizing Chengdu*. Harvard University Asia Center. 2000, p173ff; 'Events in Chengtu: 1911'. By G. A. Combe, Consul-General, Chengtu. In WCMN May 1924, pp5-18.

missionary homes in the event of increased anti-foreign sentiment.[9] Throughout the afternoon and evening foreigners streamed into the Canadian compound with what they could carry, joined by others straggling in from other affected towns over the next few days.

On September 7, Zhao invited the leaders of the Railway Protection movement for talks at his yamen and promptly arrested them. News of the arrests leaked out and, as Torrance recounted, 'Men of all classes rushed to the Viceregal Yamen or court in indignation against the Viceroy's action. A dense crowd managed to get into the outer courtyard and there, on bended knees, prayed aloud for the release of the imprisoned men. In vain were they commanded to leave. A high official named Tien-Cheng-Kuei (a man infamous for the part he played in 1900 in assisting in the massacre of missionaries at Tai-yuen-fu), nothing lothe to see blood flowing, gave the order for the troops to fire on the masses.'[10] Thirty-two people died and many were wounded.

Not knowing how long their sojourn at the hospital would be, the foreigners quickly got themselves organised and established a degree of community life, much helped by the good cooperation already in existence amongst the Chengdu missions. This was essential with 125 foreigners and a considerable number of Chinese staff all suddenly uprooted and living at close quarters in the compound. A library was established, an entertainment committee formed, and news bulletins posted for all to see. Sunday services, prayer meetings, and daily chapel services were scheduled and committees were established to oversee security, emergencies, and sanitation.[11]

The massacre was a disaster for Zhao Erfeng. As news of it spread – facilitated by wooden slats floated downstream bearing the message 'In all places, friends, arise, save and protect your land!' – a steady stream of protesters flowed into Chengdu demanding the release of those arrested.[12] The clashes continued and in their fury the Chengdu gentry switched their support away from the Qing government to the cause of anti-Qing revolutionaries. Local militias were formed across Sichuan, resentful not just of the Qing and foreign takeover of the railway project but also of the heavy tax burdens imposed to fund the

9 WCMN, Nov 1911, p9. See also Kenny Kwok-kwan Ng. *The Lost Geopoetic Horizon of Li Jieren: The Crisis of Writing Chengdu in Revolutionary China.* Leiden: Brill. 2015, pp103-4.

10 TT newsletter, January 1912. Modern pinyin: Tian Zhengkui, Taiyuan.

11 WCMN, Nov 1911, pp3-5.

12 Han, *Crippled Tree*, p 241.

Qing reforms. Rather than just protest, these militias attacked Qing troops and tried to wrest control of local government offices.[13] In the smaller towns and the countryside around Chengdu the fighting was worse than in the city and Guanxian fell to the rebels, but with nothing to match the modern rifles of the Qing troops, the thousands of rebel casualties far outnumbered Qing losses.[14] The fighting continued into October, essentially civil war, with the rebels seizing various towns and the Qing troops re-taking many of them. 'Chengdu itself, gates closed and telegraph lines cut, stood isolated in a sea of rebellion.'[15]

A fresh wave of anti-foreign cartoons appeared as part of the rebellion but the Railway Protection League had issued specific instructions that foreigners and their property should be left alone lest attacks on them harm the League's cause, and the hospital compound was an oasis of calm in the midst of everything. 'It is almost an effort of mind to realize that within a very few miles of us battles are being fought, that skirmishing is an almost daily occurrence and that the Chinese are constantly in danger and fear.'[16]

The ABS colporteurs were among those at risk, raising suspicions because they were on the road and away from their native places. Five of them were arrested in different locations and questioned as potential spies or couriers. Four didn't fare too badly but one had already had his hands tied behind his back in preparation for execution when someone was found to stand guarantee for him. Three other colporteurs were blocked by rebel militias as they tried to access the mountains in the Ya'an region and had to change their itinerary. Torrance had also heard that Miansi, in the Qiang area, was under rebel control and on October 29 a letter reached Chengdu from Charles Coates in Weizhou, to the north of Miansi, saying that the rebels had taken charge there too.

There was little love lost between the tribespeople and their Qing overlords and Torrance heard of four hundred tribesmen coming from Muping, in the foothills north of Ya'an, to join the rebels in Xinjin, one of his old CIM outstations.[17] Situated on the lower reaches of the Min River, Xinjin was on the front line where an estimated ten thousand rebels, armed with only a thousand modern rifles, were facing well-equipped Imperial troops who were lined up for several miles across the

---

13   Stapleton, *Civilizing Chengdu*, pp175-176.
14   WCMN, Nov 1911, p11.
15   Stapleton, *Civilizing Chengdu*, p176.
16   WCMN, Nov 1911, p5.
17   TT to Dr Hykes, Oct 11, 1911.

river. Torrance knew the leader of the rebels there, Hou Baozhai, who was a member of the local Elder Brothers Society, and his description of Hou gives insight into the nature of the struggle:

> Many a long talk we have had in days gone by. He is a man well over 50 years; fairly well to do; is of the merchant class; and shows considerable ability in anything he takes in hand. During the Boxer troubles he was active in protecting the church and church members. He began his career in a Yamen in Chentu. Then he turned a robber chief who made himself so strong against the officials that they were glad to pardon him and give him a small official title and made him a 'T'uan-Pao' [local militia leader] at Xinjin. For over 20 years he has been a leading, honourable and much trusted citizen there. Now his name is famous in Szechuan as the chief of the patriots who are opposing the whole Imperial strength on the banks of the Min.[18]

Torrance's choice of patriot over rebel reflected his view that the uprising had less to do with the actual railway and more to do with what he saw as the 'tyranny and rapacity' of the Qing officials, on which the railway issue had shone a spotlight.

In Qionglai two hundred soldiers killed their officers, sided with the rebels, and joined the fighting in Xinjin. On their return to Qionglai they demanded the seal of the mandarin and shot him when he refused to hand it over. Two other mandarins in nearby towns immediately handed over their seals. To Torrance's sorrow the Qing military official in Xinjin was also killed. With sadness he wrote to Hykes that 'he was one of the very few who had a reputation for the love of honesty and justice. Nearly every time I visited the place he came to see me.'[19]

With Chengdu quiet the missionaries were contemplating leaving the hospital but news then reached them that rebels in neighbouring Hubei Province had won significant victories and they feared this news might stir the Chengdu population to more open rebellion. Kerosene oil had been banned from Chengdu amid rumours that the 'patriots', with help from sympathisers in the city, would set fires burning and then storm the government yamens.

In the end Torrance and Annie returned home in late October but fighting was still continuing beyond Chengdu, with the rebels holding most of the territory west of a line stretching between Yibin

---

18 Ibid.
19 TT to Hykes, Oct 21, 1911.

and Pengzhou, including almost all the walled cities. Qing troops had managed to hold on to Xinjin but in the countryside farmers were refusing to provide food for government soldiers and were welcoming the rebels with open arms. 'I am not at all beside the mark,' wrote Torrance, 'when I say that 90 per cent of the Szechuanese on the plain are strongly in favour of the new movement. The Imperial forces because of their superior arms may win victories but the ground recovered remains seething with discontent.' If Qing reinforcements didn't arrive Torrance could see that it would be 'goodbye to the Manchu rule in Szechuan.'[20]

By mid-November, amid rumours that many of his troops were secretly supportive of the rebels, Viceroy Zhao Erfeng's position was weakening by the day. In an act of self-preservation he agreed to release the arrested Railway Protection League leaders on condition that they work with him to restore order in Sichuan, but the militias continued to fight and his position soon became untenable.

November 27, 1911, was a day many had longed for but few thought they would ever see. Viceroy Zhao relinquished his authority and the leaders of the provincial assembly declared Sichuan independent of the Qing government. 'What rejoicing there was!' wrote Torrance. 'The streets were avenues of flags. In place of the Dragon colours the new white "Han" symbol of patriotism flew gaily in the breeze. Pigtails were cut off by the thousands. Everybody was smiling. There was not a dark look or a frown to be seen on any face. At last they were rid of Manchu despotism and the Chengtu "world and his wife" were happy.'[21]

Torrance's sympathies had been with the rebel cause but not with their unruly behaviour, which had caused much distress. However, by this time he was unashamedly on the side of the revolutionaries and went with other missionaries to offer his congratulations to the leaders of the assembly.

> They were very pleased to see us. Next day the newspapers had a great account of the friendliness of the foreigners, stating how they sympathised with the popular aspirations and thanking us for our good-will. The change that came over the city was remarkable. It was as if a magic wand had been waved over the city turning despair into hope and gloom into glory.[22]

---

20 Ibid.
21 TT newsletter, Jan 1912.
22 Ibid.

By this time the revolution had spread to other parts of China with the cities of Hankou, Hanyang, Changsha, and the province of Yunnan all having fallen in October, followed by Shanghai and the provinces of Zhejiang, Fujian, and Guangdong in early November. By early December fifteen provinces had seceded from Qing rule and a provisional revolutionary government had been established in Nanjing.[23]

The rejoicing in Chengdu was short-lived. Ten days after Sichuan's declaration of independence the city was plunged into despair as unpaid Qing soldiers, many hailing from other parts of China and with no loyalty to Sichuan, flooded into the city and ran riot. In a bid to win their favour the new assembly leaders had promised the Qing forces an extra two to three months wages but rumour had deliberately been spread by those still hoping to unseat the new leaders that some three thousand 'patrolmen' were only to be paid one month extra and were to be sent out of the city to garrison the provincial counties and smaller districts.[24] On payday the rumour was discovered to be true and all hell broke loose.

Torrance was walking past the parade ground not long before the pandemonium erupted and saw the soldiers drilling with their 'bayonets glittering in the sun'.[25] A few minutes after he reached home 'the wildest excitement arose on the streets. On going out to enquire what was ado, I saw the shopkeepers hastily slamming up their shutters and companies of soldiers rushing past none knew where. The news presently came that they had revolted. They had shot their paymaster, and were now going, it was supposed, to attack the Imperial city.' The disgruntled troops headed first for the Imperial Bank of China and then moved on to the wealthy shops in the Arcade and along Great East Street. Others joined in the looting, 'scurrying off with the contents of the best business houses in Chengtu'. The streets were littered with goods people had dumped in favour of better pickings. Suddenly, huge fires lit up the night sky and rifle-fire joined the deafening roar of the chaos. 'Words fail to describe the terror that held the inhabitants that night, for fires once set a-going in Chinese cities are, as you know, often hard to extinguish and often envelop whole streets in destruction.'[26] Unable to sleep, Torrance and Annie kept close watch until dawn. In

23   Hsu, *Rise of Modern China*, p469.
24   TT to Hykes, Dec 12, 1911.
25   TT newsletter, Jan 1912.
26   Ibid.

the early hours of the morning they saw the Provincial Treasury going up in flames about two hundred yards from their front door.

To Torrance's frustration the British Consul issued evacuation orders and over the next couple of days he and Annie hurriedly packed essentials, including bedding and an oven made from an old kerosene tin, and made their way to the river bank. Annie was now expecting their first child and was loath to go but the Consul was insistent that all British and American foreigners should leave, especially women and children, until some stable form of government was in place. Giving one of his colporteurs charge of the house, Torrance was hopeful that he and Annie could wait in Chongqing and return as soon as things calmed down. Down at the wharf a man had just been shot in the face by a soldier and the wharfmen appealed to Torrance to extract the bullet. Torrance removed the man's smashed upper left molars but could find no trace of the bullet which seemed to have lodged somewhere in the man's neck. Although his ministrations were in vain 'the mere effort elicited the warmest thanks of his friends'.[27]

Delayed by various latecomers and awaiting the arrival of a provincial escort, they finally set sail on December 12 in a flotilla with 165 foreigners – British, American, German, French, Russian, and Japanese – and 120 armed soldiers, whose expenses were paid by the missionaries. At one place where Qing troops still held sway they came under fire.

> We hugged the far bank as closely as we dared, thereby putting a third of a mile between them and us, yet when a bullet found a boat it went clear through both sides of it . . . I watched the firing until we got into it and then helped the boatmen to row as rapidly as we could out of range.[28]

On the boat, with everything fresh in his mind, Torrance managed to write a full account of the situation to Hykes in Shanghai. Hykes was clearly unaware how quickly things had deteriorated and wrote the same day to Torrance asking for a stock inventory by the end of December.

Qing patrolmen were still holding Meishan so their armed escort did a detour and rejoined the foreigners further downstream, but it was clear to Torrance that those cities holding out against the new government couldn't do so for long. 'The new troops are everywhere

---

27   TT to Hykes, Dec 12, 1911.
28   TT newsletter, Jan 1912.

busy drilling and preparing. The hearts of the masses are behind them.'[29] However, there was no good news waiting in Chongqing. Everywhere was in turmoil and to their disappointment Annie had no choice but to continue alone to Shanghai while Torrance waited in Chongqing until he could return to Chengdu. At least there he could help out at the ABS depot while Wilbur Hooker, the local ABS agent, was on furlough. Dr Hykes agreed to this on condition that Torrance comply with any Consular orders, strongly advising him not to travel into the countryside. Two further letters stressed again the need to comply with Consular orders, suggesting Torrance was chafing at the bit and that Hykes knew or guessed as much.

After a short stay in Yichang, Annie reached Shanghai in mid-February 1912, much saddened that it was too late to return to Sichuan and be with Torrance for the birth of their first child. Thankfully she was able to enjoy the warm hospitality of the Scottish ABS office manager, W. M. Cameron, and his wife and two teenage boys. Cameron had been an ABS agent elsewhere in China and Annie learned much from her conversations with them. Despite the separation from Torrance she also enjoyed the Shanghai spring and kept healthy with walks down to the waterfront through a fascinating array of shops. Torrance was now planning to come to Shanghai in the summer, when it was too hot to work, and escort Annie and the baby back to Chengdu.

As Torrance and Annie awaited the birth and their reunion, events in China were moving forward rapidly. In an effort to hold on to power, on November 1, 1911, the Qing government had appointed Yuan Shikai – the former Shandong governor who had dealt so effectively with the Boxers – as prime minister. Yuan promptly moved against the rebels, not with the intention of strengthening the ailing Qing dynasty but wanting full governmental control in Beijing.

Yuan's bid for power was not uncontested. In late December, Sun Yatsen, who had been working in exile for many years towards constitutional reform and the overthrow of the Qing, returned from overseas and was elected by the rebel provinces as China's provisional president. On January 1, 1912, a new Republic was announced with Sun at its head and its seat of government in Nanjing. However, despite Sun's popularity, Yuan Shikai still had the loyalty of troops in the north and was gaining support from foreign governments, some of whom saw him as more capable of holding China together than Sun. Under

---

29   TT to Hykes, Dec 25, 1912. Entitled 'On the Yangtze'.

pressure, Sun agreed to relinquish the premiership to Yuan if he would ensure the abdication of the Qing, declare his support for the Republic, and pledge to honour the constitution being prepared by parliament.[30] In keeping with this, the abdication of young emperor Puyi was announced on February 12 and Yuan Shikai became president of the new Republic with, as he insisted, its capital in Beijing.

In Chengdu, Yin Changheng, a Japanese-trained army officer with links to the Elder Brothers Society and the Railway Protection League, became the first of a succession of military leaders. In contrast to the sober revolution hoped for by Torrance, Robert Kapp paints a bleak picture of the next fifteen years as the whole province fragmented into militia-controlled regions:

> Szechwan suffered from nearly uninterrupted war, burgeoning opium addiction, economic disruption, and ineffectual or non-existent provincial government. Constantly shifting military alliances, frequent military conflicts, and the spread of social disorder make the chronicle of events bewildering.[31]

Lacking the authority held by previous Qing-appointed viceroys, the new self-proclaimed leaders struggled even to gain control of city-wide affairs in Chengdu. Instead, 'Street headmen and new urban militias assumed responsibility for many matters of local security that the constables were unable to handle. . . . The Chamber of Commerce was no longer patronized by provincial officials and invited to contribute to Chengdu's urban development; instead it was pressured to fund the armies of rival militarists.'[32]

Far away in Shanghai, Annie's letters to Torrance at this time abounded with advice about eating well, boiling the milk from the cow, not eating any re-cooked vegetables, and finding a cleaner – amply justifying Olsen's confidence in her effect on Torrance. She was also faithfully writing from Shanghai to Torrance's mother, whom she had yet to meet.

Towards the end of March, Hykes wrote to Torrance confirming that a box of items he had requested was on its way from Shanghai to Sichuan. The list reveals something of Torrance's day-to-day life

---

30   Hsu, *Rise of Modern China*, pp472-475; Westad, *Restless Empire*, p142.
31   Robert A. Kapp. *Szechwan and the Chinese Republic: Provincial Militarism and Central Power, 1911–1938*. Yale University Press. 1973, p8.
32   Stapleton, *Civilizing Chengdu*, pp181-182.

and what was unavailable in Chengdu – or perhaps not of the desired quality. It included assorted ironmongery and stationery items along with butter, cheese, jam, Postum coffee substitute, eight volumes of Everyman's library, twenty-two Chinese books, a boot last, and a dog chain. From one of Annie's letters at this time it is clear that sections of the reports Torrance was sending to Hykes in this period were being forwarded to the ABS in New York and also to a new American-run daily newspaper, *The China Press*, which had been launched in August 1911 in Shanghai.[33] A short report by Torrance on the November 1911 uprising also appeared in the ABS publication, the *Bible Society Record*.[34]

Finally able to leave Chongqing, Torrance had reached Chengdu on March 1, 1912, to find not a queue in sight and a warning issued that those found wearing the 'Manchu appendage' after March 3 would be fined. This coincided with a fresh openness to things foreign, and using the rarity of magic lantern pictures of Europe and America to draw people in, he held meetings in the Quaker, Canadian Methodist, and American Methodist meeting halls, where he found high demand for the ABS New Testaments and other Scripture portions.

Following the success of the magic lantern in Chengdu, Torrance took it to the month-long spring fair at the Qingyang Temple where he rented a large room, which his colporteurs darkened by covering the windows and pasting over any cracks. Benches transported from the ABS meeting hall were arranged in rows, a large screen was erected to conceal the temple idols, and notices were posted announcing daily showings from 10am to 4pm. Putting his Hamilton sales experience to good use, Torrance set the entry fee at the purchase of a Scripture portion, which he sold at less than cost-price as he preached outside to attract the passing crowds while the Chinese colporteurs spoke to those inside, illustrating their talks with the lantern pictures. With an average attendance of four to five hundred people each day, by the end of April they had sold nine thousand books.

On May 10, 1912, after an 'unusually prolonged and difficult experience', Annie gave birth to a baby daughter, Mary.[35] A delighted Torrance received the announcement the following day by telegram and promptly went round to share 'the latest news from Shanghai'

33   Annie to TT, March 25, 1912.
34   *Bible Society Record* (BSR). Vol 57, Jan 1912, p4.
35   W. M. Cameron to TT, May 10, 1912.

with the Consul-General.[36] He had been busy with various repairs, planning ahead for the arrival of the new baby which, as he wrote to Annie, had been a reminder to him that 'it must be the same with the Heavenly Father regarding us.'[37] With the Yangtze at its most treacherous in the early summer months, it had been agreed that Torrance would wait a while before leaving for Shanghai so two days later he set off on a trip to Xinjin and Qionglai and from there, with an armed escort on the bandit-ridden road, to his good friends Harry and Lona Openshaw in Ya'an. Weary from the month at the spring fair, the mountain air and Lona's cooking did him the world of good. The Openshaws had found much favour with the locals, having stayed on in Ya'an through the 1911 fighting helping to care for some of the wounded, and the nightly gatherings with the magic lantern were well-attended.

Annie took a while to recover her strength. She was enjoying Mary and the restful environment in the Cameron home but she and Torrance had been apart nearly six months and she felt the separation keenly. Torrance finally arrived in early September and was overjoyed to meet his first child. After he had seen to some ABS business he and Annie set out with their precious cargo on the long journey home, by steamer to Yichang and on to Chongqing by houseboat, with a bad-tempered captain at odds with crew and passengers alike. For Annie it was one of the worst trips she ever had on the Yangtze:

> We had several hairbreadth escapes from being caught in swift currents and falling upon the rocks. One place it seemed we would be wrecked. As the men rowed against the swirling waters their faces were tense and white and I expect ours were.[38]

Reaching one particularly dangerous section, Torrance, with the weighty responsibility of a wife and baby daughter, insisted on leaving the boat to ensure that new ropes and extra trackers were available to pull it up the rapids. Although it meant clambering over boulders, Annie also chose to carry Mary and walk with Torrance and the trackers. From Chongqing the overland stretch was blissfully uneventful and they reached Chengdu on November 18, relieved to be home together again in what by now seemed, according to the WCMN, to be 'the

---

36   TT to Annie, May 12, 1912.
37   Ibid.
38   *Memoirs*, p50.

most peaceable of the capitals of the eighteen provinces which go to make up the new Republic'.[39]

After a year of turmoil Torrance could at last concentrate fully on his family and the ABS work. He was full of energy and was finding ways to get the ABS literature into all sorts of places. The Shanghai ABS depot couldn't keep up with his requirements so he had arranged for more supplies to be printed at the Canadian Methodist Mission Press in Chengdu, including new portions of Scripture and new tracts that he had begun to write in Chinese. Now and then he still itinerated, following up on the work of the colporteurs and doing his own evangelism as he travelled, and when the colporteurs were in town he was continuing to have times of Bible study with them. Aside from keeping his own records and accounts and sending regular reports to Hykes in Shanghai, Torrance was now Chengdu correspondent for *The China Press*, sending news from Sichuan and occasionally writing longer articles.

Torrance, Annie, and Mary in Shanghai, 1912

39   WCMN, July-August 1912, p29.

Chapter 6

Sichuan Begins to Fragment
1913-1916

Early in 1913 Torrance informed his newsletter recipients that 'China politically is at present neither a Republic nor a Monarchy nor anything else.'[1] He was optimistic that things would improve but for now everything was unsettled. In spite of this the ABS work was thriving and so was he. About twenty ABS colporteurs were travelling far and wide in Sichuan, even up to the mountainous Qiang and Tibetan areas in the west, as well as to Guanxian in early spring to meet the tribespeople who would come down every year to trade. Torrance had been in Guanxian recently and had treated a tribesman suffering from conjunctivitis. The leader of the group told Torrance with gratitude that 'he would be pleased to receive me any time I cared to visit the borderland.'[2]

In January Torrance was invited by Edward Toyne of the CIM to bring his magic lantern to Leshan. The meetings were so popular that people had to be turned away. Leshan's chief military official invited Torrance to show the pictures in his yamen and over tea afterwards expressed his hope that the work of the missionaries would help to raise standards in society which, in turn, would help to establish the New Republic.

On a visit to nearby Emei, Torrance and Toyne were bold in their advertising. Having put up posters, they hired a local night-watchman to walk through the streets at dusk beating his gong and stopping every fifty yards to 'call on the people to come and buy a book and see the sights of the screen.'[3] The meetings were again packed out. At a small town north of Leshan, the military commander allowed them to show the slides in a local temple where his soldiers were living. The meeting was again announced by a town crier and a large crowd gathered. Back in Chengdu in time for the Chinese New Year, Torrance held similar meetings, to which the police sent men each evening to maintain order. In March he did the same in Pengzhou, to the north of Chengdu.

1 TT newsletter, Feb 12, 1913.
2 TT to Hykes, Feb 10, 1913.
3 TT to Hykes, Jan 1913, reporting on his trip.

In June Torrance took the lantern with him on a three-week trip to the Pixian region, northwest of Chengdu, while Annie and Mary went to stay with the Hutsons in Guanxian. Annie and Torrance were expecting their second child at the end of August and Annie was thankful for the help of a faithful woman servant, Auntie Gou, who had moved with her from Guanxian and was an indispensable helper and friend. On Torrance's return they all went up to Lingyan Temple for the summer. Writing to his parents from the hills, Torrance was keeping them up-to-date with his dairy cows. To his delight, a newly acquired cow, which they had brought to Lingyan Temple for the summer, was yielding fifteen big cups of milk per day.

MISSIONARIES AND CHINESE STAFF AT LINGYAN TEMPLE
ABOVE GUANXIAN

Annie wrote to them with more of the domestic news. Torrance had become thin over the last three weeks. 'I wish I knew how to make him fat! . . . He needs too much looking after to be left alone.'[4] She told of the cook-boy who was still getting used to their kerosene-can oven. Whenever Annie baked a cake he would keep taking it out to see how it was doing and ruin it in the process. Another helper was being initiated into foreign ways of washing and ironing. 'He starched my nightdress up the other day so stiff that I could scarce get into it.' Mary was now fourteen months old and, according to Annie, just like her father. 'She is very keen and observing and knows the use of most things. If she gets hold of a piece of paper with any writing on she

4   Annie to TT's mother, July 1, 1913.

starts singing right away. . . . She tries to brush her hair and put on her shoes and walks all over the place and into every kind of mischief.'[5] Torrance's mother was sending the *Christian Herald* and the *Hamilton Advertiser* to keep them in touch with news back home.

Returning early to Chengdu for the birth, Annie had her second experience of an earthquake, during which the house 'seemed to shake and sway like a paper one' but stood firm.[6] Added to this, heavy rains had flooded the garden and, thanks to magpies and blackbirds digging under the roof tiles for moss to line their nests, the rain had penetrated to the bedroom and study, bringing some of the ceiling plaster down. Annie sometimes daydreamed of transporting a cosy little home from Britain over to Chengdu but at least the garden, when not flooded, provided some comfort. Both their mothers had sent seeds and Torrance had planted cabbages, turnips, wallflowers, primroses, pelargoniums, and thyme.

Thomas Forsyth Torrance, named after his grandfather, arrived on August 30, 1913, with Florence Olsen assisting at the birth.[7] Towards the end of September Annie wrote to Torrance's parents that Tom was thriving and although she had been slow to regain her strength she was 'getting around all right'. Their joy was overshadowed by news that a missionary wife and her baby had died in childbirth in Leshan around this time.

Tom was born against the backdrop of the threat of all-out civil war in China. In 1912, in a challenge to Yuan Shikai's authoritarian rule, a close ally of Sun Yatsen's named Song Jiaoren had founded the National People's Party or Guomindang, which in February 1913 had won an overall majority in China's first democratic elections. Song had hopes of forming a cabinet with executive authority answerable to parliament rather than to Yuan Shikai but in March, to the horror of many, Song had been assassinated and that summer seven southern provinces, in sympathy with this newly-formed Nationalist Party, rebelled against Yuan's government. Chongqing and other parts of Sichuan followed suit but the rebellion failed to reach Chengdu, which remained relatively stable. In November, Yuan Shikai firmly consolidated his power in Beijing and outlawed the Nationalist Party, despite its electoral success. In Chongqing and Chengdu he installed governors loyal to himself.

That autumn, Torrance made a short trip with the magic lantern to an American Methodist outstation. As an ABS agent he was free to

5   Ibid.
6   Annie to TT's mother, Sept 28, 1913.
7   TT to his parents, Oct 12, 1913.

work with any mission which invited him as long as the visit included literature distribution, and he made the most of this liberty. Towards the end of November he took Annie and the two children to visit the Olsens in Qionglai. They took the cow and its calf along to keep the children supplied with milk but the distance was too far for the calf so they tied its legs and carried it in a basket, which 'caused many a merry remark by the onlookers'.[8] Olsen and Torrance took the magic lantern out to a couple of towns where Torrance was known from his time at the Qionglai CIM station. They were warmly welcomed and presented with gifts of eggs and sweetmeats as well as a bag of white Indian cornmeal from an old friend who remembered Torrance's fondness for it. Robbers had attacked Qionglai a few days earlier so several militiamen accompanied them as they went from village to village. By the end of 1913 Torrance and his colporteurs had distributed a total of 110,000 tracts, Scripture portions, and Bibles. 'The colporteurs have gone forth north, south, east, and west with the Book and the message, humbly, patiently, as diligently and often as little esteemed as the obscure bees that fructify the flowers of the field.'[9]

In March 1914 Torrance was again at the Qingyang Temple fair, this time for a strenuous five weeks. With three colporteurs and his depot-manager they had half-hour meetings for five hours a day, each time addressing seventy-five people. The hardest part was controlling the crowds as one group left and the next came in but they sold over seventeen thousand books to people from all walks of life. Torrance followed this with a quieter trip south of Chengdu to Chinese churches he had often visited in his early days. Having regained his strength he then went north to the Pengzhou CIM church to help the Chinese with an evangelistic campaign, which proved to be a lively time. 'From end to end of it everybody had heard of our meetings, and thousands came either during the day or in the evening. Between the three thousand odd volumes we sold and the tracts given away, the place was flooded with gospel literature.'[10]

In the summer, with Lingyan Temple growing in popularity, there were forty-nine adults and twenty-eight children enjoying the respite from the heat. Not long after the Torrances arrived, Henry Richardson of the Chengdu YMCA was struck down with dysentery and typhoid fever and Torrance's medical training was put to the test. The WCMN

---

8   BSR, March 1914, Vol 59, p36.
9   BSR, April 1914, Vol 59, p52.
10 BSR, Oct 1914, Vol 59, p160.

TORRANCE WITH HIS COLPORTEURS

described Richardson's slow recovery as a 'long fight' and reported that Torrance had done 'excellent work nursing and caring for him in the absence of a doctor'.[11] One of the fruits of this time was the friendship which formed between Annie and Mrs Richardson, who asked Annie if she would start a weekly Bible discussion group back in Chengdu. Annie was surprised how little some of the women knew but they were eager to learn and together they studied from Genesis through to the Psalms. Annie was a born teacher and Tom would later describe her as 'a woman of the greatest spiritual depth, prayer life, and theological insight'.[12]

Just as Torrance was beginning to relax again after caring for Richardson, the community in the Guanxian hills received 'the most bewildering message in the history of modern missions . . . that practically all Europe is at war'.[13] The shocking news cast a pall over the summer as groups gathered every evening on the tennis courts to read and discuss the latest Reuters updates. With startling rapidity, by the end of the summer the tentacles of the First World War had extended to northeastern China as Japan joined Britain and her Allies with her eye on the German-controlled territory in Shandong. On November 7 German forces there yielded to Japan, giving her once again a much-resented foothold in China, which would eventually have grave consequences.

11   WCMN, July 1914, p26.
12   John I. Hesselink, 'A Pilgrimage in the School of Christ – an Interview with T. F. Torrance'. *Reformed Review 38* (1984), p50. Cited at: https:// tftorrance.org/childhoodYears
13   WCMN, July 1914, pp26, 31.

Torrance had been expecting a visit later that year from Dr von Weegmann of the Munich Ethnographic Museum, which seems to have been prevented by the outbreak of war. On his travels for the ABS he had managed to carry out further archaeological research, including of some local caves in Leshan, and had sent some grave goods to the German museum. The museum's curator, Professor Lucian Scherman, had replied hoping that Torrance would oblige them by 'continuing your excellent endeavours towards securing more specimens of trustworthy Chinese archaeological remains'.[14] Back in 1909 Torrance had also initiated what would become long-term contact with the British Museum and sent them a photograph of one of his finds. In reply they had expressed interest in 'any fragments of early pottery which you could obtain, provided they had distinctive features which might make them useful for purposes of comparative study'.[15]

By Christmas 1914 the birth of Annie and Torrance's third child was imminent. Mindful of her slow recovery after the first two births and of childbirth tragedies experienced by other missionaries, Annie was particularly prayerful as she found herself wondering how the children would cope if she didn't survive. However, in the early hours of January 7, 1915, Grace Brownlie Torrance came safely into the world assisted by Dr Hoffman, newly married to a friend of the Torrances who was a professor of English at Chengdu's Chinese University. Annie chose the name Grace having been encouraged by a passage in the book of Exodus about finding grace in the sight of the Lord.[16]

Torrance and Annie were following news of the expanding global conflict as much as possible, but in Chengdu life in the house on San-dao-guai continued much as usual. The family were quite sociable and in her memoirs Annie describes various foreigners beyond the missionary community dropping in and enjoying some home life. Some of these, like Professor Hoffman, taught in Chinese schools and colleges or worked at the Post Office. For the sake of the children the visits were eventually turned into an 'at-home' day once a week and, as the family got bigger, the visits decreased further but Annie recalls how much fun they had playing charades in the living room.[17]

In October 1915, Torrance and four of his Chinese ABS workers set out on a four-week trip to the west of Chengdu, joining the Olsens

---

14   Professor Lucian Scherman to TT, June 12, 1914.
15   Ormonde M. Dalton to TT, March 29, 1909.
16   Exodus 33:13-34:9.
17   *Memoirs*, p55.

and Chinese Christians in the town of Dayi for a convention and evangelistic campaign. In his CIM days Torrance had seen potential in the resident evangelist in Dayi when he was still a lad and had arranged for his schooling. He had then been employed by the Canadian Press until Torrance found someone to sponsor his theological training and he was now 'the most earnest preacher in all Mr. Olsen's wide district'.[18]

Torrance and his co-workers then moved on to other villages in the area. In one village almost everyone was absorbed in card game gambling, a common pastime in slack periods between market days. However, the headman was friendly and took it on himself to announce their meeting. Despite the poverty of the village, about a hundred books were sold and they had 'a very cheering evening'. On the way to the next village Torrance ran into trouble. 'It was decreed this day that I should record the shortest prayer I ever prayed and tell also of the most remarkable answer to prayer any one could have.'[19] Just near the top of a slippery uphill path his horse suddenly stumbled and fell, pinning Torrance's right leg under him with Torrance downhill from him. Afraid that he would be crushed as the horse struggled to get up, Torrance involuntarily cried out 'Lord, help me.' 'Like a flash of lightning a voice spoke within me: "Hold down his head and he can't struggle." Immediately I put every ounce of strength I could exert in his mouth to this end and, managing to keep him motionless for a second or two, I succeeded in freeing my leg.'

In this village they visited Mr Luo, a man who had studied the Bible with Torrance in Chengdu for three months and then been baptised. After a good meeting with some local farmers, Mr Luo explained that they wanted a Christian teacher both for the village children and to teach the adults on Sundays. Torrance agreed that, with Olsen's help, he would find a teacher and provide half the necessary support, on the understanding that they find the rest. In another small town Torrance met a friend who was one of the leading Christians there. At their first encounter several years before, Mr Han had paid lip-service to Christianity but had been in the grip of opium. Torrance had persuaded him to go to Chengdu and see Dr Canright. 'By his own confession the struggle was so desperate that he felt only a supernatural power could deliver him. He made his urgent prayer to the God of Heaven and He once and for all broke the power of this drug over him. He returned

18   Nov 26, 1915. A typed manuscript which seems to be a report by TT for Hykes/the ABS.
19   Ibid.

a changed man.'[20] This was followed by his wife and children being converted and his son had since become a preacher.

Torrance was glad to get back to the Olsen home, have a hot bath, read the packet of letters waiting for him, and sleep in a bed 'that seemed a foretaste of Heaven' after nearly a month on his camp-bed. Altogether he and his men had sold ninety New Testaments and nearly six thousand Scripture portions, as well as giving away many tracts. Before returning to Chengdu he gave a series of talks in Olsen's church, attended on one evening by the local mandarin who slipped in to listen with his son and attendants.

ANNIE, GRACE, MARY, TORRANCE, AND TOM

1915 had been the most peaceful year in Torrance and Annie's four years of married life but the peace was short-lived. In Beijing, Yuan Shikai had set his sights on becoming supreme ruler at the head of a constitutional monarchy but even as his monarchist movement gained ground, resistance to his grandiose aspirations was also gaining momentum. Undeterred by this opposition, on December 12, 1915, Yuan was sworn in as Emperor of the Abundant Constitution, with his reign to commence on January 1, 1916. This time, however, he had gone too far – even for some of his own supporters.

Far away in China's southwest, a National Protection Army was formed by Cai E, a former governor of Yunnan Province, and others

20   Ibid.

who were united in their opposition to Yuan. On December 23 Yuan rejected an ultimatum from Cai E to abandon his monarchist plans and two days later Yunnan declared its independence. Guizhou Province followed suit on December 27. Yuan then postponed his enthronement and ordered his generals to lead their troops against the National Protection Army. Two of his key generals refused on the grounds of ill health, an ominous sign of his growing isolation. In Shandong an anti-monarchy army was formed and on March 15, 1916, Guangxi Province proclaimed independence. Although Yuan was beginning to show willingness to compromise on his position, in April Guangdong and Zhejiang provinces declared independence and by May various anti-Yuan groups had come together to form a Military Affairs Council. It was downhill all the way after that. In May Shaanxi, Sichuan, and Hunan all declared independence, the last being Hunan on May 27. Just ten days later Yuan Shikai collapsed and died aged fifty-six.

In Chengdu, Governor Chen Yi, who had announced Sichuan's independence on May 22, was swiftly replaced by a commander from Chongqing loyal to Yuan Shikai. He lasted just four weeks before being removed by Cai E's National Protection Army, which had been joined by Sichuan militarists such as Xiong Kewu and Liu Cunhou. As troops loyal to Yuan Shikai began evacuating Chengdu, they seized locals to act as carriers and whole streets of shops closed their shutters in response.[21] Having gained this victory, Cai E, who was in need of urgent medical treatment for tuberculosis, made a hasty decision to leave two of his officers in charge in Chengdu: Luo Peijin from Yunnan as head of military affairs and Dai Kan from Guizhou as head of civil affairs. This not only resulted in tension between Luo and Dai but also created resentment among the Sichuanese militarists that their province was now in the hands of non-Sichuanese leaders.[22]

The August 1916 editorial of the WCMN indicates how fractured Sichuan was by this time. 'Probably at no other period, during these last six restless years, has our own province of Szechwan been in such turmoil, as during the past month. Seven or eight big armies with their respective generals, each somewhat independent, have held different sections . . . As to the governorship of the province, nominally at least, this has been held by five different officers in about as many weeks.'[23]

---

21   WCMN, Aug 1916, p36.
22   Kristin Stapleton. *Fact in Fiction: 1920s China and Ba Jin's Family.* Stanford University Press. 2016, Kindle Edition.
23   WCMN, Aug 1916, p1.

The sectarian nature of Sichuan at this time was also affecting the Qiang area, where Charles and Hannah Coates had been joined by CIM missionaries James and Lily Edgar at the station in Weizhou. A militarist called Yang Wei had established small garrisons in the Qiang districts of Xuecheng, Weizhou, and Miansi, and was effectively in control of the Min Valley. Things were quiet in Weizhou but in the Qiang town of Maoxian further north, where the Church Missionary Society (CMS) had a station, soldiers had rebelled and shot two of their military officers and the postmaster, creating great fear among the people.[24]

On the Chengdu plain the situation was chaotic, travel was unsafe and no foreigners were permitted to travel to the Guanxian hills that summer. Unusually cool weather in late August brought some relief from the heat of the city but once again it brought heavy rain and flooding. Stuck in the city, Torrance used the forced confinement to spend more time with his growing family and to return to his writing.

Having not had anything published since 1910 except for mission-related reports or newspaper articles, in 1916 Torrance completed a lengthy monograph, *The Early History of Chengtu: from the Chou to the close of the Shuh Han Dynasty,* which was published by the Canadian Press. Although he had yet to visit the Qiang area, the article contains what seems to be his earliest written reference to the Qiang people, noting that historically 'the Ch'iang, with their various sub-divisions, lived to the west of Shuh', which in today's terms would be in the mountains of western Sichuan and beyond.[25] Referring specifically to the Han period (206 BC – AD 220) and China's efforts to control 'the regions of the West' he then described the Qiang of that era, with his words betraying a certain admiration for their resilience:

> The various branches of the Ch'iang proved hard peoples to govern. They were quick to resent insult or oppression, and could never bring themselves to forget that the Han were intruders. Notwithstanding the schools opened in their midst, their love of liberty lost nothing of its old-time passion. The Chengtu authorities had constantly to despatch punitive expeditions amongst them. But no sooner had one withdrawn than the members of that tribe appeared as unrelenting as before.[26]

24   WCMN, Sept 1916, p25.
25   TT. *The Early History of Chengtu: from the Chou to the close of the Shuh Dynasty.* Canadian Methodist Mission Press. 1916, p1.
26   Ibid., p9.

As Torrance later explained to Hykes, it was through this reading of Sichuan's history that he had become 'keenly interested' in the Qiang people.[27]

In September 1916 the WCMN published 'The History of the Chengtu Wall', a shorter article by Torrance covering an extensive period from 300 BC through to the recent demise of the Qing dynasty. His reading for both these articles was primarily in Chinese. In the first article on Chengdu's early history he mentioned the 'common authorities' regarding this field: *The General History of Szechwan*, *The History of Chengtu*, *The Chronicles of Huayang* (a gazetteer of Sichuan compiled in the mid-4th century AD), and *The Mirror of Shu*, a weekly magazine about Sichuan. He also recommended three broader Chinese reference sources: *The Complete Literature of Szechwan*, *The History of the Three Kingdoms*, and *The General History of China*.

That same month everyone breathed a sigh of relief when a Sichuan provincial assembly was convened under Luo Peijin, the military governor from Yunnan, who was trying to restore order and had dispersed some of the robber bands plaguing the countryside. By early autumn travel restrictions had been lifted and Torrance was planning another trip to the foothills west of Qionglai with the Olsens but was delayed by a severe outbreak of amoebic dysentery in the city. The delay was timely. Annie and Mary both suffered attacks and he was able to nurse them through. Once they had recovered he was afraid to leave in case Tom or Grace should succumb, and he was then able to help save the life of another missionary who was critically ill. In early September the disease tragically took the lives of two young sisters, Grace and Dorothy Abrey.

Torrance and four of his Chinese co-workers eventually set out in October for Qionglai, their arrival coinciding with a large contingent of troops passing through who had commandeered almost every coolie in sight. Torrance and the Olsens had little choice but to hire some opium-smoking carriers – rejected by the troops – to transport their baggage, who charged them over the odds and abandoned them at the first opportunity. While the Olsens waited for more carriers, Torrance went ahead to start the meetings with the local Chinese and had the joy of seeing twelve people baptised, including the father of Mr Luo. Although he had previously opposed his son's beliefs, Luo's father had been in Chengdu in the spring and stayed with the Torrance family for several days where he had chatted to Torrance's ABS depot manager,

27   TT to Hykes, Aug 12, 1919.

a scholarly Christian named Lu Shenzhai. Having taken some reading back to his village the old man was now firm in his faith.

Chen Zuofu, the school teacher whom Torrance had found for Luo's village, was also among those baptised. Already a Christian, he had spent three months living with the Torrances and studying the Bible before moving up to the village. True to their promise, the farmers were providing half his salary and he had settled in well. The school lessons were being held in the local temple which, like other temples in the area, had been of great renown in the Ming period but had long since been abandoned. On Sundays Chen was also teaching the adult Christians and any other villagers showing interest.

Torrance returned to Chengdu in late November, glad to be with Annie and the three children in time for all the Christmas festivities, something to which Annie enjoyed applying her creative gifts. In her memoirs she recalled one Christmas party for about twenty children, for whom she made scrap books of red cloth and teddy bears out of rabbit skin muffs.[28] The crowning glory of the party was a decorated Christmas tree.

To everyone's relief the colder winter weather provided a breathing space for the city after the dysentery outbreak. Trade was returning to normal, thanks to the safer travel conditions, and with everything generally more stable Torrance sought an audience with the governor, Luo Peijin: 'I went to appeal to him to do something to eradicate the opium traffic from the province. To my surprise he began by speaking of the great work of the American Bible Society in China. He told me how profoundly he respected the Christian religion. "Our country," he said, "has so many evils and idolatrous practices that only the continued circulation of the Bible will be able to cure."'[29]

But Luo's days as governor were numbered, as was the peaceful interlude in Chengdu.

---

28 *Memoirs*, p57.
29 BSR, Vol 62, Nov 1917, p136. BSR articles were drawn from ABS sources worldwide and often appeared some time after the reported events.

Chapter 7

Chengdu Under Fire

1917-1919

In the spring of 1917 Torrance set out with James Neave and two colporteurs on his first preaching trip to the Qiang people. As they reached the edge of Qiang territory he felt a 'strange elation' and said to Neave, 'To-morrow we strike the aboriginal country and begin our work. Seventeen years before I got to this same township but no further. But now at last the opportunity has come to go on.'[1] No record has come to light of this earlier trip but it seems likely that it was in 1901 when Torrance and Johan Johanson had returned to Chengdu after the Boxer uprising and spent several weeks travelling together with freedom to plan their own itinerary. Torrance would later describe 'the real border' of the Qiang area as a place called Taoguan, ten miles south of today's Miansi, so it is possibly this village which he and Neave had now reached.[2]

Torrance's elation didn't last long. A messenger reached them the next day with news of serious fighting in Chengdu and they had no choice but to turn back, leaving the two colporteurs to continue further into the mountains. In haste they made their way down the Min Valley and across the plain to Chengdu, with Torrance's disappointment far outweighed by his concern for Annie and the children, especially as Annie was expecting another baby in September.

To his great relief he found Annie and the three children unscathed but this was no minor skirmish. The fighting had broken out on April 18 between Yunnanese troops loyal to the military governor, Luo Peijin, and Sichuanese troops loyal to General Liu Cunhou, who was popular in Chengdu. Overnight shelling on April 19 had stretched well into the next day with houses ablaze and people dead and dying. After several days of fighting Luo Peijin was ousted from Chengdu and Dai Kan, the civil governor, was left in charge, backed by his Guizhou troops,

---

1   TT to Hykes, June 4, 1917.
2   TT. 'Journeys Among the Tribes People'. Aug 22, 1923. Typed manuscript, no destination indicated.

but with Liu Cunhou now in a stronger position. In a letter to Hykes, Torrance had high praise for Liu Cunhou, 'who holds the welfare of Szechuan in his hands'.[3]

In July, to the dismay of Chengdu's conflict-weary populace, the fragile peace under Dai Kan was shattered by a worse outbreak of fighting, this time between him and Liu Cunhou. The catalyst for this was a bitter power struggle being played out in Beijing between President Li Yuanhong and Premier Duan Qirui, in which Zhang Xun, the governor of Anhui Province, had been asked to mediate. Zhang, known as the 'pigtail general' because his troops still wore the queue out of loyalty to the Qing, had never given up hope of Qing restoration, and as the price of his mediation he demanded the dissolution of parliament.[4] On July 1 young Puyi, now eleven years old, was restored as emperor. Twelve days later Zhang was defeated by Premier Duan Qirui's troops and young Puyi was once again deposed, but not before Zhang had appointed Liu Cunhou as Chengdu military governor in place of Dai Kan. Despite Zhang's defeat, Liu Cunhou refused to back down and acknowledge Dai Kan as governor.

On July 5, Dai Kan, whose 3,500 troops were horribly outnumbered by those of Liu Cunhou, retreated into the security of Chengdu's thickly-walled imperial city to prepare for battle. By that afternoon shops were closed and residents were beginning to flee the city. Just after midnight, rapid rifle fire pierced the night sky and early the next morning thick black smoke could be seen over the city as Dai Kan's men came out of the imperial city and set fire to street barriers and nearby houses, using terror to compensate for their military weakness. As the fires spread, panic-stricken people fled while troops on both sides indulged in reckless plunder. The glow of the fire was visible from Guanxian forty miles away.[5] Dai's men were pushed back into the imperial city and when Liu offered them a peaceful evacuation via the East Gate their response was to fire sulphur shells into Great East Street, killing many citizens. Torrance was shocked by the carnage inflicted as Dai Kan and his men fought a losing battle:

---

3   TT to Hykes, June 4, 1917.
4   Xu Guoqi. *China and the Great War: China's Pursuit of a New National Identity and Internationalization.* Cambridge University Press. 2005, p219.
5   W. E. Hampson. 'Shot and Shell: Events in Chengtu during July, 1917'. *Millions*, 1917, p138. Hampson was a CIM missionary in Chengdu. His article was published after his death in the dysentery epidemic which followed the fighting.

Angered at his defeat he wantonly burned about ten thousand homes in this city. . . . The terribleness of such a conflagration words fail to describe. The people were terrified. All our foreign houses were jammed with refugees.'[6]

By mid-July matters had reached an apparent stalemate with Dai Kan's men protected behind the seemingly impenetrable imperial city walls. However, unknown to Dai, Liu's men were digging a hole beneath the wall and at 10 a.m. on July 16 two Chinese coffins filled with 300 kilograms of gunpowder exploded, shaking the whole city and knocking a breach in the wall twenty to thirty foot wide. Dai's men were all forced out of Chengdu the following day. Dai handed over the seals of office and agreed to a ceasefire in return for money to pay his troops, three hundred coolies to carry their goods, and a promise of safe passage beyond Chengdu. The *North China Herald* later reported that Liu Cunhou's men had forced Dai Kan and his troops to keep marching. If any stopped they were fired on mercilessly. As their numbers dwindled and they got ever weaker, Dai Kan chose to commit suicide in an effort to save the remnant of his men.[7]

Torrance once again happened to be out of town when the July fighting erupted but Annie and the children had been under fire. 'It would go on all through the day', Annie wrote, 'but after dark it was far worse – it was one long nightmare until daylight. The bullets would rattle over our roof during the day – one or two fell into the sugar in the store room. Not wishing Mary, Tom and Grace to be alarmed I tried to amuse them and distract their attention from the goings on outside by going to one place of the house and then another according to the position of the firing.'[8]

The Postal Commissioner, an Indian Parsi called Kaoroz Doodha, was so concerned for Annie and the children that he invited them to move in with his family but in the end they moved to live at the Canadian Methodist Mission.[9] Torrance only managed to reach

6   TT, Annual ABS report, 3 Dec, 1917.
7   TT. 'Civil War in China'. BSR, Vol 62, Nov 1917, p198-199.
8   *Memoirs*, p56.
9   On Dec 4, 1917, the Edinburgh Gazette (No. 13,175) recorded that King George V had granted His Majesty's Royal licence to Kaoroz Bhicajee Doodha and the authority to wear the decoration conferred on him by the President of the Republic of China, namely the 'Fourth Class of the Order of the Excellent Crop'.

Chengdu on July 16, in time to witness the destruction caused by the coffin explosions. Entering Chengdu by the west gate he made it safely to the northern part of the city amid the sound of persistent shooting and then turned east for a mile, picking his way through stretches of burned streets until he reached home.

Having learned that Annie and the children were safe he made a quick check of the ABS property and then climbed over the side wall into the Chinese Foreign Office premises next door to get an update on the situation from Mr Qian, one of the officials. Qian was married to an English girl, Adela, whom he had met while studying in London, and they and the Torrances had become friends.[10] As he and Torrance talked they could hear the boom of big guns, the screech of missiles overhead, and an occasional thud as one landed nearby. Qian warned him to keep watch that night, afraid that incendiaries from Dai Kan's troops would set their block on fire, which also housed Chengdu's Telephone Exchange. However, the chief of police for that section of the city had taken shelter at the Torrance home and the place was well-guarded so Torrance managed to get some intermittent sleep before being reunited with Annie and the children the next day.

The scene Dai Kan's men left behind was one of devastation. *China's Millions* reported that just south of the imperial city 'a densely populated and thriving business section has been reduced to a vast area of waste, ruins and indescribable debris.'[11] Roughly one hundred streets had been set ablaze and by the end of the fighting nearly a quarter of the city had been devastated either by fire or by general destruction, leaving thousands homeless. The missions on the east side where the ABS compound was situated had mostly escaped major damage and missionaries now joined the Chinese in relief work, with thousands of refugees being fed at large temples which had escaped the blaze. The ones who had lost homes were 'raking and scraping among the ruins to see if any of their former possessions had withstood the fire, and not even a rusty nail was overlooked.'[12] Li Jieren, author and Chengdu native, would later write of this period:

---

10   Qian Weishan (Charles) and Adela (nee Warburton). Annie had been particularly supportive of Adela when she was expecting her second and third daughters, Hilda and Isobel. See https://pollyshihbrandmeyer.com/family/
11   Hampson, *Millions*, 1917, p139.
12   Ibid., p141.

We modern Chengdu people were not so foolish. We knew that in a chaotic world no one could expect a long life, so it was useless to make a 'Great Plan for a Hundred Years.' What we needed to do was just enjoy life as best we could . . . So, from the last years of the Guangxu era on, most of our houses were expected to last only twenty years or so.[13]

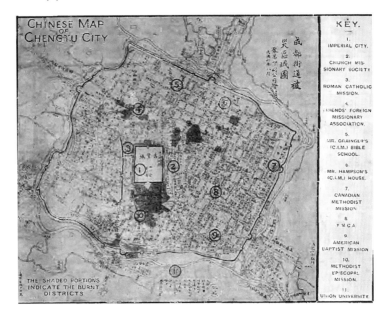

CIM MAP OF CHENGDU SHOWING AREAS BURNED IN THE FIGHTING
NO.1 IS THE IMPERIAL CITY (*Millions*, Dec 1917, front cover)

The September editorial of the WCMN described the summer as 'one replete with calamity'.[14] Alongside the burning of Chengdu, the Min River had flooded in July, breaching a dam at Guanxian and causing the worst flooding in years. On top of all that, an earthquake had also been felt in Chengdu. How Annie survived all this and gave birth to a healthy child is almost beyond comprehension but on September 30 Margaret Ramsay Torrance came into the world, her name bearing witness to their gratitude to Clarence Ramsay, whose departure from his ABS role in Chengdu had opened the way for so many things:

---

13   Li Jieren. 'Weicheng zhuiyi' (Memoirs of an Endangered City). Originally published in *Xin Zhonghua* 5, nos. 1-6 (1937). Reprinted in Vol 5 of *Li Jieren Xuanji* (Selected Works), pp96-148. Chengdu: Sichuan Renmin Chubanshe, 1986b. Cited in Stapleton, *Civilizing Chengdu*, p193, n.38.
14   WCMN, Sept 1917, p1.

Torrance's return to China, his sense of fulfilment in the ABS work, and his and Annie's deeply satisfying marriage.

In his annual ABS report Torrance mentioned in passing how much he had been able to assist fellow missionaries and Chinese during such a troubled year, thanks to his general China experience, his fluency in the language, and nearly twenty years living in Chengdu. In recognition of this, General Liu Cunhou invited him and another missionary to a dinner, which was also attended by the new civil governor and other government department heads. In deference to the missionaries Liu had no alcohol at his table, something highly unusual on such an occasion.[15]

Having been confined to Chengdu once again for much of 1917, Torrance had accepted local speaking and preaching invitations and also held a series of special evangelistic meetings at the ABS premises and at the Canadian church with James Neave. Continuing his historical research, he also had two articles on the history of Sichuan published in the WCMN, one on the Jin Dynasty (AD 219-465) and the other on the Northern and Southern Dynasties and the Sui Dynasty (AD 420-618).[16]

At the beginning of December he and some of his colporteurs joined his old CIM friend John Muir, now based in Pengshan, for a two-week evangelistic campaign in nearby Meishan, once again using the magic lantern in the meetings and distributing literature on the streets. Two encounters were evidence of how effective the literature could be. One man they met had become a Christian through reading a gospel booklet bought seventeen years previously but had only recently attended a church meeting when invited by another Christian. The other, Mr Pan, had been lent a gospel by a friend forty years before. Just before the evangelistic campaign he happened to meet a Christian who explained the gospel more fully and introduced him to John Muir. 'At one stroke he gave up the old and turned eagerly to Christ', and immediately started telling others.[17] Torrance and Muir were also received courteously by the local mandarin who asked them to show the lantern slides to some well-to-do young men from across the district who were at the yamen for meetings regarding a new police-militia system.

15   TT. Annual ABS report, 3 Dec, 1917.
16   WCMN, July 1917, pp4-11; WCMN, Nov 1917, pp5-8.
17   TT to Hykes, Dec 21, 1917.

A New Home, January 1918

Margaret's arrival in September 1917 had spurred Torrance to look for larger premises. The house at San-dao-guai had served them well but it was in a low, congested part of town and easily flooded, something Tom and Mary had turned to great advantage, floating around the garden on wooden boards. In mid-November a larger property was found in the northeastern section of the city on a street still known today as Wushi-tongtang, meaning 'Five Generations Under One Roof'.[18] Situated on higher ground near the East Parade Ground, it was nearer to the Canadian mission and hospital complex where various friends lived, and convenient for the Canadian Press which was producing an increasing amount of literature for Torrance. The previous Canadian occupants had made improvements but repairs and adaptations were needed to make it suitable for the ABS work and the family finally moved in January 1918.

Their arrival at the new residence was announced to all and sundry by large Chinese characters erected above the outer gate of the property which read: 'American Bible Society Bookstore'.[19] Between this gate and an inner gate was the gate-keeper's room, beyond which lay a courtyard with flower beds, flanked on one side by low wooden rooms used for the ABS depot and for colporteurs back from their travels. Servant accommodation and a kitchen faced these across the courtyard, beyond which lay a high-roofed hall where benches could be set out for meetings. To the left and right of this were various storerooms, a joinery workshop, and two visitors' rooms. Set further back were the stables for Prince the horse and Billy the mule.

An inner court with flower beds lay beyond the meeting hall, edged with a veranda where the family often had tea, and with accommodation on the left for Auntie Gou and a seamstress, and guest rooms for personal visitors of the Torrances. Torrance's study was on the right next to a couple of storerooms. Behind this inner court was the family home which included a laundry room, an outside kitchen and coal house, and a deep well which provided their water. At the back of the property a garden area provided space for the flower and vegetable beds, the cowshed, and an outhouse where Tom kept pigeons.

---

18 Nowadays the street (五世同堂街) bears an inscription regarding a house that was recognised by Emperor Qianlong in the 18th century for having five generations of the Zhang family living under the same roof.

19 The sign read 大美國聖經會書局.

Mulberry, persimmon, walnut, and fig trees grew near the back wall, which was adjacent to Chengdu's law school.

Towards the end of February, just as they were getting settled in their new home, Sichuan's position in the tug-of-war between north and south once again came to the fore as Liu Cunhou was ousted as governor of Chengdu by Xiong Kewu, a Sichuanese supporter of Sun Yatsen whom Torrance described as the 'commander in chief of the Southern forces in Szechuan'.[20] A few months later, Torrance sent Xiong a New Testament and a copy of a report on the history of the American Bible Society in China. In response, General Xiong sent a financial donation and a personal reply:

> Dear Mr. Torrance,
>
> I thank you for your favour of a copy of the New Testament. I know that what the Bible teaches makes men and nations great. This is what I myself sincerely believe. For this reason I wish that my countrymen might believe in the Christian religion. I herewith send a small donation to assist your Society in the printing of the Bible. At the same time it will serve as a tangible evidence to you of my faith in God.
>
> Yours sincerely, Hsiung Keh-wu[21]

Torrance was cheered by his response. Although courting the missionaries had benefits other than spiritual, particularly as institutions like the mission hospitals and the West China Union University represented significant foreign investment in Chengdu, a positive relationship was beneficial for both parties and Sun Yatsen had made Christianity generally more acceptable with his own belief that it could have a positive influence on society.

In the spring of 1918 Torrance made trips southwest to Qionglai and south to Pengshan, Meishan, and Danling. On one of these journeys he met Mr Xiong, a 77-year-old farmer and head of a reputable family who, sometime ago, had bought a copy of the book of Genesis from a colporteur. Xiong had been so moved by the story of Joseph that he asked his sons to purchase any similar books they could get and he eventually came to church and was baptised.[22]

---

20 TT. ABS report, July 5, 1918.
21 Ibid., translated by TT.
22 Ibid.

Having been thwarted the previous year, Torrance was once more making plans to visit the Qiang area but to his great disappointment he was again prevented, this time by his own ill health. Instead he spent the summer with the family up at Lingyan Temple where he had to make do with hearing reports of other missionaries' travels in the western mountains.

In August the WCMN published another of Torrance's articles, 'The History of Szechwan During the T'ang Dynasty, A. D. 618-906', which was followed in October by a lecture on Sichuanese history in the ensuing Five Dynasties period, presented at the Fortnightly Club and later published in the WCMN.[23] The Fortnightly Club, of which Torrance was an executive member, had been founded a few years before for those wanting a greater understanding of the Chinese and their culture. As explained by Daniel Sheets Dye of the university physics department, 'Each member made it a point to investigate and present some local or provincial or Chinese subject, such as diseases, temples, gods, theatricals, or local history. Knowledge and appreciation of the Chinese and their mental wealth was provoked and new lines of contact were made with our Chinese problems.'[24]

The presence of the West China Union University in Chengdu greatly enhanced such meetings, bringing an academic rigour to the research and the presentation of material. The university had been founded in 1910 as the result of cooperation between five Christian missions based in Chengdu and Torrance benefited much from his friendships with university staff. As time went on, he would diverge from some of them regarding what he saw as their liberal theology but he still valued the interaction with regard to historical, literary, archaeological, and ethnographic research.

Although Torrance's second attempt to visit the Qiang area had come to nothing, he was fit enough in late summer to make a trip to Xindu, north of Chengdu, taking the main route which author Li Jieren described as a dirt track barely five feet wide which, after heavy rain, was 'so muddy you could hardly walk a step without fastening clamps to the back of your straw sandals.'[25] Torrance had been invited by Ernest Hamilton, an Anglican minister with the Church Missionary Society, to help with some evangelistic work and, to Torrance's surprise, Hamilton asked him to give the Sunday sermon.

23   WCMN, Aug 1918, pp21-35; WCMN, May 1919, pp28-37.
24   WCMN, June 1920, p17.
25   Li Jieren, *Ripples Across Stagnant Water*. Panda Books. 1990, p42.

'Imagine me speaking in a Church of England pulpit,' Torrance wrote to Hykes. 'I waited in the pew until the rigmarole of their ritual was run off and then went up and proceeded as I should have done in a Presbyterian, Methodist or Baptist church.'[26] He was very conscious of their differences, with Hamilton a Tory and a 'decided Episcopalian' and Torrance disliking anything that smacked of clergy hierarchy and the notion of social superiority. However, he and Hamilton were united in their 'common evangelical desire to see men saved' and the visit seems to have been a success.[27] In December he took the dirt track once again to help Hamilton and his Chinese co-workers with a further series of meetings.

End of the War

On November 17, 1918, six days after Armistice Day, an English thanksgiving service was held in Chengdu for the close of the First World War. Although it had been a 'quiet war' for those who had stayed in Chengdu, Torrance's friend Harry Openshaw had worked in France with the Chinese Labour Corps, which was providing support for the Allies, and several other missionaries had gone to serve in various capacities, at least two of whom had been killed in the fighting.

Some days later Torrance had to make an unexpected visit to Qionglai. His depot manager had been kidnapped, probably in the hope of some kind of ransom from Torrance, and although he had since been released, three Christian youths taken at the same time were still being held, as well as 'two dry cows' belonging to Torrance.[28] The exact details aren't clear but the culprit behind the kidnapping turned out to be a militia leader in Qionglai who had since gone into hiding for fear of his life. From his refuge he sent a message to Torrance asking him to guarantee his life in return for the boys and the cows but warning that if Torrance pursued a case against him, the boys would be killed. The man was already guilty of other offences so Torrance sent word that if he didn't produce the boys and the cows he would be in even further trouble. In December Torrance informed Hykes that the depot manager had received compensation and the 'cow case' was nicely settled.[29]

This same letter revealed that Hykes had mentioned the possibility of a 700-mile move to Hankou in Hubei Province, for Torrance to take over

---

26 TT to Hykes, Nov 24, 1918.
27 Ibid.
28 TT to Hykes, Oct 29, 1918.
29 TT to Hykes Dec 23, 1918.

the ABS work there. It was only a suggestion but Torrance, who had a strong sense that God had called him to Sichuan, was dismayed. 'I am wedded to Szechuan as you know,' he told Hykes. 'My grip of the local language gives me a pull here. Tho' I say it there is hardly another who can talk as plainly in the current dialect as I can. Others talk as good or better but they are bookish or their "tones" are out etc. Consequently no other sphere would fit me as well. Then I am sure neither Mrs T. or I could stand Hankou. So we thought we would like to remain here until our furlough.'[30] To his and Annie's relief, Hykes abandoned the idea and they stayed in Sichuan.

Since Xiong Kewu's takeover in February life in Chengdu had been relatively calm but the struggle for power between the Beijing government and Sun Yatsen's southern alliance continued to dominate much of China. Parallel with this, the early seeds of Communist ideology were being sown amongst intellectuals as they watched developments in Russia which had led to the 1917 Bolshevik revolution. In 1915 Chen Duxiu, the eventual co-founder of the Chinese Communist Party, had founded *New Youth*, a magazine calling for radical social change and a rejection of the inequality and passivity of traditional Chinese society. In December 1916, Cai Yuanpei, another influential leader in this New Culture Movement, had become chancellor of Beijing University. Although he had been the privileged recipient of a classical Chinese education, Cai had later studied in Europe and was now advocating a more questioning, research-based approach to study, which was a revolutionary departure from the old higher education system and the easy transition it provided into the elite world of officialdom.

The following year Cai appointed Chen Duxiu as Dean of Letters and in 1918 Li Dazhao, co-founder of the Communist Party with Chen, became librarian, assisted by a 24-year old Mao Zedong as a junior staff member. That year students at the university produced another magazine, *New Tide*, with more fervent attacks on traditional Chinese culture, including Confucianism, the social class system, and cultural double standards, for example the different expectations of men and women regarding chastity. Immanuel Hsu describes these magazines as an 'intellectual bombshell' and in their promotion of public political discussion they were far more powerful in the long term than the might of any provincial warlord, producing a body of highly motivated youths and other intellectuals with a vision of

---

30   TT to Hykes, Dec 23, 1918.

China's potential unlike anything that had gone before – something which was a key factor in events which would spill over into Sichuan the following year.[31]

1919 was a momentous year for China. Feeling betrayed by the wheelings and dealings of the post-World War I conference at Versailles in France, which confirmed Japanese control of Germany's earlier territorial gains in Shandong rather than restoring the region to China, Chinese students rose up in opposition. Having supported the Allies through their Chinese Labour Corps, the Chinese were dismayed that the West was yielding to Japan's demands, even though some of the blame lay with the Beijing government which had secretly granted the Japanese the right to build two railways in Shandong and station troops there in return for a loan. On May 4, 1919, students in Beijing took to the streets in a mass protest and on June 28 Chinese students in Paris obstructed the Chinese delegates to the Versailles conference, preventing them from attending the signing ceremony.[32] The impact of what became known as the May Fourth Movement would be far-reaching as protests broke out across China and some younger Chinese, now deeply disillusioned with the West, looked towards Communist Russia as an alternative source of inspiration for China's own future development.

In Chengdu two large demonstrations were organised in May and June, the first attended by about ten thousand and the second by over twenty thousand protesters. There were, however, no clashes with the authorities. On the contrary, Governor Xiong was in sympathy with the protesters and not only encouraged his own troops to attend the protests but also made it known that he supported the rejection of the Versailles decision regarding the Japanese presence in Shandong.[33]

Xiong's measured response contributed to a surprisingly peaceful year in Chengdu. Canadian missionary Edward Wallace wrote towards the end of 1919 that 'For the first time since 1915 West China has enjoyed a year free from the terrors of civil war and largely immune from the depredations of bandits.'[34] However, he also mentioned the financial stringency resulting from the First World War and from a

---

31 Hsu, *Rise of Modern China*, pp497-501.
32 Ibid., pp502-505.
33 Chen Zhongping. 'The May Fourth Movement and Provincial Warlords: A Reexamination'. In Modern China, Vol 37, No.2 (March 2011), p146. https://www.jstor.org/stable/23053321.
34 WCMN, Nov 1919, p21.

serious drop in exchange rates. Torrance was feeling the pinch too. Bible Society donations had fallen and the amount of literature he and his colporteurs were able to circulate had almost halved. Of the roughly twenty colporteurs he had taken over from Clarence Ramsay in 1911, he was now only able to support one through the ABS and had three others who were funded directly by overseas donors. To compensate for this Torrance was encouraging other missionaries and their Chinese co-workers to distribute the ABS literature at their mission stations and on their travels.

With fewer colporteurs Torrance didn't attend the spring fair that year but instead made a short trip with George Hartwell of the Canadian Methodist Mission to the west and north of Chengdu. There had been no rain for six weeks and the earthen roads were thick with dust. 'All day we travelled in a cloud of superfine grit that penetrated the clothing, stuck to the face, and got into the mouth. What sights we were, on arrival at our first city!'[35] Torrance continued on to Guanxian to do some outreach with the Chinese Christians there but made sure he was home in time for Tom and Grace having their tonsils out. All went well with Grace but there was a fraught moment with Tom. 'I stood by until the actual operation began. After he was well under the chloroform I heard Dr. Spiers say "he has stopped breathing." My own heart nearly stopped then. But it was only for a second; he was all right as soon as the nose mask was withdrawn.' Once Tom and Grace had recovered, Torrance and his co-workers took what had become an annual journey south of Chengdu by boat to Pengshan, Danling, and Meishan.

In May, Torrance and two other executive members of the Fortnightly Club published a letter in the WCMN asking if anyone knew of a blind boy who might be educated at the Institution for the Blind in Shanghai, funded by the YMCA and local donations, in the hope that he might eventually help to start a work for the blind in Chengdu.[36] No recommendations were forthcoming but the appeal was not in vain. By December the Chengdu churches were instead looking at a joint project to establish a School for the Blind in the city, which would eventually open in November 1922 with Torrance's friend Harry Openshaw as director.

---

35   BSR, Aug 1919, pp131-132.
36   WCMN, July 1919, p14.

Chapter 8

Discovering the Qiang

1919

Despite having not yet reached the Qiang area, Torrance's interest in the people there was continuing to grow. On June 10, 1919, he sent Dr Hykes a detailed article about Sichuan which included historical references to 'a very virile race called the Ch'iang' living in the mountains to the west and northwest of the Chengdu plain in the 4th century BC.[1] During the reign of Emperor Wu of Han (r.140-87 BC) these Qiang 'were nominally made subject to China, but it was over 1500 years before they were finally crushed.' He also noted that an ancient Qiang capital had existed in the vicinity of Maoxian.

Torrance was in no doubt that the Qiang of the early twentieth century were associated with these 'renowned Ch'iang' of more than two thousand years ago and he disagreed with those who held the view that the Qiang and Tibetans were of the same stock. Alongside his references to the Qiang people he mentioned neighbouring ethnic groups in western Sichuan: the Tibetans, Xifan, Boluozi, Nosu, and also the Wasi people who had been brought down by the Chinese from Ngari in Tibet in the mid-fifteenth century to help quell local rebellions among the Qiang.

Besides his own historical reading Torrance had also heard reports from travellers to the Qiang area. James Neave had travelled there in 1907, as had Clarence Ramsay who, as the WCMN reported, had 'returned slightly worn after a book-selling expedition into the tribes country to the north-west.'[2] Torrance had inherited Ramsay's colporteurs just four years later, so not only had Torrance probably heard in detail from Ramsay about his trip but some of his early colporteurs would have already travelled in the region. The Edgar and Coates families had also lived at the CIM property in Weizhou

---

1   TT. 'Szechuan'. June 10, 1919. The article was received by Dr Hykes on July 7. No destination is indicated.
2   WCMN, June 1907, p13.

in the Qiang area and although the Coates had left, James Edgar was still travelling extensively in the wider region. In addition there were accounts of other travellers to and through the region although, as illustrated below, these tended to provide descriptions of what was immediately visible but gave little reliable detail about Qiang culture and customs. There was little clarity about Qiang identity, what language they spoke, or what they believed.

Travellers' Reports

The earliest English account of a journey through the Qiang region seems to be that of Captain William Gill, a 32-year old British army officer and explorer. In 1876, unexpectedly delayed in Chengdu on his way to Tibet, Gill decided to venture up the Min Valley to Songpan. Before leaving he was advised by Monseigneur Pinchon, the Catholic bishop in Chengdu, to take his own provisions because 'barbarians' inhabiting the Lifan region believed, according to the bishop, that poisoning a wealthy man would make them rich.[3] 'Barbarian' was the unfortunate translation of the Chinese term *manzi*, a derogatory term used historically for various non-Han groups in China whom the Chinese viewed as less civilised than themselves. Naturalist Ernest H. Wilson described it as 'a contemptuous term . . . and of no ethnological value whatever' and Gill's translator warned Gill against using it.[4] The expression had nonetheless been adopted by some foreigners, with even an editorial in *China's Millions* noting that the Sino-Tibetan border area was 'for the most part, inhabited by small, semi-barbarous tribes, each speaking its own dialect, and being scattered over mountain districts'.[5]

Undeterred by Pinchon's advice, Gill's party, with a ten-man Chinese military escort, travelled up the Min Valley to Miansi, which seemed a miserable, poverty-stricken place. On the mountainsides beyond Miansi Gill was struck by the fortress-like stone settlements guarded by high towers and 'in quite a different style to the Chinese', which reminded him of villages he had seen in the Alborz Mountains in northern Iran.[6]

---

3   W. J. Gill. *The River of Golden Sand: Being the Narrative of a Journey Through China and Eastern Tibet to Burmah*. London: John Murray. 1883, p104.
4   Ernest. H. Wilson. *A Naturalist in Western China*, Vol 1. London: Methuen & Co. 1913, p158.
5   *Millions*, April 1907, p57.
6   Gill, *River of Golden Sand*, p111.

The Chinese had a particular term, *zhaizi*, for such settlements, meaning a stockaded or defensively built village. Down in the valley burned-out homes were witness to the Chinese taking control of the main thoroughfares and pushing the tribespeople back into the mountains.

From Miansi, Gill and his party proceeded to Weizhou and then turned west along the Zagunao River to the town of Xuecheng, a market town and the administrative centre of the Lifan district. From here Gill climbed up to a village about two thousand feet above the valley and was surprised to find cultivated terraces where locals were growing barley and wheat. Returning to Weizhou his party then made the hundred-mile trek north up the Min Valley to Songpan. Along the way suspension bridges and high single rope crossings came into view, the latter graphically described by Isabella Bird, which were crossed by gripping a hinged wooden cylinder placed around the rope: 'The passenger rushes at tremendous speed, head foremost, down hill across the chasm, with an impetus which sends him a little way up the other slope. Then, letting go the cylinder, he puts his hands on the rope above his head, and hauls himself up hand over hand, slowly and laboriously.'[7]

Isabella's 1896 journey followed Gill's route to the Lifan area. With characteristic detail she described the powerful Min River 'booming, crashing, and foaming through canyons and gorges' and 'hemmed in by cliffs and mountains so precipitous as rarely to leave level ground enough for a barley patch'. The bridle paths along the valley were 'cut, not blasted, in the rock, at times on steep declivities and at times on precipices . . . not broad enough for a loaded mule to pass a chair.' It took her party nine hours to travel thirteen miles.[8]

The scenery from Weizhou to Xuecheng reminded her of a stretch of the road from Kashmir to Tibet, along the Indus River. Of the people in the Qiang area, she learned through her escort that, 'their fathers and their fathers' fathers never remember a time when they were free', something which explained the defence towers, on top of which fires were lit in times of danger to warn of advancing enemies.[9] Regarding the physical appearance of these people, she perceived a difference compared to both the Chinese and the Tibetans:

7   Bird, *Yangtze Valley,* p370.
8   Ibid., p367.
9   Ibid., p382-3.

Their handsome, oval faces; richly-coloured complexions; thick, straight eyebrows; large, level eyes, sometimes dark grey; broad, upright foreheads; moderate cheek bones; definite, though rather broad noses; thin lips, somewhat pointed chins, and white, regular teeth are far removed from any Mongolian characteristics, and it is impossible not to believe that these tribes are an offshoot of the Aryan race.[10]

Hypotheses about the origins of people groups were not unusual during this period. Diffusionism, the idea that cultural similarities had derived from a common root rather than developing independently in diverse places, was a popular anthropological theory of the nineteenth century, and in Torrance's time Western explorers such as Sven Hedin and Aurel Stein were also raising intriguing questions about the diverse ethnic origins of people who had lived centuries earlier in Central Asia and northwest China. In 1903, *China's Millions* had included a reference to Sven Hedin speaking of his recent Asian journeys at the Royal Geographic Society, and some in the missionary community – often intrepid travellers themselves – would have followed news of his and Stein's explorations with great interest.

In 1904, William Haines-Watson, assistant British Consul in Chongqing, travelled up the Min Valley to Songpan in the company of Ernest Wilson. In his account Haines-Watson referred to the locals as aborigines and mentioned the 'well-nigh inaccessible places where these strange and isolated people have built their houses', also affirming earlier observations regarding ruined 'former Manzi habitations' in the valleys.[11] Although he didn't refer to the Qiang by name, he described the people living between Xuecheng to Weizhou and extending down the Min Valley from Weizhou as 'rather European in appearance' and noted their different language.[12]

This trip was one of at least three collecting trips made by Ernest Wilson to the Min Valley, where he noted the high altitude crops grown by the mountain villagers, including wheat, barley, buckwheat, peas, linseed, and 'exceptionally good Chilli peppers', particularly in Maoxian.[13] Having witnessed fatal landslides which destroyed lives and homes, Wilson also wrote of the dangers: 'In many places rockslides are

---

10 Ibid., p458. The term 'Aryan' in this period was generally used to indicate people of Indo-European origins.
11 W. C. Haines-Watson. 'Journey to Sungp'an'. JNCBRAS, Vol 36, 1905, p63.
12 Ibid., p87.
13 Wilson, *A Naturalist in Western China*, Vol 1, p153.

constantly occurring, and warning notices to travellers not to tarry are frequently displayed throughout the Upper Min Valley.'[14] In 1910 he suffered a compound leg fracture in a minor landslide on his way down the valley, which left him with a permanent limp.

James Neave, with whom Torrance had attempted his 1917 trip, was more familiar with the Qiang region than many, having lived to the north of it in Songpan in the late 1890s, and he was perhaps the first Western traveller to refer to the Qiang by name. In a report of his 1907 summer trip to the region he referred to some tribes with more allegiance to Tibet than to the Chinese but then described another people under direct Chinese rule: 'There are also what are called the Chiang Ming, held by some to be the original inhabitants of the country, but our information is not quite clear on that point.'[15] Curious as to their origins, Neave mentioned a theory he attributed to the Sinologist, Dr Herbert Giles, that these Qiang people were 'an ancient tribe in Tangut, shepherd nomads of the Ouigour [Uyghur] race, living from early times west of Szechwan and Kansuh [Gansu].'[16]

Neave described these 'Chiang ming' as a people who avoided the main valley road, grew maize and various kinds of beans up in the hills, and were skilled hunters, with bear and deer among their quarry. However, he described their language as 'very much akin to, if not actually, a dialect of Tibetan' and their religion as mainly Lamaism, which indicates that he wasn't distinguishing clearly between the Qiang inhabitants and neighbouring Tibetan Buddhist groups like the Jiarong and the Wasi.[17]

In 1908, William Fergusson of the British & Foreign Bible Society also visited the region. Reaching Miansi, he recorded that 'On inquiry it was found that the people living on the east bank of the river are called Chang Ming, and are supposed to be the remnant of the aborigines of

---

14   Ibid.

15   James Neave. 'The Hill Tribes of China'. Chapter 9 in *Our Share in China* by George J. Bond. Toronto: Missionary Society of the Methodist Church, Young People's Forward Movement Dept. 1909, p155. In Torrance's day the common transcription for the Qiang character (羌) was 'Ch'iang'. They were also referred to as the 'Ch'iang min' (羌民), meaning 'Qiang people', but travellers often transcribed what they were hearing, hence Neave's 'Chiang ming'.

16   Ibid. Although imperial Chinese histories record various Qiang groups of the Han dynasty as pastoral nomads living in China's northwest where the Uyghur people now live, there is no suggestion nowadays of a link between the two groups.

17   Neave, 'Hill Tribes of China', p157.

the country.'[18] Like Torrance, he mentioned the Wasi on the west bank
of the Min River, being brought from Tibet to help conquer the Qiang.
According to Fergusson, these Wasi had come down the Min Valley as the
Chinese had come up from the Chengdu plain and between them they
had trapped the Qiang and pushed them up into the hills. He described
the Qiang as 'fierce warlike tribes' who had frequently raided the Chinese
on the plain and then retreated out of reach to the mountains.[19]

For centuries the Min and Zagunao valleys had been important trade
routes connecting Sichuan with regions further west and Fergusson
painted a picture of a busy thoroughfare with 'thousands of coolies laden
with furs, wool, medicines, deer sinews, brought from the Tibetan border
towns' which were exchanged for 'salt, sugar, wine, rice or bamboo and
hemp sandals.'[20] Travelling from Weizhou to Xuecheng he noted:

> There are at least 50,000 of this remnant of the ancient occupants
> of the province of Sechuan. They are now under the Chinese
> Government, and have had no chiefs of their own for nearly 1,000
> years. They are still looked down on by the Chinese, though they have
> adopted Chinese customs and habits to a great extent. They dress in a
> coarse woollen cloak which is suitable to protect them from the cold
> winds that continually blow in these mountains. The women speak
> their own patois, which is not understood on opposite sides of the
> river; the men all speak Chinese, many of them 'broken' enough;
> and very few of them are able to read the Chinese character. They
> have no written language of their own. The Chinese Government
> is establishing schools in some of these villages, and the coming
> generation is encouraged to attend them.[21]

Perhaps surprisingly, James Edgar, who was actually living in Weizhou,
had continued to use the term *manzi* for the local people but he had
also discovered that their own name for themselves was *Ri-Mi*, an
autonym still used by the Qiang today and transcribed in various ways,
for example *Rma* or *Rrmea*. In a 1915 article in the WCMN Edgar wrote:

> In the hill regions around Weichow we have the remnant of an
> unknown tribe. Their language, 40% of which seems to be T'ang
> Dynasty Thibetan, would lead me to suggest that they may be

18   William Fergusson. *Adventure, Sport and Travel on the Tibetan Steppes.*
Charles Scribner's Sons. 1911, p85.
19   Ibid., p247. This had been a tactic of the early Qiang, seen e.g. in the battles
between General Zhao Chongguo and the Qiang tribes of Qinghai Province in
the mid-first century BC, as recorded in Chapter 69 of the *Book of Han*.
20   Fergusson, *Adventure, Sport and Travel*, p86.
21   Ibid., p133.

descendants of the neolithic race who lived in the Min Valley. They seem to have been affected by early Thibetan invasions before the introduction of Buddhism. . . . They call themselves Ri-Mi, and the semi-independent market of Weichow is their business rendezvous. Their houses and hillsides are studded with small towers supporting cylindrical pieces of untrimmed quartz. . . . With their houses high up in the mountains, or deep in secluded valleys, the Ri-Mi remain suspicious, truculent and unfriendly.'[22]

In another article he described them as 'taciturn and illiterate'.[23] Edgar offered an explanation for this reticence and at the same time highlighted the lack of clarity about the Qiang:

These people have been fighting China since the year 1 A. D. and every General down the ages has dumped some remnant of his army in the vicinity. Hence at once the taciturn dispositions of the Mantze, and the grouping of their houses in high mountain positions. Hence, too, the strange features and foreign complexions, as well as a form of dress belonging to the pre-Manchu days. They speak Chinese, too, with tones and accent of another day and their local patois seems to be composed of Tang dynasty Tibetan, ancient Chinese, and something probably unrelated to any known tongue.[24]

Later that year, in a brief article entitled 'Pre-Historic Stone Implements in West Szechwan', Edgar pondered the origin of these stone relics and concluded that such simple tools could not be connected with 'the early civilization which came to the Min from India, Kashmere, [and] Afghanistan *via* Eastern Turkestan' because that was a highly developed civilization. Unfortunately he gave no further information about the arrival or existence of this apparent early civilization in the Min Valley, writing simply as if it were an accepted fact.[25] In May 1919 Torrance wrote to Hykes about a discussion he had had with Edgar about the Tibetans and other border peoples of western Sichuan. Although he enjoyed Edgar's company, he had mixed feelings about the reliability of his information: 'Edgar is a born explorer, has a decided dash of genius,

22   James H. Edgar. 'The Lifan Marches'. WCMN, March 1915, p13.
23   James H. Edgar. 'Women's work among the Red Mantze'. WCMN, July 1916, p28.
24   Ibid., p29.
25   WCMN, Sept 1916, p32. The discovery in the Qiang region of ancient beads made from the tridacna clam of the Indo-Pacific region and also faience beads, possibly associated with Egyptian or Western Asian faience production, may suggest early long distance connections with the Min Valley.

is very effusive but lets his imagination have far too much rein. Edgar knows very little about the North West tribesmen, he told me so.'[26]

According to Torrance, John Muir, who had lived in the Tibetan towns of Kangding and Batang, was also doubtful about some of Edgar's conclusions. Torrance described Muir as 'the only one in West China besides myself who knows something of the real story of the Ch'iang people, tho his reading has been confined to one or two local histories.'[27] Torrance had been told by Muir that the Qiang worshipped the God of Heaven and had a temple with some kind of white stone in it, and he also knew from James Neave that they offered annual sacrifices.

A 1917 trip by Presbyterian missionary Robert Fitch shed a little more light on the Qiang region. Describing the 'Chang Min' as inhabiting the border region west of the Min River since the Han dynasty, he wrote of a garrison of two thousand Chinese troops being sent to the region in 1753 and the ensuing destruction of 'many towns of the Mantze and the Chang Min.'[28] He also noted that they practiced cremation.[29]

To the Qiang

Early in July Torrance set out on his 'long desired journey to see this little known race' in the company of T. Edgar Plewman, a skilled photographer and manager of the Canadian Press, and Mr Lu, a Chinese preacher who worked with Torrance.[30] His initial descriptions of the journey up the Min Valley echo those of Gill, Bird, and other travellers. Dwellings were more in evidence as they neared Miansi, with the Chinese living along the river and the Qiang living in their flat-roofed stone houses on the hillsides. To Torrance they were 'another race than the Chinese' and he and Plewman 'had almost to rub our

---

26   TT to Hykes, May 19, 1919.

27   TT to Hykes, July 4, 1919.

28   Robert Fitch. 'North-western Szechwan'. *The Chinese Recorder*, Dec 1918, p788.

29   Ibid., p793.

30   This and subsequent quotes here are, unless otherwise indicated, from a letter to Dr Hykes on August 12, 1919, later printed with minor revisions in *The China Press* under the title 'A Visit to the home of the Ch'iang' (n.d.). An entry in the WCMN (Nov 1932, p13) suggests Torrance had visited the Qiang much earlier: 'In the Revolution Year, 1911-1912, agents of the Bible societies, and other missionaries, notably Revs. T. Torrance, J. Neave and W. N. Ferguson, sowed these Tribes country valleys thick with Scripture portions and Gospel literature.' However, Torrance's 'sowing' back then would have been through his ABS colporteurs and there is no doubt that his first successful evangelistic and research trip was in the summer of 1919.

eyes to make sure there was no mistake. For before us lay clusters of flat-roofed stone buildings such as one sees in pictures of Palestine and the Middle East.' From his itinerations in Sichuan and his journeys across China to Shanghai Torrance was very accustomed to both rural and urban Chinese architecture but this was something new to him.

Near Miansi they climbed up to their first Qiang village. Having heard stories of how fierce and inhospitable the Qiang could be, Mr Lu made it half-way up and then turned tail and headed back down the mountain. When Torrance and Plewman reached the village the inhabitants were reticent at first but eventually a man standing in his doorway invited them in. Speaking in fluent Sichuan dialect, Torrance said he had grown up in a stone house and was glad to see one again. The man relaxed and in the conversation that followed they 'learned much that was useful'. At the next village, one of the inhabitants was very friendly and showed them around his house, despite his wife's remonstrations. Another had previously met John Muir and welcomed them up to his flat roof to chat. He was willing to answer questions and when Torrance and Plewman turned the conversation to the gospel, to their surprise the man's older brother said he had heard twenty years earlier from a Catholic convert about Christ's death for sinners.

Glad to reach Weizhou, they were able to stay with the Edgars at the CIM mission house, where Annie had stayed with Ella Bailey in 1911. Administered from Xuecheng, Weizhou was an important commercial centre with its own resident deputy official and although most of the local farmers were Qiang, many of the town's occupants were Han Chinese or Hui Muslims. Its position at the confluence of the Min and Zagunao rivers meant that whoever controlled it had control over routes to the north, south, and west and it had long been a prized stronghold. When the Tibetan empire expanded during the early Tang dynasty (AD 618-906) the Zagunao and Min valleys had been strategic routes into Chinese territory.

The next village they visited, above Weizhou, was a disappointment to Torrance. Some of the inhabitants only spoke Chinese and there was a Chinese temple in the village dating back to Emperor Qianlong's eighteenth century military interventions. They also explored a ruined fort from the Three Kingdoms period (AD 220-280) which overlooked Weizhou.

Accompanied by Edgar, they then followed the Zagunao River to Xuecheng. One consequence of Torrance and Neave's abandoned 1917 journey to the region had been the initiation the following year of Chinese-led church work in Xuecheng. Under the auspices of the Canadian Methodist Mission, Pastor Mao Shusen had been appointed by the Chinese Home Missionary Society and had rented a house in the centre of the town. The front of this had been turned into a chapel, where Torrance preached on Sunday to a 'dense congregation'. Torrance had brought up fresh supplies of gospels for Mao.

In Xuecheng they sent their calling cards to Chief Yang, the Tibetan headman of the Qiang villages in the district, who happened to be at his residence in town and invited them to pay a visit. Torrance was

Yang Anbang, the Tibetan Chief of the Qiang at Jiuzi,
with his two grandsons

delighted with the encounter, a delight that was mutual, as evidenced by his good relationship with Yang over the next few years. He wrote:

> Rarely have I met a more agreeable person, or one who more impressed me with his keen, intelligent grip of a question. What was more he was natural in his manner and free from that affectation and suave diplomatic air which Chinese officials so commonly assume. As he told us of the religious rites of his [Qiang] people my whole heart went out in deciphering to him the meaning of the ancient sacrifice they so faithfully maintain. The interpretation was new to him.

Yang held an influential position. Although Miansi, Weizhou, and Maoxian had been under Chinese administration since pre-Qing times, the Lifan area had historically been part of a larger Zagu region ruled by a Tibetan chief (*tusi*). The final Tibetan chief had stirred up so much unrest in the region that he was removed by the Qing who, in 1752, established Lifan Sub-Prefecture, composed of five military districts (*tun*). Five Tibetan headmen were given hereditary positions over these districts, four of which were populated mainly by the Jiarong people, with Yang's district of Jiuzi the only Qiang district. Within each district, men were given military training in order to serve as government troops when required.[31] Yang's visiting card presented him as the commander of the fifth battalion. He invited Torrance and the others to come up to his family home on the mountainside when they returned from their visit further along the valley to Zagunao.

The Qiang population gave way to Jiarong as they travelled further west and Torrance noted the architectural similarity between the Jiarong and Qiang villages, often differentiated only by the Tibetan Buddhist flags fluttering on the houses. He had initially suspected that the two peoples 'in prehistoric times . . . sprang from one stock', with the Jiarong only yielding to Buddhism as a result of the expansion of the Tibetan empire. However, this idea was dispelled by the difference in their languages and because 'the Ch'iang are insistent that they are quite different from their neighbours which the Nya-Rong [Jiarong] themselves positively confirm.' In Torrance's own view 'the Ch'iang, the Nya-Rong and the Tibetans are as distinct today one from the other as the British, Germans and French.'[32]

---

31   Liu Biyun. 'From Kinship to State and Back Again'. Chapter 2 in J. Wilkerson and R. Parkin (eds), *Modalities of Change: The Interface of Tradition and Modernity in East Asia*. Berghahn Books. 2013, pp8-39.
32   Although the Jiarong or rGyalrong people are adherents of Tibetan Buddhism, it is only since the Chinese ethnic classification of the 1950s that

To illustrate this he provided Hykes with a list of the numbers 1-10 in the three languages.

In Zagunao, a market town frequented by Chinese, Qiang, Jiarong, and Tibetans, Edgar was in his element selling Tibetan literature and attracting people's attention with his fluency in Tibetan. Although it was an area rarely visited by foreigners, the secretary to the Zagunao chief told them he could remember the visit of the Russian ethnologist and traveller, Grigory Potanin, over forty years before, as well as Isabella Bird's visit in 1896. The secretary's name was Ren and he and his son, a local school teacher, had become Christians through literature given them by Fergusson and through contact with Pastor Mao in Xuecheng. Ren, whom Torrance described as 'a very gentle, unassuming individual of mixed blood', was a scholar with an interest in archaeology and he took them to an old fort where Torrance helped him date some pottery fragments. On his return to Chengdu, Torrance sent Ren some Christian literature and in reply Ren recounted more of his spiritual experience, explaining that two months before Torrance's visit he had been studying the gospel of John and, having lain down to rest, had had a vision of Christ.[33]

Torrance found Chief Gao of Zagunao less impressive than Chief Yang. With a 'rakish look', he was 'affable' but seemed to lack depth of character. From him they obtained an introduction to Chief Sang of Ganbao, whom they hoped to visit on their way back to Xuecheng. Word was sent to Sang who came out to meet them with his deputy, Mr Gou. There was an immediate rapport between them all and they talked for hours. To Torrance's surprise, Gou was 'a constant reader of the Bible', having bought one in Chengdu several years before. Torrance waxed lyrical about Chief Sang's residence, which was 'a magistrate's office, a castle, and a farmhouse combined. Where else would one find such a blend? We felt we were back in the age of the Patriarchs.' Sang told them of the animals they hunted in between busy agricultural periods, including takin, cliff sheep, goral, wild boar, and a dark-haired monkey.

Parting from Chief Sang they took up Yang's invitation to visit his village of Erwa, an 'eagle eyry' which required an upward trek of several

---

they have been classified as a sub-group of the Tibetan people. Torrance refers to them simply as Jiarong and clearly saw them as distinct from Tibetan groups he encountered.

33   TT. 'The Story of Ren Jen-Bang'. Chapter 19 in *Conversion Stories of Chinese Christians*, (unpublished). Available at https://tftorrance.org/tt-1935-1

miles.[34] There was a Chinese temple in the village and Yang, being a Tibetan, had a lamaist chapel in his residence but, as Torrance noted, the Qiang villagers paid little heed to either. 'Sandwiched between two foreign faiths they recognise both in this way yet keep their own.' Yang and Torrance had a highly enjoyable conversation about the history of Sichuan and Torrance promised to send him *The History of Shu*, which Yang hadn't read.[35] After another visit three years later Torrance would describe Yang as 'a most likeable man and a walking encyclopaedia on everything pertaining to the border and its peoples'.[36]

With limited time spent among the people and his lack of Qiang language, Torrance knew he could only present Hykes with an outline of the religion of the Qiang but one advantage he did have was a good understanding of Chinese Buddhism, Daoism, and local folk religion in Sichuan, so, as with the architecture, it was clear to him he was seeing something different:

> They have a bare, simple, sacrificial house. It is a true temple though not in the ornate worldly sense of this word.[37] In it stands a White Stone. The White Stone is called a Lopee. It is the emblem of Deity. The Deity is variously spoken of as The Spirit, The Spirit of Heaven, The King of Heaven, The Spirit of the Mountains, the King of the Mountains. He is One – of this there is no doubt. One who has personality for He is a King. And He is holy, for the Lopee represents purity.
>
> The temple stands apart in a copse or grove. The grove is sacred. It is called God's grove. There is a bare square or patch of ground where the sacrifice is slain. Some groves have no temple, only the White Stone and the clear patch of ground.
>
> The White Stone is taken and set up in its natural state. Those we saw were all pieces of white quartz. Where there is a temple, a plain slab of stone rests in front as an altar. No metal tool may be used to fashion it. It may simply be broken to a usable size by another stone.

---

34   Erwa (尔瓦寨) is in the hills north of today's Muka town, east of Xuecheng.
35   蜀志: Chapter Three of the mid-4th century *Chronicles of Huayang*.
36   TT. 'A Trip to Lifan and Songpan'. WCMN, Sept 1922, p17.
37   David C. Graham writes of 'a typical Ch'iang temple or sacred shelter' and provides a sketch of a simple one-room construction with two small shelves, a central fire-place formed by three stones, and a sacred white stone in one corner. (*The Customs and Religion of the Ch'iang*. Smithsonian Miscellaneous Collections. 135 (1):1-110. 1958, p46.)

The Deity though a Unity is also a Trinity. He is sometimes represented by three White Stones. We ourselves saw a shrine with three. Behind one temple stood two built pillars with a white stone. Ch'iang houses show three White Stones on their highest wall behind. They look like ornaments but have a religious significance. (Some Tibetan houses, we observed, had three small white Chortens on the same part.)

There is a religious officiator. He is called a priest, also an Exorcist. This latter term implies that he is also the healer of his peoples' diseases. The manner of the sacrifice is handed down orally from one priest to another. The Ch'iang have no written language.

There are, at least, two leading festivals in the year. One begins at midnight as the old year closes and the new comes in. It lasts until the third day. Their New Year is in the late autumn. The second is a spring festival. The dates vary according to the locality. At one place they were respectively the 1st of the 10th Chinese moon and the 2nd of the 2nd Chinese moon.

A bullock is offered in the evening at the Spring sacrifice. It must be three years old and without spot or blemish. Neither must it have been used for work of any sort. In sacrificing it no bone is broken. A cut is made and the heart removed. The blood is sprinkled on the Lopee and on the Altar. The priest prays to the Spirit. Incense is simultaneously burned and white paper hung on bamboo sticks inserted in front. A ritual is chanted to the accompaniment of a small drum.

The head of each family must be present. Distance is no excuse. No women come. That all, however, may share in the benefits of the service each one takes home part of the flesh and apparently also of the blood for it is not poured out but eaten. At the temple each worshipper drinks a very small cup of wine while eating the sacrifice. No more than one is allowed.

The sacrificial fire, on which the offering is prepared, gives light to the worshippers. Then the White Stone shines with an effulgence significant of the character of the Spirit of Heaven and of the mountains. In other words His Shechinah is supposed to be seen at this time of sacrificial communion.

At New Year time goats and cocks are said to be offered. The goats must be full grown young males. The numbers sacrificed depend on the size of the community or communities. Two or more villages may unite. If so the rite is celebrated at each place in turn. The priest secures the head, the shoulder, and the skin as his portion. The horns of the bullock are placed on the altar.

At other times special sacrifices may be presented. I saw grain on an altar and blood and feathers on the Lopee. In cases of sickness there is a custom of liberating an animal. A bullock or goat is devoted or made a scape-offering. It is given its liberty and life and driven into the wilds beyond the habitation of men. Sometimes these creatures live for years but no one will ever claim or use them. In one district where the hinterland was limited this practice was discontinued because they returned and spoiled the crops.

We secured a good photograph of a sacred grove. The burned out embers of the fire lay in the centre. Three stones had been used to support probably a cooking vessel. The White Stone was to one side. The incense and white paper were inserted at the edge under a tree. We were given variations of the above description. The details, however, were insignificant. The rites essentially were the same. They were all that of a monotheistic religion which cuts the Chinese worship of idols to shame.

Torrance had been struck by the biblical similarities he was seeing in these practices, which he assumed had been diffused world-wide from the earliest sacrifices recorded in the Bible: 'There is no need for me to say how marvellously alike in many respects the Ch'iang ritual is to that of the Old Testament. That it should continue so pure is a fine tribute to the constancy of the race. And surely here is a proof of the unity of worship. As Christians we believe that a certain manner of sacrifice was once divinely delivered to men. To this we owe the world-wide belief in its efficacy. The many creeds on the globe are but variations or corruptions of the original standard. That after thousands of years the Ch'iang religion should today show such close resemblance to it is almost miraculous.'

Regarding the physical appearance of the Qiang, although the Qiang of every district they visited had certain Chinese characteristics, to Torrance they were still distinguishable from the Chinese, particularly with their longer faces and stronger jaws and 'a basic resonance in their voices the Chinese have not'. Torrance found them initially shy but 'jovial on acquaintance' and in his wider reading about the Qiang he had discovered that 'Chinese writers admit the staunchness of their character'. They were very loyal to each other and could live independent of outside produce, relying on their own agriculture, hunting, and other skills which included weaving linen and woollen garments.

Coming to the end of their trip, Torrance preached on Sunday at the Weizhou CIM station and seven men came forward at the end wanting to know more. The following day they headed back down towards Miansi, hoping to visit the chief of the Wasi people, known as King Suo. He was away but they visited his house, temple, and village and Torrance was struck by the contrast between the 'devilish' Tibetan deities in the temple and the 'pure worship' of the Qiang.

QIANG MAN WITH BACK BASKET[38]

In Miansi they met with more Qiang people who came back to their lodging, wanting to continue conversations started on the street. Torrance was able to help them with minor medical complaints, prompting many more to come the next day, wanting treatment for

---

38   Photo by W. R. Morse. (In The Thomas F. Torrance Manuscript Collection, Special Collections, Princeton Theological Seminary Library.)

sore eyes, upset stomachs, sprains, and various other ailments. When they offered payment he said that he might turn up at their villages one day and claim a cup of tea from them. Their reply was 'Come soon.'

Reaching Guanxian it seemed to Torrance that he and Plewman 'had left part of our hearts behind us' but he was glad to be reunited with the family at Lingyan after more than a month on the road. Annie and the children were equally glad to see him. The children had had some scrapes and Grace had a nasty cut on her forehead that threatened to leave a scar whilst Tom had been the unintended target of a stone-throwing incident and was sporting a cut on his eyelid.

Knowing that the family's forthcoming furlough would prevent a return visit the following summer, Torrance sought out Chen Bingling, an ex-colporteur laid off due to lack of funding, and asked if he would go and work among the Qiang, supported directly by Torrance and a few friends. Chen was to live at the CIM mission in Weizhou and itinerate among the Qiang along the Min and Zagunao rivers. Torrance also asked the Canadian Methodist Mission if a Qiang boy could be educated at their mission school in Chengdu if he could find financial support for him.

In September Torrance received a request from the West China Union University (WCUU) to speak about the Qiang at a monthly lecture attended by many of the foreigners in Chengdu. Given in December, the lecture resulted in requests for printed copies of the lecture and a further invitation to speak about the Qiang at a Sunday evening service for the WCUU students.

Still maintaining his other interests, that winter Torrance made an archaeological collecting trip to the caves near Leshan with Daniel Sheets Dye. Over the years he had built up good relationships with locals living near the caves and Dye, who was in charge of the new university museum, wanted to see the caves for himself.[39] This time they were able to obtain a burnt carved clay coffin for the museum, which was transported to Chengdu by boat. The museum was opened early in 1920 with Torrance as one of the key contributors, having provided pottery and coins from the Han, Tang, and Song periods.[40]

---

39   TT to Hykes, Jan 7, 1920.

40   D. S. Dye. 'The West China Union University Museum'. WCMN, June 1920, p18. Many of the exhibits from those early years are still part of the collection in what is now the Sichuan University Museum.

In preparation for his December lecture Torrance seems to have pursued further Qiang research and both his lecture and subsequent paper, *The History, Customs and Religion of the Ch'iang: An Aboriginal People of West China*, were of a more academic nature than his summer reports. The paper was published by the *Shanghai Mercury* as a 36-page monograph, illustrated with Plewman's photographs.[41]

In the historical section of the paper Torrance touched on the sparse pre-Qin history of the Qiang but then focused more on official Chinese records dating from the Qin and Han dynasties (221 BC – AD 220). He mentioned various Qiang groups, including the Yak (Maoniu) Qiang, the Dark Clothing (Qingyi) Qiang and the White Horse (Baima) Qiang, who inhabited regions stretching northwards from the Ya'an region in southwestern Sichuan to the Min Valley and up to southeastern Gansu and eastern Qinghai. He also noted the Han era policy of transferring Qiang to other regions, hence Wudu in southeastern Gansu and some parts of Shaanxi Province becoming a mix of Qiang and Han inhabitants. Later, the Qiang found themselves in a precarious position between the Chinese and Tibetans as the Tibetans pushed eastwards into China. Gradually, the Qiang in the regions closer to the Chinese became assimilated whilst those in the more remote mountain regions managed to keep their own customs and religious practices. Torrance made particular reference to the Xuanzong period (1425-1435) of the Ming Dynasty when Qiang tribes in western Sichuan refused to pay taxes, resulting in the arrival of the Wasi Tibetans who acted as a kind of military police. Tensions between the Qiang and the Chinese had lasted into the mid-eighteenth century when Emperor Qianlong's interventions led to the establishment of Chief Yang's Qiang district of Jiuzi.

Although Torrance referred to the Qiang as 'aborigines' he was clearly curious about their origins: 'Who they are and where they come from no one knows.' Whatever their roots, Torrance's Scottish background seems to have given him a sense of identification with their upland existence and their years of conflict with the Chinese: 'Such was their prowess that it took several Chinese to match one of them. In handicraft and religion the highlanders also took a commendable place, and the knowledge of this preserved them against that submission of spirit which so often follows political submission.' His biblical metaphors continued, with comments on

---

41   TT. *The History, Customs and Religion of the Ch'iang.* The Shanghai Mercury. 1920.

the similarity with Middle Eastern architecture and likening Sino-Qiang relations to Cain and Abel: 'There was an eternal Cain and Abel hostility between the two races, and it was the shepherd Abels of the purer sacrifice that slowly perished.'

In the next section on Qiang customs his sympathy for the Qiang was equally evident. Describing the notched tree trunk used as a ladder in their homes he likened it to the Qiang themselves:

For having been grown in the mountains, shorn of its pristine beauty, wounded many times with sorrowful blows, continuously trodden over and oppressed, yet withal retaining its strength and rugged usefulness, it remains forever as a symbol of the patient, sturdy character of this wonderful people.

He also commented on the plough, which was 'more of a knife or prong style and more vertical' than the Chinese plough. Other distinctive customs included the presence of a cremation ground in every village; the keeping of accounts and making formal agreements by using knots on a string and carved marks on wood; an old tradition of pillars set up as witness of oaths made; and the Qiang custom of sealing a forest for fifty years, when no tree could be cut until the opening ceremony at the end of that period.

QIANG CHILDREN ON A LADDER

The final section of the paper was similar to his August 1919 letter to Hykes in its description of the religious beliefs and rituals of the Qiang. He emphasised that the colour white was associated with holiness, with the white stone marking a place of worship and white streamers signifying 'the desire of the worshippers to approach Him in the way of holiness'. To Torrance the presence of the white stone, which the Qiang cleaned once a year, was much less oppressive than the idolatry of the Chinese. 'We feel that the lover of the sacred quartz is much more nearly related to us than the worshipper of the mud gods.' He did, however, acknowledge that 'some parts of their ritual are strange' and that some of the priests had 'borrowed of the deceptive corruptions of the Chinese exorcists'.

The sacred grove where religious rituals were performed was sometimes near the village but could be a mile or so away or on the mountain top. Torrance had discovered a third major religious festival on the 24th day of the 6th lunar month, a festival date shared by other tribes such as the Lolo people (part of today's Yi minority), and he also mentioned a triennial sacrifice of a bull without blemish. In his description of the goat released into the wilderness he made a connection with the Old Testament Azazel or scapegoat ceremony in the book of Leviticus, in which one goat was sacrificed whilst another – the scapegoat – was presented to God but then released into the wilderness, bearing the iniquities of the Israelites.[42] Another Qiang custom was to sacrifice a goat when someone died.

Aware of Chinese and Jiarong influences on the Qiang who lived down in the main valleys, Torrance encouraged future researchers to go up to the more remote villages for a purer version of Qiang religious customs. 'The best plan is to desert the main roads and climb the mountains. Up there . . . he will find the old true Ch'iang who will tell him that his God is in the heavens and he owns no other.' He was also aware that different groups of Qiang perhaps had their own distinctive habits and he knew that this initial research was just a beginning. It was hard to be leaving on furlough with such an inviting new field opening up before him.

---

42 Leviticus 16:8-10.

Chapter 9
Furlough and Return
1920-1921

Furlough was long overdue for Annie and by now she was so rooted in Chengdu that she had 'almost lost the desire to leave'.[1] Having left Britain at twenty-three she was returning aged thirty-five, married, and with four children aged between two and seven who had never been beyond the borders of Sichuan, except for Mary's birth in Shanghai. Concerned for Annie's health, Torrance had suggested to Hykes that she and the children leave before him: 'I thought she should go as she is suffering from tingling of the nerves. . . . She had a trying nervous time two years ago before Margaret was born when the fighting was going on in Chengdu and I was away. She has never fully recovered from the shells flying over the house.'[2] But Annie had been unwilling to go without him.

In January 1920 Wilbur Hooker and his family arrived from Chongqing to take over the ABS work, releasing the Torrances to leave for the coast. After the overland trip to Chongqing they had safe passage on the river to Yichang, despite the occasional presence of bandits on the river banks. From Yichang to Shanghai the children were thrilled to have their first experience of travelling on a steamer, with the novelty and luxury of a 'large white bath, plenty of hot water, . . . real home porridge, carnation milk and heaps of other things'.[3] During the journey Annie began preparing them for a western world where people would speak their language but wouldn't necessarily share their outlook on life or understand anything of their lives in China.

Reaching Shanghai, the children already felt they were in a foreign country. Sikh policemen in red turbans directed the traffic and the roads and buildings were of a magnitude not seen in West China. Dr Hykes had arranged for someone to help with the children so

1 *Memoirs*, p62.
2 TT to Hykes, March 8, 1919.
3 *Memoirs*, p59.

that Torrance and Annie could make some visits together and get necessary shopping done. Torrance had been concerned for some time about Dr Hykes' health and it was precious to have time with this man who had been so instrumental in turning his life around and re-establishing him in China.

The family sailed from Shanghai on April 2, 1920. Annie's half-brother was now living in Vancouver and Hykes had arranged for them to travel via Japan to Canada, from where Torrance would make a brief visit to the ABS headquarters in New York. On the ship two of the children picked up whooping cough and after a dull, grey voyage across the Pacific, with a couple of fire drills thanks to a rather disturbed gentleman setting fire to his bedding (twice), it was a relief to disembark in Vancouver. Annie's brother had booked a hotel room for them but whether due to the sound of a whoop or the sight of four young children, the manager refused to take them so they squeezed into the brother's home and together toured the city, enjoying Vancouver Island in blossom and their first experience of an escalator in a large downtown department store.

Hykes had offered to pay for a first class train compartment for their onward journey but everything was fully booked so they travelled tourist class and took their own supplies. The other passengers proved to be pleasant company and with a kitchenette at the end of the carriage for boiling water and seats which became bunks at night, they settled in for the journey across Canada. Travelling through the towering, pine-fringed Rockies to Calgary was an unforgettable experience. Between Calgary and Toronto they had to change trains at a bitterly cold station and only found room in a large, cold saloon car on the next train. By the time they reached Toronto 'the whooping cough manifested itself without any mistake' in all four of children.[4]

While Torrance went on to New York, Annie and the children enjoyed a whole flat to themselves at the top of a Toronto boarding house run by Mrs Urquhart, a Scottish lady who was understanding of the children's whooping and even took care of them one day so that Annie could take a look around the city. Once Torrance returned they took a sleeper train to Montreal and set sail for Plymouth. On the train to London they had a compartment to themselves and the children went from side to side as the unfamiliar countryside flashed past. Annie was in her element:

4   Ibid., p62.

The banks along the railway track were covered with primroses and
violets and the hedges in May blossom and the fields in buttercups
and daisies . . . I had not seen these things for over twelve years and
I thought England was the loveliest country I had ever seen! . . . It
was all so peaceful and quiet too – away from all the fighting and
turmoil which had been so much part of our life in China.[5]

At Paddington they piled all their luggage on to a horse-drawn cab
which took them through the busy streets to catch their train to
Bromley, where they stayed with Cousin Jeannie. Annie's mother lived
nearby and it was a time of precious reunions as well as introductions
for Torrance and the children. Torrance was rather anxious about the
contrast between Bromley, so pretty and peaceful, and his parents'
current home. His mother and father (also named Thomas and Annie)
were quite frail by this time and had moved from their small farm
to the coal-mining and ironworks town of Shotts. Torrance warned
Annie how different it would be.

Annie was in no hurry to leave such a lovely oasis down south
but it was nine years since Torrance had seen his family and in the
end he went north with Tom and Mary while Annie and Jeannie took
Grace and Margaret to Worthing for a fortnight's holiday. The lovely
walks and time on the beach were a tonic for Annie's 'tingling nerves'
but in Shotts Mary and Tom fared less well and a telegram arrived in
Bromley from Torrance's mother and niece saying the children needed
their mother, so Annie and the two little ones promptly took the train
to Scotland. Despite Torrance's attempt to prepare Annie, the contrast
was still hard to take. 'We were no sooner out of the station when I saw
smoke and flames billowing out of an iron furnace and my heart sank.'[6]
There would be some compensation in the rough beauty of the moors
beyond the town, where Torrance had loved to roam as a boy.

In China the family had called Britain 'Grandmother's country', a
reflection of how faithfully Torrance's mother had corresponded with
them. Annie now met the woman she knew only through letters, as
well as the various relatives and friends she had heard about over the
years. Torrance's parents had moved to 42 Station Road to live next
door to his sister Maggie. Sadly Maggie had since died but her teenage
daughter, Annie Thompson, still lived there with her father and semi-
invalid stepmother and helped to care for her grandparents. With

---

5   Ibid., p63-64.
6   Ibid., p64.

Torrance's mother, sister, niece, and wife all named Annie, it is perhaps not surprising that in the early days of their marriage Torrance and Annie had decided he would call her Betty, from her middle name Elizabeth, hence the 'Dear Betty' in all their personal correspondence.

Torrance and Annie had hoped to find other accommodation but in the end they stayed the whole time with his parents. After the help Annie was used to in China it was a challenge for her to be cooking and cleaning for eight and assisting her parents-in-law with their needs, but she gradually settled into a routine and developed a close bond with Torrance's mother. For Tom and Mary, Calderhead primary school was a new experience – and equally so for their classmates to have newcomers who spoke Chinese and could tell stories of far-away places. In Chengdu they had had some tutoring from one of the Graingers' Chefoo-educated daughters and had also attended a new kindergarten run by Mrs Plewman but entry to the Canadian primary school in Chengdu was from age seven so this was their first experience of formal education.

For Torrance this home-going was in complete contrast to his return in 1909, when his future had hung in the balance. Now he was a settled husband and father, playing a significant role in the work of the ABS, and he had with him a letter of commendation from Hykes expressing his 'unqualified satisfaction' with Torrance's work. Hykes' letter mentioned his good character, his work with different denominations in their evangelistic services, his excellent reputation amongst Chinese and foreigners, and also his archaeological research, describing him with pride as 'our missionary antiquary'. Hykes' final sentence was somewhat poignant: 'I cannot think of any greater pleasure than having you associated with me in the work until I am ready to put off the harness.'[7]

One of the fruits of the time in Scotland was the completion of *The Beatitudes and the Decalogue*, a book Torrance had been working on for some time. Published in 1921 with a foreword by the prominent Baptist preacher F. B. Meyer, it was a study of the parallels between the blessings listed in Christ's Sermon on the Mount and the ten commandments in the book of Exodus.[8]

The family's nine months in Britain culminated in their 1920 Christmas celebrations in Shotts and they now faced what was to be their final farewell to Torrance's parents. His father would die a year

---

7   Hykes, March 23, 1920.
8   TT. *The Beatitudes and the Decalogue*. Skeffington & Son, Paternoster House, London. 1921.

later in December 1921 and his mother in March 1922. Annie was first to say good-bye as she, Grace, and Margaret left for a last visit to Bromley and to make preparations for the return to China. Staying with Jeannie, Annie visited her mother every day and, again, it was a painful parting. Torrance, Tom, and Mary joined them eighteen days later and on February 18 they sailed on the *SS Soudan*, glad of a quiet few weeks to prepare for the transition back to life in China.

Shanghai and Home

Their arrival in Shanghai on April 4 coincided with the departure of James Neave who, sadly, was returning to England with his children after the death of his wife. Torrance was glad to see Dr Hykes again but sorry to see that he was still weak from a serious attack of flu some months before. A delay in the departure of the Yichang steamer provided them with some extra time together and also gave Torrance a chance to buy some Southern Song coins in Shanghai for the WCUU museum.[9]

To Torrance's frustration, the delayed start meant that they missed their Yichang connection to Chongqing but news then came that the steamer had hit a rock and been wrecked and they were deeply thankful to have been spared. Their own passage to Chongqing was uneventful and the captain was full of praise for the children's good behaviour. Annie was dreading coping with the wayside inns from Chongqing to Chengdu with the four children but they soon got back into China mode and Torrance was happy to be dealing with everything in the Sichuan dialect once again. The older three children often walked along with him while Annie rode with Margaret in a sedan chair.

Despite the joy of being back, their homecoming was tinged with great sorrow. Dr Hykes died on June 14 from flu-related complications after forty-eight years in China, eight of which had been as a US Consul. Two weeks later another devastating blow struck the ABS. Wilbur Hooker, who had left Chengdu with his family for their own furlough before the Torrances arrived, was drowned in Yichang when the small boat ferrying the family to their steamer capsized. His wife and twin sons survived. Wilbur had been in China since 1892, first with the CIM and then the ABS, and his death was a great sadness for many who had come to know him over the years.

Settling back into the house on Wushi-tongtang Street, Annie now entered the busiest period of her life in China. Shortly after the family's return, Dr Retta Kilborn invited her to take a Bible class for the

---

9   TT to Daniel Sheets Dye, May 24, 1921.

Chinese nurses at the Canadian Women's Hospital and other teaching opportunities soon followed, facilitated by Annie once again having help in the home and the children being at school, or at least in kindergarten for part of the day. The opening of the Canadian primary school in 1916 on the university campus had been an answer to prayer as she and Torrance desperately wanted to avoid sending the children away to boarding school. At first the children travelled to school by sedan chair but then graduated to riding Billy and Prince. Once Margaret was old enough to join her siblings there, Annie heard tales of Tom galloping at top speed on the campus with 'wee Margaret' on his back.

Tom, Mary, Grace, and Margaret holding the dog

Over the next few years Annie also taught English language and literature at a Chinese school where many of the students were sons of military men. Although it was a secular situation, there were some good discussion opportunities with the students and the principal was keen to keep her, recognising her gift for clear communication. Closer to her heart were classes she taught to Chinese women at the Canadian Women's Bible School, many of whom were pastors' wives and Christian workers. The teaching was in Chinese and took Annie hours of preparation, sometimes with the assistance of Torrance's Chinese tutor, as she focused on the Pentateuch, the minor prophets, and Paul's missionary journeys. She also taught grammar and rhetoric in the Canadian Girls High School, where the students were boarders and mostly daughters of Chinese pastors, evangelists, and teachers out in the rural areas.

Torrance was eager to get back to the Qiang area. Chen Bingling had been down to update him on the work and reported that some Qiang had already 'professed belief'. Having seen the family settled at Lingyan Temple he set off up the Min Valley. This time he was hoping to get off the beaten track, not only to learn more about the Qiang but also to help Chen explore new routes for his itinerations. Chen joined him on the road to Weizhou, where several Qiang were waiting to meet him. One of them, who had just become a Christian in June, was Gou Pinsan, a scholarly man who would become one of Torrance's closest Qiang friends and co-workers. Two others had recently been baptised, one by Chen and one by James Edgar, who had visited a couple of weeks earlier. Torrance was disappointed to have missed what were, to his knowledge, the first ever Qiang baptisms.

On his first Sunday in the mountains he preached in the CIM mission to a full church of Chinese, Qiang, and 'old Mohammedan settlers'.[10] A stream of people came for medicine in the afternoon and later they handed out tracts on the street, attracting the attention of a Chinese official who took one, got into conversation with Torrance, and then went for a walk with him.

The next morning Torrance, Chen, Gou Pinsan, and Mr Lu, who had accompanied Torrance on his first trip, set out in the direction of Maoxian to visit two Qiang villages northeast of Weizhou. Gou's presence prompted a warm welcome from the headman of the first village who was a good Chinese scholar. They left with a promise that Chen would return with books for him. A steady upward trek took them on to the lofty village of Luobozhai. The locals working in the fields stopped to stare, fascinated to see a foreigner. Torrance and the others offered them tracts and some came over to have a look and chat. One man asked for medicine and accompanied them up to the village, which assured them of a good welcome from the other villagers. As they sat and talked, Torrance explained the gospel to them and in return they explained more of their religious practices to him. At Torrance's request, one of the villagers offered to show them the sacred

10 All quotes in this trip description are from Torrance's article, 'Report of a Journey to the Heart of the Ch'iang Country', in *The China Press*, Sept 25, 1921.

grove half a mile above the village and Torrance was intrigued on the way to hear Gou and the villager discussing the correct shape of the bread which formed part of the sacrificial ceremony, each maintaining that 'the shape used in his own district was the correct one!'

The descent from Luobozhai was much harder than the ascent. Torrance had brought Billy with him this time and the mule boy surpassed himself getting Billy down to the valley, from where they continued northwards to Maoxian. There they found lodging at the CMS station, which was run by a Chinese evangelist who joined Gou, Chen, and Lu distributing tracts and selling literature on the street. Beyond Maoxian Torrance had an ambitious plan to go northwest to some Qiang villages in the Heishui valley before turning south over the mountains to the Zagunao valley. This would take them 'through the very heart of the Ch'iang country' where perhaps no foreigner had been before.

VIEW FROM LUOBOZHAI DOWN TO THE MIN RIVER
(Photo: author, Nov 2013)

The road that followed the Min River north of Maoxian was 'a wild difficult road' with landslides and precipices, most of it not fit for mule riding, so after some miles the mule boy turned back to Maoxian

with Billy. The few travellers encountered on the road were transporting opium down from the independent states still beyond Chinese jurisdiction. They informed Torrance's little party that the Qiang dwelt along the Heishui River as far as Waboliangzi village, three days journey from Maoxian, where they bordered the Xifan people.[11]

The first night in the Heishui Valley was spent at an inn on the bank of the river which Torrance described as 'purgatory intensified' due to an abundance of

Torrance & Billy on a mountain path

highly athletic fleas, but the landlord was 'kindness personified'. At Shaba, near the entrance to the valley, Torrance noticed a Chinese proclamation against opium but found that on the same street Chinese officials were profiting from the banned trade, having set up a checkpoint to tax any opium being transported out of the valley. One local Qiang man told him they had been ordered to plant opium the previous year and were then heavily fined for doing so. Whilst in Shaba they met and talked with some Qiang from 'the opposite mountain' who, when they realised that Torrance was familiar with their beliefs, responded with great openness.

11 Sifan, Hsifan or Xifan (西番), meaning 'western foreigners', was a general term for groups in this region who had adopted Tibetan Buddhism but did not belong to distinct Tibetan groups like the Amdo or Kham. Here the term was used for the tribespeople in the Upper Heishui-Songpan region.

Leaving the Heishui River and turning southwest into Longping Valley they could see Qiang villages on the slopes above. The only blot on the beauty of the landscape was the ubiquitous opium but as they ascended to higher altitudes the cultivation gave way to virgin forest. At two of the higher villages, Kayu and Lafu, they asked how far it was to the first houses over the mountain ridge. The answers were inconclusive: a strong walker could do it in a day but there again they might need to find a rock for shelter overnight and light a fire to keep wild animals away. To their delight a local hunter offered to serve as a guide and a young farmer also joined them. Stopping overnight at Diaohua, the highest village on the northern side at about 8,000 feet, they set out again as soon as daylight broke, following the stream up into the forest. The beauty was awe-inspiring. 'Words fail me to describe the fairy-land aspect of the way. Our eyes were ever upwards and through open gaps the grand mountain sides were tremendously impressive. Only a poet could do them justice.' By mid-morning, having passed a waterfall and negotiated a large landslide, they reached a plateau and rested. From here the upward track was easy to see and Torrance, Chen, and Gou went on ahead, taking short rests every two hundred yards to cope with the steepness and the high altitude. After six hours of climbing Gou was the first to reach the 13,750 foot summit.

Torrance was elated. 'What a magnificent view we had up there. On the south side especially it was captivating. Great mountains on every side: one near by and about our own level with a small patch of snow, another beyond and higher with two huge snow-fields. The tops were bare, then come green stretches of grass; succeeded by great virgin forest belts, below which came human residence and cultivation. I can never hope to see a fairer vista than we so rapturously gazed upon. This was the heart of the Ch'iang country.' On this southern side of the ridge a small, emerald green lake lay glistening in the sun. 'Though only 200 yards or so long the inhabitants regard it with great awe. They say it sometimes cannot be seen, so perfectly does it reflect its surroundings on a calm day. Should any unwary traveller dare to disturb its perfect surface by stone-throwing, heaven immediately will rain on him terrible showers of hailstones.'

The grassy slopes below the lake 'dazzled with innumerable flowers' in the short grass – foxgloves, bluebells, aconite, various kinds of edelweiss, and others that Torrance didn't recognise. Some locals who were digging for herbs and roots to sell told them not to tarry if they wanted to reach habitation, they had another twenty miles to cover.

Beyond the flowers the descent led through bush and forest with open grassy areas 'that could have grazed thousands of cattle. And the air was so exhilarating that one wished for a tent to camp here for a fortnight. It was an empty paradise for the holiday maker.'[12]

THE LAKE *(Courtesy of Yu Yongqing, 2007)*

It was late afternoon when they reached the first cultivated fields and soon afterwards a mill belonging to the village of A'er came into view.[13] It took another half hour to reach A'er itself, which the aneroid measured at 8,700 feet. Finding lodging in a Qiang home, their host was incredulous when they said they had come from Diaohua over the mountains in a day. Torrance's straw sandals were in tatters and his socks were sodden but he soon warmed up by the fire. Gou bought some local eggs and these were cooked with the farmer's potatoes, assuaging their hunger. Torrance was impressed by the kitchen area:

> A Ch'iang kitchen is a great institution. A sunk square in the floor serves as a fireplace. In it stands a heavy flat iron ring three yards in circumference resting on three legs that curve inwards so that a pot can rest on them in the center of the log fire. Round the edges of the square sit the inmates resting their wearied limbs and gazing at the crackling flames.

---

12   In recent years a campsite has been developed lower down the valley.
13   This is mis-typed in the *China Press* article as Ori but in later letters and reports Torrance writes of it as Oir. Its current Chinese rendering is A'er (阿尔).

In the morning they followed the Longxi stream down to Dongmenwai, a village at the junction of the Longxi and Zagunao valleys which would become home from home for Torrance in the coming years.[14] At one point they encountered a landslide and had to rely on a local Qiang woman who 'led us round the face of a precipice that no one but a Ch'iang or a wild goat would have attempted'.

From Aèr to Weizhou was about fifteen miles and they reached the CIM mission house late that afternoon, thankful after a whole week of tramping and climbing that the next day was Sunday – a day of rest – although Torrance and Chen both spoke at the morning church gathering. On the Monday they left the Zagunao Valley and went south to Miansi where they crossed the Min River and walked up to the village of Heping. One of the villagers had met Torrance in 1919 and invited them into his home. Relatives

DONGMENWAI VILLAGE

crowded in and with the host translating into Qiang, Torrance was able to tell them 'the old, old, story of Jesus coming as the Lamb of God, illustrating the necessity of His work by the very sacrifices they themselves had used from time immemorial.'

The trip was a huge encouragement. Chen now had access to new places, in part through the high esteem Gou Pinsan was held in

14 Dongmenwai or 'Beyond the East Gate' was so named because the village lay just outside the eastern boundary of the Tang dynasty district of Bazhou (霸州).

locally, and because Torrance's medical knowledge had opened doors. People also liked to hear a foreigner speaking fluent Chinese. Torrance suggested that Chen try and find some Qiang who would be interested in going down to Chengdu for an extended time of Bible study, for which Torrance would provide travel expenses and day to day needs. His hope was that they would then return to their villages with more understanding of the 'inward meaning of their olden-time religion' and of Christ being 'the Lamb of God, the Fulfiller of all their sacrifices and the Savior of men'. Chen asked Torrance to send copies of Leviticus and Hebrews to help him communicate these truths. He already had copies of Exodus and during the past year he had distributed about a thousand gospels.

As far as Torrance was concerned, this 1921 visit confirmed his earlier findings, that the religion of the Qiang was essentially monotheistic, with rituals similar to those of the Old Testament.

> Investigations by myself and others have shown what I wrote, far from being exaggerated, was a very moderate statement of their belief. The sacrifice of he-goats or rams at their festivals which are held three times in the year; the sprinkling of the blood of the sacrifice for remission of sins; the eating of the flesh with unleavened bread; the significance of white as typical of the holiness of the Deity, etc, etc, are the prevalent elements in their worship. And they speak of worship as paying their vows to the Lord. They even have an infant dedication which resembles circumcision. A white cord round the infant's neck is severed after the offering of a special sacrifice and the part severed placed on the altar. The sprinkling of blood is done by means of grass or straw.

People were beginning to ask about the origins of the Ch'iang but Torrance's response, despite the apparently 'Jewish-like religion practice', was that 'they have been here for thousands of years, indeed from the dawn of Chinese history.'

Torrance's travels and research bore fruit in two different directions later that year. On November 21, as a result of both his ethnographic and his archaeological research, he was elected as a Fellow of the Royal Geographic Society. The second was that, thanks to Chen Bingling's encouragement, several Qiang took advantage of the slack agricultural period in the winter and came down to spend some time studying the Bible and sharing more about their own customs. It was a 'rare pleasure' for Torrance 'to have them night and morning at our family worship, and to see them grow daily in grace.'

Chapter 10
Further Discoveries
1922-1923

Sichuan in the 1920s was vastly different from Torrance's early days in China when Chengdu's Viceroy had been subject to the imperial court in Beijing. In 1921, a call of 'Sichuan for the Sichuanese' had been followed by a fresh declaration of independence by Sichuan's provincial assembly, wanting to stay out of the ongoing conflict between the Beijing government and the new, self-proclaimed government in the south, centred on the city of Guangzhou and led by Sun Yatsen.

This self-declared independence was not, however, a recipe for provincial peace. Although Sichuan was now governed by Liu Chengxun in Chengdu, it was still at the mercy of various generals vying for power and in a review of 1922 for *The China Press* Torrance didn't mince his words:

> Szechuan at present is parcelled out among seven or eight military magnates who rake in the many provincial incomes and shamelessly divide these among themselves. Power and money form their sole aim. No love of country or sense of moral decency has any weight in their deliberations. . . . A General with thousands of men at his back will lie idly in a city leisurely devouring its produce and at the same time allow numberless bandits to overrun the countryside looting villages, robbing boats, holding up travellers and kidnapping the well-to-do.[1]

On the wider scene, the First World War war had so diverted the attention and resources of western nations that their imperialistic influence in China was on the wane. By 1918 British imports to China had halved in value and the decline in Western trade was giving China's own industries more opportunity to develop.[2] This

---

1   TT. 'China in 1922'. *The China Press*, Feb 1923. Despite its title the article was primarily about Sichuan.
2   Hsu, *Rise of Modern China*, p495.

freed the missionaries in some measure from being judged for their own nations' actions in China, but they were finding themselves up against a fresh challenge as China's openness to Western thought was introducing new social influences. The philosopher and educator John Dewey had lectured in Beijing in 1919 and Bertrand Russell stayed for almost a year in 1920-21, following a visit to Russia. An advocate of socialism, Russell was highly critical not just of Western missionary endeavours, which he saw as cultural imposition, but of religion in general, whose inherent conservatism he viewed as an obstacle to reform.

Despite his socialist views, Russell's experience of Russia had made him wary of the excesses of the revolution there but his warnings about this had little effect on the growth of Soviet influence in China, with many Chinese impressed by the speed of social change in Russia. The result was a period in which Western and Soviet influences vied for supremacy in China, as reflected in the power struggle played out between the Nationalist and Communist parties.[3]

Over the next few years the missionaries would find themselves caught up in this struggle with, broadly speaking, the Nationalists relatively friendly towards them and the Communists increasingly anti-Christian. However, in these early days Torrance still had hopes that the current educational reforms and greater freedom of thought might result in a better future, especially if there was a greater turning to God. 'Given unselfish, avarice-free men to lead the state and guide it along the lines of peace and not war China in fifty years could become the wealthiest nation on earth.'[4]

In the spring of 1922 the clash between Christianity and its opponents came to the fore with the decision of the World Student Christian Federation to hold a conference in Beijing from April 4-9. In response to this decision, an Anti-Christian Student Federation was formed in Shanghai, proclaiming that mankind and religion were incompatible and that China needed deliverance from the poison of religion. Although this federation failed in its goal of preventing the Christian conference, its efforts were nonetheless rewarded. On the final day of the conference, a series of anti-Christian lectures was launched at Peking National University under the auspices of the 'Great Federation of Anti-Religionists', including a lecture by university chancellor Cai Yuanpei. Other Beijing colleges then issued

---

3   Ibid., p511.
4   TT. 'China in 1922'.

their own anti-Christian declarations and in May 1922 the 'First Great National Congress of Socialist Youth Organisations in China' also voiced its support for anti-Christian and anti-religious organisations. After several years of relative calm, the future of mission work was once again looking precarious.

The repercussions of all this had yet to reach Sichuan and for now Torrance's life was continuing as normal. Much of his working day was spent with the Chinese ABS staff and visitors to the depot but his involvement in the museum, the Fortnightly Club, and the newly-established West China Border Research Society, founded in March 1922 to increase awareness and understanding of Sichuan's border peoples, was bringing him into frequent contact with university staff and giving him far more academic interaction than many missionaries in China had access to. In May and July Dr William Morse, one of the founders of the West China Union University and a medical doctor with a keen interest in anthropology, gave lectures at the Fortnightly Club and at the more social Saturday Night Club, one of which was entitled 'Anthropological Notes on Aboriginal Tribes of the Thibetan Marches'.[5] Torrance was clearly in good company for discussions relating to his own interests.

Continuing his research into the history of Sichuan, in May and August Torrance had two articles published in the WCMN, both of which were 'free translations' from the *History of Shu* in the fourth century *Chronicles of Huayang*.[6] In his introduction Torrance explained some of the difficulties of such a translation: 'Chinese scholars differ in the interpretation of certain characters and passages so that translation is not always easy. Then there are admitted discrepancies in the text owing to copyists writing wrong characters.'[7] Seen as reliable ancient history by local scholars, the *History of Shu* indicated that the state of Shu, centred on the region around Chengdu, was highly civilized before it was conquered by the state of Qin in 316 BC, something which has since been confirmed by archaeological discoveries at Sichuan's ancient Sanxingdui and Jinsha

---

5   Mentioned in WCMN, May 1922, p31; WCMN, July 1922, p30.
6   TT. 'The History of Shuh, or West Szechuan (蜀志)', WCMN, May 1922, p15-18; 'The History of Shu', WCMN, Aug 1922, p26-28.
7   TT. 'The History of Shuh, or West Szechuan (蜀志)', p15. Torrance had referred to this work as 'The Annals of Shu' in his Aug 12, 1919 letter to Hykes, which is a more literal translation.

sites. Torrance's August article contained a story of romance between a King of Shu and a woman from Wudu, which Torrance described as an ancient Qiang kingdom in southwest Shaanxi and eastern Gansu, to the north of Sichuan.[8]

In the summer of 1922 Torrance was on the road again among the Qiang, a trip that was recorded in two articles, one published in the WCMN as 'A Trip to Lifan and Songpan' and the other published in *The China Press* with great fanfare (thanks no doubt to the editorial staff) as 'Blazing the Gospel Trail In Back Blocks of China Among Pagan Aborigines. Chiang Tribes Gladly Hear The Message Brought To Them By Ardent Pioneering Missionaries.'[9] Wanting to learn more about different groups of Qiang, one of Torrance's goals this time was 'to find out exactly the Northern and Western borders of the Ch'iang and see how their manner of life compared with their kindred farther South.' Writing for a more familiar audience in the WCMN, he expressed a more emotive reason for the trip:

> This year I wanted to get back again among the Ch'iang. For millenniums they have been so staunch to the monotheism and sacrificial ritual of their fathers and put up such a grand fight against their enemies that one's heart warms spontaneously to them.[10]

He was accompanied this time by Chen Bingling, a colporteur named Liu, and Gou Pinsan, who had had been down for Bible study in Chengdu the previous winter. Gou had shown such a clear grasp of things and such a zeal that he was now itinerating with Chen. Reaching Miansi they were met by three Qiang Christians who had walked down from their mountain homes to welcome them.

For the first time Torrance had brought his magic lantern and gave two evening showings of 'foreign countries, foreign life and of the Life of Christ'. Most locals had never had such a window on the

---

8 According to the *Book of Han,* completed in the first century AD, Wudu, in today's region of Longnan in southeastern Gansu, had a mixed population of Qiang and Di (氐) but was more often mentioned in relation to the Di people. In the *Book of the Later Han*, Wudu had a Qiang district (羌道) but also suffered attacks from Qiang groups.

9 TT. 'A Trip to Lifan and Songpan', WCMN, Sept 1922, p15-18; 'Blazing the Gospel Trail', *The China Press,* Sept 10, 1922. All quotes regarding the trip are from the *China Press* article unless otherwise indicated.

10 WCMN, September 1922, p16.

world before and when he showed some Chinese and Qiang photos at the end 'they applauded uproariously', delighted to see such familiar scenes projected in front of them.

Chen Bingling was still living at the CIM mission house in Weizhou and the magic lantern pictures were received there with equal enthusiasm. At the end of a well-attended Sunday service Torrance asked four of the new Qiang Christians to tell the others about the change in their lives, which they all did 'unfalteringly'. In the afternoon they climbed up to one of the Qiang villages where Chen and Gou Pinsan were well-known. Sitting on the flat rooftops they chatted at leisure with the villagers and Torrance was hopeful that at least one of them would come to Chengdu for the winter Bible study and return to teach his own people. Although James Edgar had experienced the Qiang reserve towards strangers, Torrance was increasingly finding them warm-hearted and 'profuse in their kindness once they realise your friendliness'.

As they moved north towards Maoxian, Torrance continued to make enquiries about Qiang customs at various villages along the way. He found the Qiang far more open to the Bible and questions of faith than the Chinese generally were, and their Qiang sacrificial customs were a natural entry point for discussion and comparison:

> With their system of sacrifices resembling so closely those of our Old Testament they have a foundation on which to build . . . To tell a Ch'iang that Christ was the Lamb of God to take away the sin of the world is to tell him what he can understand at once . . . The Ch'iang . . . speak of God, as the Spirit of Heaven and the Father-Spirit. Their religion is called the White Religion – white meaning righteous; and the worshippers go to their sacrifices clad in white, i.e. seeking righteousness.

The white stone played a key role in all this as 'the symbol of the Divine character and the mark of the White Religion'.

In the Maoxian region Torrance made an interesting discovery. 'One thing that surprised me at Mongchow [Maoxian] is that locally, though admittedly Ch'iang, they are not called by this name. The Chinese term them Ri-Ih-Tsze. It means, they say, the second or lesser barbarians and is intended as a name of contempt. The Ch'iang detest it.' It seems likely from this description that this term would be 'Er-yi-zi' (二夷子) in today's pinyin, combining 'two' and 'Yi', which was a common Chinese term for non-Chinese.

In his 1920 monograph on the Qiang, Torrance had described their language as monosyllabic, with an unusual juxtaposition of consonants and apparently with some tones.[11] He now described each district as having its own dialect, with altogether six or seven varieties, and people having difficulty understanding each other. North of today's Maoxian county town he noted that 'people on both sides of the Min talk Ch'iang, though with the usual difference of pronunciation.'[12] Like the Qiang of Weizhou and Lifan, these people beyond Maoxian also observed the three annual sacrificial festivals and their ritual was similar too. One practice they had maintained which had been lost further south was the wearing of a multi-coloured robe by the priest in the sacred grove.

In one place to the southeast of Maoxian the people identified themselves as Chinese but still observed one annual sacrificial festival and had a syncretic religion which seemed to combine aspects of the 'White religion' and some idolatry, which was uncharacteristic of Qiang religious practices. Despite their claim to be Chinese, Torrance assumed from their 'faces, customs and their yearly sacrifice' that these people were a mix of Qiang and Chinese through intermarriage.

As they travelled on up the Min Valley towards Songpan the Qiang population gradually decreased and became mingled with Xifan inhabitants, which made the northern Qiang boundary difficult to determine. As for the western boundary, Torrance's enquiries didn't seem to yield new information but he already knew that the Qiang extended some distance along the Zagunao and Heishui valleys.

Reaching Songpan, over eighty miles north of Maoxian, Torrance found the climate particularly refreshing and 'as like home as any place can be' with its sunny days and early morning chill. Among those coming to trade in Songpan from the wider area Torrance noted Tibetans, Qiang, Boluozi, Heishui people, and Goloks. He understood the Boluozi to be Lolo people who had been brought north as carriers by a Chinese general in the early Ming period and had stayed and married local women. As for the Golok, they were a fiercely independent nomadic people in the Qinghai-Sichuan border region. In the town itself the Muslim residents outnumbered the Chinese. In the wider Songpan area no-one knew of locals who were called Qiang and Torrance didn't have time to enquire further afield,

---

11 TT. *The History, Customs and Religion of the Ch'iang*, p15.
12 WCMN, Sept 1922, p17.

although he was told of 'a tribe with similar characteristics who lived to the West of Gansu'.[13]

Torrance gave no detail of the return journey but he seems to have returned straight back down the Min Valley through Maoxian, Weizhou, and Miansi to meet up with the family for a rest at Lingyan.

Torrance was not the only one on the road that summer. Dr Morse of the WCUU had planned a major research expedition with several others to the tribal country between Ya'an and Kangding. The areas of expertise in the group included medicine, anthropology, botany, and surveying, augmented by James Edgar's diverse knowledge as 'the versatile Genius of the party'.[14] The results of their investigations were to be presented to the West China Border Research Society, of which Morse was president. The society's first public meeting with lectures was in January 1923 and the first volume of its journal was published by the Canadian Press that same year, a large part of which was focused on 'the tribes country'.

One of the contributors to the journal was T. Edgar Plewman who had travelled with Torrance in 1919. In the summer of 1922 he decided to travel north over the mountains from the Zagunao Valley to the Heishui region, a route further west but roughly parallel to Torrance's own trip over the mountains with Gou and Chen the previous year. Starting from Xuecheng and crossing over a 14,500 foot pass with his cook and two carriers, the sight of a white stone on a stone platform raised Plewman's hopes that he might be in Qiang country but he soon discovered that the locals, who called themselves Krehchuh, were Buddhists, although their language 'while distinct seems akin to the Ch'iang'.[15]

Further down they reached a village called Yadu where Plewman was surprised to hear a Qiang dialect which seemed almost identical to that spoken in the Qiang villages of Chief Yang's Jiuzi district. His surprise was compounded by the knowledge that the Qiang dialects of Jiuzi and nearby Tonghua were considerably different and he wondered if there had been a migration between Jiuzi and Yadu. To illustrate his

13 Possibly Pingwu County, east of Songpan, on the Sichuan-Gansu border, which still has a Qiang population.
14 Dryden Linsley Phelps. 'An Expedition Through Bati-Bawang'. WCMN, Sept 1922, pp5-15.
15 T. E. Plewman. 'A Journey into the Heofan Valley'. In the *Journal of the West China Border Research Society* (JWCBRS), Vol 1, 1922, p21. Krehchuh, nowadays rendered as Khro Chu, is the Tibetan name for Heishui.

findings he included a word list comparing the languages of the Qiang of Jiuzi (*Kiutzeteng*), Tonghua, and Yadu, and of the Krehchuh and Jiarong peoples.[16]

	Kiutzeteng Chiang	Tunghua Chiang	Yahtu Chiang	Krehchuh	Kiarong
One	arguh	ngaiguh	arguh	aow	gaychoh
two	nerguh	neguh	nerguh	i-yiu -	gayness
three	cheeguh	cheeguh	ksurguh	k'siu	gayswom
four	gurguh	zrerguh	gurguh	griu	gogee
five	warrguh	hwayguh	warrguh	oh-wu	gemngoh
six	strughguh	strughguh	strughguh	strugh	gaydroh
seven	schnerguh	hsinguh	schnerguh	shiu	geshniss
eight	qrerguh	bihguh	zrerguh	cra-ow	waherryih
nine	ih'gwerguh	ihgwillee	ihgwerguh	erguh	gengoo
ten	hadrugo	haluguh	hajugo	hao-jiu	sjay

James Edgar, the 'versatile Genius' who was a Fellow of both the Royal Geographic Society and the Royal Anthropological Institute, was also continuing to write about the Qiang and the wider ethnic picture of western Sichuan. Like Torrance, he was a keen reader of Chinese history and in a paper published that year he explored the names of non-Chinese groups in Sichuan's history, including the Qiang, Di, Rong, Tibetans, Yi, and Man.[17] His Chinese sources included the official Chinese histories of Wenchuan, Lifan, and Maoxian, the first century BC *Historical Records* by Sima Qian, and a more recent illustrated geography of Tibet.[18] Edgar had first encountered the Qiang on a trip with John Muir in 1907 and observed how different they were from the Chinese in language, religion, and customs.

Noting that the Qiang were 'well-known to readers of Chinese History', Edgar had found differing views as to their identity. One Chinese view was that they had an ancient Chinese origin as a branch of the San Miao people of Hunan province.[19] On the other hand, Sima Qian's *Historical Records* described how Qiang in Xinjiang and Gansu had obstructed the Chinese in their attempts to reach Graeco-Bactria

---

16 Ibid., p34. Later linguistic research has shown that the population of the lower Heishui valley, including Yadu, are speakers of a cluster of dialects broadly labelled Northern Qiang, also referred to as 'Rma.'
17 J. H. Edgar. 'Notes on Names of Non-Chinese Tribes in West Szechwan'. JNCBRAS, Vol 53, 1922, pp61-69.
18 *Xizang tukao* (An Illustrated Research Report on Tibet). Compiled by Huang Peiqiao in 1885-86.
19 See Rachel Meakin, 'Qiang 羌 References in the Book of Han 汉书, Part 1', p2, for a discussion of the San Miao connection. (www.academia.edu)

and how, in the late 2nd century BC, the Han envoy, Zhang Qian, had recommended avoidance of this route because of the Qiang. Admitting that it was 'difficult to find the true value of the term Ch'iang' and aware that he was not offering clear answers, Edgar described them as 'the great fugitives of Chinese History', often found 'split up into divisions which, if they had been united, would have given China an uneasy time'.[20] As regards the practices of the Qiang, Edgar was insistent that the Qiang were animists and that they worshipped the white stone, a view shared by Plewman but firmly rejected by Torrance, whose research had led him to understand that the stone was a reflection of the character of their Deity and not an object of worship.[21]

Acknowledging that his article would 'do little but suggest difficulties', Edgar wondered whether the Qiang were actually of 'pure stock' and whether the name Qiang had persisted more because of its use by Chinese authorities than as a term used by the people themselves. At the end of the article he added a 'Note on Chiang Sacrifice' which, for some reason, he provided only in Chinese. This was from 'a Qiang leader' in Weizhou and reads as a transcribed verbal account. Despite Edgar's claim that the Qiang were animists and worshipped the white stone, the note corroborated and added to Torrance's own findings:

A look at the annual sheep sacrifice of the people of Weizhou, Sichuan[22]

Each village or *zhaizi* uses stone to build a sacrificial altar at the foot of a cliff or on the wooded mountainside, or in the open country. This is about 5-6 feet high or 4-5 feet high (it varies), and a white stone is erected on it. Each year, either in the first or sixth lunar month, some a bit earlier, some a bit later (they vary), or in the tenth lunar month – more so in the tenth month – a young sheep is used as a sacrifice, a set practice passed down from generation to generation, that when a ram without blemish is offered in sacrifice, flour is used to make an unleavened bread and after this has been offered up as a sacrifice, it is shared out with the meat of the lamb

---

20 J. H. Edgar. 'Notes on the Names of Non-Chinese Tribes in West Szechwan', p63. The Qiang did historically give the Chinese 'an uneasy time'. Significant Qiang uprisings in Gansu during the Eastern Han dynasty were a contributing factor in the fall of the Han dynasty.
21 Ibid.
22 J. H. Edgar. 'Note on Chiang Sacrifice and Litholatry'. JNCBRAS, Vol 53, 1922, pp68-69. Translated from Chinese by the author.

and eaten. Once the sheep is sacrificed a slice is cut from the tongue and from each of the four feet and the tendons are removed and offered in sacrifice on the altar. Before the sacrifice of the sheep several grain stalks are put in a bowl in preparation for use in sprinkling the blood. The meat of the sheep cannot be eaten by those who are not local and also those locals who have not gone through the cutting ceremony are not allowed to eat it.

When a local person is a young boy, he leads a sheep to the place of sacrifice and when the sheep is sacrificed a white thread is placed round the child's neck and tied with a knot – about one foot and several inches long. Then a knife is used to cut several inches and this is called the cutting ceremony.

The practice of removing the tendons from the sacrifice was not something Torrance had mentioned in his own Qiang research, which is surprising considering his interest in finding biblical parallels in their culture. It is a practice described in the book of Genesis and although there is no suggestion of a connection between the Qiang and the Chinese Jewish community of Kaifeng in Henan province, the Kaifeng Jews were traditionally known by the Chinese as those who follow 'the doctrine of extracting the tendon'.[23]

1923

By the end of 1922 Torrance's own writings on the Qiang had reached a wide audience among foreigners in China through his publications in the WCMN, the *Shanghai Mercury,* and *The China Press.* In January 1923 Carleton Lacy, John Hykes' successor in Shanghai, read a new paper by Torrance to members of the Royal Asiatic Society entitled 'The Religion of the Ch'iang'. This was reviewed in the *North China Daily News* under the title 'China and the Old Testament', with the subtitle, 'Some Remarkable Parallels in the Religion of a Primitive Western Tribe'.

The paper, which was subsequently published in the *Journal of the North China Branch of the Royal Asiatic Society* (JNCBRAS), showed that Torrance's recent travels and enquiries had added significantly to the information in his 1920 paper.[24] These two papers essentially laid the

23 挑筋教. In Genesis, Abraham's grandson Jacob had been left with a limp after a struggle with God and "Therefore, to this day the sons of Israel do not eat the sinew of the hip which is on the socket of the thigh." (Genesis 32:32)
24 TT. 'The Religion of the Ch'iang', JNCBRAS, Vol 54, 1923, p150-167. All quotes in this section are from this article unless otherwise indicated.

foundation for all his research and it would be 1930 before he published anything further on the Qiang, even though his understanding would increase in the meantime.

In this paper Torrance explained that, having once been a great nation, the Qiang now only numbered about 250,000, with their survival as a people in large part due to their distinct religious practices. Their two principal names for God were Ma-Be-Ch'ee (God of Heaven) and A-Ba-Ch'ee (God the Father). A third name, only used in prayer, was La-Ts'a. Ma-Be-Ch'ee was a holy and supreme being who controlled everything and rewarded good and evil. A common Qiang remark was that 'Ma-Be-Ch'ee will requite you.' The white stone, representing the character of this Deity, was sometimes set amidst twelve small white stones. Worship was divided into annual public ceremonies and private ceremonies in family homes, which could include weddings, funerals, and healing sickness.

Public Ceremonies

The public worship took place in the sacred grove with the stone altar and the white stone, where no cutting of trees was permitted. Stones for the altar could be broken with another stone but not with any metal tool. The animal sacrifice was preceded by the purification of the participants and followed by prayer – the making of petitions to God. The animal could be a ram or he-goat, or a young bull, or a fowl. In some places, if a bull was sacrificed, it should never have been used for ploughing. Whatever animal was used, it had to be free of any blemish. With no Qiang script and no written scriptures, the priest was the only one to memorise the ceremonial chants, which were passed down orally from generation to generation in the priestly family. He also served as an exorcist.

There were three annual festivals. Two of them, referred to by Torrance as the Peace Festival and the Feast of Thanksgiving, could be attended by 'privileged outsiders'. The third was their New Year festival, which was held on the first day of the tenth lunar month and was the most important. It could only be attended by the men of the community, with attendance mandatory for each head of household. Ten days ahead of the ceremony a ram or male goat would be chosen. If a white one wasn't available a white cock would be sacrificed to atone for this deficiency. The men who attended the ceremony had to purify themselves three days before the ceremony – bathing, washing their clothes, and abstaining from garlic, onion, and anything seen as unclean. Anyone not purified was not allowed on the path to the sacred grove and villagers watched to make sure no-one trespassed there.

The day before the ceremony, the ram or goat would be washed and cypress incense waved around it. On the day of the ceremony, late in the evening, a procession made its way to the grove with torches and the ram or goat was led with a new rope by someone who had been chosen as a worthy villager. His responsibilities included the slaying of the animal and he would receive an extra portion of meat for his services. On the way to the grove the animal was cleansed again and water poured in its ears. If it didn't react to this by shaking its head, it would be rejected. On arrival at the grove it underwent a third cleansing.

In the grove a Ma-Be-Ch'ee white banner with a miniature bow and arrow attached to it was placed on the altar, along with a large round flatbread and a jar of local wine.[25] A bonfire was lit in the open space and the priest chanted to the beat of his drum and prayed, recalling instances of divine deliverance and giving thanks for the preservation of his people.[26] This continued into the night, interspersed with pauses for rest. The priest was usually dressed like the other participants, in homespun white hemp, but with the addition of a monkey-skin cap. However, Torrance had managed to obtain a robe which had traditionally been worn on such occasions: 'the body of which is blue, and the plaited skirt of green. The collar shows bands of blue, scarlet, green and fawn and on the back is a shieldlike adornment, which probably had once a religious significance.'

The actual sacrifice took place at about three in the morning. The smoke from burning cypress branches was wafted around the white stone, the rope was removed from the animal and wound around the receptacle for the blood, and the priest and elders knelt down and placed their hands on the animal's head, followed by the other villagers. At this point the priest prayed a prayer, the content of which Torrance included in his paper, based on a Chinese translation provided for him from the Qiang language. The miniature arrow was then removed from the bow and the priest's knife was given to the one chosen to slay the

---

25 This was probably *zajiu* (咂酒) or sipping wine – a traditional, sweet, beer-like alcohol made from local grain. At ceremonies it is often drunk through long bamboo straws from a communal jar.

26 The legend of the battle between the Qiang and Ge people (羌戈大战) is one of the best known Qiang legends, told as part of the Qiang priest's chants. There are many variants of the story but it tells of the Qiang trying to settle in an area occupied by the Ge or Geji people and gaining the victory through divine assistance.

goat. The blood was drained into the basin and sprinkled over the altar as well as on the bread, wine, white stone, banner, and all around. After this the white banner was removed from behind the white stone and placed above it, with one of the goat's ears placed on the tip of its staff. Apart from the main banner, each participant took four small white paper flags to the grove. These were also sprinkled with the blood and taken home, with two of them later set up in the fields.

The sacrifice was then divided up. The head, heart, liver, and kidneys were roasted at the grove, the intestines cleaned, minced, and cooked, and all was then eaten with small flatbreads brought by the people. The bread and wine on the altar were also shared out. The horns, a paring of the hoofs, a thin portion of the lips, and the genital glands were all presented on the altar. The priest was given the skin, breast, a foreleg, and the lower jaw. The one who had led the goat or ram to the sacred grove received his extra portion and the loin fat, and the rest was divided up amongst the other participants to be taken home for their family members. The ceremony finished with final prayers without any beating of the sheepskin drum. Later that day the villagers would gather to sing and dance together around a fire in the presence of a white banner, 'assured of prosperity in their fields'. The ceremony was followed by two days of rest.

Private Ceremonies

In the private ceremonies, held by individual households, a worthy member of the family would be purified to assist the priest. Seven days before the ceremony he would cut a three-pointed branch which was not allowed inside the house and had to be raised up to the roof, where it was inserted behind the white stone. The priest would come at noon, pray outside the closed front door, burn incense to purify the home, and then enter, go up to the roof, and waft incense over the white stone. In the afternoon he chanted intermittently to the beat of his drum. In the evening a white cock or goat was slain as a preliminary offering. A large white sheet of paper was put up on the wall and three white banners placed in front of it. At midnight the head of the house laid his hand on the head of the sacrifice and it was then slain. The rest of the ceremony was similar to that in the grove. At dawn the family members ate the meat with the flatbread and the priest then prayed a final prayer and departed. The horned skull of the animal would be preserved in the main room of the house.[27]

---

27 The sheep's horned skull is still a dominant symbol of the Qiang, sometimes seen above Qiang doorways and in their embroidery designs.

In what Torrance referred to as a large or extraordinary family sacrifice, there were additional traditions such as the outside wall of the house being whitewashed and one or two tree outlines drawn on it; a cross within a circle being drawn 'about the doorway' and blood sprinkled on the door frame; and two single-pointed branches placed at the corners of the back wall, either side of the three-pointed branch. Sometimes a goat was slain in front of each branch. On the wall inside the house twelve sheets of paper were put up, sometimes with a multitude of small white banners placed in front of them.

A GOAT
BEING LED TO
SACRIFICE

Torrance also mentioned the naming of a new baby boy after forty days and the public cutting ceremony at three years old in the sacred grove, which he had referred to in his 1921 *China Press* article. He now added that blood and burned fat were daubed on the child's forehead after the sacrifice of a goat or cockerel and the cutting of the cord. Unsurprisingly, he found more orthodoxy in the ceremonies of the remoter villages but even then there were variations from place to place.

The Qiang marriage ceremony was always performed by the priest. The bride and groom would exchange large round flatbreads which were placed in front of the white paper in each of their homes. Another flatbread would be given by the groom to the priest, who placed it on some corn and inserted a small white banner in it. The arrival of the bride at the groom's house was announced with antiphonal singing by the relatives and the priest prayed as he led the bride and her escort over the threshold into the house. He then stood in front of the white paper to pray and burn incense. The bread placed on the corn would be divided among the guests and eaten with meat. A marriage feast followed this and three days later the newly-weds would visit the wife's parents, taking two flatbreads, one of which might be half-moon shaped.

In cases of sickness the priest was called, the traditional view being that sickness was caused by 'the Evil One'. Although the use of medicine had become more widespread, the prayers and rituals of the priest were still seen as effective. An animal chosen for the healing ceremony would be released into the wild in the hope that it would take the sickness with it. When a death occurred in the village a drum was beaten on the housetop and three goats were sacrificed, one when the drum was beaten, one at the sealing of the coffin, and one the night before the funeral. Burial and cremation were both practiced. The priest would only pray in the house, not on the roof or at the grove. At the burial of the body or of the cremated remains, the priest would scatter grain over the relatives, who picked it up and took it home.

There was also a ceremony for cleansing of the fields which included a sacrifice, the sprinkling of blood, and a procession through the fields accompanied by incense and the beat of the priest's drum. The hope was that this would bring blessing on the crops and protect them from blight. Commenting again on the plough, Torrance described it as of the Persian type with 'little more than an iron blade' and noted a Chinese saying about Qiang farming methods: 'They plough with a knife and sow with fire.'

Like Edgar, Torrance had read local Chinese histories concerning the Qiang and had found descriptions of them which were much in keeping with his own views. According to the Lifan history, 'The men are strong and obstinate but their disposition is simple and sincere. They make expert hunters. Their land is hard to cultivate and the people are poor. In their habits they are frugal and diligent. In their dealings they are honest and litigation is rare. The scholars among them are well informed and self respecting.'[28] The Wenchuan history was equally positive: 'They are accustomed to hard work on

---

28 TT. 'The Religion of the Ch'iang', p163. Torrance doesn't give the precise names of these histories but each county had their official annals.

their unproductive lands, nevertheless, they are correct in their moral principles. Their kindly disposition makes them respond quickly even to small kindnesses. The men farm, the women weave, the husband sings, the wife responds; mirth and laughter come naturally to them.'[29]

Some people familiar with Torrance's research were beginning to ask if the Qiang were perhaps part of Israel's lost tribes or had even converted to Judaism at some point but Torrance was still insistent that the Qiang had been in China 'from before the dawn of history' and that other groups in China shared some similar customs. Among these he included the ancient Di people who had been neighbours of the Qiang; the ancient people of Shu who had apparently had a white stone; the Jiarong who still had white stones; the Yi people who had some similar customs; and others, including the Miao, Tu, and Yao, who had sacrificial rituals. Pointing out that sacrifice in the Bible was pre-Moses and only received its accompanying rituals in the Mosaic period, he asserted that 'West China faiths do not spring from Judaism. The only satisfactory conclusion is that the religion of the Ch'iang represents a very primitive faith from which both it and our Old Testament ritual are directly descended.'

At the end of the paper Torrance listed the parallels he could see between the Qiang rituals and biblical beliefs and practices, including the unity and holiness of God; the need for sacrifice to deal with sin; repentance and prayer as an integral part of the sacrificial ceremony; separation of the holy and the profane; the rest days accompanying the sacrifices; and the taboo on any non-participants eating of the sacrifice (except for family members of those present). He also provided specific Bible references for suggested similarities: altar stones not hewn (Exodus 20:25); a lamb without blemish (Leviticus 22:19-24); purification at Sinai in preparation for God coming down to the Israelites on the third day (Ex 19:10-11); the scapegoat (Lev 16:21-32); three annual festivals (Ex 13:14-17); unleavened bread in sacrificial ceremonies (Ex 23:18); arrows as a symbol of God's judgment (Psalms 64:7, 7:13); and worship referred to as 'paying their vows to God' (Psalms 141:13-14, Isaiah 19:21).

One aspect which had particularly impacted Torrance was the cloud of incense over the white stone, the significance of which the Qiang couldn't explain but which he likened to the smoke over Mount

---

29 Ibid.

Sinai when God appeared to the Israelites, as recorded in the book of Exodus.[30] For Torrance their ceremonies demonstrated a 'desire for the manifestation of the Presence and Glory of God', which to him was the 'crowning conception' of their religion. Another distinctive feature was the lack of idolatry among the Qiang in a nation where idols were a normal part of life for so many. He also pointed to the similarity between the Qiang character (羌), consisting of 'man' and 'sheep', and the Chinese character for righteousness (義) which, surprisingly for a nation in which sheep were not particularly significant, consisted of 'sheep' above the character for 'me' or 'I', suggesting the sheep was somehow connected with righteousness – and perhaps raising the possibility that it was an imported concept.

---

30 Exodus 19:18.

Chapter 11

Diverse Confrontations

1923-1924

On February 3, 1923, a long-desired brother for Tom arrived with the birth of James Bruce Torrance and Annie was healthy enough to continue her teaching commitments almost up to the birth. When Torrance told the children of the baby's arrival, Grace asked excitedly, 'Oh, does Mummy know?' So Torrance went in to ask Annie – and she did![1]

Three weeks later fighting broke out in Xindu to the north of Chengdu as Liu Wenhui, who would become one of Sichuan's most powerful militarists, sought with other allies to unseat Governor Liu Chengxun. In early April a shocking report from A. G. Lee at the CMS mission in Xindu described the ferocity and folly of the conflict. 'Wars and fightings have monopolised nearly all our attention during the past six weeks . . . This fighting has been the most determined that I have seen in China, and the killed and wounded are numbered by thousands. Bayonet fighting has been quite common at times, and bravery has been displayed which would call forth our admiration if it was only on behalf of some better cause.'[2] Sadly these were Sichuanese killing Sichuanese, enlisted by opposing generals and mostly without any strong sense of allegiance, sometimes fighting friends on the other side. One of Lee's colleagues in the nearby town of Deyang had died of typhus while attending to wounded soldiers. By April Liu Wenhui had Chengdu in his sights and the city gates were closed for about ten days, but fighting was sporadic and eventually subsided. In May the WCMN reported that almost all the generals concerned were in the city and had supposedly reached some kind of settlement.[3]

By this time the situation in Chengdu was calm enough for Torrance to visit the ABS depot in Chongqing, for which he had oversight, and meet with Carleton Lacy, who was paying a rare visit from Shanghai. While Torrance was away, Annie fell ill with malignant malaria. She

---

1 *Memoirs*, p76.
2 WCMN, May 1923, p35.
3 Ibid., p38.

had suffered several bouts of malaria over the years but had stopped her daily quinine while nursing James and the consequence was a particularly virulent attack. A message reached Torrance asking him to return immediately and in the meantime Annie and baby James were cared for in the home of Dr and Mrs Kelly while the other children went to stay with friends. Annie was eventually moved to the Canadian hospital where she spent several weeks, hovering at times between life and death. For Annie it was not just a physical illness but also the beginning of a spiritual 'dark night of the soul'.

While Annie was in hospital, news came in from the CMS mission in Mianyang, north of Chengdu, that their schools had been in the firing line for a week.[4] In June further fighting broke out to the east as the troops of General Yang Sen, who had just taken control of Chongqing, pressed westwards with their eye on Chengdu. Yang Sen's advance was checked and Liu Chengxun managed to hold on to power but in July he was replaced by Liu Xiang, a relative of Liu Wenhui and a major contender for control of Sichuan. In genteel fashion and in somewhat surreal contrast, the birthday of King George V was celebrated on June 3 at the British Consulate in Chengdu, with all foreigners invited by the new Consul-General, G. A. Combe, to drink to the king's health at noon.

Despite the lawlessness Torrance was still planning a summer trip to the Qiang, much encouraged by Dr Morse who was urging missionaries to use their summer breaks to add to the growing pool of research on western Sichuan: 'Men like Edgar, Muir, Torrance, Ferguson, and others have done much good work, but more is needed.'[5]

Annie was still recuperating when it was time to leave for the hills but it was good to get out of the city and with the children pitching in they managed to get everything ready. This was no small undertaking, as the WCMN would later describe: 'The house is entirely given over to the work of packing. Bamboo boxes and baskets have invaded the rooms and passages . . . Chairs, tables and even the floor itself are all littered with clothes, curtains, towels, bedding and the miscellaneous paraphernalia of travel and holiday-keeping in unfurnished abodes.'[6] The challenge was to take enough but not too much and it was a miracle if it all arrived intact and on time.

There were more than forty children that year at Lingyan and the Torrance children were delighted to have the run of the temple

4   WCMN, July 1923, p42.
5   WCMN, June 1923, p27.
6   WCMN, July-Aug 1932, p1.

grounds and the anticipation of various activities arranged for them. It was also a welcome break for Torrance before his travels but for Annie it was a different story. Despite appreciating the change of scenery, she was still stuck in her post-malarial 'dark night' with no apparent way out. To her infinite relief the breakthrough came in the most simple of circumstances. Her eyes lit one day on a calendar bearing a verse from the book of Isaiah: 'With everlasting kindness I will have mercy on you', and in that moment the darkness lifted:[7]

> Suddenly I felt like a captive released, a healing of blind eyes. It seemed as if a rush of life-giving blood was pulsating through my whole body. All those terrible three months darkness and black-out and captivity to the devil had at last disappeared. It seemed to go away as suddenly as it had come. I <u>knew</u> it was completely gone, that I was restored to my Blessed Saviour's Presence.[8]

The Bible, which had been a stranger to her during this time, suddenly became her 'living companion' and for the rest of the summer she pored over it at every opportunity.

As Torrance prepared to set out for the Qiang area, with Annie yet to experience this breakthrough and James only five months old, Grace vocalised what the whole family were probably thinking: 'Father, why can't you stay at home this time?'[9] However, the thought of delaying his research and waiting another year to further develop friendships among the Qiang was too much for Torrance to contemplate and he took comfort that the family were safely away from any trouble in Chengdu and had the company of their Chinese house helpers and other missionary families. Apart from the research, one of his goals was to establish what he described as a 'church union' for those who had become Christians. A total of fifteen men from various villages had by now been down for winter Bible study in Chengdu and there were also seven young lads studying at the Canadian mission school. Gou Pinsan had committed to providing some of the Qiang boys with education and was raising funding for this himself. He would continue to do this over the next few years, even renting a house in Chengdu for

---

7   Isaiah 54:8 (New King James Version®. Copyright © 1982 by Thomas Nelson. Used by permission. All rights reserved.)
8   *Memoirs*, p79.
9   TT. 'Journeys Among the Tribes People', Aug 22, 1923. Typed manuscript, no destination indicated. All quotes regarding the trip are from this unless otherwise indicated.

them to live in until Torrance provided them with a large room on the ABS premises.[10]

As Torrance and his helpers headed up the Min Valley they passed a mule train bringing wool down from Songpan and a group of Turkic Muslims coming all the way from Xinjiang Province in the remote northwest to sell their wares in Chengdu, testimony to the valley's significance as a trade route. To Torrance's surprise, a while later they saw the mule train coming back up still carrying its loads. The muleteers had been warned that the military in Guanxian were seizing men and transport animals for army use, something they couldn't risk despite the loss of trade.

Chen Bingling, who had now moved from Weizhou to a rented house in Miansi, was waiting for them ten miles down the valley at Taoguan. With him was Gou Guanding of the Wasi people, a Tibetan Buddhist who spoke Chinese and Tibetan and had recently become a Christian. Four Qiang Christians from the hillside villages opposite Miansi had also come down to meet them and stayed in Miansi for the weekend. Torrance then went on with Chen and Gou Guanding to Weizhou where they were joined by other Qiang folk, including Gou Pinsan. This time, although Torrance sent three of his colporteurs further up the Min Valley to Maoxian, Diexi, and Songpan, he decided to spend all his time in the region around Miansi and Weizhou, letting the locals plan his itinerary – with, as he put it, 'just a shade of fear and trembling. For Ch'iang roads are often bad enough to take one's breath away. It is not a case of taking your life in both hands, but of taking it in both feet!'

His first visit was with Chen, Gou Guanding, and Gou Pinsan, over the mountain to a valley east of Weizhou, where they were an unusual sight with their mixed group of Scottish, Chinese, Wasi, and Qiang. At Lower Baishui village they visited the local Qiang priest. His drum and ceremonial hats hung on the wall, including a three-eared monkey-skin hat with a white bone ornament on the front and other 'dangling oddities', as well as a 'triple-storied felt hat' worn when a cock was sacrificed. Further down the mountainside they were met by a Chinese school teacher who had been a fortune teller before becoming a Christian through Chen Bingling. He took them to Maidi Village, where they chatted to people and gave out literature, and then to the village where he taught. The local priest was among the villagers who

10 TT. 'The Story of Isaac Whiteheart'. Chapter 21 in *Conversion Stories of Chinese Christians*. With Gou Pinsan's consent, Torrance used the English name Isaac Whiteheart for him, perhaps to protect his identity.

came to listen and he took Torrance up to see their altar, which was in marked contrast to what Torrance had seen elsewhere: 'I found the ritual to be yet more decadent than across the valley.' It was becoming clearer to Torrance how much the ceremonial rituals varied even within short distances. Some were purists keeping the old customs and some had let other influences in, possibly as a result of intermarriage with Chinese.

Moving on up the Min Valley they crossed a bamboo suspension bridge to Moutuo Village on the west bank of the river. This was the seat of Chief Wen, the local Qiang headman, who welcomed them graciously. During the Qing era Wen's family had been given the right to rule in perpetuity but the Chinese had 'nibbled away' at his territory and not much was left. Wen possessed an ABS Bible obtained a few years before and he had also read a tract written by Gou Pinsan explaining the meaning of sacrifice. He and his son were both in the grip of opium addiction and Torrance encouraged them to come to Chengdu for help but Chief Wen wanted to 'consult another tribal chief' regarding the wisdom of a visit to the city, which Torrance understood as a question of political sensitivities.

The tract Wen had read was in the form of a letter from Gou to his fellow Qiang, stressing the difference between their culture and that of the neighbouring Tibetan and Han peoples, although Gou also acknowledged that the Qiang no longer understood the significance of the customs they had inherited from their ancestors.[11] Focusing particularly on the Qiang sacrifices for the paying of vows, Gou explained that he had bought the books of Genesis and Exodus and the four gospels and as he read about the Israelite sacrifices and about Jesus' sacrifice as the lamb of God he had reached the conclusion that their own Qiang sacrifices stemmed from the same source. The parallels of sacrificing a lamb or sheep without blemish, the sprinkling of the blood of the sacrifice, the removal of guilt, the prayers to the God of heaven, the communal eating of the bread and the meat of the sacrifice, as well as their use of the white stone and white paper banners to represent the holiness of the Deity, were all too similar to be coincidental.

Chief Wen, when asked about the nature and meaning of the Qiang religion, was 'very decided that the White Stone on the housetop and

---

11 Produced by the Canadian Mission Press, the English title on the Chinese tract was 'The Origin of the Sacrifices of the Ch'iang'. The Chinese title was 'A letter to the Qiang discussing the origin and fulfilment of the paying of vows' (达羌人通信论还愿本末). An English translation of it is included in David C. Graham, *The Customs and Religion of the Ch'iang*, pp98-100.

above the altar represented the Spirit of Heaven – the Father Spirit – and that the object of the sacrifice was release from sin with securing of divine protection.' Torrance also noted that "The great cry of their priests at a sacrifice is that the "Abba chee", or Father Spirit, will come down to them in their grove.' Wen also acknowledged that in some places the religion had lost much of its earlier purity because the priests were losing their ancient knowledge. He was insistent that the white stone was not an object of worship in itself, proof to Torrance that James Edgar's claim of litholatry could not accurately be applied to the Qiang.

Edgar had wondered whether some Qiang exorcist practices were connected with monkey worship, possibly influenced by Tibetan legends of a monkey ancestor.[12] Torrance, who disagreed, wondered if the monkey-skin hat worn by some priests had contributed to this notion. He described the hat as a recent innovation, something possibly seen as efficacious in the driving out of evil spirits. The suggestion that the Qiang worshipped a monkey was greeted with much laughter by the Qiang themselves.

Returning from Moutuo to Dongmenwai, they had a good Sunday gathering at the school house and Torrance was delighted to see that all those who had been down to Chengdu for study were standing firm as Christians except one who had become addicted to opium, sadly the result of doses administered by his mother during a serious attack of dysentery. Each of the men had been invited to Chengdu from a different location and they were now teaching others back in their own villages.

Monday was spent in the home of a Christian family and was 'a time of feasting, preaching, and healing of the sick'. On Tuesday they went further up Longxi Valley to a village at the junction of two streams where they were welcomed by the father of one of the mission school students in Chengdu. To show his appreciation he sacrificed a goat on the roof-top and served it to his guests. That same day a request came for them to visit a sick woman in the village of Kuapo and the student's father accompanied them on the steep two-and-a-half-mile climb. Torrance administered quinine and aspirin and the woman's temperature went down from 105° F to 101° F. The following day she requested breakfast and continued to improve. No foreigner had been to Kuapo before and the woman's speedy recovery ensured they were made very welcome and were given opportunities to speak to the villagers, with the Qiang Christians preaching in their own language.

---

12 J. H. Edgar. 'Notes on Names of Non-Chinese Tribes in West Szechwan'. JNCBRAS, Vol 53, 1922, p63.

After a night in Kuapo they descended to the valley again and undertook an equally strenuous climb up the opposite mountainside to Longxi Village, 'a row of houses built along the edge of an almost perpendicular declivity' which 'made a stranger afraid to look down thousands of feet into the chasm below'. This was the home of Gou Pinsan's older brother, a scholar who had passed county-level imperial exams in the latter days of the Qing dynasty. Torrance described him as 'the head of the militia for the whole Lifan district, and the most influential Ch'iang of today' but sadly he was also addicted to opium. The villagers here showed Torrance something he had not seen before – an old suit of armour made of 'stiff leather plates fastened in place by leather thongs'.

LONGXI VILLAGE, PERCHED ABOVE A STEEP DROP

Their next stop was Bulan, a village several miles along the mountainside and the home of Chen Guangming, who had studied in the Torrance home. He had opened the main room of his house as a classroom where the local boys were being taught by a Christian teacher. Many people crowded in that evening to meet the visitors. The next day an old priest 'with a fine Aryan face' came for eye lotion. Torrance spoke with him of prayer being a direct conversation with God, something which was an alien notion for the priest, whose memorised chants were used only in the context of ritual ceremonies. That night, at an altitude of nearly nine thousand feet, Torrance had the joy of sleeping on the flat roof of the house. 'In the rare, clear air the stars shone like a blaze of jewels. But next morning lying in bed watching the sun catch peak after peak in his wakening beams was even finer still.'

The following Sunday marked the official establishment of the first
Qiang church. It had been decided that the Dongmenwai school house

QIANG ARMOUR

was the best place to hold a
regular Sunday gathering, to
which people from five other
Qiang villages could come.
Two men had already been
baptised, another ten were
baptised that day, and a total
of thirty-six enrolled as part
of the church. The thought
uppermost in Torrance's mind
was that the 'Lord had found
His lost sheep'. He was hoping
that some Qiang women would
go down to Chengdu that
winter for Bible study, as well
as men of other villages from
which no one had yet come,
and he was heartened to hear
that two Qiang Christians in
Heihu village, west of Maoxian,
were still doing well having
studied with him in Chengdu.

Returning to Weizhou
they crossed the Zagunao River and climbed up to the villages of Mayi,
Zengpo, and Yangtou (meaning 'sheep's head'). Dysentery was rife at Mayi
so they didn't stay long but Torrance was able to meet the local priest who
showed him some of his rituals and emphasised that he would not dare
present any offering that might be seen as imperfect or unsuitable. The
priest's explanations gave Torrance a better understanding of the Qiang
procedure at the sacred grove and he was once again impacted by the
biblical parallels and keen to dispel any impression among his readers that
this was merely a subjective interpretation. 'So much of their ceremonial
illustrates what we find in the Bible that some, when they hear of it, at first
almost refuse to credit it. They think we read into their religion parts of
the Old Testament, while the very opposite is the case.'

In Zengpo they had a good welcome from the schoolmaster, who
had become a Christian through the visits of Chen Bingling and Huang
Hanqing of Dongmenwai. Along the mountainside at Yangtou they

visited Mr Shang, the local headman who, with his brother and father, had also shown interest in their preaching. The uplands beyond Yangtou provided good hunting and enough pasture for the locals to raise cattle and horses but to Torrance's dismay he discovered that, as elsewhere, the local government had ordered all farmers to grow opium and was then demanding taxes from them. Torrance's visit coincided with the arrival of some officials to check how much was being grown and he was saddened to see the locals 'scratching and scraping the exudation from the poppy bulbs'. To his surprise there were two fairly new Chinese temples in this area. The locals explained that after the 1911 revolution some Chinese had insisted on them conforming to Chinese religious practices but the temples were not in use. At a Chinese shrine on the cliff top some local lads had placed a white stone in front of the resident idol to block it from view.

After a couple of days in Miansi Torrance returned to Lingyan to the distressing news that two CMS missionaries, Frederick Watt and Richard Whiteside, had been murdered by bandits on August 14 while travelling from Mianzhu, north of Chengdu, to the Qiang region of Maoxian.[13]

Having seen first-hand the destructive effect of opium in the Qiang area, Torrance was keen to take action. Earlier in the year, as a member of the executive council of the West China Missions Advisory Board, he had been commissioned with two others to prepare an appeal urging the Chengdu government to take steps against opium and this was now submitted. Commending Sichuan for having previously almost suppressed the trade, the appeal acknowledged that it was the Yunnan troops under Luo Peijin who had reintroduced it to the region. Torrance was then able to use his evidence from the summer:

> The Lifan magistrate this year forced the people there to grow opium, and those who refused were fined as high as fifty or sixty dollars. The five chiefs of the T'eng[14] tribesmen refused and he put two of them and the son of a third in prison. The T'eng soldiers had to enter Lifan to secure their release. In collecting the opium tax the extortion was so great on the poor mountain farmers that they became exasperated beyond measure.[15]

---

13 WCMN, Sept 1923, pp1-7.
14 *T'eng* here is today's *tun* (屯), meaning military district. The five *tun*, as mentioned in Chapter 7, were the four Jiarong districts and Chief Yang's Qiang district of Jiuzi.
15 WCMN, Dec 1923, pp20-22. Signed by Thomas Torrance, Kenneth J. Beaton, and Esther B. Lewis.

The appeal also attributed much of the current unrest in the Heishui area to weapons the Heishui people had procured from the Chinese in exchange for opium – thought to be at least fifteen hundred modern rifles.

Torrance and his co-authors urged a united response to the problem throughout the ranks of both military and civil officials but they knew full well that many were benefiting from the trade – even as the British had. An English translation of the appeal appeared in December's WCMN with a postscript by Torrance noting that an official proclamation had since been issued against opium growing. He asked missionaries to let him know whether or not this had been posted in their districts.

1924

With Liu Xiang as governor in Chengdu, assisted by Xiong Kewu as a key army commander, the city had been quiet for the last few months, despite continuing turmoil elsewhere in the province. However, early in 1924 General Yang Sen's troops, loyal to the Beijing government of Wu Peifu, defeated Xiong Kewu's men in Guanghan, north of Chengdu. Xiong managed to retreat to Chengdu which, on February 3, was shut up tight against the approaching enemy. The WCMN reported that, 'The fighting approached nearer and nearer till the nights were accompanied with the roar of cannon, the whine of bullets and the shouts of battle.'[16] The siege lasted until the evening of February 8 when Xiong, who was closely allied with the Nationalists in the south, led his troops out of the south gate and Liu Xiang stepped down as governor. The next day Yang Sen took charge of the city, a move described by Kapp as an 'intervention by proxy' of the Beijing government, which undermined Sichuan's efforts to stay out of politics beyond its borders.[17] Yang quickly imposed order on the streets by the beheading of looters, whether soldiers or civilians, and the heads were displayed for all to see.

Kristin Stapleton tells of the remarkable extent of Yang's disciplinary style of leadership: 'He urged Chengdu's residents to exercise regularly and launched attacks on footbinding, long fingernails (unsanitary and a sign of sloth), card games (they make strong men weak, whereas ball games make weak men strong), men who failed to wear shirts in public (uncivilized), and men who wore traditional long gowns (they waste cloth, and short jackets promote martial spirit by allowing freer

---

16 WCMN, March 1924, p43.
17 Kapp, *Szechwan and the Chinese Republic*, p21.

movement).'[18] Yang's modernising extended less to personal matters – he is reputed to have had twelve wives.

Yang also had grand plans for the modernisation of Chengdu. One of these was the building of a motor road between Chengdu and Guanxian, something which would greatly reduce the journey time to the hills in the summer, although it would take two years to complete. Another was the construction of Chunxi Road, now one of Chengdu's best-known downtown shopping areas, as well as plans to change various temple grounds into public parks. His interest in social projects extended to Openshaw's school for the blind and with Yang's help classes were moved to 'a splendid Temple property'.[19]

Torrance was thankful that his work could continue largely uninterrupted amidst all these political fluctuations. In the spring he rode out on Billy to the Qingyang Temple fair, where he found the atmosphere more welcoming than on some previous occasions. 'One of Chengtu's brightest scholars and best calligraphers, seeing me there purposely stopped to bow and shake hands. It was merely the work of a minute, but ah how it cheered!'[20] He was also visiting the hospital once a week to talk with the patients, give tracts, and pray with any who asked. One man, who had been shot in his side and arm by robbers, already possessed a Bible and asked Torrance how to pray. Another patient, a Buddhist priest with his foot in plaster, entered into lively debate with Torrance to the delight of the other patients who listened avidly.

In his spare time Torrance was continuing his historical research and had two articles published in the JNCBRAS in 1924. In the first, which looked at the early history of the famous Dujiangyan irrigation system, he pointed out that although Li Bing, governor of Shu in the 3rd century BC, was rightly accredited with his remarkable large-scale development of the system, the earliest irrigation works there should be attributed to Kai Ming, a king of Shu before it was conquered by Qin.[21] The other article was a continuation of his translation of the 'The History of Shuh'.[22] In her memoirs Annie recalled Torrance at work in his study at Wushi-tongtang

18 Stapleton. *Civilizing Chengdu*, p222-223, n.14, with reference to Ma Xuanwei and Xiao Bo, *Yang Sen*, Chengdu: Sichuan renmin chubanshe, 1989, p41.
19 H. Openshaw. 'The School for the Blind'. WCMN, July 1927, pp35-36.
20 TT. 'A Day's Work'. April 2, 1924. Written for an ABS report.
21 TT. 'The Origin and History of the Irrigation Work of the Chengtu Plain'. JNCBRAS, Vol 55, 1924, pp. 60-65.
22 TT. 'The History of Shuh – A Free Translation of the Shuh Chï'. JNCBRAS, Vol 55, p66-77.

writing Chinese tracts and translating Chinese historical texts, which were often borrowed from libraries in Chengdu. On one occasion he was given a letter of introduction to a Chengdu scholar, Fu Anlan, whose library contained over ten thousand books. Torrance was searching for an ancient book of Sichuan history which turned out to no longer exist but he was well-received by Fu Anlan and their conversation roamed far and wide. A few days later Fu Anlan paid him a reciprocal visit.

CHUNXI ROAD

On June 22, 1924, the last of Torrance and Annie's children, David Wishart Torrance, was born, with a middle name chosen in honour of the sixteenth century Scottish Protestant reformer George Wishart. This time Annie had kept taking her quinine and, conscious of her own physical weakness, had frequently knelt and committed each of her children to God. There was no return of the malaria but the bedroom was oven-hot and David soon developed prickly heat. To get them up to the cool of the hills as soon as possible, Torrance had a long wicker chair fitted up to transport Annie with David, while the girls travelled with young James in a sedan chair and Tom rode with Torrance on Billy. As usual, the cows came with them to provide a regular supply of milk.

Torrance set out for the Qiang area this year with a new companion, ten-year-old Tom, again riding with him on Billy. As he explained to Lacy, 'He pled so hard to accompany me that I could not refuse him, though truth to tell, I wanted his company: it is cheerier to have someone to whom you can talk English.'[23] Irene Hutchinson of the Friends Mission in Chengdu also travelled with them and went straight to Weizhou, having offered to hold Bible classes at the mission house for some Qiang women who were showing interest.

TORRANCE IN HIS STUDY AT WUSHI-TONGTANG

News from Chen Bingling had been encouraging. Back in February twelve men had joined him in the rented Miansi property for Bible study, three of whom had become Christians. Torrance and Tom were now able to lodge with Chen and on the first Sunday afternoon the three of them, along with Gou Guanding of the Wasi, crossed the river to Qiangfeng, a sizeable but secluded Qiang village overlooked by walnut trees.[24] The people gave them a warm welcome, with the women telling Torrance they would all go to church if only Annie would come and visit them. The following day they climbed up the mountainside to visit King Suo, the chief of the Wasi people, who had been away when Torrance first visited in 1919. Some years earlier Suo had received a leather-bound Bible from James Edgar and he immediately engaged Torrance in religious discussion, advising him that the Qiang would be

23 All summer trip quotes are taken from Torrance's letter to Carleton Lacy, Sept 17, 1924, unless otherwise indicated. The letter was sent on to Dr Haven at the ABS in New York.
24 Qiangfeng sits at the junction of the Min River and Cutou Gully (簇头沟), south of Miansi. In Torrance's day its Chinese name was Cutou, transcribed by Torrance as Tsayto.

more open to Christianity than other groups 'for they had no religion'. The comment revealed how differently the Qiang were perceived by those around them, having resisted pressure to yield to Tibetan Buddhism or the Daoism and Buddhism of the Chinese.

Returning to Miansi they continued up the Min Valley to Weizhou to stay a night in the old CIM house, which was being used by the Chinese Home Missionary Society, under the supervision of Pastor Mao in Xuecheng. Pressing on to Xuecheng, they met up with Mao and had some encouraging meetings together. Torrance was disappointed that Mao had little contact with the Qiang villages in the vicinity and asked him for a list of villages so that his own colporteurs could visit them in the future.

Chief Yang of Jiuzi was up at his mountain residence in Erwa but his son, Yang Jisheng, who was acting as chief in his stead, was down in Xuecheng and visited them, as did Chief Sang of Ganbao. Having mentioned their situation in his anti-opium appeal the year before, Torrance had then rightly assumed that officials in Xuecheng wouldn't pay attention to the anti-opium proclamation issued in Chengdu and he had sent a copy of it to Chief Yang, who had put it on display in his mountain yamen. Yang Jisheng and Sang now told him about their refusal to plant opium and the unrest that had followed, which had succeeded in stopping the Chinese pressure on them. No opium was being grown this year in either of their districts.

Another matter close to Torrance's heart, having grown up on a dairy farm, was the university's project to improve local stock. Some time ago a foreign bull had been brought to Chengdu from Shanghai and more recently the university had announced that the bull's two-year-old half-bred offspring was available for anyone wanting to improve the dairy stock of a local community. In the autumn of 1923 Torrance had sent a half-foreign bull up to the Qiang which, sadly, had fallen down the mountainside and died. This summer he had arranged for a local Jiarong tribesman, who was training as a colporteur, to bring another bull up, which was put out to pasture in a more secure area. This seems to have been a Jiarong man who had come to Chengdu for Bible study and whom Torrance had hoped would itinerate in the Jiarong region. To Torrance's disappointment the man 'did so well that when his Chief saw the improvement in him he imagined he could not spare him and recalled him for his own service.'[25]

From Xuecheng they returned along the north bank of the Zagunao River to Dongmenwai. Since the formation of the church the previous year, the Christians had taken a mortgage on half a house with a

25 TT. 'My Work Among the Tribes'. WCMN, Feb 1934, p17.

downstairs room for meetings and lodging upstairs for a visiting preacher. They had raised the funds themselves with Torrance giving a small amount towards some repairs.

DONGMENWAI: THE FIRST QIANG
'GOSPEL HALL' (福音堂)

There were now thirty-nine men signed up as enquirers and the Dongmenwai Christians had all sorts of plans. They intended to build their own church and to store in it 'a record of the old Ch'iang religion so that future generations may know the nature of the faith of their fathers, and how it passed away only at the coming to them of Christianity.'[26] Torrance was looking forward to reading this record and comparing it with his own research findings. On this trip he had been able to obtain 'an ancient priest's staff, which resembled a long rod with a snake wound around it: Moses' rod, as one of the Christians put it.' He also secured an unfamiliar kind of ancient burial urn for the university museum, where he was serving as interim curator that year.

---

26 This reflected Gou Pinsan's understanding that the efficacy of Jesus' sacrifice meant animal sacrifice was no longer necessary.

Between Dongmenwai and Weizhou they stopped off at the village of Keku where a man invited them in for a cup of tea. He had been reading a Bible that his father had obtained from one of the ABS colporteurs and it was clear that he wanted to talk:

His earnestness of manner showed he had something to say. He seated us in his best room, which was well furnished, and particularly bright for a native house. After tea was brought in he began to speak of the Ch'iang religion and its intimate resemblance to Judaism. He had been reading Genesis and Exodus. From this he launched out into the unknown origin of his race, at the same time strongly maintaining their equality with the Chinese, and superiority to the tribes further west of them. He was so well read and spoke so fluently that it was a pleasure to listen to him.

He was very receptive when Torrance talked to him about Christianity and they discussed sending one of his three sons to the mission school in Chengdu.

In Weizhou they met up again with Irene Hutchinson who had been much impacted by the 'warmth of feeling and heartiness' of the Qiang women. Ten women had attended the Bible classes from various villages and she was hopeful that one of them, who was particularly keen, would come down to Chengdu for further teaching.

They also coincided in Weizhou with David Graham of the American Baptist Mission in Yibin, who had been on a collecting trip for the Smithsonian Institute. Having collected several hundred birds and many boxes of insects and butterflies, he was now on his way to Miansi to hunt for rare animals. He was thankful to be able to dry his insect collection on the foreign stove in the Weizhou mission house and also took photos of 'Chiang aborigines' in the town.[27] On August 5 Graham wrote in his diary of his good fortune at meeting Torrance: 'He knows this region, and will put me in touch with a king of the aborigines who is a great hunter.'[28]

Above Miansi Graham had found a piece of skull and a jawbone, possibly from two different individuals, which he showed to Torrance. 'Mr. Torrance, F.R.G.S. thinks they are of the Sui Dynasty, at least 1,000 years old. He thinks they were mummified. The skin and flesh did not rot but dried on the bodies. Mr. Torrance sent a specimen of

27 H. Walravens (ed). *David Crockett Graham (1884-1961) as Zoological Collector and Anthropologist in China.* Opera Sinologica documenta 1. Weisbaden: Harrassowitz Verlag. 2006, p46.
28 Ibid., p63. Possibly referring to King Suo of the Wasi.

a hand to the British Museum. This is a very dry spot, and either they were mummified or else they dried up instead of rotting. The coffins, well preserved, are of wood.'[29] Graham added a further comment which was indicative of the speculation among foreigners about the history of this region. 'I would like to know what Dr. Hrdlicka finds about these bones. Are they Mongolian, Aryan, or aboriginal in type?'[30]

Leaving Miansi they headed back down the Min Valley. Despite suffering acutely from flea bites, young Tom had coped excellently with the trip and it left a deep impression. Years later he could still recall swimming in the fast-flowing Longxi stream with Torrance holding a rope tied round his waist, and sleeping in the open air next to his father on the roof of Huang Hanqing's family home. Huang's son was a similar age to Tom and a good playmate. Tom also enjoyed seeing the monkeys clambering around the rocks above the village and the shiny pieces of nephrite in the stream. Annie and the children were delighted to see them safely back at Lingyan, in time to enjoy the remainder of the summer in the hills.

They returned to Chengdu to find General Yang Sen proceeding apace with his reforms. On October 10 all the foreign residents were invited to the East Parade Ground to watch military manoeuvres, which included a march-past of about twelve thousand troops, thankfully followed by a luncheon. In November the WCMN reported that 'Our city is almost ready for rickshas! Our progressive Government have done much to hasten the day of faster communications, by widening and improving the surface of many streets.'[31]

It was with some relief that Torrance summed up 1924 for his ABS report: 'All's well that ends well. We began our year's work in Szechwan amid strife and turmoil and bloodshed. Yet, we have ended it in peace, and with a larger circulation than we at first anticipated.'[32] Positive sentiment towards the missionaries from many of the military and civil leaders had been a significant factor in their safe passage through an unpredictable year.

---

29 Ibid.
30 Ibid. Aleš Hrdlička was a Czech-American anthropologist and curator of the physical anthropology collections at the Smithsonian Institute. He would later develop the theory that the native Indians had reached America from Asia, crossing the Bering Strait.
31 WCMN, Nov 1924, p44.
32 BSR, June 1925, p101.

Chapter 12

'China for the Chinese'

1925-1926

In marked contrast to Torrance's optimistic 'all's well that ends well' at the end of 1924, he would describe 1925 as 'the gloomiest since 1900, the year of the Boxer uprising', and as events unfolded they were disturbingly reminiscent of that period, particularly the growing anti-Christian sentiment in some quarters.[1]

In the early 1920s Sun Yatsen's Nationalist Party and the Chinese Communist Party, founded in 1921, were both supported by the Soviets, who had encouraged Chinese Communist Party members to also join the Nationalist Party. In 1923 the Soviets sent Mikhail Borodin and other advisers to organise the Nationalists into a more effective revolutionary force and that same year Sun Yatsen sent a young general named Chiang Kai-shek to Moscow to study 'the Soviet military system, the political indoctrination of the Red army, and the methods of discipline in the Bolshevik Party'.[2] After his return to China Chiang was appointed by Sun to establish the Whampoa Military Academy outside Guangzhou, whose troops would eventually become the backbone of the Nationalist Party.

The Nationalists and Communists shared common goals in their desire to deliver China from foreign imperialism and from the fragmented warlordism it had suffered since 1912. However, the ultimate goal of the Soviets and the Chinese Communists was full control of the Nationalist Party, whereas Sun Yatsen was hoping that Communist support would facilitate his own form of revolution based on his 'Three People's Principles' of national independence, democratic rule, and a government concerned with the well-being of the Chinese people. In January 1924 the closeness of their early cooperation was clearly to be seen at the first Nationalist Congress when Li Dazhao, co-founder of the Communist Party, became a member of the new

---

1   TT. 'The 1925 Report of the American Bible Society in Szechuan'. In WCMN, Dec 1926, p16. Reprinted from the General Report of the A.B.S. for 1926.
2   Hsu, *Rise of Modern China*, p521.

Nationalist executive committee alongside Sun Yatsen, Hu Hanmin, Wang Jingwei, and Lin Sen. In July 1925, following Sun's untimely death from cancer, the left-leaning Wang Jingwei would become president of the 'National Government of the Republic of China' in Guangzhou, in opposition to the now highly unstable Beijing government, and with Chiang Kai-shek holding the military reins.

Although this mistrustful marriage of convenience between the Nationalists and Communists wouldn't last long, for now it brought a more radical element into the southern government, strengthening anti-Christian sentiment and increasing Soviet influence. A new Anti-Christian Federation was established, the old one having lost momentum, and a branch was opened in Sichuan. One of their activities was the production of anti-Christian literature and in December 1924 a week of demonstrations and literature distribution was organised in various cities to coincide with Christmas.[3]

By May 1925 the WCMN was reporting that the anti-Christian movement had 'come very close to some of us in its outward form of propaganda and noisy effort. It has invaded our schools and attracted some of our students.'[4] The same edition carried a translated extract from a pamphlet on sale in Chengdu, produced by The Young Men's Anti-Christian Society in Shanghai. Describing Christianity as an instrument of imperialism, its author argued passionately against the church, Christian education, and religion in general. In response, the WCMN editor urged readers to examine whether they were guilty of any accusations levelled at Christians in the pamphlet and later that year the president of the China Christian Educational Association, Timothy Tingfan Lew, also advised missionaries to emphasise the errors of their own nations rather than highlighting China's shortcomings, even if militarism and corruption were contributing to China's problems.[5]

At the end of May an incident in Shanghai took things to a much graver level. Following the death of a Chinese participant in a strike at a Japanese-owned cotton mill, a group of students were arrested in Shanghai's International Settlement as they made their way with banners to the worker's much-politicised funeral. On May 30, the day of their trial, more than two thousand students marched through the International Settlement, protesting against the trial and as a general

---

3   T. and S. Yamamoto. 'The Anti-Christian Movement in China, 1922-1927'. *The Far Eastern Quarterly*, Vol 12, No 2, Feb 1953, p135.
4   WCMN, May 1925, p2.
5   WCMN, Oct 1925, p20.

anti-foreign protest. More students were arrested and as feelings ran high some of the marchers surged towards the Settlement police station. Eventually members of the British-run police force opened fire and several students died, including one from Sichuan. Further clashes followed, leaving two dozen more dead and others wounded. Outrage erupted, spilling over to other cities where huge nationalistic demonstrations were held, protesting against imperialism and foreign privilege and fuelling the fire of anti-Christian sentiment.

Chongqing, home to the Communist Party headquarters in Sichuan, was one of the worst affected cities outside Shanghai. In early July all British women and children in the city were evacuated to Yichang by consular order and the men were gathered outside the city near the British naval moorings, dependent on city authority supplies because the locals refused to sell them any food. In Chengdu, protests extended to the West China Union University and although the situation was contained by Yang Sen and the unrest soon subsided, the effects would still be far-reaching.

As the WCMN noted succinctly, 'The shot from a rifle on Nanking Road in Shanghai was the period point to an era.'[6] In solidarity with those killed, many Chinese Christian students now adopted a stronger nationalistic stance and became greater advocates of 'China for the Chinese' and stronger opponents of the extraterritorial privileges still granted to foreigners. At the WCUU only twenty students enrolled for the 1925 summer courses compared to eighty the previous year. Nationalistic appeals were made to the WCUU students and others to leave Christian educational institutions and by November the Ministry of Education in Beijing had ordered all mission schools to come under government control, with the added requirement that all school heads must be Chinese and there should be no compulsory religious teaching.

A remark overheard by a Chongqing missionary from a usually friendly group of coolies brought home the gravity of the situation: 'They say we may kill foreigners if we wish.'[7] When one of Torrance's colporteurs was robbed by bandits they accused him of being a 'foreigner's proselyte' and 'a slave that had forgotten his country', epithets also thrown at Chinese Christians by students in Chengdu. Disappointed that the colporteur's load was literature rather than valuable merchandise, the

---

6   WCMN, Jan 1926, p3.
7   'The Anti-Christian Movement in Chungking in 1925'. (Anon.) WCMN, Feb 1926, p17. (The main articles in this issue were all anonymous, perhaps a precaution taken due to the prevalent hostility.)

bandits took his money and spare clothing, leaving him dependent upon the kindness of others to make it back to Chengdu.

Annie wrote in her memoirs that, 'The communists seemed to be active everywhere and they were exceedingly anti-foreign. Life was getting precarious in many ways and we began to wonder if we could possibly stay on.'[8] Going to teach at the Chinese boys' school one morning she experienced the hostility first-hand. As she went past in her sedan chair some young Communist sympathisers shouted 'Kill, kill'. Knowing that some of her own students had Communist leanings she was loath to continue her classes but promised the principal she would complete the term. To Torrance's surprise, while Annie was at school one day, some of the students came to ask him to persuade Annie to stay on and teach them the following year. Never one to miss an opportunity, he gave them all a New Testament, promised he would try, and she continued to teach without any further problems.

Alongside the student uprisings across China, Sichuan was facing its own provincial problems. In May 1925, Duan Qirui, head of the northern government in Beijing, had dismissed Yang Sen as Sichuan's military governor and appointed Liu Xiang in his place. Yang had refused to step down and instead launched a major offensive to take control of the whole of Sichuan. However, at a critical point in the conflict Yang's commander-in-chief defected to Liu, and Yang was forced to retreat, fighting as he went. As his troops retreated to Leshan the conflict was, as the WCMN reported, 'never so severe, and never have the soldiers been so lawless and cruel, nor the people so unmercifully taxed as these last few weeks . . . the stories of suffering are enough to make one's hair turn grey.'[9] In October's WCMN, Leshan was described as 'a little hell' that was 'black with flies' as hundreds died of starvation and the remaining population suffered nightly bombardments. The editor justified the inclusion of such a grim description because 'it should be known that this province is practically in a state of lawlessness. There is very little real government and less protection.'[10] Dr Leslie Kilborn, a lecturer at the WCUU who was passing through Leshan on his way to Chengdu by boat, was shot in the back and spent weeks in hospital.

In a section entitled 'Shall We Go Home?' that same editorial echoed Annie's concerns. Unable to work effectively amidst all the troubles it was a question in many missionaries' minds, perhaps more so because

8 *Memoirs*, p93.
9 WCMN, July 1925, p34.
10 WCMN, Oct 1925, p2.

Bishop Mowll and others at a CMS hill retreat near Mianzhu, north of Chengdu, had been kidnapped by bandits in August and held with minimal provisions for over three weeks. Mowll attributed their capture and the general chaos in Sichuan to Yang Sen's loss of power. The editor concluded that it seemed best to stay unless consular orders came to leave.

There were no references to a trip to the Qiang in Torrance's 1925 ABS report and it seems to have been too dangerous for him to travel. Instead, he had sent his colporteurs to the Miansi region and the Zagunao Valley, where eight locals had become church members, two of whom were from a 'fresh tribe, whose chief is anxious I should go personally and extend the work among them.'[11] It was clear that much was happening in Torrance's absence.

Added to this, Gou Pinsan, who had been a Christian four years by this time, had written a record of Qiang customs in his native area, comparing them with lamb sacrifice in the Old Testament. In it he encouraged people to examine the similarities for themselves and gain understanding of another people who pay their vows.

A Special Report on Lamb Sacrifice in the Old Testament and Similarities in My Native Area[12] by Gou Pinsan (Hongru)

The place where our ancestors set up their sacrificial altar to pay their vows had to be at the top of a rocky mountain. This signifies Jehovah God meeting with Moses at the top of Mount Sinai and revealing himself to the people of Israel. (Exodus 19:16-25)[13]

Our public meeting place for the paying of vows must be in a special grove of trees which is called 'the sacred grove', or it can also be in a place where there are just several trees. This signifies Jehovah appearing to Abraham at the oaks of Mamre. (Genesis 18:1)

The place where we sacrifice and pay our vows must be a place with thorns and stones. In front of these a fire is lit. This signifies Jehovah God appearing to Moses at Mount Horeb in the burning thorn bush. (Exodus 3:1-11)

---

11 TT. 'The 1925 Report of the American Bible Society in Szechuan'. WCMN, Dec 1926, p19.
12 Translated by the author.
13 The Bible references are in Gou Pinsan's original document. The Chinese verb, translated here as 'signifies', is *biaoming* (表明), also 'to show' or 'to indicate'.

When we sacrifice and pay our vows, we must erect a stone at the place where we slay the sheep. This signifies Jacob at Bethel, where he had a dream from God and erected the stone he had used as a pillow to serve as a pillar of remembrance, marking the location as God's house and a permanent place of sacrifice. (Genesis 28:10-22)

On our rooftops we build a platform and set up a pointed white stone to the only, most revered, true God. This signifies Jehovah God coming down and appearing on the top of Mount Sinai (the point of the white stone representing the mountain top). (Exodus 19)

When we pay our vows to heaven, we insert one or three tree branches behind the white stone. This expresses the tree of life and the tree of the knowledge of good and evil in the Garden of Eden, which Jehovah God prohibited to Adam, the first ancestor.

When we pay our vows on the rooftop, we light a fire in front of the white stone, which signifies Jehovah God coming down in fire on Mount Sinai. (Exodus 19:18)

When we offer the sacrifice, we take grass and dip it in the bowl of sheep's blood, and sprinkle the blood on the sacrificial altar and on the white flags. This signifies that with the sprinkling of the blood of atonement, great calamity can be passed over. (Exodus 12:8-20)

When we offer the sacrifice and pay our vows, we make round unleavened flatbreads of barley flour and offer them in front of the white stone. This signifies the observance of the feast of unleavened bread, when food must not contain yeast. (Exodus 12:8-20)

When we offer the sacrifice and pay our vows, we make large white paper flags with one long point and two short points, signifying the triune nature of Jehovah God, the three in one.

During the sacrifice and paying of vows the lamb is slain and after the blood is sprinkled, the head and tail of the sheep and the fat next to the loins and around the innards, in their entirety, are cut up a little and burned on the altar. This signifies making a burnt offering to Jehovah, as a fragrant burnt sacrifice. (Leviticus 3)

During the paying of vows some blood is smeared on the lintel and on the door frame. This signifies when Jehovah brought disaster on Egypt and commanded the Israelites to smear blood on the door frame as a mark so that He would pass over them when he saw the blood. When disaster strikes it won't come near us. (Exodus 12:7-15)

During the sacrificial paying of vows, we take a handful of fine flour and shape it into images of cattle and sheep. These are placed on a stone platter of burning cypress branches and offered on the altar to be burned along with the branches. This signifies the meal offering or an offering by fire. (Leviticus 2:1-3)

During the sacrificial paying of vows, we use a measure of wheat, or it can be highland barley, both are acceptable, and when the beibu[14] prays, he sprinkles several handfuls of this on the altar. This signifies ripened produce serving as a grain sacrifice offered to Jehovah. (Leviticus 2:14-16)

During the sacrificial paying of vows, after the sheep meat has been divided up for eating, the beibu burns the fat on the altar. He also takes a leg and breast and lifts them above the platter with the burning cypress branches and waves them in a circle three times. This signifies the offering of a leg as a wave offering before the altar of the Jehovah. (Leviticus 7:30-34)

On the parapet of every home, twelve white flags are inserted and twelve sheets of white paper are hung up. This signifies the twelve tribes, representing their twelve rods. (Numbers 17)

In the ancient rituals of our ancestors, seven days, one month, or forty days after the birth of the first-born son, the baby is brought before the white stone on the rooftop and the priest is asked to pray. He takes a white thread and ties it around the child's neck. He then cuts the thread and names the child. This signifies the rite of circumcision and that the child is offered to God. (Leviticus 12)

When we have a male child, no matter what age they are, they are not allowed to go to the public altar and share the meat of the sacrifice until they lead a sheep or bring a chicken. According to the protocol for the paying of vows, when this sacrifice is offered on the public altar the priest is asked to pray and a white thread is placed on the child's neck and then cut. Oil is then daubed on the child's head. This signifies bringing a circumcised, anointed person as an offering to God. The people all give the child an unleavened wheat flatbread as a sign of honour.

Whenever an individual household pays their vows to heaven, they use a white clay paste to paint several trees on the outer walls of the home. This signifies that they are in obedience to God. The sheep's blood has atoned for their former sins, so they draw the tree of life on the wall, which signifies that they are following God's command to be pure white and sinless.

---

14 Beibu (被不) is the Qiang term used here by Gou Pinsan for the Qiang priest. Nowadays the term shibi (释比) is commonly used.

In ancient times, when the Beibu (commonly referred to in Chinese as *duangong* or *wushi*)[15] performed the paying of vows ceremony, he would wear ceremonial sacrificial clothing. On the back of this an altar was embroidered, with a tree above the altar. A study of the meaning of this shows that it signifies Adam, the first ancestor, who went against God's command and was tempted by the devil and ate the fruit of the tree of the knowledge of good and evil, a sin which was then passed down to his descendants. The priest, in accordance with God's will, used the sheep's blood for atonement of sin and this was an ancient foretelling of the Saviour coming into the world and shedding his precious blood to atone for the sins of all people. For this reason the priest has the tree of life embroidered on his garment. It is something which draws people's attention, warning them to avoid breaking Jehovah's commandments.

The sheep which is offered as a sacrifice must have all six aspects without blemish: the horns, ears, tail, legs, eyes, and nostrils. This signifies when Jehovah, in ancient times, carefully instructed Moses that the Passover lamb must be without blemish. (Exodus 12:5)

The sheep offered in the paying of vows to heaven must be mostly white, and if that is not the case, then a white chicken must also be offered to compensate for this deficiency. This signifies Jehovah's acceptance of pure white.

The Beibu has a 'Jizu' deity.[16] In ancient times coarse grass would be bunched together, tied in the form of a person, and white paper would be wrapped around it. Whenever a sacrifice was held another layer of white paper would be added. In recent years the skull of a golden monkey has been used instead. This signifies 'Jizu' coming down from heaven and atoning for people's sins. Therefore, at the sacrificial paying of vows, it is taken to the altar with the lamb and set up there. The lamb foretells the atonement of sin. 'Jizu' coming into the world means the actual atonement of sins.

---

15 In brackets Gou gives terms which, to the Chinese, were the closest equivalent to the Qiang priest. The terms *duangong* (端公) and *wushi* (巫师) indicate someone dealing with the supernatural and are sometimes translated as 'shaman' or 'sorcerer' but neither is an exact equivalent of the Qiang priest, who serves as a mediator between the villagers and the spiritual realm and officiates at ritual ceremonies but does not traditionally go into a trance. His daily work is often farming like many of the villagers.

16 This 'Jizu' (姬租) is Gou Pinsan's choice of Chinese characters to represent a Qiang term for this roll of white paper and its contents. Torrance had come across various pronunciations for the 'Jizu' which he transcribed as 'Je-Dsu', 'Nee Dsu', 'Jay Dsu', and 'Gee Dsu'.

Anyone training to be a Beibu priest must study in depth how the priest prays, offers sacrifices, and pays vows. When the study period is complete, a day is chosen when the old Beibu priest is asked to go to the sacrificial altar in the sacred grove, where the trainee is officially accepted in this role. On the preceding night the old Beibu priest takes the trainee to a gully with water in it. If there is not enough water, a pool is dug in advance, and the trainee is washed in the water. This signifies getting rid of the old dirty stains and that he can now go to the sacrificial altar and be accepted. Only then can he pray to God.

After the older Beibu priest has led the trainee through this washing, they go up to the sacrificial altar in the sacred grove to complete the offering of sacrifice. They go up to the mountain top and the older priest daubs some oil on the forehead of the trainee and then places a 'Beida' hat[17] on his head. This signifies being anointed for the office of priest. Only after the new priest has been anointed can he wear the priestly hat. In earlier times the older priest would cleanse the trainee priest in the water the day before the ceremony.

In an added note Gou made it clear that he saw the Old Testament sacrifice of a lamb as a foreshadowing of Jesus' atoning sacrifice, which meant that animal sacrifice was no longer needed for being cleansed from unrighteousness. He also included a lengthy tribute to Torrance, praising his courage and persistence in bringing the gospel to the Qiang area with its 'myriad mountain paths, twisting and winding like sheep intestines'. Noting Torrance's own discovery of the biblical similarities, Gou expressed gratitude for the Bible study classes and the establishment of the Qiang church and also recognised Chen Bingling's work among the Qiang. At the end of the tribute he made clear that this was just a first draft which would later be carved in stone and placed 'within the gospel hall as a permanent memorial', suggesting plans were already afoot for a purpose-built church building.

In the autumn Torrance had to go to Chongqing on ABS business but was back in time to attend the West China Missions Advisory Board conference in November, as representative for the Bible Societies.[18] The conference reflected the changing times, with increased Chinese participation at leadership level, including two graduates of the WCUU, and when the question of opium was raised, it was suggested that any

---

17 被达帽.
18 There were three in Sichuan at the time: the American Bible Society, the British & Foreign Bible Society, and the National Bible Society of Scotland.

further petition to the provincial government about the matter should come from Chinese members of the Sichuan Christian Council rather than the foreigners.

In December, despite another Christmas week of aggressive anti-Christian activity in Chengdu, there was a glimmer of hope regarding the wider political situation in Sichuan. In an effort to end the military chaos, General Liu Xiang convened a lengthy Sichuan Reconstruction Conference which began on December 26 and concluded on February 11, 1926, two days before Chinese New Year. This brought together representatives from civil organisations such as the Chengdu and Chongqing chambers of commerce, as well as agricultural and educational bodies and delegates from each of Sichuan's 148 districts. Indicating just how fragmented the province was militarily, there were military representatives from 'thirty-five divisions, twenty-nine mixed brigades, and nineteen independent brigades, plus sixteen other military leaders'.[19]

The impact on Chengdu of this gathering of generals was considerable. 'Each general, fearing treachery, brought all his ragamuffin soldiers. Like the rats of Hamelin, they flooded shops, schools, private residences – more than one hundred thousand of them.'[20] In one instance, four soldiers tried to commandeer an old man's kitchen. When he protested they tied him up, beat him, and sent him to their captain, who was shocked to see that the man was one of his former teachers. He released the man and had the soldiers shot.

Yang Sen took the risk of accepting an invitation to the conference – to his cost. Camped out on Chengdu's southern parade ground, his men found themselves surrounded before dawn by troops of Liu Wenhui and forced to surrender. Yang had been sleeping elsewhere and managed to escape but many of his men were enlisted by Liu Wenhui. Tragically, some students in a school next to the parade ground were killed by stray bullets in the fracas.

The conference resulted in a rather optimistic commitment to 're-establish a locus of legitimate authority in Szechwan and to restore stability to Szechwan's disrupted political and social affairs.'[21] Civil war was to be renounced by the Sichuanese armies and a clear legal divide was to exist between the military leaders and the civil administration.

19 Kapp, *Szechwan and the Chinese Republic*, pp21-22.
20 'The Chengtu Incident'. WCMN, March 1926, p16.
21 Kapp, *Szechwan and the Chinese Republic*, p22.

Military abuses of the local population were addressed, with more streamlining of currency and tax systems, and a supposed end to any military cooperation with local militias and robber bands. Having cast off any allegiance to Beijing, the province was now also paying lip-service to the southern government whose energies were directed elsewhere, leaving Sichuan in practice still relatively independent.[22]

1926

For the missionary community 1926 began with a degree of stability. Anti-Christian sentiment was restricted mainly to student circles and normal activities were able to continue. Over Chinese New Year, the missionaries and Chinese Christians went ahead with a city-wide literature distribution which was well received but there was no doubt, after the events of 1925, that many of the missionaries were feeling pressure to re-think their approach to things. Several of the missions had annual conferences early in the year where serious discussions were held regarding the government move to regulate Christian education and the growing pressure to abolish extraterritoriality. The foreigners understood Chinese resentment of their privileges but many feared, in such a lawless and politically volatile environment, that a removal of extraterritorial concessions would leave them at the mercy of potentially subjective and whimsical Chinese law enforcement.

That spring Torrance deemed it safe enough to make an evangelistic trip to the south of Chengdu in the company of Gou Pinsan, who had come down in the winter to get some experience working alongside him.[23] Together with two colporteurs and Mr Lu – a highly educated and gifted speaker who was secretary of the YMCA – they travelled to the Meishan region. In most places they were warmly welcomed but in one particular town, where they stayed three days, their preaching didn't go down well with some military officers and well-to-do gamblers on the town's main street. To Mr Lu's surprise, Gou Pinsan – the 'tribesman' – gave the street audience 'such a learned address on the descent of the Chinese into idolatry, quoting classics and histories so easily' that he took Lu's breath away.[24] At another place Gou opened the meeting and 'discoursed earnestly on the fact of the Old Testament sacrifices foreshadowing the work of Christ'. In a later short biography of Gou, Torrance recalled once asking him in Chengdu what he thought of a

22 Ibid.
23 TT to Carleton Lacy, April 15, 1926.
24 Ibid.

trainee Chinese preacher's sermon about the Cross. 'Ah,' replied Gou, 'he has not arrived there himself.'[25]

Edith Sibley

On Monday, June 7, the missionary community was shocked to its core. Passing close to the ABS depot on his way home for lunch, George Hartwell came across the body of a foreign woman so badly mutilated he didn't at first recognise her. One of the Torrance servants ran to ask Torrance if Annie was home 'because a foreign woman is lying dead on the street not far away'.[26] George Franck then rushed in asking for a sheet and hurried back with Torrance to where the woman lay, by which time the Consul had been sent for and the body was taken to the Canadian hospital. The victim was Canadian missionary Edith Sibley, aged forty-seven and a talented musician. She and her husband William were on a short visit to Chengdu from their station in Rongxian, south of Chengdu. Edith had gone out shopping when suddenly, according to eye-witnesses, the assailant cursed and slapped her and, as she turned away, attacked her from behind with a long knife. He managed to flee but was then caught and shot while resisting arrest. The wild Boxer-like appearance of the assailant led officials to conclude that he was disturbed but some suspected he had been hired to attack a foreigner.[27]

Edith had visited the Torrances just the day before and their sorrow was great. The situation became even more poignant when they discovered that the assailant had been sitting in a teashop near the ABS and Annie, who had arrived home just before the incident, realised she could easily have been the victim. Once again she was hesitant to continue her various classes and on her next visit to the Canadian girls' school her Chinese pupils were clustered at the windows, waiting to see if she would turn up. The British Consul advised foreign women not to go out unescorted and for a while Torrance accompanied Annie to her classes but this took too much time out of his day. She then tried going with one of their long-standing servants but it was too hard on him, with accusations such as 'foreign devil's servant' thrown at him on the street. Eventually she decided she would have to trust God and go on her own, taking her umbrella to inspire bravery! One educated, middle-aged man had taken to regularly cursing her as she passed his home.

25 TT. 'The Story of Isaac Whiteheart'. Chapter 21 in *Conversion Stories of Chinese Christians*.
26 *Memoirs*, p96.
27 WCMN, July 1926, pp53-55.

The children were also affected and it was arranged for those living in the city to be escorted to and from their school on the WCUU campus. Annie was sometimes part of the escort and was startled one day by a woman catching hold of her arm and pulling her to a fruit stand at the side of the road. But it was nothing hostile. She recognised Annie from her visits to the women's hospital and wanted to buy her some fruit in gratitude for her kindness.

Possibly in response to Edith Sibley's death, Torrance wrote an article in 1926 entitled 'The Chinese Cat', which contained veiled criticism of the lawless situation across China.[28] At first glance it seemed to be a light-hearted exploration of Chinese cat-lore, with references to the Book of Rites and Book of Odes, and it was a good illustration of Torrance's cultural curiosity and his sense of humour. Confessing at the outset his own lack of affection for cats and that the paper was more about a Chinese perspective than the cats themselves, Torrance noted that cats were kept to control the despised rat population and then discussed the optimum kind of cat for rat-catching.

He concluded the article with a reference to cats and rats sleeping together, a Chinese idiom for collusion between enemies, which was aimed at the current political turmoil. Not only were the rats (bandits) and cats (soldiers) colluding but the rats were actually becoming cats, which now came in all sorts of colours, with even a 'new breed of reds in Canton'.[29] This last comment revealed how left-wing Torrance perceived the Nationalist government in Guangzhou to be at this point. Coincidentally, a cartoon in a Nationalist magazine that May depicted the Communists as a large rat gnawing through the pillars of the Nationalist Party.[30] Alarmed at the growth of Communist influence, Chiang Kai-shek was already introducing measures to restrict their power.

That summer, Tom, nearly thirteen, accompanied his father again to the Qiang area and was particularly impacted by their visit to A'er, the village eight miles up the Longxi Valley from Dongmenwai, which Torrance, Gou, and Chen had visited in 1921. This time the Qiang priest wanted to meet Torrance for a discussion about religious customs. He described their annual sacrificial ceremony where, after three days of purification, the village headman and the priest would

28 TT. 'The Chinese Cat'. JNCBRAS, Vol 57, 1926, pp113-122.
29 Ibid, p121.
30 Donald A. Jordan. *The Northern Expedition: China's National Revolution of 1926-1928*. University of Hawaii Press. 1976, p58. The cartoonist was Liang Yuming, the magazine was the *Geming Huabao* (*Revolutionary Pictorial*).

take two goats to the sacred grove. Present at the ceremony were the priest's sacred rod and the sacred roll of paper, around which the new piece of white paper was wrapped every year, symbolising purity. One of the goats would be killed on the first day and its blood sprinkled on the low stone altar to the accompaniment of the priest's chants. On the second day, they would lay their hands on the other goat and then release it into the wild.

When the priest finished describing the details of the ceremony, Torrance read to him in Chinese the annual Jewish atonement ritual, as recorded in chapter sixteen of the book of Leviticus, with its strict guidelines for purification. The Levitical ritual included the presentation of two goats before the Lord as a sin offering, one of which was sacrificed while the other was released into the wilderness after Aaron had laid his hands on its head and confessed the sins of Israel. The priest was deeply impressed by the similarities and declared that these were the lost Scriptures of the Qiang, represented now by the sacred scroll which was always present at their annual sacrifice. Torrance then took the opportunity to talk of the parallels with Jesus as the Lamb of God who had atoned for sin.

When Torrance and Tom returned to Lingyan the atmosphere seemed less relaxed than usual and the local authorities, concerned about anti-foreign sentiment, had stationed several Chinese soldiers in the area. At the end of the summer, for the first time, the family travelled back by bus on the newly completed road from Guanxian to Chengdu – much quicker but with a driver who 'drove like Jehu'.[31]

In the autumn things took a severe turn for the worse in Sichuan, particularly for the British. Yang Sen, who was now governing part of eastern Sichuan from his headquarters in Wanxian on the Yangtze River, had been in dispute with British shipping companies over their refusal to transport Chinese troops. Reports vary regarding the details but in late August, following attempts by Yang's troops to board the British steamers docked in Wanxian, one steamer, the Wanliu, tried to get away and in so doing caused the sinking of two sampans carrying troops out to the steamer, which resulted in considerable loss of life.[32] In response,

---

31 *Memoirs*, p94. In 2 Kings 9:20 Jehu is recorded as driving his chariot furiously.
32 See A. R. Williamson, 'The Wanhsien Incident'; A. K. Lortsen, 'The Battle of Wanhsien'. Both at https://www.naval-history.net/WW1xMemoir-Wanhsein.htm

Yang seized two other steamers, the Wantung and the Wanhsien, each with a Chinese crew and three British ship's officers on board.

Negotiations to release the ships proved fruitless and the British Navy sent gunboats to intervene. In the fighting that followed, Commander Darley, in charge of the operation, was killed, as were two other officers and four regular marines. Still failing to release the ships and coming under heavy fire from Yang's men on the river bank, the British turned their guns on the shore and on Yang's yamen. The fighting lasted less than two hours but resulted in the death of civilians as well as a serious fire in the business section of the city. The Navy then retreated but made it clear that they would return with greater force unless the ships were released. Despite pressure from the local chamber of commerce to back down, Yang initially refused and by the time he released the steamers on September 23 the incident had become a major point of contention between China and Britain, and the casualties and destruction in Wanxian had further fuelled anti-foreign sentiment.

THE LOONG MOW, RENAMED SS WANLIU IN 1923.[33]

Compounding this, in July the Nationalist Party, still united with the Communists, had begun their Northern Expedition in a bid to defeat Wu Peifu's northern forces and bring all of China under Nationalist control. As they moved north from Guangzhou, with a very active left-wing contingent heading for Wuhan, the leftists among them 'began an active campaign against Christianity. Looting and killing began. Property of Christians was plundered and destroyed, churches and schools were

---

33 This photo, perhaps originally a postcard, appears on the back cover of *Glimpses of the Yangtze Gorges* by Cornell Plant, Kelly & Walsh Limited, 1921. The photo here is in The Thomas F. Torrance Manuscript Collection at Princeton Theological Seminary Library, Special Collections, Box 200.

occupied.[34] In Sichuan, the Nationalists had also been courting Liu Xiang and Liu Wenhui, wanting to preclude any hostility on their western flank, and the two Lius were now openly supportive of them.

In line with this, Liu Wenhui, who had control of the army in Chengdu, was moving his own men into top posts at local schools, giving him influence over the student population and enabling the Communists in Chengdu to act more freely. In response to the Wanxian incident, and with the lines between political ideology and straightforward patriotism becoming increasingly blurred, a boycott of foreigners was called for – with Liu's approval. At the WCUU, which was a primary target with so many foreigners on staff, more than thirty students left and pressure was exerted on other students to boycott classes.[35] Although this was rejected, pressure was then brought to bear on the servants' union on campus to call a boycott, with a daily payment promised to any servant who refused to work for their foreign employers.

An appeal was made to General Deng Xihou, who was in charge of the Chengdu police force, to intervene but he was in a fragile power-sharing agreement with Liu Wenhui and didn't want a confrontation with Liu's men. Deng was officially superior to Liu but had been appointed by Wu Peifu in Beijing so the recent announcement by Liu Wenhui and Liu Xiang of allegiance to the Nationalists had made his position less secure. In the end he instructed his police to watch over the foreigners in the city but didn't obstruct the boycott.

Torrance would later write to the ABS in New York in praise of Deng and his actions at this time: 'General Teng [Deng] the leading militarist there was a warm friend of ours. He came to our A.B.S. place and had tea with us when the agitators were straining every nerve to undo our influence in the city. And at a public function in the full glare of all the leading men in the place he escorted me once to the very front of the big audience and put me in his own seat there.'[36]

As the boycott spread from the university to the city, anyone found still working for foreigners or selling them food was fined or beaten. A few were paraded during street demonstrations, labelled with the crime of being foreign lackeys. The Torrances' cook and other house staff apologetically said they too would have to obey the boycott but not before they had baked several loaves of bread to keep the family going. Annie had encouraged them to leave for their own safety but

34 Yamamoto, *Anti-Christian Movement in China*, p135.
35 Stapleton, *Fact in Fiction*, Kindle Edition.
36 TT to Dr Haven, June 22, 1927.

one or two nonetheless turned up secretly with food for the family. Another young man who liked to talk with Torrance turned up with a small suitcase of vegetables and on one evening the cook and his young assistant slipped in after dark and insisted on baking all night. They stole away before dawn, leaving enough bread to last until the boycott was over. Thankfully, there were many Chinese who did not support the protest and several exerted their influence to help resolve the situation. In the end, the boycott, accompanied by anti-foreign posters pasted around the city, lasted about two weeks.[37]

It was a time of great complexity for both the foreigners and the Chinese Christians, something which was very evident at the annual conference of the National Christian Council (NCC) that autumn, held in Shanghai and attended by 51 Chinese and 39 foreigners, including Harry Openshaw. The gathering was a watershed moment for the missionaries and the Chinese church, as illustrated by two addresses in particular, one by Dr David Yui of the YMCA and the other by Leung Siu-choh, also a YMCA representative and chairman of the local NCC council in Guangdong, the home of the Nationalist government.

Whilst acknowledging the church's gratitude to the missionaries, both Yui and Leung were anxious to see them take a back seat and let the Chinese church take the lead. Leung used the analogy of scaffolding being dismantled once a building could stand independently. They also emphasised the need for a patriotic church, aligned with the Nationalists and supporting the removal of foreign privileges. Yui felt that winning the approval of the Nationalists was a key to the expansion of church influence and although Openshaw described his address as 'in an entirely friendly spirit', Yui took the opportunity to express his discomfort with the superior attitude of some missionaries, the excess of imported Western church traditions, and the nationalistic attitude of some with regard to their own home countries.[38]

Leung's address went further. Outlining three stages in missionary work – pioneering, co-working, and the move to local independence – he suggested practical steps which could be taken to hasten the transition to the third stage, essentially advocating that all mission work and funds, except for missionary salaries and expenses, come under the administration of the national Chinese church, with the

---

37 WCMN, Dec 1926, p41.
38 H. J. Openshaw. 'National Christian Council Annual Meeting'. WCMN, Dec 1926, p7.

missionaries in support roles under the Chinese, unless democratically elected to leadership. Although he still foresaw a role for missionaries in this third stage, he anticipated the Chinese Church dealing directly with overseas mission boards, administering funds in accordance with the wishes of foreign donors, and being involved in the placement of missionaries. He recognised that some missionaries would need convincing that the Chinese were ready for overall leadership but, he warned, 'we may sometimes be so absorbed in doing things ourselves that we have neglected to read the signs of the times.'

Leung knew that his suggestions would be a step too far for many: 'I am not at all surprised that some of you think that what I have outlined above sounds almost like heresy or bolshevism.'[39] Part of his argument was that he had seen such transition work successfully in the YMCA but this was seen by some as particularly liberal in its Christianity and many were wary of a political, cerebral Christianity which had lost the essence of the gospel message. And while many missionaries, like Torrance, wanted to see the growth of a self-governing church, they wanted to see a self-supporting church taking increasing responsibility for its own finances rather than dependent on overseas giving. Torrance was also worried that a single national church structure might be vulnerable to political subversion, even though some saw it as preferable to the denominationalism of the foreigners.

One thing about which the conference delegates were unanimous was their conviction that 'all provisions in the treaties with foreign countries for special privileges for the churches or missions should be removed' and also that 'the present treaties between China and foreign powers should be revised on a basis of freedom and equality.'[40]

The climate of change was spreading fast and in Chengdu, at the annual meeting of the Sichuan Christian Council in December, it was recommended that church buildings should simply be known as Chinese Christian churches and no longer bear the names of the foreign missions with which they were affiliated. It was also acknowledged that 'the progress of the Chinese church from now on will not depend on missionaries or funds from abroad but on the Chinese themselves.'[41] Another recommendation, which would eventually become a

---

39 Leung Siu Choh. 'How May the Missions and Missionaries Best Serve the Chinese Church at the Present Time?' WCMN, Dec 1926, p29.
40 H. J. Openshaw. 'National Christian Council Annual Meeting'. WCMN, Dec 1926, p9.
41 WCMN, Jan 1927, p9.

significant part of church policy, was that all churches should engage in social service.

The combination of Edith Sibley's death, the street demonstrations, and the boycott, had placed Annie and Torrance under great strain, not least because of their concern for the children. That winter some of the Qiang came again to stay for Bible study and to help Torrance with his research. On Christmas morning, stockings emptied and presents opened, Annie was having a late breakfast when Mary ran in to say that students were at the front gate giving Torrance a bad time. Annie found Torrance and the Qiang gathered at the ABS entrance where a 'great crowd of hostile folk were clamouring and shouting led by students', some of whom were from the law school next door.[42] Taking turns to stand on a wooden bench they had brought with them, the students were boldly delivering their declamations against foreign Christians. As the children peeped from behind the inner gate, Annie joined Torrance and the Qiang. Together they stood their ground and kept silent, fearing an attack if they turned their backs. Suddenly one of the students launched a tirade against the Bible and without stopping to think, Annie pointed at him and said, 'God will punish you for those terrible words.' That somehow defused the situation and the students slowly dispersed.[43]

It was a relief to retreat safely inside. A while later the front gate opened again and they held their breath. To their surprise, in walked a group of women whom Annie had taught. 'We have come to protect you,' they said. Annie was afraid they would pay the price for their courageous support but they were a welcome sight. From that time on she often lay awake at night, torn between the danger of staying and the worry of returning home with no idea how they would manage financially. But the thought of being back in Britain was becoming a very real prospect and 'though we have to live in a slum – it will be heaven for the children's sake.'[44]

---

42 *Memoirs*, p97.
43 Torrance would later discover that this student was one of fourteen who were shot in the spring of 1928 having been involved in the death of a school principal in Chengdu. See TT, March 24, 1929, diary to children.
44 *Memoirs*, p98.

PART THREE

Chapter 13

Unrest and Separation

1927-1928

As Torrance and Annie pondered the best course of action for the family the decision was taken out of their hands. That winter the left-leaning Nationalist government, led by Wang Jingwei and much influenced by Russian adviser Mikhail Borodin, had established itself in Wuhan, with the departments for workers and farmers placed directly under Communist leadership. As a result, 'political activism more radical than any seen in Guangzhou now inflamed Wuhan and its province.'[1] On January 3, 1927, Chinese crowds forced their way into the British concession in Hankou, which was part of the newly created Wuhan metropolis. Not wanting to add to the ill-feeling generated by the May Thirtieth and Wanxian incidents, the small group of British marines guarding the Hankou concession withdrew, marking a turning point for the Chinese that they had wrested control of a foreign-administrated area.[2]

Shortly after the Hankou incident Annie arrived home from her classes one day to the news that the Consul was ordering all women and children to leave Chengdu. Word then came from Shanghai that the ABS had brought the family's furlough forward so that they could travel as a family to Scotland. The sense of relief was palpable but as they rushed to pack, Annie and the children had the heartache of sudden and perhaps final good-byes to foreign and Chinese friends, not knowing if they would ever return. Hearing the news, Annie's Chinese friends came again for a sorrowful farewell. 'As I passed out of the compound and gate,' wrote Annie, 'I felt I was leaving a large part of myself behind – I felt it dreadfully. We were leaving behind all that had been so dear and we knew not where we should go and what home we might have in the homeland.'[3] It was also a sad farewell

---

1 Robert Bickers. *Out of China*. Penguin Books Ltd. 2017, p63.
2 Ibid., p64. Under the Chen-O'Malley agreement the concession was placed under a joint British-Chinese administration until 1929.
3 *Memoirs,* p98.

to the animals – Billy and Prince, Rover the dog, and Tom's pigeons. Annie and Torrance had already made the hard decision that Torrance would probably return alone after the furlough and he now stayed a little longer in Chengdu to sort out ABS affairs and temporarily close the house down before joining the others in Shanghai.

FAREWELL TO BILLY, JANUARY 1927

The departure was China-wide and few remained of the more than eight thousand Protestant missionaries in China, with barely twenty in Chengdu by the end of January. The sudden exodus meant boats were scarce but Annie and the children eventually set out for Chongqing as part of a flotilla of evacuees, thankful that Jiu Si, one of the servants who often took care of David, had insisted on coming too. Before long it was clear that their boat was badly lagging behind. Once it got too dark to travel the captain wanted to drop anchor but men were gambling on the bank and Annie urged him to keep going. He refused at first but after waiting quietly until the moon was bright enough, they weighed anchor at 3am and moved off undetected.

With the six children in her care it was a testing time for Annie and to make matters worse, the boat was sitting unusually low in the water and leaking. The boatmen managed to stuff the cracks with wadding from their padded garments but it was a struggle to keep going. All was revealed when the boat reached a customs station just outside Chongqing and the crew were arrested for concealing an illegal cargo of saltpetre, used in the manufacture of explosives.

The family had hoped to wait in Chongqing for Torrance but anti-foreign feeling was running high and they had no choice but to continue. Under the watchful gaze of British gunboats they were transferred to a waiting steamer, relieved that the frightening journey from Chengdu was over. It was a tearful parting for Jiu Si as he carried David on to the ship and said good-bye. Thankful for a cabin to themselves, large and basic with wooden plank beds, Annie and the children settled in for the journey down the Yangtze.

As it emerged from a stretch of turbulent rapids, the ship suddenly came under fire from the river bank, sending Tom diving to the deck as a bullet whizzed past. The captain ordered the family up to the steel-plated bridge and told them to lie on the floor as noisy firing came from both sides of the river. David, not yet three, refused to lie down and Annie knelt to shelter him, suddenly sensing as she did that God would protect them all even as she was protecting David. In the end no-one was injured but the ship was peppered with bullets, two of which came home with Tom. After transfers at Yichang and Hankou they finally arrived in Shanghai where Annie got the children vaccinated against scarlet fever and diphtheria, a timely decision as they heard later that two missionary children had caught diphtheria on their way home. As another precaution, once Torrance arrived he and Annie both wrote wills, each bequeathing everything to the other, and in the event of both dying, leaving everything in the hands of Cousin Jeannie in Bromley who, as the children's guardian, was to use the funds for the children's support and education.

With several other missionary families they sailed on the *City of Calcutta*, an old part-cargo ship which had served as a troop carrier in the First World War. Stopping at Saigon, Singapore, Colombo, Port Said, and Marseilles, the older children had the excitement of going ashore with Torrance, whilst Annie usually stayed on board with James and David. It was a particularly happy time and a tonic for them to relax as a family, enjoying the on-board activities and the company of other passengers.

On arrival in England, Torrance and Tom went straight to Scotland to start house-hunting while Annie and the other five children stayed in Bromley. On June 22 Torrance sent an update to Dr Haven at the ABS in New York from 96 Calder Road in Mossend, between Shotts and Glasgow, where Annie and the children would live for the next two years. By this time they were all together in Scotland and had been catching up with friends and relatives after their six-year absence but they were also still dealing with culture shock and the sorrow of leaving Chengdu so suddenly. As the year progressed the children settled into local schools and Torrance had speaking engagements at various Bible Society meetings around Scotland, but he confessed to Dr Haven that 'our hearts are back in China' and he and Annie were avidly following developments through the British press and in letters bringing news directly from Sichuan.[4]

Not long after the Torrances' departure from Chengdu, General Liu Wenhui had written a long letter to Dr Beech of the WCUU, assuring him that the foreigners remaining in Chengdu would be protected. However, making his position clear, Liu declared that China was moving away from any kind of inequality or Western imperialistic imposition and that, as a dedicated Nationalist, he was placing much hope in Soviet Russia who 'would treat us with fairness and justice' and 'abolish for us all the hardships or injustice'.[5]

As Communist intentions became clear, Chiang acted decisively. On Across China the Nationalists, Communists, warlords, and the ailing government in Beijing were all vying for control of the nation. On March 3, 1927, in an effort to increase Communist influence in the Nationalist Party, Stalin issued an order to the Chinese Communist Party 'calling for the intensification of mass movements, arming the workers and peasants, and mobilizing the masses'.[6] However, although the leftists were dominating the Nationalist government in Wuhan, a rival Nationalist power-base was growing in the east under Chiang Kai-shek, who that same month managed to take Shanghai and Nanjing.

As Communist intentions became clear, Chiang acted decisively. On April 12 before dawn, a large-scale purge of Communists was launched in Shanghai and beyond. According to Hsu, 'Nationalist troops, police, and secret agents raided Communist cells, shot down suspects on sight, disarmed the workers' pickets and eliminated the labor unions'.[7] The

---

4   TT to Dr Haven, June 22, 1927.
5   WCMN, March 1927, p14. Written Jan 28, 1927.
6   Hsu, *Rise of Modern China*, p527. KMT: the Kuomintang (Guomindang) or Nationalist Party.
7   Hsu, *Rise of Modern China*, pp527-528.

Wuhan government promptly dismissed Chiang as head of the National Revolutionary Army, to which he responded by setting up an alternative Nationalist government in Nanjing. In a further blow to the Wuhan faction, two powerful northern warlords, Feng Yuxiang and Yan Xishan, put their support behind Chiang Kai-shek.

The final straw for the Wuhan government was Wang Jingwei's discovery of a secret telegram from Moscow, ordering the Communist Party to establish its own armed forces. In July, Wang, who was politically left but not Communist, cut ties with the Communists and Borodin was forced to return to the Soviet Union. By early 1928, following a gradual rapprochement between the two Nationalist factions, Nanjing had become the seat of a united Nationalist government, with Chiang Kai-shek at its head. With the help of Feng Yuxiang and Yan Xishan, Chiang took Beijing in June 1928 but chose to make Nanjing China's new capital. In July 1928 the Nationalists were recognised by the USA as the legitimate government of China and the one that offered the best hope of stability.

Much of the fighting during the advance of Chiang's Northern Expedition had been focused on controlling the Yangtze valley and in July 1927 the WCMN had reported that trade on the river was almost at a standstill, with tens of thousands of men laid off and facing possible starvation.[8] One of Torrance's colporteurs wrote saying that literature supplies were not getting through. In September letters came from Mr Liu at the ABS depot and from another colporteur with news that Communist activity in Sichuan had been suppressed but even so, a carrier with some ABS literature had been attacked by activists and later died of his wounds.

The Nationalist Party's expulsion of the Communists had paved the way for a crackdown by Liu Xiang on the Communists in Chongqing, and other leaders in Sichuan followed suit. In Chengdu, protests by students and workers were suppressed, which helped ease the climate for local Christians. However, a letter sent to Torrance in October by one of the Qiang Christians, Wang Jiechen, was pessimistic about the future: 'Taking a general view of the situation in Szechuan the outlook is not very good. There is much opposition from agitators and from a certain class of students. They call us Christians "slaves who forget their country" and curse us.'[9] He also told Torrance that part of the

8   WCMN, July 1927, pp1-2.
9   Torrance included a translation of Wang Jiechen's letter in a letter to Dr Haven on Oct 8, 1927.

Weizhou mission property was now occupied by the local military commander, with Pastor Mao receiving a small rent which was helping to support Pastor Ren in Zagunao.

Torrance was encouraged to hear that the Dyes had managed to return to Chengdu in mid-September 1927 and found a more friendly environment than when they had left in January. Faculty, students, and servants alike all gave them a warm welcome, with students even happy to acknowledge them off campus. The university also seemed generally less foreign than previously, with more equal cooperation between the Chinese staff and the few foreign staff members who had stayed behind. Added to this, in December 1927 Chiang Kai-shek married Soong Meiling, the American-educated sister of Sun Yatsen's wife, and daughter of a highly influential Chinese Methodist businessman. Chiang had made it clear that Chinese Christians were welcome within the Nationalist Party and were not to be discriminated against.

A FAREWELL FAMILY PHOTO 1928

Return

In early March 1928 Torrance said a painful good-bye to the children and travelled with Annie down to Southampton. He sailed on March 8 and, in the first of many letters crossing the divide, wrote to Annie the next day of how hard it was to watch her 'fading away in the distance'. It was a great consolation that she and the children were now safely home but they would live the next few years with the uncertainty of when and even if they would eventually be reunited. The expectation was that Torrance would complete another seven years and then retire but they both knew to hold such expectations lightly.

Annie had a few precious days in London visiting Ella Bailey and other friends before returning to all that lay ahead of her in Scotland. The day after Torrance sailed, Tom also wrote the first of many letters from the children, saying how well James and David were behaving and that they were both sending love and kisses. This separation was something none of them wanted and David would later recall Annie wondering long after if it had really been for the best, but their options had been few, especially as they were so opposed to sending the children to boarding school.[10] Back in Britain employment opportunities would have been scarce for Torrance, who was now fifty-seven, so it also made financial sense for him to continue working for the ABS.

On board ship Torrance was pleasantly surprised to have a cabin to himself. Adapting to his role as long-distance father and husband, he wrote reminding Annie to give the children cod liver oil and brown bread and reassuring her that he was taking his quinine regularly. As the ship docked at the various ports he hoped eagerly for letters from home and began a habit that would last through the next few years, writing diary instalments for the children about the people and places on his travels. From Singapore he sent Annie an Indo-Persian rug for the house.

In late April, waiting in Shanghai for onward travel documents, Torrance was surprised to hear from Annie that she had received a tribute to him from the Qiang. It turned out to be a version of the 1925 tribute but this time it was handwritten on white cloth and included the names of about sixty church attendees in the districts of Miansi, Lifan, and Maoxian.[11] It had been written on Christmas Day 1927.

Finally able to leave Shanghai on May 4, Torrance travelled up the Yangtze with two other missionaries who were also returning without their wives. In Hankou he remembered to buy two packets of special paper for David's fourth birthday: 'You dip a white sheet in water then lay it on the red sheet and press together on the palm of the hand and the picture will show itself.'[12] Annie had mentioned that Tom was looking thin so he sent an extra ten shillings to pay for trips out to

---

10 Revd David W. Torrance in conversation with the author, August 29, 2011.
11 Stored with the Thomas Torrance Papers (RG 16) at Yale University Divinity School Library (b.Ovd-5).
12 TT to Annie, May 12, 1928, from Hankou.

the countryside and suggested Tom might have a couple of weeks in the summer at the farm of relatives at Cairneyhead, outside Shotts. Torrance had been dreaming of Annie.

In his letter from Hankou – scene of the conflict which had precipitated the previous year's mass evacuation – he described the current sense of normalcy but at the same time he was concerned by the levels of bribery and corruption under the Nationalists, as well as the rising cost of living, higher taxes, and general ongoing lawlessness. Steamers were still travelling in convoy from Hankou to Yichang under the protection of a British gunboat and boats continuing west from Yichang had an armed guard.

It was clear from a letter sent from Chongqing on May 29 that Torrance was not going to spare Annie any mention of danger or unpleasantness, although any news would be several weeks old by the time she read it. He described to her the chaotic stretch from Yichang to Wanxian where robber groups and so-called 'Red Spears' – with certain Boxer-like traits – controlled several places. At one point his steamer came under fire from both sides but although fierce while it lasted, they were through in fifteen minutes and suffered no casualties, thanks to the response of their ten-man naval escort.

Whilst in Chongqing Torrance had some valuable discussions with Daniel Diao, the ABS depot manager there, whom Torrance held in high regard. Diao had been a mission school student and then worked with various missionaries in Chongqing, followed by a stint at the Asiatic Petroleum Company. He had eventually returned to work with Wilbur Hooker at the ABS and when Hooker drowned in 1921 he had taken responsibility for the depot.

From there Torrance went overland to Chengdu with another missionary couple, Gordon and Mary Agnew and their young son Robert, greeted all along the way with friendly smiles and nods.[13] About fifteen miles from Chengdu they were surprised to see a motor car draw up alongside them and more so when the chauffeur got out and presented Torrance with General Deng Xihou's card welcoming him back. The chauffeur had orders to drive Torrance and the Agnews on this last stage of their journey so they arrived in style on the new wide road into Chengdu.

On June 15 Torrance wrote the first of his weekly Chengdu letters to Annie. That same day, Deng Xihou, whose home was near the ABS

---

13   The Agnews, who worked at the WCUU, would carry out significant research into the role of vitamin D and phosphorous in the prevention of tooth decay.

depot, came for a chat and said he was organising a welcome dinner for Torrance. Sichuan's military leaders were considerably younger than Torrance and his seniority, together with his ease of communication and his broad interest in their culture, history, and current affairs, were all positive factors in these relationships. Torrance had brought presents from Scotland for General Deng and two of his officials, Liao and Diao, for which 'all seemed pleased'.[14] Diao, one of Deng's senior men, had been taking care of Billy and came over for a chat, as did various Chinese friends. Billy was 'as fat as butter'.[15]

Torrance's chats with Deng gave him more insight into the political situation. He had noticed a lot of troop movement around Chongqing and Deng told him heavy fighting was expected there between Yang Sen and Liu Xiang. Sichuan was currently divided up between several generals: Liu Xiang to the east in Chongqing; Yang Sen further east in Wanxian but now marching against Liu Xiang; Liu Cunhou and Tian Songyao both in northern Sichuan; Liu Wenhui in the south and sharing control of Chengdu with Deng Xihou; and Deng holding the area north and west of Chengdu, which included the Qiang region. Tian Songyao also had a foothold in Chengdu alongside Deng and Liu Wenhui.

It was a delicate balance. As Torrance explained to Cameron in Shanghai, although 'latterly all hoisted the revolutionary flag this in no way changed their sentiments.'[16] Whilst Liu Xiang and Liu Wenhui had moved closer to the Nationalists, Yang Sen had been closely allied with Wu Peifu in Beijing, and Deng Xihou, Liu Cunhou, and Tian Songyao were trying to tread a more neutral path but were anxious to prevent the two Lius gaining the ascendancy and therefore didn't want Yang Sen defeated by Liu Xiang. With perhaps grudging admiration, Deng had been given the nickname 'crystal monkey', a play on his name and a reference to his skill at avoiding conflict while other generals fought. Although some saw this as a weakness, many, including Torrance, had cause to be thankful for it. Torrance was also thankful that it was Deng who had control of the Qiang area.

For Torrance, life in Chengdu now felt very quiet and it was strange to see so few missionaries.[17] At a welcome meal for him and the Agnews

---

14   TT to Annie, June 15, 1928.
15   TT to Annie, June 22, 1928.
16   TT to Cameron, June 16, 1928.
17   TIME magazine reported that of the 8,250 missionaries who had been in China in January 1927, only 3,183 were at their posts a year after the exodus, mostly on the coast. 'Religion: Christianity in China', TIME, April 28, 1941.

there were nine other men, one single lady, and one other couple. Rather than have the burden of running their own households, several of the Canadian men were living very basically together in a rather subdued atmosphere without their wives and children. The arrival of young Robert Agnew had raised the number of missionary children in town to seven, a drastic change from the days when Lingyan Temple had echoed with shouts of dozens of young missionary children playing together. Torrance was waiting until after his summer travels to make longer term housing decisions and was temporarily boarding with his old CIM co-worker George Franck, who was now working for the British & Foreign Bible Society. He was glad that friends like Harry Openshaw and the Dyes were still around – such friendships meant a lot in the absence of family.

Despite having just arrived, Torrance could hardly wait to leave Chengdu where the temperature was at least 36°C and he had been 'in a bath of sweat morning, noon and night.'[18] Setting out for Lingyan on July 6, his journey to Guanxian took four hours with much jolting and excitement in a bus with wooden planks roped to the sides for fording the many ditches along the way. Up at Lingyan he discovered that the military had commandeered some of the furniture the family had kept up there but he managed to retrieve various pieces. One of the priests was enjoying Annie's rattan rocking chair. Finding in their rooms traces of previous summers, he wrote to the children: 'I, and a boy's cap and one long hair instead of a family of eight as before! Would you not call that living in reduced circumstances?'[19]

A few days later he set off up the Min Valley with Billy and the carriers, giving medical advice and treatment at the roadside villages. Approaching Miansi he came across a group of Qiang carriers resting at the spring. When they heard he had visited their village of Upper Baishui a few years before and seen their sacred grove they relaxed and talked freely with him. At Torrance's request, Chen Bingling was helping with the ABS work in Chengdu this summer but Gou Pinsan and a friend were waiting to meet him in Miansi. Gou Guanding, the Wasi Christian, then joined them and others followed, many asking after Annie and the family, whom some knew from their winter study periods in Chengdu. On Sunday they had a good worship service with Qiang, Wasi, and Chinese all present. In the afternoon Torrance wanted to visit the village

18   TT to Annie, July 5, 1928.
19   TT's summer 1928 diary for the children. All summer trip quotations are from this unless otherwise indicated.

of Qiangfeng across the Min River but the folk in Miansi pressed him to stay with them and talk. As they chatted, two Qiang men from west of Maoxian turned up who barely spoke Chinese. One of them 'with a typical Jewish cast of face' was in need of medicine.

On Monday they continued to Weizhou where Torrance was confronted with the dismal state of the mission property under its military occupation. Soldiers had removed the doors and much of the glass, as well as the benches in the chapel room. Unable to stay there they pressed on to Keku Village in the Zagunao valley and found lodging in the home of a young man who had stayed with the Torrances and attended the mission school in Chengdu.[20] Early on Tuesday they made the narrow and precipitous climb up to Gou Pinsan's village of Mushang, where the annual summer sacrifice was due to take place. Normally taboo for outsiders, Torrance had never witnessed this but he now had a personal invitation from Gou and described the event in detail in his diary for the children:

> July 17: I changed my clothes almost at once, putting on a high drab suit to be ready to attend the sacrifice as soon as it began. The immemorial custom is that the worshippers should bathe and wear white at this occasion. I, therefore, did not want to offend any of their susceptibilities. There is usually a Sacred Grove. Here it was only an over-spreading tree behind an altar on which stood the usual White Stone. The White Stone, if you have read my booklet, you'll remember represents the holiness of God, or, in their language, the purity of His character. I remained here to-day for hours minutely watching the service.[21] I did not anticipate the priest's preliminary prayers would be so long. Though I could not understand what he said I could distinguish that certain sections of the ritual he chanted over and over again. There was a lot of repetition. At length came the killing of the lamb with all its attendant ceremonies. I had learned nearly all about it before but was most interested now to see it myself. And to think to-day I was the first white man to witness this pre-historic custom of theirs. It demonstrated how they have learnt to trust me. The priest himself told me they forbade any outsider coming.

20 It seems likely this was the home in which Torrance had stayed in 1924 where the host had been reading Genesis and Exodus and discussed sending one of his sons to the mission school.

21 The author attended the preliminary part of a Qiang New Year ceremony in early November 2013. The main part, attended only by men of the village, lasted through the early hours of the morning.

The lamb stood tethered at one side. Near by were three paper banners, one with a small bow and arrow attached to the top. The arrow was first let go as the mark of the divine vengeance on sin. A little of the lamb's wool was now looped into the cord holding the bow to the banner. The meaning of this is ambiguous. The lamb, the Sacred Roll, a large round scone of unleavened bread, and the White Banners were next taken in front of the altar. The priest's assistant slew the victim while the priest chanted his prayers. The blood was received into a basin. Two straws (the orthodox means is a wisp of grass) were used to sprinkle it on the altar, the banners, the Sacred White Roll and the ground. An ear was cut off and placed on the top of the pole of the banner with the bow. A paring of the lips, a certain gland and cypress twigs incense were now burned as the priest continued his supplications. The sprinkling gave him the right to pray for mercy. For the lamb had been slain in the sinners' stead. Not only for mercy, but for blessing and general prosperity. The foreleg and the breast were given to the priest. Ko Pin-San [Gou Pinsan] purposely brought his portion for me to see. (Exodus 29:27, 28; Leviticus 7:31, 37.) A large "Ko" or boiler stood over a wood fire already burning. It was to cook the flesh of the sacrifice. The worshippers ate this with the unleavened bread and drank a cup of wine.[22]

Torrance was invited by the priest to partake of the meat, bread, and wine but he declined and explained that Jesus was his sacrifice, his own 'Nee Dsu' or sin-bearer. He explained to the children that the sacred roll of plain white paper – the 'Nee Dsu' of the Qiang – symbolised a sin-bearer who would come from Heaven, die for them, and save them. Their term 'Ga-gee' – meaning 'my' in the Qiang language – which they placed in front of 'Nee Dsu', indicated 'My own Sin Bearer!'

Gou Pinsan thought it unlikely that anyone would attend an evening meeting once the ceremony was over but more than twenty came, with several responding to Torrance's message from the first chapter of the New Testament book of Hebrews, in which he described the significance of Jesus' sacrifice in the light of passages in the Jewish scriptures. By the end of their time in Mushang, twelve villagers had enrolled their names, wanting to learn more about the Bible, and the ones who could read were given a New Testament.

The next morning the priest let Torrance write a transcription of the opening invocation of his chanting: 'Gagee Chee Imbeea; Chee bo ge; O jo ge; Kuay ro ge; Jo chee ge; Kuay Kay lama; Jo Kay lama,

22 Probably Qiang *zajiu* or 'sipping wine'.

Ts'ze Kay lama; Me Kay lama. Keay da me da; Jay Ke da; Jay ke kuay ro; Jay ne neer o; Ma me shih.' The meaning of the first two lines was explained to Torrance as 'Our Spirit who is in Heaven, according to Thy Will we now offer Thee our Sacrifice' but the priest was unable to clearly explain the rest. The ancient sounds and forms had been preserved without clear comprehension of some of the inner meaning. Nonetheless, it was clear to Torrance that they strongly believed that the sacrifice was connected with the 'vicarious expiation of sin'.

On the following day Torrance witnessed a sacrificial ceremony for the consecration of a young boy. The priest's assistants were young men and the priest wore an older style hat 'like an inverted Chinese basin' rather than the three-horned skin hat worn at the previous ceremony, which Torrance understood to be a recent invention. He discussed the two ceremonies with Gou Pinsan, who held the view that the sacrifice was connected with righteousness and that the presentation of the white paper banners indicated the worshippers' desire to ask forgiveness for any sins committed. He had no explanation for the release of the arrow. Torrance had been told by priests in the Miansi region that it was the arrow of God's judgment and to emphasise this, in their ritual they pretended to hide for a moment to avoid the judgment. Those same priests had also described the white banners as the 'clothes of God'.

LEADING A SACRIFICE TO THE SACRED GROVE.[23]

(*Note the white paper roll or Nee Dsu, the priest's wide-brimmed hat, the small paper banners, and the sheepskin drum*)

On his final night in Mushang Torrance managed to sleep through an earthquake which shook the house for several seconds. Thankfully the path down the mountainside was still intact and as they reached the

23 TT. *China's First Missionaries: Ancient Israelites*. Thynne & Co. Ltd. 1937, opp p68.

valley and turned towards Dongmenwai they were delighted to see some of the villagers coming to meet them. After two good evening meetings and a well-attended Sunday morning service Torrance met with the main leaders to discuss the work. This resulted in the appointment of five men as overseers: Gou Pinsan, Huang Hanqing, and Chen Zhisan in Dongmenwai and Wang Tingxiu and Gou Guanding in the Miansi area – four Qiang and one Wasi. (Two years previously Wang Tingxiu's eyesight had been saved by Dr Cunningham in Chengdu.) The plan was for all the villages to be visited in rotation and for schools to be established in Dongmenwai and in the Miansi area. With so much to encourage it was a sadness to Torrance that two of the Qiang Christians were smoking opium.

Saying farewell to the Qiang at Dongmenwai, Torrance went up the Min Valley to Maoxian for a few days rest with the Spreckleys at the recently re-opened CMS station. Old Gui,[24] a Christian from Heping village, accompanied him and continued on to Heihu village, west of Maoxian, to enquire about two Qiang Christians who had been down for the winter Bible study in 1921. Torrance was hoping to see them but Old Gui returned with the sad news that both had recently died.

At a lunch stop on the way back down to Miansi Torrance encountered a Qiang woman walking along with her granddaughter, who was suffering from leg ulcers. He offered them some tea and, as with other Qiang, felt an inexplicable sense of 'fellow feeling' with the woman as they fell into easy conversation. They travelled on together to Miansi where Torrance gave the girl a box of zinc ointment and some bandages. 'It was all I could do for her.' The following Sunday the girl's grandfather came to the meeting in Miansi.

From Miansi, Torrance, Gou Guanding, and Old Gui crossed the river and went up to visit Wang Tingxiu in a small hamlet above Qiangfeng, which Torrance always referred to as the 'Glen'. Wang was away but some of his relatives invited them in for a meal and Torrance found it easy to explain the gospel to them, noting in his diary that evening that the notion of redemption through sacrifice was part of the Qiang people's 'own religious language'.

On Monday they climbed up to Heping, the village of Old Gui and also of Old Su, the first Qiang Christian in the Miansi region, who had died since Torrance's last visit. Torrance was able to give some medical help and people then gathered in the home of Old Su's daughter to hear

---

24 'Old' as a prefix to an older man's surname was a term of respect rather than indicating that he was elderly.

him speak. One man there declared excitedly that 'they and we belong to the same God' – something Torrance had already heard others express.

Apart from a rather cool encounter with the Chinese magistrate in Maoxian, Torrance had been well-received wherever he went on this trip but on his last evening in Miansi a proclamation in Tibetan and Chinese was pasted up describing the 'high noses, green eyes, yellow hair and white skins' of the British and declaring that they must be hated 'like poisonous snakes and wild beasts'.[25] The author was Yang Fuquan, the Chinese military commander in Songpan, who was officially under Deng Xihou, although in practice only loosely so according to Torrance.[26]

Heping villagers

The lengthy proclamation was an effort to win over the Tibetans and local tribespeople and unite them against a common British foe, with a reminder that they were all Buddhists and part of the 'Yellow race'. Torrance assumed the proclamation was in part a bid to ease the current Tibetan hostility towards the Chinese in the regions west of the Zagunao Valley.

Thankful that the proclamation had only appeared at the end of his travels, Torrance was still much encouraged by the whole trip. He was already planning ahead to the winter Bible study and it was agreed that Chen Bingling, now back in Miansi, would keep a record of all the villages he and others visited and see who might be interested in coming down to study.

25   WCMN, Nov 1928, p36.
26   TT. 'Work Among the Ch'iang Tribesmen'. *The Chinese Recorder*. 1930, p103.

Back in Scotland, Annie was busy keeping the family together and still adjusting to having left China. Her last few years there, with the diverse teaching opportunities, had been the most satisfying. She had once been told that it took twenty years to really learn the language and know the Chinese well and she was just in her twentieth year when she left. But it was not safe to keep the children in Chengdu and she had seen the negative effects on some children who had been left in their home country while both parents returned to the mission field. Her days were now filled with housework and the needs of six children from pre-school to mid-teens. The older ones were having to work hard to catch up in some subjects at school and it was a relief when they all did well in their first end-of-year exams. Having prayed throughout the summer for Torrance's travels they had a frustrating two-month wait for his diary to reach them but it was a delight to receive some of Torrance's photos, including one with Billy.

Torrance with Billy 'as fat as butter' at Lingyan Temple

Torrance was much missing Annie's companionship. Realising it was impractical for him to run the Wushi-tongtang home as a fully-functioning household, he decided to continue living with Franck. It was good to have some company and his room at Franck's faced the parade ground where the air was fresher. A Chinese couple, the Tangs, were taken on as resident caretakers for Wushi-tongtang. Torrance would move back there whenever the Qiang came in the winter and in the meantime he could still use his study when he needed quiet. He was currently working on a Chinese tract about eternal life which had to be gone over again and again to get it right.

Adapting to single life again and not wanting to dwell on his loneliness, Torrance maintained a busy routine and was glad when visitors called in at the ABS depot. One of these was Deng Xihou's officer, Liao, who liked to practise his English and to whom Torrance had given his copy of Robert Burns' poems. On Thursday evenings he attended a Chinese prayer meeting and on Fridays an English one. He was also much in demand as a preacher and Norman Amos and Pastor Pan of the CIM had asked him to speak at their street chapel one evening a week and wanted him to visit some villages with them. Pastor Pan told Torrance he knew of no-one else who could speak so clearly or plainly, especially in his exposition of Bible passages.

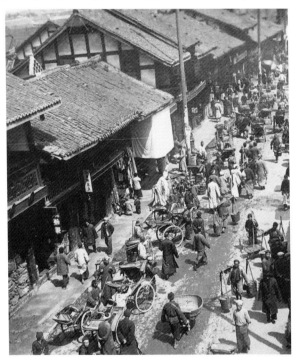

Great East Street

On Wednesday evenings, encouraged by Harry Openshaw, he spoke regularly at the American Baptist meeting hall, something which would become a main feature for both of them over the next few years.

The hall was situated on Great East Street, one of Chengdu's busiest streets, which stretched from the centre of town to the East Gate.

Sunday was a day of rest when Torrance would often visit friends and play tennis, or perhaps play draughts with George Hartwell, known affectionately as 'Dad' Hartwell, who had been in Chengdu since 1891 and was for Torrance that rare kind of friend who could be called on at any time. He also visited patients at the Canadian hospital on Sunday mornings and was surprised on one occasion to see the Lifan magistrate, who had been shot in the thigh. Having previously seemed to Torrance a 'haughty patronising sort of fellow', the magistrate was now far more friendly and to Torrance's astonishment he accepted some tracts and a New Testament and eventually expressed a desire to attend church.[27]

There was a sad story behind his shooting, a story Torrance had heard that summer and in which he would later play a minor role.

CHIEF GAO WITH HIS WIFE, SUO DAIYU, AND CHILD
(Photo: Sidney Gamble, 1917)[28]

Torrance's initial understanding was that Chief Gao of Zagunao, whom Torrance had first met in 1919, had refused a request from the previous Lifan magistrate for a woman from his tribe and the magistrate had then ordered the killing of him and of his son, Gao Liang. However, Torrance later heard what seemed a more accurate account from a military official in Songpan. In 1927 tensions had arisen between Chief Gao and his brother-in-law, King Suo of the Wasi, whose sister,

27 TT to Cameron, Nov 21, 1928.
28 Sidney D. Gamble Photographs Collection, Duke Digital Repository, Duke University. Roll 56A: Mr. & Mrs. Kao (Gao) and child. (CC0 1.0 Free Re-use.)

Suo Daiyu, was married to Gao. Both men were claiming the right to a vacant chieftainship in Heishui for their sons and King Suo had apparently made a deal with the Chinese to do away with Gao, and with his son Gao Liang. The son had been killed in the Weizhou mission property, where Torrance had seen the bullet marks in the wall and blood stains on the floor. Chief Gao was then also captured and killed, despite having previously helped the Chinese in their attempts to regain control of Songpan from the Tibetans. Furious at this betrayal the tribespeople in Zagunao and beyond had risen up in rebellion and it was in fighting to quell this unrest that the current Lifan magistrate had been injured.

That summer, on his way back down the Min Valley, Torrance had met a Chinese official who was on his way to try and reassert Chinese control in the region. He acknowledged to Torrance that the murder of Chief Gao had been a huge mistake and had stirred up a hornet's nest – an accurate assessment as Gao's wife, Suo Daiyu, sought over the next few years to avenge his and her son's deaths.

In the autumn Torrance had annual financial and general reports to complete and he was also continuing to research and write. A lecture he had given to the Fortnightly Club was published in November by the WCMN as a twenty-page article entitled, 'Religious Life in China from Ancient to Modern Times'.[29] The editor's opening remark in his editorial expressed regret that such a useful paper had not been available years ago to help missionaries gain a better grasp of China's religious history.

Referring to John Ross's book, *The Original Religion of China*, Torrance asked how it was that, unlike other early peoples, Israel and China, on the western and eastern edges of Asia, both had the concept of a most high God: Jehovah in Israel and Shangdi in China.[30] Looking first at the characteristics of Shangdi and at the Chinese concept of Tian (meaning Heaven but also conveying deity), he then moved on to the advent of a fuller code of ethics with Confucius, the development of Daoism and Buddhism, and the introduction of religions such as Manichaeism and Zoroastrianism from Persia, followed by the arrival of Nestorian Christianity, the coming of Islam overland from Central Asia and by sea to southern China, and finally the Catholic and Protestant forms of Christianity. Although Buddhism originated in

---

29 TT. 'Religious Life in China from Ancient to Modern Times'. WCMN, Nov 1928, pp5-24.

30 John Ross. *The Original Religion of China*. Oliphant, Anderson & Ferrier. 1909.

India, Torrance noted that Buddhism, Daoism, and Confucianism, all of which he viewed as atheistic for their lack of Deity, were perceived as Chinese religions. He was most positive regarding Confucianism, observing that its emphasis on the clan or family and on filial piety had 'kept family life comparatively wholesome and given to the public administration a strong steadying influence'. He did, however, lament the burden it placed on the Chinese to serve their ancestors, who had 'the power to prosper the dutiful and punish the negligent'.

Returning to the early imperial tradition of annually sacrificing a young bull at the Temple of Heaven in Beijing, he pointed out that the significance of this had been lost, despite it being 'the only case of survival from ancient times of a sacrifice to the Supreme God'. Wondering whether this sacrifice in Beijing once shared a common source with the sacrifices of the Qiang, Torrance suggested that the Chinese could have learned more about the significance of the sacrifice from the Qiang, whose rituals he then described in detail, also pointing interested readers to his 1923 article, 'The Religion of the Ch'iang'.

October 23 was Annie's birthday. There had been a gap in mail from the family and Torrance was worried that something was amiss. He wrote her a letter and kissed her photo on the mantelpiece, finding 'a trifle of comfort in that'. Nothing was seriously amiss but Annie was homesick for China and regretting that James and David were missing out on what the older ones had gained from growing up in Chengdu. She had obviously mused aloud about the possibility of returning with the two boys, and Mary, now sixteen, mentioned this in a letter to Torrance. He was torn in his response, feeling he would function so much better in China if Annie were with him but concerned about the children's safety if they came and the difficulty of finding someone suitable to care for the older ones in Scotland. On top of this was his own fear that Lacy might suddenly decide to move him elsewhere. In the end his response was ambiguous: they would need the Lord to make a way but perhaps Annie might come out for a while and return home to see the older ones into university. Annie's own longing would have been accentuated by news that more women were now returning to Chengdu, including friends of hers. For now the matter was placed in 'wait and see'.

Two days after Annie's birthday, Torrance and the other foreigners were guests at a feast held by Deng Xihou, Liu Wenhui, and Tian Songyao – the 'three big guns' as Torrance described them – who shared control of Chengdu.[31] Attended by many Chinese officials, the banquet was ostensibly to celebrate the birthday of the Chinese Republic but Torrance also saw it as designed to cultivate good relations with the foreigners now that Chiang Kai-shek's Nanjing government had been officially recognised by other nations. National anthems of various countries were played by a military band and a three-minute silence was held in commemoration of Sun Yatsen and in honour of his Three People's Principles. As usual, speeches were an important part of the proceedings, with Harry Openshaw representing the Americans and Dr Clifford Stubbs, vice-president of the university, speaking for the British. Openshaw described the evening as 'a distinctly friendly gesture on the part of the leading Provincial officials' and he was 'hopeful that a new day is beginning to dawn'.[32]

Towards the end of November, seven Qiang – four men and three women – arrived from the mountains for the winter classes. Wang Tingxiu, from the Glen above Qiangfeng, came early. He had a lot to discuss with Torrance as he wanted to get baptised and was also hoping to open an outstation in Qiangfeng with a properly designated schoolroom. Torrance offered to provide half the funding for this if the locals could raise the other half, which Wang thought was possible. Yu Chengbing from Keku had come down to train as a colporteur and was working in the daytime and coming to classes in the evening. Another, Old Wang, was from Gou Pinsan's village of Mushang, and Old Gui was also down from Heping and wanted to get baptised. He was cooking for the group. One of the women was the young wife of Wang Jiechen in Weizhou, who had written to Torrance in Scotland about the state of the Weizhou property and who was now working as a colporteur. The other two women were older ladies, Mrs Chai from Upper Baishui Village and Mrs Yang from Weizhou, neither of whom had ever been to the city before.

On some evenings Torrance took the men to the CIM and Great East Street meetings after which they would come back and join the women for their evening class. Chen Bingling was helping with the teaching, going over the topics again after Torrance had spoken. Torrance often drew on their own environment for analogies in his teaching: 'Yesterday morning I had a great time with them over the exposition of John 4:46 to end – the 3 steps of faith. I compared it to the storeys in their Ch'iang houses; the three rising over one another

31 TT to Annie, Oct 23, 1928.
32 WCMN, Nov 1928, p34.

but even these were not enough without the roof. The house of faith needed a roof of love to Christ before it was complete and so on. They sat and thoroughly enjoyed it.[33] In the end, three of the men and one of the women, ranging in age from twenty-two to sixty-eight, were baptised at the CIM baptistry.

The study period with the Qiang was a good end to the year for Torrance but their departure on Christmas Day was timely. The following day anti-Christian posters were put up around Chengdu, naming four leading Chinese Christians. Further afield, Torrance was disturbed to hear that the Nanjing government had appointed a committee of generals to discuss the situation in Sichuan, dissatisfied with the Sichuan generals, who were not heeding their authority. 'I hope they let us alone,' he wrote to Annie.[34]

THE SEVEN QIANG STUDENTS WITH TORRANCE
CHRISTMAS MORNING 1928   (*Photo: T. E. Plewman*)

33 TT to Annie, Dec 13, 1928.
34 TT to Annie, Nov 29, 1928.

Chapter 14

A (Relatively) Calm and Fruitful Year 1929

Torrance's first Christmas in Chengdu without the family was not a particularly happy one. The Qiang had left, he was missing Annie and the children, and he was concerned for the Chinese Christian leaders named on the anti-Christian posters. Torrance and Openshaw were the only foreigners on the Executive Committee of the Sichuan Christian Council at that time and they knew the men well.

On December 26 Torrance was due to speak at the Great East Street hall and some assumed he wouldn't show up for fear of opposition but he and Openshaw 'got the place jammed full and had a rousing meeting' with fifteen signing up as enquirers.[1] New Year's Day was spent at the Mulletts' home with an excellent dinner, although the coffee, he told Annie, wasn't as good as hers. As the other guests were enjoying a game of tennis Torrance suddenly heard a noise outside and discovered some students pasting anti-Christian posters on the Mulletts' doorway. He pulled the posters down and sent the students on their way.

Thankfully the activists were a minority. From early January, Torrance, Openshaw, Franck, and Amos of the CIM joined with some Chinese Christians in a city-wide distribution of literature, including Torrance's tract on eternal life. Apart from the opposition of a few students they were generally welcomed and visited everywhere, from mansions to the poorest dwellings and from street traders to factories and banks. At the close of the campaign Torrance sent tracts covering the essentials of Christianity to each of Sichuan's 133 magistrates, hoping that these would help to dispel false rumours and misunderstandings.[2]

Following this, Torrance and Openshaw held a season of nightly meetings at the Great East Street hall, handing out tracts on the street and inviting people in as they passed by on their way home from work.

---

1   TT to Annie, 27 Dec, 1928.
2   A magistrate in the Republican period was similar to a county head.

HARRY OPENSHAW AT THE GREAT EAST STREET MEETING HALL

Large character posters with songs and Bible texts were pasted up at the front for all to see and when the hall was about half-full Torrance would go in and lead some singing, accompanied by the skilful organ-playing of a young man from the school for the blind. Once the hall was full, Openshaw would, 'in his own inimitable way', put everyone at ease with a welcome chat and a prayer, followed by Torrance giving the main address.[3] Gospels were given to those who wanted to know more and a New Testament to those bold enough to put their names down as enquirers.

After four weeks of nightly meetings interest was still increasing and Openshaw and Torrance were loath to stop, but they were beginning to provoke opposition. On one evening a group of young 'Bolshevists' tore up a tract in Openshaw's face, stood on a bench shouting insults, and smashed the lanterns hanging at the door. Deng Xihou sent police the next day to keep order. This afforded some protection inside but didn't deter a concerted effort to disrupt the meetings from outside over the next few days. Regardless of this, the hall continued to be packed every night. One man told Torrance he hadn't missed a meeting the whole month. Openshaw was delighted with the success of the meetings and suggested he and Torrance continue to work together.

In February Torrance took on new staff: a new depot manager, Li Youren, who had good English and would become an invaluable right-

3   TT. 'Evangelism in West China'. *The Chinese Recorder*, Vol 61, Dec 1930, pp767-771.

hand man; a cook-boy, Yang, whom Torrance hoped to train up to cook on his summer travels; and Jiu Si, the house servant who had been so fond of David. Jiu Si missed the family too much and only stayed a couple of months but came back again a while later.

There was change at the West China Missionary News too. Lewis Havermale of the university's Faculty of Religion had taken over as editor and seems to have been a man after Torrance's heart. In the February editorial he wrote bluntly of missionaries using tactics other than spiritual ones to entice people and also criticised the gap in lifestyle between many missionaries and the poorer Chinese, emphasising the danger of bad racial and personal attitudes and the need for missionaries to nurture their own spiritual life. Unlike some missionaries, the Torrances had always lived in a Chinese-style home and Torrance had expressed frustration with missions that paid Chinese salaries in excess of local levels of pay. Rather than focusing on numbers of converts, he also greeted with caution anyone asking to be baptised, wanting to ensure that the significance and implications of such a step were clearly understood.

At the end of February Torrance had an unexpected visit from Yang Jisheng and his wife and invited them to stay at Wushi-tongtang. Yang, who had succeeded his father as chief of Jiuzi, brought news that Deng Xihou's men had lost the town of Songpan, defeated by Muslim troops from Gansu. Deng Xihou later told Torrance that soldiers were being sent up to re-take the area. Chief Yang and his wife seemed in no hurry to leave and to Torrance's surprise stayed until early summer. Yang was smoking opium but he attended some of Torrance's Monday night Bible studies, held for enquirers from the Great East Street meetings. Torrance appreciated the connection with Yang and knew the hospitality would be reciprocated.

An unforeseen result of the Yangs' stay was revealed in a letter to Annie later that year noting the numerous rats at Wushi-tongtang and saying that Yang's brother had gone off with their main rat trap. Perhaps imported, this was not easy to replace and Torrance was considering getting a cat. It seems likely that the brother was Yang Jizu, who would have been nineteen at the time. Despite the Yangs' Tibetan Buddhist background, Jizu had come down in 1923 to study at the American Huamei Mission School in Chengdu. In 1931 he would become chief of the Zagunao district, having married the widow of Chief Gao's son, who had been killed in the Weizhou mission house. The deaths of Chief Gao and his son were still contributing to unrest between the Chinese and the tribespeople.

In mid-March, happy to get out of Chengdu for a couple of weeks, Torrance and three Chinese helpers travelled south by boat to Jiangkou, passing through a patchwork of golden rapeseed, wheat, and beans and

BRICK WITH ELEPHANT DESIGN
(*The other two brick carvings were of a horse and a chariot*)

stopping at riverside villages on the way. Jiangkou was an old haunt where locals had often helped Torrance with his archaeological collecting. This time he bought some heads of Han dynasty figures and also had a chance to visit a recently discovered ancient tomb with three vaults and a fine central pillar. 'All the bricks showed designs I had not seen before. Those on the pillar gave it a rare spiral effect. I brought away 3 bricks for the University museum.'[4]

On his return to Chengdu Torrance sent his Qiang colporteur, Yu Chengbing, to get news from Miansi and Dongmenwai and to find out how Wang Jiechen was, having heard that Wang was too ill to take up

his pastoral and preaching position in Miansi. In early February Torrance had sent him off with a supply of cod liver oil, concerned by his persistent cough and hoping the change to a drier climate would help. News came back that Wang wasn't well at all and had been spitting blood. This was a great sadness for Torrance who had known him as a youngster at the mission school in Chengdu

WANG JIECHEN AND HIS WIFE
IN CHENGDU

---

4   TT diary to children, March 24, 1929.

and knew of his high hopes for the work in Miansi. Torrance sent some money up to help support Wang and his wife but news came towards the end of May that he had died. At a Sunday service Chen Bingling had read from chapter 14 of the book of John: 'In My Father's house are many dwelling places; if it were not so, I would have told you; for I go to prepare a place for you.'[5] Wang had died the next day.

A while later, Chen Bingling came down to Chengdu for a minor eye operation and brought news that the new schoolroom in the Glen above Qiangfeng was open. Zhu Fuhuan, a Qiang from Jiuzi who had trained as a colporteur, was teaching there in return for food provided by the locals and Torrance contributing towards his wages. His classes included general subjects, the gospel, and a catechism of core Christian beliefs, a model Torrance hoped would be established in other mountain villages. Chen Bingling returned to the Qiang area commissioned by Torrance to oversee the building of the long-awaited church in Dongmenwai.

In April, in a box marked 'Sundries' to avoid the exorbitant Chinese postal taxes, Torrance received a welcome package from home: shortbread, oatcakes, pencils, peppermints, blotting paper, shaving soap, and a fine family photo. The following month he sent a rather different package to Scotland: a fur rug for Annie's bedside, two cushion covers, two bamboo trays, three fireside brushes, a Chinese coat (for the girls – in fashionable kimono-style), a Song bowl (with a bag of chilli pepper in it for the children), two strings of amber beads, a piece of amber on a silver chain (for Margaret from 'Old Tooth'), a stone cicada representing immortality for Tom's watch chain (so he would have time at one end and eternity at the other) and an old spear head. The Song bowl and spearhead were for loan to the Edinburgh museum.[6]

In contrast to the activity and diversity in Torrance's life, Annie was finding all her time taken up with running the household and she was still missing the wider stimulation of life in Chengdu. Had she and Torrance left together they would have shared the process of grieving and moving on, but with him still in Chengdu and sending news of friends and familiar places, the 'half-in, half-out' was emotionally challenging. The time-lag between letters didn't help either, especially when big decisions were to be made. In mid-March she wrote to Torrance, 'I often wonder if you get all my letters. You hardly answer

5   John 14:2
6   TT to Annie, May 30, 1929.

many important questions I ask you – which is disheartening sometimes.' She was still contemplating coming to China with James and David, even just for a couple of years, and wondered if Cousin Jeannie might look after the older children, who were more settled now.

Torn between the desire to have Annie with him and what was best for the children, Torrance suggested for now that she get some house-help to free her for other things and also reminded her not to underestimate her spiritual impact on the children's lives, which, as Tom would later testify, was immense.[7] A while later, Annie happened to meet a representative of the National Bible Society of Scotland who told her bluntly that the situation in China was deteriorating as the Communists gained ground and was no place for her or the children right now.

In May Annie managed to find a nicer house at a much reduced rent due to competition from a new housing scheme and they moved to North Road, Bellshill, right opposite a new primary school for James. The Baptist manse was almost next door and the church members, who had taken the family to heart, helped them move and were praying regularly for Torrance.

Such prayers were much appreciated by Torrance, especially on his summer trips. This year he wanted to re-visit Songpan and Dr Morse from the university had asked to accompany him, wanting to continue his collection of anthropological data in western Sichuan. Gordon Agnew of the university dental department was joining them and he and Morse made plans to meet Torrance in Miansi.

On July 3 Torrance's helpers set out for Guanxian: a new young colporteur named Hou Li-de, Yang the cook-boy, and the mule man with Billy. Torrance went by bus the next day, leaving Li Youren to supervise the ABS depot. Li had recently sacked the grass cutter and one of the servants and Torrance was thankful he was taking that kind of responsibility. These things were never easy to deal with and he was increasingly valuing Li's judgment.

In Guanxian Torrance stayed a few nights at the CIM station with the Glittenbergs, taking some meetings, buying supplies, and hiring carriers. While there he visited Auntie Gou, Annie's old helper, who was now eighty-three and in poor health. He gave her some medicine and eggs and left some money with the Glittenbergs for her. She gave him some onions and sent word to Annie that she would never forget her kindness. She died later that year.

7   Hesselink, 'A Pilgrimage', p50.

The journey up to the Qiang area was uneventful except for a rockfall on a road round a precipice, where they had to wait while sixty mules picked their way across the fallen rocks, followed by the hardy muleteers carrying the mule-loads over separately. Reaching the spring below Miansi they were greeted by the sight of thirteen schoolboys from the Glen who had come to accompany them to the Miansi mission house where their teacher, Zhu Fuhuan, was waiting with Wang Tingxiu.

The next morning Chief Yang and his wife and servants unexpectedly turned up having just left Wushi-tongtang. Yang was travelling with his neighbour, Chief Sang of the Ganbao tribesmen, who had visited Torrance in Xuecheng a few years before. In his diary Torrance recorded that Chief Sang's people seemed to be 'a mixed race of Ch'iang and Rong though they talk Rong'.[8] Sang had been buying rifles in Chengdu and was accompanied by forty of his men, some of whom came to the evening meeting.

Morse and Agnew reached Miansi a couple of days later and provided the locals with medical and dental help. There was a good meeting in the evening and the whole party left for Weizhou the next day, stopping at Banqiao for a dip in the stream and at Qipangou for some lunch. In Weizhou they were hoping to stay at the mission house, having been provided with a copy of an order issued by Deng Xihou, banning troops from church property, but every room was full of soldiers and two large Tibetan mastiffs were chained up outside. Dismissing the paper, the military official told them to leave.

Thankfully they found lodging again in Keku, three miles along the Zagunao Valley, where Gou Pinsan was now teaching. Gou arranged for them to sleep on the roof of Mr Yang's house, which Morse and Agnew much enjoyed. They were both continuing to give medical treatment, leaving Torrance free for conversations. Pressing on to Xuecheng the next day they stopped in Dongmenwai to see the new church building in progress. Situated on a plot of land across the stream from the village and designed to serve as both church and school, its walls were now halfway up and the door was in place. Torrance mentioned in his diary that a marble slab had been placed in the wall 'giving the name of the man who gave them the gospel'. The slab and the building are long gone but it seems likely that this inscription was based on Gou Pinsan's 1925 tribute to Torrance.

8   Summer diary to children, July 12, 1929. All summer trip quotations are from this unless otherwise indicated. 'Rong' here would be Jiarong.

Morse and Agnew were curious about the door, which was typically Qiang with a hole to the right of the doorway for a wooden key. Torrance showed them how a hand could reach through the hole and grasp a large wooden key slotted into the end of the door bolt. At night the door was locked and the key removed. He pointed them to the biblical parallel in the Song of Solomon where the Lover tries to visit his Beloved at night and extends his hand through the hole by the door, hoping in vain to unlock it.[9]

Chief Yang had warned Torrance that the Tonghua bridge between Dongmenwai and Xuecheng was too precarious to cross, especially for Billy, but on examination Torrance decided it was worth a try. They tightened the loose boards, found flat stone slabs to fill the spaces, and Billy went over without hesitation – to Yang's amazement when they told him that evening in Xuecheng. The next morning, with the favour of Chief Yang upon them, Morse set to with his head-measuring project, wanting 'to have the cephalic index of as many tribesmen as possible', while Agnew did dental examinations which also seem to have been for research purposes. Some days later Torrance noted in his diary that Morse 'from his measurements of the Ch'iang is firmly convinced of the accuracy of my assertion that they come of an Aryan or non-Mongolic stock. Many have traces more or less of an admixture of Chinese or Rong blood, yet there is no mistaking their early relationship to ourselves.'

Among their Qiang visitors the following day was a priest who shed some new light on their practices. 'He told me something I had not heard before,' wrote Torrance, 'that should he dare to offer sacrifice merely as a ceremony and not with its integral purpose of seeking the removal of sin he himself should warrant death.' Morse then asked the priest about Qiang perceptions of the relationship between sin and disease and although the priest was cautious in his response, it was clear that while acknowledging natural causes he saw sin as a significant underlying factor. One of the Qiang Christians in Torrance's party chatted further with the priest about their rituals and Torrance overheard the priest say, 'Don't let us talk here where others can hear lest they deride us.' In his diary to the children he commented that 'All Ch'iang are most secretive about their religious practices and frequently mislead the Chinese when pressed with questions.' At a rousing evening meeting Torrance discovered that one man present had attended the Great East Street meetings in Chengdu.

9   Song of Solomon 5:4-6.

Tonghua Bridge

They had hoped to cross the river the next day at Xuecheng and go up to Chief Yang's village of Erwa but the bridge had been burned by soldiers some time ago and only a single beam of the new one laid, so they had to go back and renegotiate the Tonghua bridge before making the ascent. Arriving hot and breathless, they were welcomed with special honour by Yang and invited to watch a traditional Qiang dance with the men and women lined up opposite each other singing antiphonally. After such a climb and such a reception Torrance was sorry to leave the next afternoon but he needed to prepare for the Sunday meetings in Dongmenwai.

Morse and Agnew stayed on in Erwa for further research and arrived in Dongmenwai in time for the service, which was a good full house. Their departure from Erwa was timely. Torrance wrote to Annie of rumours that Deng Xihou was sending troops to 'disarm the two Yangs'.[10] The letter gave no further detail but this seems to have referred to Chief Yang and a relative of his who was headman in the next valley, which controlled a strategic route connecting with the Heishui valley.

Edgar Plewman, who was also travelling in the area that summer, had heard similar reports. As he set out from Guanxian on July 18 for the Suomo region beyond Zagunao, he encountered Chinese troops heading towards Weizhou. Their commander had spread the word that they were heading for Maoxian but Plewman found out that they were going up to deal with the tribespeople in the Zagunao valley in response to the unrest stirred up by Chief Gao's widow, Suo Daiyu, and the attack the previous year on the yamen of the Chinese magistrate in Xuecheng, whom Torrance had met in the hospital.

10 TT to Annie, Aug 5, 1929.

While the troops rested in Weizhou, Plewman continued to Zagunao where it became clear that the troubles were mainly to the west of the Yangs and that the tribesmen had been forewarned of the Chinese expedition and were 'holding strongly all the points of approach'.[11] Changing his plans, Plewman turned north to Heishui and learned later that the Chinese troops had regained control of several villages west of Zagunao after two years of insurgency. In his trip report he made the prediction that, 'The next big task of the Chinese is the subjugation of the Heishui district . . . and we doubt if the Chinese military authorities are prepared to tackle it.'[12] He would prove right on both counts.

On Sunday afternoon, Morse and Agnew climbed up to Bulan village to continue their research while Torrance stayed in Dongmenwai to talk with the church elders. On Tuesday they all returned to the Weizhou property to find that the officer had moved his regular soldiers elsewhere but his gun-makers were still there with the mastiffs. Stopping only to pick up letters from Annie and the children at the Post Office, Torrance and his party turned north up the Min Valley and trekked up to Luobozhai, spurred on by the marvellous view of the surrounding snow-capped mountain peaks. In its lofty seclusion the village was abuzz with the news of their arrival and many came to talk and receive medical treatment. As with Jiuzi, it was a long climb to stay only one night but they were still hoping to reach Songpan and the next day was a cooler day for travel after rain overnight.

To their disappointment, in Maoxian they were warned of serious problems further up the Min Valley. The Luhua people of upper Heishui had been carrying out raids and, as Yang Fuquan's proclamation had indicated the year before, there was also a decidedly anti-Christian attitude among the officials up towards Songpan. Morse and Agnew decided to head back to Chengdu. Sorry both to lose their company and not to reach Songpan, Torrance revised his plans and went west from Maoxian with Chen Bingling and a Qiang Christian to the secluded Qiang village of Heihu.[13] Torrance was enchanted by it. 'Nature here is at its apex of beauty and sublimity. The village lies

---

11 T. E. Plewman. 'Unrest in the Tribes Country'. WCMN, Dec 1929, pp37-38.
12 Ibid., p38. (Pinyin updated.)
13 Heihu means Black Tiger. Torrance refers to the village by its original name of Heimao, meaning Black Cat, which was presumably still in use locally. The change to Black Tiger occurred during the Qing dynasty when one of the villagers, known as the Black Tiger General, led the area to victory in battle.

on the virgin line and behind it tower heaven-touching peaks clad in forests of deepest green.'

The Heihu residents seemed to be more ethnically mixed than those of the Weizhou and Lifan districts and Torrance noted that, unlike the square watchtowers in many Qiang villages, about half of their towers were octagonal with round interiors. Although this was his first visit, the Heihu people knew of him through the two villagers who had been to Chengdu for Bible study and who had died the previous year. A steady stream of people came by, some just curious, some for medical treatment, and some interested in their message. At noon a good number attended a service. At night wild pigs got into the maize crops and there was a lot of 'noise-making' as the villagers tried to chase them away.

Heading back to Weizhou via Maoxian the sun was so hot that it burned Torrance's umbrella to shreds. Deciding to leave the main road, where settlements were predominantly Chinese, they climbed up to some of the higher villages. At one village the people indignantly showed Torrance where soldiers had cut down the trees of the sacrificial grove, a serious violation of their taboos. In Weizhou, still unwelcome at the mission house, they stayed a couple of nights across the river in a less populated area and chatted with some of the Chinese soldiers now billeted there. One of the soldiers was a Catholic and another had heard Torrance preach at Great East Street.

On August 1 Torrance visited Mayi village, looking for 'lost sheep', as he wrote to the children. Mayi, high up across the Zagunao valley from Keku, was where he had first come across the white paper scroll in 1923. Once again, he had a long talk with the aged priest:

He said it was the blood that atoned for sin, not the body of the ram. The sprinkling of the blood was the efficacious part of the sacrifice. He was firm on this point and I put his view-point on record for you. His father, who lived till he was 87, charged him to be careful in his duties. He was to suffer no disorder or carelessness to take place in the ritual. The personal name he gave to the Sacred Scroll was Jay Dsu and not Gee Dsu or Nee Dsu as in other places. He added that He was the Mediator between the Father Spirit and the sinner, for He was the real Sin-bearer and the Forgiver of sin. This last was new to me.

He is 75, and one of the few old surviving priests. The younger ones know much less and I was glad to learn when we had the chance of what he had to tell me. He took me to the Sacred grove.

It had the usual altar under a sacred tree with a White Stone in the centre of the altar. Nearby were the three stones for the resting of the cauldron for the cooking of the sacrificial meat.

Having cancelled the trip to Songpan, Torrance was able to spend extra time in the Miansi area, happy to be away from the military presence in Weizhou. Across the river in Qiangfeng the locals were exceptionally welcoming, delighted that they now had their own school in the Glen, with Zhu Fuhuan as teacher. They killed a chicken and cooked a meal for the visitors. Torrance left in the rain after the evening meeting, promising to return a borrowed umbrella in the next few days.

After a good Sunday in Miansi, they climbed up to Heping to a warm welcome from Old Su's daughter. They stayed in Old Gui's home and Torrance had a long talk with the priest who maintained that 'when the Father Spirit saw the blood, there was no sin. It was done away with.' He also told Torrance that the name of the sacred scroll was Abba-ma-lah and that 'it was his mediatorship that made the sacrifice acceptable. He could not explain why, simply made the plain statement.'

Although the Qiang customs in the Miansi district were less pure than in some of the more remote villages, Torrance still found it remarkable that what remained had been preserved, especially in such close proximity to Chinese influence and Tibetan Buddhism. At the evening meeting in Heping he mentioned their tradition of breaking a stone in two for the making of a covenant, both sides needing to produce their half as proof of the agreement, and then pointed to how Christ's sacrifice fitted together with their sacrifices as a fulfilment of their rituals.

Between Heping and Qiangfeng lay the village of Gaodongshan (High East Mountain), where the girl with the leg ulcers lived with her grandparents. She had since married and Torrance was delighted to find that her legs were now better. He had a talk with the priest here too:

> His version of Abba-ma-lah was that it is He who witnesses the sacrifice and carries the worshipper's prayers up to God. He is the indispensable agent in all worship.

Moving on to the Glen where Wang Tingxiu's family lived, they held an evening meeting and the next morning were invited into the home of Wang's sister, who was married to the priest. One villager whom Torrance had met the previous year confided to him, 'All you told me last year, I have still in my heart and I mean to abide by it. You gave me the words of life and good.'

After a final night in Miansi, they headed back down the Min Valley with Torrance feeling much encouraged by the trip. The schools in Dongmenwai and the Glen were making progress, the young colporteur, Hou Li-de, had done well, and Chen Bingling's preaching had a 'good new tone'. Torrance had also received positive reports from the Qiang colporteur Yu Chengbing and his Chinese co-worker, who had taken their literature to the Jinchuan region west of Lifan, where there were various tribal peoples.

GAODONGSHAN VILLAGERS

Back in Chengdu the autumn proceeded fairly peacefully despite rumbling tensions among Sichuan's generals and, on a national scale, Chiang Kai-shek still fighting to consolidate his power. Earlier in the year Liu Xiang had defeated Yang Sen and was now controlling much of eastern Sichuan, with Yang reduced to a small garrison area in Guang'an, north of Chongqing, and many of his men enticed into Liu Xiang's own ranks.

On September 7, General Deng Xihou invited some of the foreigners for dinner and Openshaw returned the hospitality a few days later, with several missionaries present, including Torrance. Deng gave him a lift home afterwards and came for tea at Wushi-tongtang a couple of weeks later. He and Torrance seem to have talked on quite a personal level and not long after this Torrance wrote in a newsletter to friends and family of 'a big General in Chengtu whose foster-mother was a Christian. He is the one who protects us and lets our work go on. . . . Were he to be defeated or driven out we should have much harder times.'[14]

DENG XIHOU[15]

In mid-September Torrance had a museum committee meeting at the university with Beech and Dye. The Plewmans were planning to move out to the university campus and Torrance's comment to Annie that 'They'll be in Society there' sheds light on the contrast between life in the city and life as part of the university community. Torrance enjoyed his campus visits and sometimes stayed with the Dyes when attending West China Border Research Society evenings. From 1929 to 1930 he was vice-president of the Society, and an executive member from 1930 to 1931.

A particular delight for Torrance was having Qiang folk come to call in Chengdu. This wasn't a frequent occurrence but in October Chen Wenping, a Christian from Dongmenwai, paid him a visit and confirmed that the Chinese troops who had gone up in the summer had driven the tribespeople back. Later in the autumn two Qiang men from Heihu came to visit having been in Mianyang on business. They hadn't met Torrance before but knew of his Heihu visit that summer and had been assured by others that he would welcome them. They came to one of the Great East Street meetings and then stayed on at Wushi-tongtang for a while, wanting to learn more.

In Scotland things were proceeding less smoothly. Towards the end of October Annie fell ill with a serious attack of malignant malaria. From the lack of letters Torrance knew that something was wrong but had no idea what. The first news he received was on January 2, 1930, written by Mary on November 3. Now seventeen, Mary had been taking time

---

14 TT newsletter, October 31, 1929. Deng Xihou's parents died while he was still young and he was raised by relatives.
15 https://commons.wikimedia.org/wiki/File:Deng_Xihou1.jpg Source: Fu Runhua, Zhongguo Dangdai Mingren Zhuan, Shijie Wenhua Fuwu She, 1948, p269.

off school to care for Annie, with help from Torrance's sister Annie. Tom had then written in mid-November to say that Annie was on the mend but thin and weak. Although this was old news by the time it reached Torrance, he described it as 'the hardest blow yet', knowing full well that such attacks could be fatal.[16] Mary and Grace had both had milder attacks whilst on a family holiday in Arran that summer.

Deeply concerned for Annie and also for Mary's schooling, Torrance was wondering whether to return to Scotland but a letter finally arrived from Annie on January 15, saying she was slowly regaining her strength and that Mary was back at school. Troubled that both Annie and the children still seemed to be carrying malaria in their systems, he urged Annie to have their blood tested and arranged for a thousand quinine tablets to be sent to her with detailed instructions. Annie was now anxious about Torrance because, 'The papers are rather alarming in their reports of political conditions in China.'[17]

In the midst of all this, Torrance had had a sociable Christmas Day in Chengdu, enjoying lunch, tennis, and dinner with friends, as well as a morning visit to the boys at the school for the blind and an early evening meeting at Great East Street. The anti-Christian movement had kept up its annual Christmas week activities and once again Torrance caught some students pasting their placards up outside the Mulletts' home, one of which was a parody of the Lord's Prayer.

16 TT to Annie, Jan 2, 1930.
17 Annie to TT, Dec 11, 1929.

Chapter 15

'Unusual Difficulty, Danger and Encouragement'

1930

The first few days of 1930 were unusually cold with the rare sight of severe snow in Chengdu. And it started on a cold note for the foreign community. At the Canadian hospital Dr Peterson was treating a student who suddenly tried to stab him in the eye. Protected by his glasses, Peterson nonetheless needed several stitches below his eye.

The anti-Christian activity had, for much of December, been particularly aggressive at the WCUU campus, which had become a target of students from the nearby Sericulture School. Writing his January editorial for the WCMN, Lewis Havermale observed that 'anti-Christians from a neighboring college are parading the campus with flags and yells. The walls and windows of the Library and Administration Building have been plastered with ugly posters calling upon all and sundry to "Strike down Christianity". Certain groups of students in these outside institutions have taken oath, like Paul's enemies of old, to rest not until the Union University has been utterly destroyed or death relieves them of their oath's obligation.'[1] One Chinese pastor was paraded through the streets by a group of students who forced him to carry a flag bearing the epithet 'foreign slave'. Things only quietened down when Deng Xihou's men clamped down heavily on the unrest, arresting students and keeping five of them in prison.

Although some of this hostility was specifically anti-Christian, the Christians weren't the only ones affected. David Graham, in Yibin, 170 miles south of Chengdu, noted that during Chinese New Year fewer than half the Chinese homes had put the traditional red-paper inscriptions on their door frames and even fewer had pasted door-gods on the doors – perhaps an indication that the Chinese were increasingly uncomfortable expressing any kind of religious 'superstition' in public.[2]

---

1 WCMN, Jan 1930, p1.
2 WCMN, May 1930, p37.

For General Deng Xihou, the Communists weren't the only problem. Rumour had it that Liu Wenhui was planning to seize his arsenal and Deng's men were mounting a nightly watch at the East Parade Ground, which Torrance could see from his room at Franck's. In the end the threat abated. In February the politically resilient General Yang Sen was in town staying with Deng and he and Torrance had a brief chat. Yang was disappointed to see that some of the municipal projects he had initiated in his time as governor of Chengdu had been abandoned since his removal in 1925.

That month *The Chinese Recorder* published an article by Torrance called 'Work Among the Ch'iang Tribesmen'.[3] Combining an overview of his contact with the Qiang since 1919 and a description of their culture and history, this was Torrance's first published work on the Qiang since 1923 and his first Qiang article in *The Chinese Recorder*. His opening comment revealed that he had encountered some scepticism regarding the parallels he had drawn between Qiang and biblical practices: 'Few people have heard that we have in West China a tribe of aborigines with a monotheistic faith and religious practices which resemble in many respects those of the Old Testament. And of the few who have heard, some find it hard to credit the assertion. Yet such is the case.'[4]

Some had asked if the Qiang might be descended from the Israelite tribes of the eighth century BC Assyrian dispersion but in response Torrance said there was no proof of this, despite the similarities he had found. However their features and customs indicated to him that they were 'an early immigration from Asia Minor' and he thought that they had probably come to China via Central Asia and then skirted the states of Qin and Shu to reach their present location.[5] As James Edgar had discovered in his reading of Sima Qian's *Historical Records*, Qiang groups had clearly been recorded living in late BC between the Chinese and Central Asia, where they had obstructed Chinese efforts to reach Bactria, in today's Afghanistan.[6]

---

3 TT. 'Work Among the Ch'iang Tribesmen'. *The Chinese Recorder*, Vol 61, 1930, pp100-104.
4 Ibid., p100.
5 Ibid., p101.
6 J. H. Edgar. 'A Chinese Ulysses (130-100 B.C.) and the Result of His Wanderings'. WCMN, May 1920, pp5-9; 'Graeco Bactria and China'. WCMN, June 1920, pp23-27. See also 'The Account of Dayuan', Chapter 123 in Burton Watson, *Records of the Grand Historian of China. Translated from the Shiji of Sima Qian*, Vol II. Columbia University Press. 1961.

Some of Torrance's critics had accused him of interpreting Qiang rituals through the eyes of the Old Testament but he assured them this was not the case. Having talked to various priests and other Qiang in several different locations, and having attended three sacrificial ceremonies, he had 'often been staggered by this sameness of thought on different parts of their ceremonial . . . Everywhere there is the unanimity that it is the blood that atones for sin.'[7]

As to how his own interest in the Qiang started, Torrance explained that he had 'found his clue to their religion by the reading of local histories and discovered by travel among them what it is.'[8] It was fascinating to him that the Qiang were particularly impacted by the early Old Testament books, which was an unusual starting point for anyone new to the Bible. 'The reading of Genesis and Exodus went further than anything else in winning them.'[9] He recalled King Suo's comment to him back in 1924 that the Wasi people 'had a religion and did not need another' and that Torrance should 'go entirely to the Ch'iang who had no religion!'[10] Giving a general overview of the work among the Qiang, Torrance observed that they were also more receptive to the gospel than the Chinese because when he talked to them about Jesus being 'the Lamb of God who took away the sin of the world' it was a religious language that they had no difficulty understanding, something Gou Pinsan had testified to in his 1925 article about Qiang-Old Testament parallels and Christ's own sacrifice.[11]

Torrance had been feeling unwell but medical tests in March showed nothing amiss and he was probably just run down after an intensive month of Great East Street meetings over Chinese New Year. The doctor advised him to take it easy for a while but approved a visit to Daniel Diao in Chongqing as long as he rested on the boat trip. Travelling with 'Dad' Hartwell, who was retiring to Canada, and Plewman who was going to Chongqing on business, the journey was a delightful break with two Chinese helpers, plenty of food, beautiful spring weather, and passes provided by Deng Xihou for the tax stations along the way. Eleven days later, after a stop in Yibin to see Torrance's old friends the Olsens, they reached Chongqing where Torrance said a sad final farewell to Hartwell.

---

7 TT. 'Work Among the Ch'iang Tribesmen', p102.
8 Ibid., p103.
9 Ibid.
10 TT letter to Carleton Lacy, Sept 17, 1924.
11 TT. 'Work Among the Ch'iang Tribesmen', p104.

On a happier note, the ABS work in eastern Sichuan was thriving under Diao, although the book depot was looking rather drab so Torrance organised a spring clean and a fresh coat of paint for the bookshelves.

He returned to Chengdu on April 16, disappointed to have just missed seeing a group of about forty Tibetans from the Songpan region who had been visiting the city. The visit had been initiated by Yang Fuquan, the commander in Songpan and author of the anti-foreigner proclamation, as part of his efforts to promote Chinese-Tibetan relations. The delegation had travelled down on horseback and set up camp outside the city where, as official guests of Deng Xihou, they were 'feted and given presents for 20 days'.[12] The visit included a tour of the university where they 'seemed to enjoy the library, the several laboratories, the medical rooms, and the tea and cakes. They had to recite several charms, especially in the Physics laboratory and in the dissecting room, to overcome the baneful influences abroad, but they were very appreciative.'[13]

Feeling better after his time away, Torrance was busy again with the ABS work. The Hankou Tract Society had printed a tract he had written on the four gospels and were adding it to their own stock. Franck had ordered twenty thousand copies for the B&FBS and John Kitchen, the current manager of the Canadian Mission Press, had asked Torrance to write a tract with a Christian perspective on dying, following the death of one of their young Chinese members of staff.

While Torrance had been in Chongqing the shopkeepers in Chengdu had gone on strike for several days in protest at a new tax proposed by Deng Xihou, who, with loss of face, had relented. In early May Torrance invited Deng to join several of the missionaries for tea and tennis. He had heard that some of Deng's men had moved to Pixian, northwest of Chengdu, and asked if they were drilling in preparation for a fight – something which would explain Deng's attempt to raise taxes. They were, and for a time it seemed that the troops might get caught up in a critical confrontation between Chiang Kai-shek and an alliance of military commanders in other provinces who were challenging his authority. The fighting, which became known as the Central Plains War, raged for months but even though Deng, Liu Wenhui, and Tian Songyao all declared support for the anti-Chiang coalition whilst Liu Xiang came out in support of Chiang, Sichuan managed to stay out of

---

12   Xiaofei Kang and Donald S. Sutton. *Contesting the Yellow Dragon: Ethnicity, Religion, and the State in the Sino-Tibetan Borderland*. Brill. 2016, p38.
13   WCMN, May 1930, p32.

the conflict and Deng's troops did no more than drill. Chiang would emerge victorious towards the end of 1930 and gain a declaration of loyalty from the Sichuan militarists, who still had no intention of actually relinquishing their independence.[14]

Trouble was also rearing its head in other directions. On May 8, Torrance wrote to Annie that the Communists in Sichuan were growing bold, something he attributed to the lack of national government authority in the province and the infighting among the generals.[15] He also mentioned the foothold the Communists had gained in Hubei, little knowing that from them would come the Fourth Front Army which, just three years later, would cause havoc in Sichuan.

Clifford Stubbs

In the second week of May, Torrance and Openshaw left together for a week of meetings with a Chinese pastor in Jianyang, southeast of Chengdu. A week after their return it was the fifth anniversary of the May Thirtieth incident, when a Sichuan student had been among those killed in Shanghai's International Settlement. In the afternoon about a hundred students suddenly converged on the WCUU campus clock tower to commemorate the incident but dispersed without causing any disturbance. That same afternoon, Clifford Stubbs, Dean of Science and Vice-President of the university, had gone for a picnic on the river with his wife, young son, and some friends. In the evening he cycled across campus to visit some colleagues. At about nine o'clock, two students were returning to their dormitory when they heard someone groaning and found Clifford lying on the ground. He had been stabbed six times in the chest, hit on the head, and his face 'had been crushed into the cinders on the path'.[16] With help from friends the students constructed a makeshift stretcher and got him home. He was in such pain that the doctors on campus decided he shouldn't be moved immediately but the next day he was taken, unconscious, to the Canadian Hospital where, despite seeming to rally slightly, he died on Sunday evening.

People were stunned at the news of Clifford's death. Not just the foreign community but the university students too. Presbyterian by upbringing and Quaker by choice, he was one of the most integrated foreigners in Chengdu, adept in the Chinese language but also with a

---

14 Kapp, *Szechwan and the Chinese Republic*, p73-4.
15 TT to Annie, May 8, 1930.
16 Charles Tyzack. *Nearly a Chinese: A Life of Clifford Stubbs*. Book Guild Pubishing. 2013. Kindle Edition.

great facility for communication and with socialist politics far more in harmony with Chinese developments than the views of many others in the mission community. After the foreign exodus in 1927 one of his colleagues in Shanghai had written, 'People out here feel that Clifford should be amongst the first to go back because of his proved ability for friendship with the Chinese.'[17] The Chinese service before the funeral was filled to overflowing as speaker after speaker mourned his loss. Torrance wrote to Annie, 'Never before has any one seen such widespread mourning among the Chinese for a foreigner . . . Stubbs by universal consent did not have a single enemy anywhere.'[18] Chinese and foreigner were drawn together in their common grief and on June 5 the University Senate wrote in tribute to him, 'Real friendship, based upon a generous justice in all relationships – personal, industrial, international, racial – was his ruling passion.'[19]

There was no indication that Stubbs had been personally targeted. Like Edith Sibley, he just happened to be the first foreigner to come along. Not long before the attack some figures had been seen in the dim evening light with a carrying pole. Although his bike was missing, nothing else had been taken and robbery alone didn't account for the brutality of his injuries. In the end it was the discovery of his bike at a repair shop that led to the arrest and execution of the supposed culprits – something Stubbs would have abhorred, and Torrance had his suspicions that they were scapegoats rather than convicted on any solid evidence.

Students from the Sericulture School were seen as the main agitators in the incident although the Chinese Literature School, and even some WCUU students, were also under suspicion. Torrance heard a rumour that the one who wielded the knife was a student at the Literature School and that several students had fled the school immediately after Clifford's death. About fifty left-wing students were arrested but Chengdu had the second largest student population in China, with around thirty thousand students above middle grade, and it was hard to keep track of all such activity.[20] In the summer, further protests were held in reaction to the construction of a wall around the WCUU campus. The grounds had originally been an open space for people to enjoy but in the current climate the students themselves had requested more protection and officials were in agreement. After several attempts

17 Ibid.
18 TT to Annie, June 5, 1930.
19 Tyzack, *Nearly a Chinese*, Kindle Edition.
20 WCMN, Oct 1930, p24.

by a vociferous minority to destroy parts of the wall, calm was restored and it was finally completed.[21]

Torrance had already left for Lingyan Temple by the time these summer protests broke out. Delayed in Guanxian for several days by heavy rain and 'sundry matters', he eventually set out for the mountains on July 14. One of his loads had already gone up thanks to a Qiang woman who happened to be in Guanxian with Wang Tingxiu and two others and insisted on taking it. Torrance had acquiesced but not without some discomfort: 'Imagine a woman carrying it – she was young – not 20 yet.'[22] He then travelled up with the colporteur Hou Li-de, Ting Si the cook, and Chen Bingling, who had been in Guanxian on business.

Torrance was delighted to be back in 'the Ch'iang lands'.[23] Unaware of the delay, some of the schoolboys from the Glen had waited in vain for them at the spring a few days earlier and then gone home, but they turned up for the first evening meeting, sitting at the front and answering Torrance's questions with great enthusiasm. Hou Li-de also spoke at the meeting. Chen Bingling's wife and child were now living with him in Miansi and Torrance was pleased to see how well his wife was fitting in with the locals, without the airs and graces he had seen some outsiders bring with them.

The next day they crossed the river to Qiangfeng, where the 88-year old village headman was celebrating his birthday. The headman's son was the local priest and people gathered to listen to his conversation with Torrance. The previous year the priest had explained that their 'Abba Malah' was the sin-bearer to come from Heaven. Although the term was used for the sacred roll of white paper, it seemed also at times to be used for the sacred rod of the priest. Torrance had since perceived what he saw to be a linguistic similarity between *malah* and the Hebrew word *mal'akh* – meaning angel or messenger – and drew the priest's attention to verses in the Old Testament book of Malachi describing the Messiah as the messenger, or *mal'akh*, of God's covenant.[24]

Moving on to Weizhou, they found that the local magistrate was now living in the mission property. With Clifford Stubbs' death fresh in his mind and no desire to create enemies, Torrance decided to continue

---

21 WCMN, Sept 1930, p27.
22 TT to Annie, July 14, 1930.
23 TT diary to children, July 16. All summer trip quotations are from this unless otherwise indicated.
24 Malachi 3:1.

straight on to Keku. 'It is not well these days to be ostentatious, seeing it is hard to determine who are our friends.' At Keku there were many wanting medical treatment. One of these was Yu Chengbing who had worked as a colporteur the previous year and was now very ill.

Reaching Dongmenwai early the next day Torrance was delighted to see the completed church and school building. 'It resembles a large Ch'iang house. There is thus no outlandish appearance about it to excite antipathy . . . It lacks the prominent White Stone on the top of the back wall: we may even put that up yet.' Built near the foot of an imposing precipice and not far from the junction of the Longxi and Zagunao valleys, the building had about two and a half acres of land behind it, some of which was to be planted with trees while the rest would be a garden. In local style, a ladder led to an upper room, which was for visiting preachers and opened on to a flat roof.

Church and school building, Dongmenwai
(*Torrance on the roof*)[25]

At the Sunday morning service Torrance spoke of how the prophets had foretold the coming of Christ, and in the evening meeting of the good shepherd mentioned in Psalm 23 and the New Testament, an analogy they could easily relate to. 'The picturing to them of the wayward sheep, lost, exposed to attack, representing straying from God, they understood

25 TT. *China's First Missionaries*. Frontispiece.

perfectly.' The villagers had all had times when a sheep or goat needed carrying home and they all knew their own.

Word had spread that Monday was to be a dispensary day and people came down from the various villages. A Christian school teacher from Keku, who had replaced Gou Pinsan there, also visited. Knowing of Torrance's interest in archaeology he had brought several artifacts to show him. One was a small earthenware figure that Torrance judged to be from the Han dynasty. Thanks to the dryness of the climate it had retained its colours and was well-preserved. The locals also drew his attention to some stones high up on the precipice facing the church, which seemed too ordered to be natural. With his binoculars Torrance could see that they were part of a tomb, which suggested there might be others up there too.

DONGMENWAI CHURCH MEMBERS

To Torrance's sorrow, Gou Pinsan's older brother had died. Like Gou he had been a scholar, but he had succumbed to opium. Gou had been asked to replace him as headman but had no desire for such a position and said he would rather leave the district than accept it. He was now leading the school in Dongmenwai, replacing the previous teacher there, a Chinese Christian named Xiong who had moved to teach at the school in the Glen.

On Tuesday, just as they were setting off for Jiuzi, a man turned up needing medical treatment. He had fallen on one of the steep mountain sides and had 'a nasty hole in his head'. Torrance attended to the injury and they set off again, calling at Taoping to chat with the villagers and then stopping further along to chat with a group of farmers resting by the Tonghua bridge and later with another group, several of whom were playing traditional Qiang mouth harps.

CROSSING A LANDSLIDE

At Muka, about two miles before Xuecheng, they turned off the main route and climbed the precipitous path to Erwa, negotiating stretches of sliding rubble. Chief Yang was delighted to see them, glad of a chance to get any social or political Chengdu news, knowing full well, as Torrance wrote, that 'what takes place below has its repercussions sooner or later in his district'. The next morning the only two Christians in the village came to visit and in the afternoon Yang took Torrance for a walk in a deep gorge nearby and showed him a grove of sacred oak trees which were 'consecrated afresh every spring by the sacrifice of a cock. No one is allowed to cut timber or firewood in it.' That evening they held a meeting in Yang's spacious guest hall. Sadly, Yang and his wife had lost their two-year-old son to dysentery since Torrance last saw them.

Returning to Dongmenwai by a longer but safer route, Torrance held another dispensary day, which included lancing a large abscess for Huang Hanqing, and in the evening he walked up beyond the village for a dip in the stream. The following day they climbed up to Bulan, high above Dongmenwai, where they were welcomed by Chen Guangming, the only Christian there. Torrance was dismayed to see how many of the villagers were addicted to opium. 'Poverty and misery are in evidence everywhere.' He was reminded of a verse from the book of Ezekiel: 'Can these dry bones live? O, Lord, Thou alone knowest.'[26] Chen Guangming's mother had left the village to become a religious devotee in a temple but Chen had been one of the first to visit the Torrances in Chengdu for Bible study and had kept his Christian faith since then.

From Bulan they took a high path along the mountainside to Longxi Village, where one of the villagers offered Gou Pinsan the use of his main room for a gathering – to which the man invited the school teacher and some other villagers. Torrance was moved to see how Gou 'left a strong impression on all. Having a wide and very fine reputation his testimony goes far.' Gou also 'skilfully used their ancient customs to commend Christ to them. They admitted freely the decline in their own olden time religion: the younger priests knew very little of its meaning and often varied among themselves.'

Back in Dongmenwai, Gou's son and the colporteur, Hou Li-de, were baptised and for the first time the bread and wine of Communion were shared, something which Torrance never did lightly. In celebration, Gou Pinsan killed a sheep and invited Torrance and many others to a feast, after which the Qiang set off back to their villages.

The next day Chen Bingling and Hou Li-de climbed up to the village of Kuapo, with Hou needing all the courage he could muster on the ascent. Kuapo was where Torrance had treated a woman seven years before who had been near death's door and she came to listen to Chen and Hou. Torrance and Gou had stayed behind in Dongmenwai to discuss the future of the work, for which Gou was now taking responsibility. Torrance had suggested providing funds for Gou to mortgage land in his own name so that he could support himself and continue preaching but Gou turned this down, knowing that any indication of personal wealth might draw unwanted attention.

Stopping at Keku for a night, Torrance was pleased to see that Yu Chengbing, though still thin and weak, was on the mend. The evening meeting was well-received and Gou had hopes that a room on the village street might be used as a chapel. Torrance also offered to send a half-bred foreign bull up to improve the village stock and four of the men agreed to share its care. Above the cultivated slopes there was good pasturage where the bull could graze with the herd.

---

26   Ezekiel 37:3.

Back in Weizhou, Torrance decided to call on the young magistrate at the Weizhou property and see if they could stay a night or two. He was granted a room which the magistrate was using as a study and the others slept in an unused room. The next morning Chen and Hou climbed up to Luobozhai while Gou and Torrance went over the mountain to Upper Baishui village, from where Mrs Chai had come to Chengdu for Bible study in 1928. They reconvened in the evening after long days of walking. Torrance had fallen on one of the descents, sliding on some loose stones, but thankfully escaped with some bruising and a swollen knee. The following day Gou returned to Dongmenwai with plans to get the church grounds in order, build a small kitchen outhouse, and arrange for Huang's son to take over the daily school classes, releasing Gou to travel and preach.

Qiang priest with drum, scroll, and monkey-skin hat

Moving down to Miansi, Torrance, Hou, and Chen crossed the river with Gou Guanding, the Wasi Christian, and went up to a warm reception in Heping, one of Torrance's favourite places. 'Beautiful Heping. So bewitchingly lovely in the evening, so glorious in the early morning. Half-way up a great mountain the view is unsurpassed. Away down below, the river is roaring.' Before leaving the next morning Torrance took two photos, one of a Qiang hunter with his dog, gun, powder flask, and knife, and one of a Qiang priest with his drum, sacred scroll, and skin hat. On their return to Miansi, Torrance was pleased to find that photographs he had sent to Chengdu for developing had arrived. They were to be given to those in the photos, a precious gift that was highly valued.

At the Sunday service in Miansi, three Qiang men enrolled as enquirers. The next morning Torrance went up to see King Suo who was 'exceptionally gracious'. His visit coincided with that of four young teachers from the Chengdu Agricultural School, apparently interested in local stock-raising. Torrance and King Suo had doubts about this, which were confirmed when the Miansi chapel door was plastered with Communist posters overnight.

King Suo was fortunate to still be alive. He had been part of the Chinese force encountered by Plewman the previous year, sent up to suppress the ongoing unrest stirred up by his sister, Suo Daiyu, and one of her sons. On this visit Torrance found out that Suo Daiyu had tried to have King Suo assassinated because of his collusion with the Chinese against her. In her desire to avenge the murder of her husband, Chief Gao, and their son, she had caused havoc but had sadly lost another son in the fighting. In the end, Deng Xihou had sent orders for her to be brought down to Chengdu, in part for her own protection and also to prevent further incitement against the Chinese. Torrance found out later that she had called on him in Chengdu earlier that summer but he had already left on his travels.

Another visit to the Glen was extended to three nights due to heavy rain. The villagers insisted they stay and entertained them with stories of the local animals, including bear, leopard, lynx, deer, takin, golden monkeys, wild cattle, and the particularly destructive wild boar. In return, Torrance told biblical stories of a lost sheep, a lost coin, and a prodigal son, and mentioned again in his diary for the children that, 'In the Ch'iang country the thought is insistent with me that I am assisting in the search for sheep gone astray.' On Friday they ventured into the recesses of the Glen with locals who were herding their goats, sheep, and two bullocks. Beyond the grazing grounds a waterfall tumbled out of a hole in the cliff face and further on a Wasi temple gazed down on them from the heights. Urged by the villagers to come back next year, they left for a brief visit to Qiangfeng before returning to Miansi.

Torrance noted in his diary that evening that before leaving the Glen 'a foreboding of trouble had come over me. It is strange how one gets these premonitions.' As they reached Miansi they saw some students from the Agricultural College standing by the bridge. A group of seven of them were now lodging opposite the church and that evening they held a meeting after Torrance's gathering had finished and denounced him to their audience as an American capitalist whose preaching was a cover for his true aim of stealing precious stones. Torrance and Chen went to the yamen and asked the officials to come and listen. The men slipped in at the back and were alarmed enough by what they heard to suggest Torrance sleep in the yamen that night.

The following evening Torrance held a final meeting behind closed doors and although some tried to enter and disrupt things at the end, it concluded without serious incident and in the morning they slipped out at 4 a.m. to avoid any further confrontation and set off down to Guanxian. Clifford Stubbs' death and other incidents had put matters in a much more menacing light. It was a timely departure for other reasons too. Soon after they left severe flooding cut the road off in places and washed bridges away.

With his mind full of the events of the last month Torrance was shocked to find a letter from Carleton Lacy waiting for him at Lingyan, asking if he would consider a move to Yunnan Province. The New York headquarters had approved a proposal from Lacy that the ABS be amalgamated with the B&FBS, represented by Franck in Chengdu, and the National Bible Society of Scotland, whose nearest office was in Chongqing, and they were looking at staff reassignments. Torrance wanted neither the amalgamation nor a move to Yunnan. He feared the amalgamation would reduce the work to something less personal and also bring it more under the sway of the National Christian Council, which, as he had anticipated, had become too aligned with Nationalist politics for his liking.

Torrance had already expressed his misgivings about the amalgamation to Lacy so he replied on a more personal note explaining why he would rather not move to Yunnan. Stressing how clearly he had seen God's leading to Sichuan back in 1896 with the CIM, he then pointed to how the door, having seemed to slam shut in 1909, had, against all expectation, been re-opened by Hykes offering him the ABS job in Chengdu. On a purely practical level, he argued, his Sichuan dialect would not be fit for preaching in Yunnan, he wasn't sure he had the physical endurance to start in a new field, and he didn't have that long before retirement – so why move him somewhere where he would be less productive, especially as there was still so much work to do among the tribes. Concerned that Lacy had perhaps heard more from him about the Qiang work than about his daily ABS work among the Chinese, he then gave details of the evening meetings with Openshaw, the New Year campaign, and the thousands of privately funded tracts distributed throughout the year by both paid and voluntary colporteurs in Sichuan. Last but far from least, he noted how his relationship with 'certain Generals and officials' had helped facilitate the work of various missions in Chengdu in recent years.[27]

A heartening reply came from Lacy at the end of September: 'A lovely letter came in to-day from Mr. Openshaw urging that we leave you in Szechwan to carry on the fine work you have been doing.'[28] Lacy reassured Torrance that they had no intention of arbitrarily tearing him up by the roots. Perhaps prompted by this interaction with Lacy, Torrance submitted an article on 'Evangelism in West China' for publication in *The Chinese Recorder*, describing his and Openshaw's work at the Great East Street meeting hall.[29]

In October, Torrance and Openshaw went southwest of Chengdu to hold some meetings with local Christians in Cuqiao and Shuangliu. In contrast to the left-wing posters in Miansi, both places were displaying anti-Communist posters and about three hundred Communist supporters had apparently been arrested.

A couple of days after returning to Chengdu they were on the road again, this time on a muddy journey to Guanghan, about thirty miles north of Chengdu, to visit Vyvyan and Gladys Donnithorne at their CMS station. On their first evening together, Vyvyan, who had a first in classical Chinese from Cambridge, had also invited to dinner 'the only Christian magistrate in Szechuan', along with an army major who enjoyed meeting foreigners.[30] With Torrance and Openshaw both fluent in Chinese it was an evening of easy conversation. Having seen pro-Communist posters on their way to Guanghan, Torrance asked

27 TT to Lacy, August 27, 1930.
28 Lacy to Torrance, Sept 30, 1930.
29 TT. 'Evangelism in West China'. *The Chinese Recorder*, Vol 61, 1930, pp767-771.
30 TT to Lacy, October 31, 1930.

the major about Communist influence in the town but the major was dismissive.

Torrance and Openshaw retired to bed as soon as the guests left but were woken abruptly by the Donnithornes at 11.30 p.m. with the news that a well-orchestrated Communist uprising was underway. The telegraph and telephone wires had been cut and, after thirteen strikes on the Middle School bell, the Communists, who had infiltrated the local troops, had attacked, killing six officers and any soldier who resisted. They then 'raided the courthouses, looted the military quarters, released all the prisoners including forty robbers and burned the land-tax records. Secondary officials and leading citizens were seized and heavy sums wrung from them. Their houses the soldiers ransacked leaving nothing portable or of value.'[31]

The next morning, looking out through some shutter slits, Torrance and the others could see soldiers with their rifles and their spoils from the looting. To the sound of bullets they had a prayer time together, knowing they were potential targets, and Vyvyan asked Torrance to read that morning's entry in his *Daily Light* devotional: 'You shall hear of wars and rumours of war but see that you are not troubled . . . The very hairs of your head are numbered so do not be afraid.'[32] As Torrance prayed he was 'sensible that the Spirit definitely led me. A supernatural calm came down on our souls.' That night they slept fully-clothed and ready to flee if necessary but woke early the next morning to find that the 'Reds' had disappeared, taking the army horses and merchants' mules to carry their plunder.

The magistrate with whom Torrance and Openshaw had dined had managed to flee the city and raise the alarm but the yamen had been wrecked, several wounded soldiers were in the hospital, and the wife of a Christian lieutenant came to see Vyvyan and Gladys with news that her husband had been killed and she had lost everything. Torrance heard later that the magistrate attributed his escape to their dinner together. On returning home he had stayed up late to attend to some duties and was able to escape at once.[33]

With the rebels gone and troops arriving to protect the city, they continued with their outreach, warmly welcomed by people on the streets. The Donnithornes were deeply thankful that Torrance and

---

31 Ibid.

32 *Daily Light on the Daily Path*, first published c.1875 by Samuel Bagster & Sons, having been compiled by the Bagster family.

33 Torrance mentioned this in a letter to Annie on 29 Nov 1933, by which time the magistrate, Tao, was a Brigadier General in Deng Xihou's army.

Openshaw had been with them at such a critical time. Back in 1925 they had experienced the trauma of being kidnapped and held for nearly a month so they were keenly aware of what this round of hostility could have led to. Although mindful of the tragedies, in his letter to Lacy about the episode Torrance wrote, 'Certainly we all had a new and most intimate vision of His glory and the vision abides with us.'[34]

The incident had shaken the wider region and repercussions were severe in Chengdu. A WCMN editorial reported that the attack 'was followed by a period of ruthless suppression by the authorities, when many suspected persons were executed or imprisoned. Several schools have been closed because they were found to be centres of Communist activity.'[35] Many of the missionaries found the severity of action being taken against the Communists hard to bear, especially as guilt was not always proven. 'Many executions resulted, including some girl students whose faces were familiar about the Union University campus. Both the adjoining Sericulture School and the Art School have been sealed by the government and the furniture sold at auction . . . One's compassion goes out toward the innocent who have to suffer for the guilty, and one wonders just what will be the result of scattering the other agitators, if any, whose idle hands may now be freer to work mischief.'[36]

In his ABS report at the end of November 1930 Torrance described the year as 'one full of unusual difficulty, danger and encouragement. All through it, the Communist menace has been most threatening.' But perspectives differed and there was no doubt that the Communist message was attractive to some of the students. Earlier in the year, Dr T. Z. Koo, a prominent Chinese Christian leader in the YMCA and soon to become vice-president of the World Student Christian Federation, had written of the diverse political and literary influences impacting students in China.[37] In his opinion, the Nationalist Party's insistence that Sun Yatsen's 'Three People's Principles' be taught in schools was having little practical effect. In contrast, the Communists had a clear political creed: the end of imperialism and foreign ownership; a united, independent China; the end of Nationalist Party rule; a committee system of governance including representation for farmers and industrial workers; protection of workers' rights; an end

---

34 TT to Lacy, October 31, 1930.
35 WCMN, January 1931, p4.
36 WCMN, Dec 1930, p32.
37 Dr T. Z. Koo. 'Student Thought and Activity in China Today'. WCMN, April 1930, pp14-18.

to unjust taxes; and cooperation with Soviet Russia and the 'proletariat' worldwide. In comparison to China's tradition-bound, hierarchical society of the Qing era, and the current chaos and high taxation of the militarists, it seemed to some that the Communists had much to offer.

As usual, news of the Guanghan incident reached Annie and the children long after the event, as did Torrance's account of the summer trip. In Scotland they were in full swing with the autumn term and other activities. Grace was top of her class for the third year in a row and Tom, now in his final year at school, was excelling in his studies and had come first in Latin and won a prize in Greek. He was already clear in his mind that he wanted to become a Christian minister. In the autumn Annie wrote to Torrance, 'I often wonder what you would feel like among ours again. It is not by any means a quiet family. Often it seems an incessant round of activity. Conversation, arguments, discussions, etc. Waxing pretty lively some times.'[38] Although Torrance had eventually suggested that Annie might bring James and David out for a six month trial period, Annie had decided to stay in Edinburgh for now, a decision much influenced by the heart-to-hearts she was having with the older ones as they faced adolescent challenges and life decisions.

David, aged seven, had started writing his own letters to Torrance and, as Annie explained, 'He prefers to compose and spell them out on his own and feels quite proud when he gets through . . . quite original as you can see.'[39] Annie had also sent a heart-warming letter about the boys earlier in the year. At bedtime one day James had asked what 'converted' meant. As they talked about it David said, 'It's better to be converted at five isn't it' and insisted that was what he wanted. After he had knelt down and prayed with Annie, James told him that he should also say, 'Write my name in the Book of Life.' David promptly added that and then said, 'Now James' – and James followed suit.[40]

38 Annie to TT, undated.
39 Annie to TT, November 23, 1930.
40 Annie to TT, May 7, 1930.

Chapter 16

Turned Back at Diexi

1931

'I'll be needing an introduction by the time I come home.' So wrote Torrance on New Year's Day 1931 in response to Annie's description of the children growing fast and developing their own circles of friends and activities. The separation didn't get easier for any of them. Young James had taken to writing little poems, one of which read:

> I have a father and mother,
> My father is far away,
> He worries to see my mother,
> I worry to see my father.[1]

Torrance also admitted feeling low at times and wrote that it was their letters that helped keep him going.

As time went on some of the children wrote less often. Annie explained that Tom was not a good letter writer because 'he becomes absorbed in theological study'.[2] However, when he did write it was with discussion of doctrinal issues and theological books, some of which he sent to Torrance, which helped to maintain their long distance relationship. Tom was currently against infant baptism whereas Torrance, drawing a parallel with Old Testament infant circumcision, accepted it as long as it was more than just a sprinkle of water. Photos were also a treasured means of connection. In February Torrance sent a photo of Guanxian, always close to Annie's heart, with the street she had lived on now widened and well-paved, and in March a photo of the sitting room, a simple but poignant reminder of their daily family prayers there.

At the end of February Torrance wrote to Annie that the Chinese New Year meetings had been the best ever. The Great East Street hall had been packed out and at the end Torrance sent a copy of John's gospel and a new tract, 'The Greatest Question on Earth', to every civil

1 Annie to TT, Feb 2, 1931.
2 Annie to TT, April 1931 (n.d.).

magistrate in Sichuan. He was also planning to send his colporteurs to all the main towns around Chengdu by the end of the year. Xiong, the Chinese teacher in the Glen, had come down for two months to gain more experience and help with the meetings. The school had now moved from the Glen to Qiangfeng and at the beginning of March Xiong headed back up to resume his teaching. A while later Torrance heard that Communist posters had once again been posted around Miansi, including on the mission house.

In Chengdu, the depot manager, Li Youren, had decided to move into the servant quarters at Wushi-tongtang and Torrance, who was still living with Franck, was happy to have someone so dependable on site. One of the servants had been caught stealing coal and selling it to the cook at the Canadian Press. About 150 kilos had been retrieved and the servant had promised to repay the remaining debt but then disappeared. Jiu Si, who had left and got a job as a rickshaw-puller, had wearied of that and came asking Torrance for help finding a job. Torrance found him rather temperamental but he was 'poor and down and out, almost as a tramp' so he took him on again.[3] Another member of staff, not long a Christian, needed treatment for syphilis. Torrance paid for injections for him and kept him on, trusting that it was a momentary lapse and that he would be a good worker, a trust which proved to be merited.

In early March Torrance gave a lecture on Chinese pottery and porcelain at the university and on March 12 he celebrated his sixtieth birthday, a rite of passage in China marking the beginning of a new life stage. Mrs Plewman baked him a cake and representatives of the Chengdu foreign community presented him with a Ming dynasty earthenware jar and a birthday tribute in appreciation of his 'wonderful researches in the realms of amber beads, jade, etc.'.[4] The tribute also commemorated his narrow escape in Guanghan with Openshaw and the Donnithornes.

Continuing his interest in local history, Torrance had been working on a two-part article for the WCMN, telling the dramatic story of Zhang Xianzhong, a rebel leader from Shaanxi who ruled over Sichuan for less than three years in the mid 1600s as the Ming dynasty gave

---

3   TT to Annie, April 16, 1931.
4   The tribute was signed by P. J. Keating (the Postal Commissioner), James Neave (Pastor of Si-sheng-ci Church), Dr Retta Kilborn (Women's Missionary Society), and H. J. Mullett (Commissioner of Oaths, and chairman of Sewers and Drains Committee).

way to the Qing.[5] His brief and bloody reign resulted in a large-scale depopulation of Sichuan, with multitudes killed or fleeing. Zhang met his death at the hands of advancing Manchu troops, leaving behind a sad legacy: 'He found Chengtu one of the finest cities in China; he left it a city of the dead – a smoking, blackened, desolate ruin.'[6]

Glad of an opportunity to be out of the city in springtime, Torrance went to help with some CIM meetings in Pengzhou and then spent a week working with a Chinese pastor in Qionglai. It felt good to be back in familiar haunts and he continued to encounter people who had been to the Great East Street meetings. Quite a few soldiers attended the meetings in Qionglai and responded enthusiastically to the preaching. He was also visited by an ex-B&FBS colporteur who was now working as an official and wanted help to kick his opium habit.

Back in Chengdu, Torrance gave a lecture on May 20 to the WCUU students about the border tribes. That same week, Homer Brown, in his address at the annual meeting of the West China Border Research Society, looked at different areas of research and mentioned Torrance's study of the Qiang as a good example of research into the history of groups with distinctive religious traditions. A few days later Torrance vented his frustration to Annie regarding a recent newspaper article by Edgar Plewman: 'I see from the China Press that Plewman had been speaking in Shanghai on his border trips and told them again that the Ch'iang worship the White Stone. He likes to spread abroad this fallacy. It seems to sound well. The White Stone is only a symbol.'[7]

Encouraging news had come from Gou Pinsan that the Dongmenwai work was going well, with the Christians regularly attending Sunday services. Torrance was hoping the political situation wouldn't derail his summer plans. The territorial agreements between the five main generals in Sichuan were becoming increasingly fragile and Torrance complained to Annie that Liu Xiang was encroaching on Deng Xihou's territory. In March some of Chengdu's city gates had been closed for a few days, with soldiers encamped outside the north gate who were loyal to a minor militarist wanting more territory and troops of another, Li

---

5   TT. 'The Spoiler of Szechuan', Part 1, WCMN, March 1931, pp29-39; Part 2, WCMN, April 1931, pp36-45. Torrance's sources included these works by Sichuanese historians: *Shu Bi* by Peng Zunsi of Danleng (18th C); *Shu Po Jing* by Sun Ji of Pixian (1787-1849); and *Shu Jing Lu* by Ouyang Zhi of Guang'an (17th C).
6   Ibid., Part 2, p43.
7   TT to Annie, June 3, 1931.

Zhixiang, purportedly in the city. Li was supposedly subordinate to Deng but was now stirring up trouble, which some locals saw as part of a plot by Liu Xiang and Liu Wenhui to squeeze Deng out. Deng had done much to keep the peace in Chengdu and Torrance reiterated to Annie that he was 'the man who has done most for us. It is to him we owe our liberty to work here.'[8]

The WCMN editorial in May was extremely gloomy about the situation:

> After six years of comparative peace, based on a nicely adjusted balance of power, it looks as if Szechuan is in danger of another flood of war such as was all too common ten years ago. At the time of writing there is fighting on the Suining river and considerable apprehension that it may spread to other parts of the province.[9]

The fighting resulted in parcel shipments being blocked and Torrance was down to his last ten gospels. The price of rice had doubled and people were afraid of famine despite good harvests. In the end the fighting was kept away from Chengdu but tensions were still simmering.

In early June Torrance had a visit from General Huang, one of Deng's top military men and an uncle of Liao, to whom Torrance had given his Burns poetry book. Last summer Huang had been cured of dysentery in the Canadian hospital and had also received help to give up opium. Torrance had visited him a couple of times in hospital and there was now a good rapport between them. Huang was an art expert and Torrance was keen to show him a painting he had bought for the university museum. Liao was out of town, having been sent in April as Deng Xihou's delegate to a Nationalist Congress in Nanjing. As in Sichuan, the Nationalists were also dealing with deep divisions and instability.

As Torrance was preparing for his summer travels amidst all the political uncertainty, a more positive upheaval was happening in Scotland. For several months Annie had been making enquiries about houses in Edinburgh and had found something almost too good to be true. In June they moved to 25 Warrender Park Road, a flat on two floors above a ground floor flat, with spacious rooms and big windows. Although the rent was higher than in Bellshill, the move meant Tom and Mary could live at home when they started at Edinburgh

---

8   TT to Annie, April 16, 1931.
9   WCMN, May 1931, p1. The six years of relative peace dated from the Sichuan generals' conference in the winter of 1925.

University that autumn so it still made financial sense and it was also in easy reach of the younger children's new schools and just a five-minute walk from The Meadows, where David and James could run to their heart's content. Three other China missionary families lived nearby and Charlotte Baptist Chapel was just a twenty-minute walk, where Annie quickly felt at home under the ministry of Dr Graham Scroggie. Torrance was delighted that the family would be able to stay together.

In late June Torrance set off for more than six weeks in the mountains, pleased to be joined by Leona Thoering, an American missionary with the CIM in Guanxian, and Mrs Wang, a gifted speaker and wife of a Chinese preacher. With them were Jiu Si attending to Billy, Liang Si as cook, and Tang, one of Torrance's best book-sellers, as colporteur. Hou Li-de was bringing up two calves for stock-breeding in Miansi and the Glen and would then return to Chengdu. One of these was from Torrance's own cow and the other a half-foreign one from Frank Dickinson's university breeding programme.

The plan this year was to go north to Songpan and also west from Weizhou along the Zagunao Valley. In Songpan Torrance wanted to visit a new worker, Ong Guangming, who had recently moved up there. Years ago, Ong had worked for Clarence Ramsay as an ABS colporteur but after the death of his wife he had taken a job with the police and a sad series of events had brought many troubles his way.[10] Eventually he had moved up to the mountains and started afresh, selling medicine for a living and preaching the gospel. When Torrance discovered this, he had asked if Ong would work for him up in the Songpan region. After all that Ong had been through, Torrance perceived a rare spiritual depth and prayerfulness in him and an ability to talk with ease to whoever he met.

Rain overnight, so common in the summer, provided them with a cool day for the main trek up the Min Valley, made easier by recent road improvements. Late spring lilies dotted the hillsides and Torrance was in his element serving as tour guide for Leona and Mrs Wang as they passed places of interest and enjoyed the fauna and flora of a climate so different to that of the Chengdu plain.

After a night in Yingxiu and another at Taoguan, where the women set their cot-beds up in a temple and the men had a flea-bitten night

---

10 Ong Guangming's story is told in Chapter 18 of Torrance's *Conversion Stories of Chinese Christians*.

in a rudimentary inn, they reached Miansi. That evening Leona and Mrs Wang led a meeting for the local women, with any men attending relegated to the back. During the night some local students chalked graffiti on the mission house using Torrance's Chinese name, Tao Ranshi,[11] and he was now an imperialistic dog rather than the American capitalist of the previous year. 'Truly my titles are increasing on me,' he wrote to the children.[12]

The next day was busy with visits from Qiang friends and Leona and Mrs Wang strolled around the town, chatting with the women and children in their homes and helping with health issues. Torrance wrote to Annie that Leona's 'heart is truly in the work and already she is in love with the Ch'iang. Their kindliness and gratitude have taken her by storm.'[13] In the evening the ladies preached again, following which Torrance let some rather rowdy lads in and also spoke. They listened quietly and although once outside again there were a few shouts of 'down with Christianity', there was no further graffiti.

Torrance had brought a gramophone with him this time and played a few records before the meetings, a novelty much enjoyed by the regulars and others who came to listen. As usual, people also came for medical treatment, many with intestinal trouble and dysentery, which was particularly prevalent that summer due to a plague of flies. It gave Torrance great satisfaction to be able to alleviate their distress but even greater satisfaction when people responded to their message: 'Can there be anything better under the sun than a gospel meeting where men respond to the claims of Christ? If there is I have yet to find it.'

Across the Min River in Qiangfeng the elderly village headman whose birthday they had attended last year was delighted to see them and expressed his desire to become a Christian. A less positive development was the closure of the school in Qiangfeng, much to the disappointment and indignation of the villagers. The Chinese official in Miansi had ordered the students to come down and attend the government school in a local temple but it only had a primary school teacher so the older boys were losing out. One of the Qiang farmers provoked much laughter with his description of the lessons: 'This is an

---

11 陶然士, a phonetic transliteration of Torrance but also meaning happy, carefree, and a scholar.
12 TT diary to children, July 2, 1931. All summer trip quotations are from this unless otherwise indicated.
13 TT to Annie, July 6, 1931.

egg, a goose egg is larger than a duck's egg, a duck's than a hen's, etc. Why do our boys want to be taught what everybody knows.'[14] Moving up to the Glen, Torrance presented one of the Qiang farmers with eggs from some Leghorn chickens raised in Chengdu by Irene Hutchinson, which were immediately placed under two sitting hens.

After a Sunday in Miansi, with services morning and evening, Leona and Mrs Wang left Torrance to spend a week visiting the women in Qiangfeng, the Glen, Gaodongshan, and Heping, accompanied by Chen Bingling's wife and Teacher Xiong, who was free now that the school had been shut down. The others set off for Weizhou where they found the mission house still occupied by the magistrate and about thirty of his staff. Torrance was able to rest a while there and told the magistrate of their plans to visit Songpan. They then continued to Keku where Torrance's usual quarters on Mr Yang's roof were ready for him. Yang's central room quickly filled up for the evening meeting at which Torrance spoke of Jesus' sacrifice, using as illustrations the purity of the lilies on the mountainsides and the holiness required at Qiang sacrifices.

On arrival in Dongmenwai the next day, Torrance was disappointed to hear that the bull brought up the previous summer had died. 'It fell into a crevice and had to be pulled out. It managed to walk home but died afterwards.'[15] He was also disappointed to find that Gou Pinsan wasn't at Dongmenwai. Despite his resistance the previous year, Gou had been obliged by the local Chinese official to become headman of his district – something which would bring him trouble in time to come – and he was away at an official conference in Maoxian. The villagers were anxious for his return. Two days earlier, heavy rain and hail had destroyed most of the crops up in Longxi Village, and in the valley the stream had swelled to such a height that it had destroyed the water channels from the Dongmenwai mill to the lower fields and swept away part of the road between the church and the village. Gou was needed for reconstruction decisions to be made.

On Sunday it was a moving sight to see people wending their way down the valley to the weekly service, even from the more remote villages. Using the surrounding mountains as his setting, Torrance spoke of the mountain top transfiguration of Jesus and contrasted the radiance of the transfigured Christ with the whiteness of the Qiang sacred stone in the light of their sacrificial fire.

---

14 TT to Annie, July 6, 1931.
15 TT to Annie, July 17, 1931.

Gou returned on Monday from Maoxian and on Tuesday Leona and Mrs Wang rejoined them after a highly enjoyable week in the Miansi villages. The plan now was for the women to hold meetings in the old meeting room while the men met in the new church building. On Wednesday Gou took Torrance for his first visit to Upper and Middle Keku where Torrance enjoyed watching the wheat-threshing on the roof-tops, particularly one blind man who was the most skilled with his flail. At Upper Keku Torrance was surprised to see a woman with bound feet, not usually a practice of the Qiang. She explained that she was from Guanxian but her parents had married her to a Qiang farmer. She was a ready listener and it turned out that she had known the Hutsons and been to church as a girl. As they chatted with the villagers, Gou likened the ancient customs of the Qiang to 'a map or drawing of the benefits of the gospel', pointing to Jesus' own sacrifice.

Returning to Dongmenwai, Gou and Torrance set out along the Zagunao River to the neighbouring villages of Kongdiping and Taoping. At Kongdiping news of their arrival spread and many came for medical treatment. Seeing so many women among them, Torrance offered to send Leona to treat them the following day. In Taoping Torrance left most of the speaking to Gou Pinsan. 'He was perfectly in his element to-day. Never have I heard him speak in better form. He made a great impression.' Heading back along the river, the bank suddenly gave way under Billy. Torrance quickly rolled out of the saddle and managed just in time to get his legs away from Billy's scrambling hooves as he regained his footing. They had been seconds away from tumbling into the fast-flowing current.

Quite a few people came down to Dongmenwai from Mushang village on Saturday to be in time for the Sunday service so an impromptu meeting was held that afternoon. Gou spoke on the similarity between Jesus as mediator between man and God and the Qiang sacred roll of paper, their 'Je-Dsu' or 'Nee-Dsu', which also had a mediatory role. The following day the church was full to overflowing with 'old and young, far and near, all sorts and conditions of people', so they chose to hold the service on a nearby grassy slope. Three women and four men were baptised in the Dongmenwai stream, including Xiong the teacher and Tang the colporteur. The two other men were Gao, in his fifties and from Qiangfeng, and a 19-year-old lad, Wang, from the Glen. Chief Yang happened to be in the area on business and came to watch the baptisms.

A couple of days later Leona and Mrs Wang returned to Guanxian and Torrance set out for Luobozhai with Chen Bingling and Tang.

Remembering Torrance's medical treatment two years earlier, many Luobozhai villagers came to have ailments treated and an attentive crowd gathered to listen as the three men took turns to speak. Several were 'strongly impressed' and New Testaments were given to two of the villagers who showed interest and could read.

Moving on the next day, Torrance described the beauty of the approach to Maoxian: 'The city lies in a basin . . . Great mountains surround it. The lower slopes of one were a vast rich brocade of various coloured fields of ripe grain, blooming buckwheat, young maize, with ridges and slopes of grass and bush.' The Spreckleys were away on furlough and the CMS mission house had been commandeered by a Colonel Liu who avoided any contact with Torrance's party. Despite this, Torrance was able to set his cot-bed up in a reception room there and early the next day they moved on to the village of Musubao, half-way between Maoxian and the town of Diexi. Here they spoke in the evening to a mixed group of Qiang, Chinese, and Muslims who were amused at the ease with which Torrance could distinguish between them. Always curious about differing local customs, Torrance learned from one of the Qiang that their priest wore a leopard skin robe at the sacrificial ceremonies in their village. He was also told that the Qiang here were called 'Er-yi-zi', the much resented Chinese term meaning 'second barbarians' which he had encountered in 1922 in the Maoxian area.

Pressing on the next day to Diexi, a small town whose name two years later would be on lips across China, the road was rough and steep as it led over a mountain pass but Torrance was cheered by the sight of a group of Qiang singing as they harvested wheat in their fields. As they neared the house of a man whose eyes Torrance had treated back in 1924, the man suddenly came out, recognised Torrance, and asked for more lotion.

Bad news awaited them in Diexi. As they entered the town they were met by two armed soldiers with orders from Maoxian to turn them back – an indication that anti-Christian sentiment was still strong there. They took Torrance to see a local official who asked to see Torrance's travel permit, which was clearly valid for all of Sichuan, and then told him that to continue to Songpan he needed a special letter from the Chengdu generals or a permit from Maoxian. Torrance explained that General Deng knew of his trip and asked the official for a note explaining the reasons for his actions but this was refused. However, when Torrance agreed to return to Maoxian, the official, perhaps uncertain as to who had originally issued the order, suddenly changed his mind and said they were free to continue to Songpan but he would accept no responsibility for their safety. Knowing this would leave them too vulnerable, Torrance decided to turn back despite his deep disappointment once again at not reaching Songpan, which was compounded by not being able to see Ong Guangming.

Retracing their steps to Maoxian they passed two men, one of whom recognised Torrance and turned out to be a Christian who had heard him preach in Chengdu. He was a senior officer under the Songpan commander, Yang Fuquan, and was on his way to visit the official in Diexi. He was indignant when he heard about Torrance being turned back and as they parted he gave Torrance his visiting card.

In Maoxian the local Christians took Torrance and his companions to visit some local gardens, where they happened to encounter Colonel Liu. Although Torrance was certain it was Liu who had intervened to prevent them reaching Songpan, they had a civil conversation, with Liu complimenting Torrance on his good reputation in the region and Torrance expressing appreciation of the new roads and other social improvements.

The unexpected change of plan gave Torrance time to visit several villages around Maoxian that were new to him. One Qiang villager he talked with initially denied that they still kept their old rituals, despite the existence of a sacred grove above his village, but once he realised how much Torrance knew of their traditions he acknowledged that they were still observed. 'He told me how some time ago the Chinese military wantonly cut down the great trees in their grove. But they now only observed one festival in the year viz in the second moon.' Further down the valley they stopped to visit the village of Yangmaoping, meaning 'Sheep-Wool Flat'.

In Weizhou Torrance was able to stay overnight at the mission premises. Knowing that the magistrate had a telephone connection with Liu in Maoxian, Torrance guessed from his lack of curiosity about their early return that he was well aware of what had happened in Diexi, but he proved affable. They found common ground in discussion of agricultural matters and Torrance was pleased to be shown the nursery where the magistrate was experimenting with various kinds of American maize seed and other imported grains and plants. Torrance appreciated his friendliness but the sight of the chapel room now being used as a stable was hard to bear. 'The only sign of its former sanctity was a sign still on the wall with the words on it "God is love". Immediately underneath was a pile of horse manure!'

The rest of the trip went as planned. Tang had gone ahead to sell literature in Xuecheng and Zagunao, preparing the way for their arrival. Taking the good road on the south bank of the Zagunao River, they went straight to Tonghua where many came for medical treatment. Thanks in part to Gou's influence, some of the villagers there had lost their earlier reserve and said they wanted to open a place of worship. In Xuecheng they were welcomed by Pastor Mao and had obviously been spotted coming along the valley as an invitation promptly arrived to visit Chief Yang in Erwa but Torrance decided against the long climb this time, wanting to make the most of time in Zagunao after a ten year gap since his last visit.

On August 1, Torrance and Annie's twentieth wedding anniversary, they moved on to Zagunao, crossing into predominantly Jiarong territory at the junction of the Puxi and Zagunao valleys. Although Old Ren, the secretary to Chief Gao, had died several years ago, his school-teacher son was now leading a church of about twelve members in Zagunao, closely connected with Pastor Mao. Torrance joined the younger Ren at his meetings and there was an encouraging response to his preaching. After the Sunday gathering they visited the local lamasery. Torrance was convinced that the Qiang and the now Buddhist Jiarong had once shared the same customs. In his diary to the children he wrote that they had 'long been Lamaists. Tibetan influence finally swamped them. Yet here while the old customs have changed they have not died out. They have been perverted. White Stones are seen on the roofs, but the sacrifices are offered to Buddha and not to God. A Lama officiates when a ram or an ox is slain. Most plainly the Rong once held the faith of the Ch'iang.'

After a rainy journey back to Xuecheng they took the narrow track along the north bank to Taoping where they happened to meet Albert Brace and Cecil Hoffman. Torrance was glad of some English conversation over lunch with them. Brace had replaced Plewman as secretary of the Canadian Methodist Mission's tribes work and they were on their way to visit Mao and Ren. One more night in Dongmenwai gave Torrance and Gou Pinsan time to discuss renting meeting rooms in Tonghua and also in A'er, eight miles up the valley from Dongmenwai, where Torrance and Tom had had such a memorable encounter with the priest in 1926. After the wettest summer trip he had experienced, Torrance was now keen to start his journey back before the road became impassable. Crossing the stream at Banqiao the water was up to Billy's belly.

TAOPING

To Torrance's astonishment the small town of Miansi was in a state of
high excitement over the expected arrival of Wu Peifu, the powerful
northern general who had once been the hope of the foreign powers
for a stable China, and whose face in 1924 had graced the cover of
TIME magazine.[16] Defeated by Chiang Kai-shek's Nationalist forces in
1926, Wu had taken refuge in eastern Sichuan with his allies, Yang Sen
and Liu Cunhou.[17] However, now that Sichuan was paying at least lip-
service to the Nationalists, that had ceased to be a safe place and he
had been given right of way by Deng Xihou, whom he had appointed
as civil governor of Sichuan back in 1924, to pass through his territory
away from the reach of Nanjing.

Wu Peifu and his entourage were expected on Sunday and
Torrance thought few would risk coming to the morning service for
fear of being impressed as carriers, but the meeting hall was quite full.
In the end, Wu arrived late afternoon and Torrance, who was out for
a walk, watched the procession into town from his vantage point on

16 TIME, Sept 8, 1924.
17 TT to Cameron, May 31, 1928; TT to Annie, June 17, 1928.

the hillside. Staying only one night, Wu departed the next morning to a roar of firecrackers. He acknowledged Torrance as he passed by and Torrance, who considered Wu one of China's more honourable leaders, wished him a prosperous journey.

General Wu Peifu, Sept 8, 1924[18]

With the excitement over, Torrance and the others paid a brief visit to Heping. Here they found that three villagers had been pressed into carrying loads for Wu but all had managed to escape by the time the procession reached Weizhou. They laughed when Torrance said he had come to impress them all to go to the Kingdom of Heaven with him. Torrance was delighted that the youngest son of Old Su wanted to become a Christian. One of the other villagers, whose father was a Christian, explained his own reticence to Torrance. He was afraid he would find it too difficult to handle the taunts of the Chinese, something which illustrated the courage of those who persevered regardless, when there was little to be gained of any temporal nature.

Stopping only to say farewell to Chen Bingling and others at the spring below Miansi, Torrance then set off towards Guanxian. Dysentery was still rife and several people approached him for

---

18 https://en.wikipedia.org/wiki/Wu_Peifu (Public domain)

treatment along the way. Two children he had treated on the way up were doing well but in one place he was asked to help a young boy and a woman who had both been ill for nearly three weeks. He didn't hold out much hope for either but did what he could and left some extra medicine for them.

At Lingyan it was 'sweet to rest again, to relax in body and mind' and enjoy some soft baked bread. On his return to Chengdu he set about getting the colporteurs stocked up with batches of books and was soon back in his usual round of ABS work, Great East Street meetings, and hospital visiting. In quiet moments he was writing a paper, 'Notes on the Cave Tombs and Ancient Burial Mounds of Western Szechwan', which Daniel Dye had requested for the JWCBRS.[19] In a WCMN review of the whole journal it was described as 'one of the most interesting articles' and was also praised in *The Chinese Recorder* as a 'deeply interesting and beautifully illustrated article'.[20]

Towards the end of September Torrance received an unusual request from the British Consul in Chongqing, asking to be kept informed about a man named Trebitsch, who was on his way to Chengdu in the garb of a Buddhist priest. A few years younger than Torrance, Trebitsch was a gifted linguist, would-be politician, sometime aspiring clergyman, and, apparently, a con-artist. Born to Jewish parents in Hungary he had fled to London on the run from the Hungarian police and supposedly converted to Christianity through someone who, after Trebitsch had stolen some of his wife's jewellery, described him as 'thoroughly bad, a genius, and very attractive, but taking the crooked way always for choice'.[21] After a brief spell as MP for Darlington in 1910, followed by rejections from Britain and Germany of his offers to spy for them in the First World War, and three years in a British prison for forgery, he decided, in the early 1920s, that China would be a good place to start afresh. There he ingratiated himself with various militarists, including Yang Sen for a brief period, and in 1931 he was officially ordained as a Buddhist monk, something which had clearly failed to convince the British Consul of any character reformation.

---

19 JWCBRS, Vol IV, 1930-1931, p88-96.
20 WCMN, Nov 1932, p24; *Chinese Recorder*, Jan 1933, p53.
21 Phillip Knightley. 'Reverse Discrimination'. *London Review of Books*. Vol 10, No 10, May 19, 1988. (A review of *The Secret Lives of Trebitsch Lincoln* by Bernard Wasserstein. Yale. 1988.)

Nor was Torrance persuaded when Trebitsch paid him a visit a few months later:

> He walked right in and into the middle room unannounced! . . . I told him he had no right to come in and I took him outside. Three callers were then with me . . . I said I knew all about him and he should not be here in Chengtu, he ought to leave, and go where he could get a job. I felt sorry for him he was so tramp-like. I advised him to repent and become a Christian. He maintained he was, for his parents every evening taught him out of the Bible.[22]

Torrance gave him some money for food and Trebitsch moved on, eventually dying in Shanghai in 1943 after further dubious exploits.

A more welcome visitor arrived in October. Having been prevented from seeing Torrance in the summer, Ong Guangming had come down to discuss the work in Songpan, where he had rented a simple property with a bedroom at the back and a room facing the street. Five people were now joining him for worship on Sundays. Keenly aware of the opposition up there, Torrance advised Ong to keep the meetings low profile and not put any signs up to attract people. Together they chose various tracts to be sent up and Torrance gave him a list of people he could visit on his way back up, including the Christians in Miansi and Dongmenwai, and others Torrance had met on the way up to Diexi. Gou Pinsan had sent news from Dongmenwai that Old Gui from Heping had moved into the new kitchen outhouse at the church to care for the building and garden area, for which Gou was giving him a bushel of wheat each month.

More news from the region came at the end of October. As Plewman had predicted, government troops had been sent in to subdue the Heishui tribes and their powerful leader, Su Yonghe. Initially, Colonel Liu, who had blocked Torrance's trip to Songpan, had sent a force of three hundred men to subdue them, dismissive of their fearsome reputation, but his men had been easily defeated with many casualties. Now a further attempt with a thousand soldiers had once again been repulsed. Towards the end of the year reinforcements were sent up and a force of about three thousand men went in but they too were defeated and Deng lost several hundred men overall. Colonel Liu was wounded and in disgrace, having initiated the costly fiasco, and the people of Maoxian demanded his removal.

---

22 TT to Annie, Feb 11, 1932.

Some time later Torrance heard more detail and described the final fierce clash:

> The Heishui warriors, seeing it was to be a life and death struggle, chased all Chinese merchants out of their country, and resolved at all costs to preserve inviolate their land and their homes. They allowed the main force to move in a long distance practically unmolested. Then they cut off the rear and surrounded an auxiliary detachment of several hundred men who were guarding the stores and money behind. These they held in a position where no water could be had and after seven days, when all were weak, rushed the camp and left not one alive. The main force had now to fight its way back and out. Had it not been for the prowess of a Gansu Lieutenant and his men all should have perished.

News also reached Torrance that King Suo had been killed in the fighting. He and his men had been pressed into joining the Chinese forces against the Heishui people. In the final attack on Heishui, Suo had been in charge of this rearguard which was isolated and annihilated by the Heishui men in the vicinity of Weigu. One of the eleven Wasi who died alongside Chief Suo was a son of Gou Guanding, the Wasi Christian. He had been sent by Suo's wife with a message for Suo and was killed almost as soon as he got there.

Mrs Gao, King Suo's sister, was still under house arrest in Chengdu and had offered to go and negotiate for peace with the Heishui fighters but the Chinese suspected that once she was back with her people she wouldn't stick to her word. In early December Mrs Gao sent a woman to Torrance with a request, as he explained to Annie: 'Deng seems to be thinking of appointing her to Heishui. His troops have been defeated apparently . . . and a truce has been arranged. But Deng wants some one to guarantee her. This woman wanted to know if I would lend my name to help to guarantee her.'[23] Several months before, Torrance had lent Mrs Gao $15 but she had apparently told Deng he had lent her $2000, presumably to convince Deng that Torrance considered her trustworthy. She wanted Torrance to back up her story of the large loan but he declined. To Annie he explained, 'Mrs Gao has a poor name here. It may not be deserved, of course, but there it is. All she owes me is $15.'[24]

---

23 TT to Annie, Dec 4, 1931.
24 Ibid.

Not long after this, Torrance and Openshaw went to visit Mrs Gao, who had been moved from a house on Huaxing Street to the police station prison. She appealed to them to intercede with Deng Xihou on her behalf. She had made sure her daughter was in a safe place but was convinced that the Chinese wanted to kill her whole family and seize her lands. When Torrance and Openshaw went to talk with Deng he was unsympathetic and held Mrs Gao responsible for the Heishui unrest, which had cost him so dearly. Torrance withheld his own opinion that Colonel Liu in Maoxian was largely to blame for the troubles but they urged Deng to give Mrs Gao a better place to live, reminding him that her husband, Chief Gao, had been unjustly killed.[25] Deng was immovable and Torrance later wrote to Annie that one of Deng's men, Deng Juezhang, was thought to have secretly sanctioned Gao's murder.[26]

The year concluded with a conference for Chinese Christian leaders, together with the annual meeting of the Sichuan Christian Council, which gave Torrance a chance to see some of the Chinese Christians he knew from across Sichuan. On one evening he invited some of them over for a big dinner, in part to get to know them better but also wanting to express his continued concern about their vulnerability to political control and the difficulties this might create for anyone thought to be putting their allegiance to Christ before political loyalties. A letter to Annie in early 1934 shows what a weight this was on his mind: 'Just as sure as all the churches in China are grouped into one organization then it becomes a government tool for political ends. Hitler in Germany is doing this.'

For the family back in Scotland the Christmas holidays were a welcome rest. Tom and Mary had just completed their first term at university, Tom in Classics and Mary 'buried in old English and Anglo-Saxon stuff'.[27] Both were glad to be living at home and often invited friends back on weekends so the house was becoming a hub of activity. Taking after his father, Tom had been leading some Christian meetings and also participating in open air gatherings on the corner of South Charlotte Street and Princes Street, where he often spoke to quite a crowd.

25 TT to Annie, Jan 4, 1932.
26 TT to Annie, March 31, 1932.
27 Annie to TT, Nov 10, 1931.

Annie's own circle of friends and connections was ever expanding and she was becoming much in demand as a speaker, even going away for the occasional weekend now that the older children were able to care for the younger ones. In October she had spoken at a week-end gathering in Falkland, a National Bible Society of Scotland meeting in Mid Calder, two large women's meeting at St Cuthbert's Presbyterian Church in Edinburgh, and at an annual missionary exhibition at Charlotte Baptist Chapel.

But Torrance was never far from their thoughts and the political tensions and the difficulties on his summer trip were much on Annie's mind. 'We yearn to have you home and safe with us once again. There is a big big welcome waiting for you both in our home and hearts and once with us again it will be difficult to let you go ever again.'[28] She was conscious that Torrance might be forced to leave China any time and despite Britain being in the grip of the Depression, she had reassured him that they would manage somehow without the ABS income. Torrance wasn't so sure and wrote to Annie on the last day of 1931, 'Were I to come home now all your prospects would indeed be gloomy. When the Lord wants me home I am sure He will make His will plain.'[29]

---

28 Annie to TT, Oct 4, 1931.
29 TT to Annie, Dec 31, 1931.

PART FOUR

Chapter 17

Songpan Again – and the Shadow of War

1932

In January 1932 Edgar Plewman set up his own radio receiver in Chengdu. An avid listener, he would tune in late at night to stations around the world and send printed news updates to the various missions. For Torrance, always keen to keep abreast of local and global political developments, this was a welcome addition, especially in the light of current events.

In North America and Europe the Great Depression was cutting deep into the home economies of the missionaries, a situation aggravated for many of those in Chengdu by low dollar exchange rates. The Canadians had been given a ten percent reduction in salary and Lacy warned Torrance that a cut was imminent. Torrance was looking for ways to prevent that affecting Diao's salary in Chongqing but to his relief, Lacy not only found a way to offset the cuts but also sent the welcome news that the ABS was extending the children's allowances until they graduated from university.

Plewman's radio brought disturbing news in late January of increased Sino-Japanese tensions in eastern China. That winter, foreigners across China had been waiting with bated breath to see if Chiang Kai-shek would implement a promise made on May 4, 1931, to remove their extraterritorial rights. The date had been chosen in remembrance of China's 1919 humiliation at Versailles and the regulations were due to come into effect on January 1, 1932, bringing all foreigners and foreign enterprises under Chinese jurisdiction. In Manchuria, Japan's Kwantung Army, almost a law unto itself, saw this as a threat to their interests in the northeast, which were vital to Japan's struggling economy, and in September 1931 they had taken matters into their own hands. On the false pretext of a Chinese bomb attack on a Japanese railway in Manchuria – in fact carried out by a Japanese soldier – the Kwantung Army had launched a successful bid for full control of the long-coveted territory. The Chinese responded to this aggression with a huge outpouring of patriotism. Students rushed to

Nanjing to join the fight and universities promptly introduced military and first-aid training. Even in Chengdu, 1,500 miles away, a city-wide student demonstration had taken place in October 1931, this time with WCUU students joining the crowds, united with other students in their indignation and patriotism.

Looking to strengthen their hold in China, at midnight on January 28, 1932, the Japanese attacked Shanghai. Annie was following the news in Scotland and wrote to Torrance on February 19 that 'the Japs and the Chinese are massing great numbers along an extensive battle line and unless there is some intervention which at present seems quite unlikely, there is going to be a terrific war and horrible bloodshed.' Her fears were confirmed. Edmund Sugg, a CMS doctor who was treating the wounded at an emergency hospital in a Shanghai temple, wrote in mid-March that thousands of Chinese were fleeing as Japanese aerial bombs and shells from heavy artillery hit the villages and districts around Shanghai. 'As many as twenty thousand houses were destroyed in just one night. Consequently there were several thousands wounded and killed, and what had previously been prosperous villages and districts were reduced to heaps of ruins.'[1] A truce was eventually signed in May, resulting in a Japanese withdrawal from Shanghai and followed ten days later by the assassination of the Japanese prime minister, Inukai Tsuyoshi, by young Japanese naval officers angry at his attempts to restrain the military.

Despite the truce, the Japanese still controlled Manchuria where, in early March, they appointed Puyi, the infant emperor installed by Cixi in 1908, as a puppet ruler. Although this was opposed by a League of Nations commission of enquiry later in the year, which advocated Japanese autonomy but not sovereignty, Japan rejected the commission's ruling, left the League of Nations in March 1933, and a year later proclaimed Manchuria as an independent republic, with Puyi elevated to emperor.[2] Annie feared that the situation would provoke general anti-foreign sentiment again but in their struggle against Japan the Nationalist government was keen to maintain good relations with the other foreign powers.

Another hindrance to the implementation of Chiang Kai-shek's new regulations was the growing conflict between the Nationalists and the Communists. Fighting on two fronts was so undermining the power

1   Letter from Edmund Sugg written March 15, 1932. WCMN, Sept 1932, pp35-37.
2   Bickers, *Out of China*, 2017, p136.

of the Nationalist government that it would be unable to guarantee protection of foreign nationals on its soil once it removed their extraterritorial privileges. In the end the extraterritorial provisions stayed in place for the time being and Torrance was relieved that for now, amidst all the political insecurity, the extra layer of protection still remained. But it was clear that Chinese tolerance for such things was diminishing.

Far from the war in the east, in early March Torrance was invited by Daniel Dye to give a lecture at the university on Chinese pottery, which he illustrated with various pieces, including some porcelain he had borrowed from Deng Xihou.[3] That same week he had a visit from Huang Hanqing who had come down from Dongmenwai with an unusual request for help. The previous March, Chen Guangming, the only Christian in Bulan village, had been down to stay a few days with Torrance having been released from prison in Xuecheng after Torrance had interceded with Deng on his behalf. The details are not clear but Torrance told Annie he had been accused by 'two scallywags'.[4] Chen had still had to pay a significant fine for his release, something Torrance saw as plain bribery. Now Huang's son had been detained by the Xuecheng magistrate, having been summoned as a witness in connection with Chen's arrest the previous year. Torrance saw this as a trumped up anti-Christian charge and sent a note to ask if Deng Xihou would intervene again.

In a typical example of reciprocity or Chinese *guanxi*, Deng wrote to the Xuecheng official asking him to put things right and then asked Torrance to find someone to teach his daughter English, which Mrs Wilford agreed to do. Torrance then discovered that in response to Deng's request, the Xuecheng official had simply agreed to reduce the fine he was demanding from Huang's son. Deng wrote again with orders for the son's release and asked Torrance to find an English teacher for one of his sons, who had been studying in Japan until the situation had turned sour. George Franck obliged and that was the end of the matter.

Having not been out of town since last September, Torrance made a trip south to Renshou and Jiangkou in the spring with three of

3   The Princeton Theological Seminary archives contain a 1933 manuscript by Torrance entitled *Porcelains: The Outline of Pottery and the Making of It*. Among the Chinese books he kept on his return to Scotland was one on Jingdezhen porcelain and another on the history of China's fine arts.
4   TT to Annie, March 2, 1932. The letter indicates that Torrance had mentioned this in an earlier letter, not found by the author.

his colporteurs. The weather was beautiful and they met with little opposition, selling 2,500 gospels and giving out 10,000 tracts, including a particularly popular one written by Torrance with a title in the style of a Chinese proverb: 'The Universality of Heavenly Truth'.[5] In Pengshan he met up with Daniel Dye who was leaving for furlough in America and due to stop off in Britain. Dye already had a box for Annie and to this Torrance now added an old sword found in one of the local caves, which Dye was to pass on to Robert Hobson, a specialist in Oriental ceramics at the British Museum to whom Torrance had sent various artifacts over the years.

On his return to Chengdu Torrance and a young CIM doctor named Howard Jeffrey went out to the spring fair at the Qingyang Temple, accompanied by Hou Li-de and two other Chinese workers. They had forgotten that it was a school holiday and as they strolled among the crowds their Chinese companions overheard a group of students discussing whether or not to attack Torrance and Jeffrey. Thankfully, a nearby soldier also heard and issued a sharp warning: 'If you do, you'll soon have no head left to eat your rice.'[6]

Torrance had been suffering from a sore throat for some time and in early June Dr Peterson successfully removed one of his tonsils. After a brief convalescence with the Joliffes he made plans to go early to Lingyan for a rest. He was missing Annie's presence as he packed: 'Wish you were here to do it and go along. I feel I am needing to rally my courage and vim now to go on. I have nobody to chatter to.'[7] On June 22 he sent a touching letter for David on his eighth birthday:

> Almost my first thought this morning was that your birthday had come round again . . . I cannot forget my youngest son . . . I could not but let my heart and thoughts go out to our Benjamin.[8]

Annie had started thinking again about bringing James and David, now eight and nine, out to China but the fighting in Shanghai and the widespread general instability once more put such thoughts to rest.

Various missionaries were planning trips to the mountain regions that summer, some to the Yi people in the Liangshan region, some to the Tibetan area of Kangding, and Brace was going to Xuecheng to see

---

5   天道不分中外.
6   TT to Annie, March 31, 1932.
7   TT to Annie, June 14, 1932.
8   TT to David, June 22, 1932. A reference to Jacob's youngest son in the biblical book of Genesis.

Pastor Mao. Torrance had been looking forward to the company of another missionary and his son as far as Weizhou but they had to pull out at the last minute. In the end he travelled up with Chen Bingling, Jiu Si looking after Billy, Yao Si as colporteur and cook, and Ong Guangming, who had been visiting again from Songpan. Yao Si, who had worked for Torrance before the family left in 1927, had turned up in the spring looking for a job.

The party reached Miansi at noon on July 6 after an easy journey. The drab town was looking more attractive with trees now planted along the edges of the main street and the dilapidated main temple undergoing renovations. As they gave out literature they were accompanied by some children who told Torrance they had been threatened with a thrashing by one of their teachers if they accepted any Christian tracts. Despite this, some of the children came to the meeting in the evening.

After his experience the previous year, Torrance was travelling with a special military pass approved both by Deng and by the British Consul and he was determined to go straight up to Songpan. Stopping for just one night in Weizhou, he visited the mosque and was invited in by 'an old Mohammedan friend' for tea and for a chat with the imam.[9] They spent the next night at Shigu, stopping at the villages of Yangmaoping and Baishui on the way. At Baishui the headman said his New Testament had been stolen and Torrance promised him a whole Bible in its place.

In Maoxian Torrance had hoped to see Dr and Mrs Lechler, now in charge of the CMS station, but they had gone up to a big religious tribal fair at Huanglong temple, east of Songpan. Instead, they were welcomed by the local Chinese pastor and, with Colonel Liu no longer around, it was a more relaxed time than last year. Paying his respects at the government office, Torrance was welcomed cordially by one of the scribes who had heard him speak at Great East Street. On Sunday he spoke at the morning service and in the afternoon one of the local Christians took him to a temple where they chatted with some Heishui people lodging there. They seemed to be refugees and Torrance got the impression that their eviction from the Heishui valley was the result of trying to stay neutral in the previous year's fighting.

After a long hard trek, they had a flea-bitten night in Musubao but were happy the next morning to discover a new river valley route that

9   The friend seems to have been the father of Wang Xichun who later became a government archivist in Weizhou. Born in 1925, in his later years Wang could still recall Torrance's conversations with his father in their home.

avoided last year's steep climb over the pass to Diexi. However, they hadn't gone far when travellers coming down the valley warned them that a rockfall had blocked the new road and they would need to climb up to the old one. Not realising there were two alternative paths, Torrance and Jiu Si, who were ahead with Billy, waited at the second turning for the others, who had taken the first path – with all the food and bedding. Torrance and Jiu spent a cold night sharing Jiu's 'bit of scone' for dinner and sleeping on boards in a two-sided shack they had found. Torrance was moved to see how enterprising and considerate Jiu was as he sought to make the situation as comfortable as possible. 'I shan't forget what he did for me for a long time.'[10] Setting out at 4.30 the next morning, they found the rest of the party at the first village they came to and tucked into a good breakfast.

The following night was pleasantly different. Stopping to give medical treatment at several villages along the way, they reached the village of Pingding Pass where they were greeted by a Qiang man who had been to the Torrance home for Bible study. Originally from a village visited by Torrance on his trek over the ridge to A'er in 1921, the man was now renting a shop here and insisted they stay with him. As they sat and drank tea together, the heavens opened and they were grateful for such hospitable shelter. They held a meeting in the evening at which several locals responded and the schoolmaster took a New Testament.

The next stop was Guihua, now Minjiang Township, and Torrance was in his element in the beauty of his surroundings. 'The scenery the past three days has been sublime. I wish I had English enough to describe to you its grandeur and surpassing loveliness.' He had found wild strawberries and blackberries along the way and was enjoying the sight of wild roses. He stayed that night at the local mosque while the others stayed in a Chinese inn. The imam was a Hui Muslim from Gansu who had lost friends in fighting in Gansu a year or two back and was feeling bitter against the Chinese, hence his hospitality not being extended to Torrance's companions.

About twenty miles south of Songpan, Torrance was resting in a teashop when 'in came an old Ch'iang with a very Jewish face'.[11] Torrance offered him some tea and discovered as they talked that the Qiang people in that area had kept most of their old religious customs,

---

10 TT diary to children, July 13, 1932. All summer trip quotations are from this unless otherwise indicated.

11 TT to Annie, July 16, 1932.

despite living in close proximity to their Tibetan Buddhist neighbours, the Xifan people.

After ten days on the road, they finally reached Songpan on July 15 and were escorted into town by several of the Christians who had come out to meet them. Torrance, who had only been there once in 1922, painted a colourful picture of the town:

> Songpan is a great trading centre. Its city population is half Chinese and half Mohammedan. Around the city for a distance, roughly, of 25 miles live the Xifan people. They are of Tibetan origin but had long settled in the neighbourhood as farmers, shepherds and cattle-raisers. On the outside border of the Xifan live different tribes, the Ch'iang on the South, the Boluozi on the South-west, the Aba Tibetans on the West, 'the grass lands' nomads on the North and different peoples on the East. All these come to Songpan for trade and barter.
>
> Guanxian sends tens of thousands of bales of coarse tea, each 80 lbs in weight, every year for sale to the Xifan and the Tibetans. The latter and grass lands nomads bring in immense quantities of lamb skins for the Chinese fur-market, and wool and other skins, [and] mule trains of such merchandise and yak or cross-bred yak trains are daily coming in and moving out of the city. You get, therefore, a big floating population all spring, summer and autumn. In winter the cold is severe and folks have to 'hibernate' for a time.

Over the next ten days they were out on the streets daily, giving Tibetan gospels to the lamas, Tibetan traders, and the Xifan people, as well as treating sore eyes and other ailments, preaching when and where possible, and chatting with whoever was interested. The Christian official whom Torrance had encountered on the way down from Diexi last year was now in Songpan and his good report of Torrance resulted in quite a few military officers coming for medicine or to chat. In his diary for the children Torrance wrote, 'I enjoyed having them see the poor among men, the despised Boluozi and the Xifan, come to call and note how I made no difference in the reception or treatment of any one. My services were equally at the disposal of those in need whatever their race or condition might be.' He also met and talked with Tibetans from Aba County, which he described as 'south of the Golok country'.

One particularly memorable occasion was a visit to the sick wife of a Xifan chief, who provided Ong with a mule so that he and Torrance could ride out to their home, about ten miles outside Songpan. As they passed through the upland countryside with its abundance of wild flowers, Torrance was reminded of the Scottish highlands and their ancient chieftains. The chief's daughter-in-law, with features 'of a perfect European type', served them with a lunch of hot milk and a kind of local bread whilst the chief drank the more traditional buttered tea with *tsampa* or roasted barley flour. Torrance described their home as a place of 'beauty, refinement and charm'. Years ago the chief had been to Beijing to pay tribute at the Qing court and had seen Emperor Guangxu. The wife seemed to have a contracted tendon and sadly all Torrance could do was suggest the possibility of hospital treatment in Chengdu.

Xifan chiefs outside Songpan

Yang Fuquan was still the commander in Songpan. Under orders from Deng Xihou, he had recently joined efforts to help restore power to Nationalist allies over the border in Gansu but had returned after a defeat and many of his men had drowned as they retreated.[12] Torrance's visit coincided with the arrival of one of Deng's deputies to inspect the remnants of the army and Commander Yang had planned a welcome reception on the drill ground outside the town. Having gone to the town gate to take some photos, Torrance was promptly asked by his Christian acquaintance on Yang's staff to take photos for them too. It was quite a scene. All the Xifan chiefs had been summoned to the welcome and were gathered on horseback outside the town with their guns. Unexpectedly, Torrance was able to have a long talk with

12   Kang & Sutton, *Contesting the Yellow Dragon*, p138; TT to Annie, July 16, 1932.

Yang, who was surprisingly friendly, in spite of his 1928 proclamation denouncing the hateful British.

The Boluozi people, whom Torrance had met on his Songpan trip ten years ago, made a deep impression on him during this visit. From Lesser Heishui, north of the Heishui valley, many of them would come in the summer to work for the Xifan farmers and stay in Songpan at night. They were a poor people, looked down on by others as raiders and cattle-thieves, but they were independent and 'strong enough to make it disagreeable to any one meddling with them'.

A GROUP OF BOLUOZI PEOPLE, WITH LANBU,
THE FIRST CHRISTIAN, SMILING IN THE BACK ROW.

Remarkably, Mrs Zhang, a Chinese woman in Ong's small group of Christians, had grown up among the Boluozi and was able to serve as interpreter so on one evening a meeting was held just for them. 'They were sitting jammed together on benches and in rows on the floor,' wrote Torrance. When he asked if any were interested in his message they said impulsively, 'You need not ask us one by one if we are willing to believe – we are all willing to do that; what you have said fits in to what our mothers and fathers have counselled us, there is no disagreement; your words are all good and every one is ready to do as you say.' Chen, Ong, and Torrance were very moved by this and Torrance wrote to his children, 'I confess I too fell in love with them.

They are often unwashed and uncouth looking; they very rarely wear sandals, shoes or stockings; their garments are of dark coarse serge but in their faces you can see nature in all its simplicity and unspoilt charm.' Before they left Songpan, baptisms were held for a diverse group of five: Lanbu, who was the first Boluozi Christian; the Zhangs; a shoemaker called Huang; and the scribe in Commander Yang's office.

On Monday, July 25, Torrance and his companions set off back down the Min Valley to the Qiang area, thankful that Torrance's military pass had opened the way to Songpan. It was hard to say good-bye to Ong and his little group but Torrance had been encouraged by their time together and it had been good to see Ong conversing easily with such a variety of people. He was hoping Ong would come down the following winter to teach a Bible class at Dongmenwai, where the weather would be less severe than in Songpan. When they reached Diexi, unaware of the disaster that would befall it the following year, Chen Bingling and Torrance 'took a holy delight in scattering gospels and tracts through the streets'.

After several days on the road it felt good to be back in Dongmenwai, in time for the Sunday service. Having known some of the villagers since his first visit in 1919, Torrance had come to regard his friends there as family and 'there was no welcome like the one the Ch'iang give.' Glad to rest, he took some time alone in the shade of a large rock and read letters from Scotland which had come via the Weizhou post office.

On Tuesday Gou Pinsan, Chen, and Torrance went to Taoping for the day where a family called Chen were the first to welcome them in, one of whom had been to Chengdu for Bible study. At the school house other villagers gathered for medical treatment and to hear them speak. The following day they went up the Longxi Valley to A'er where they stayed in the school house. Many of the villagers gathered in the small village square and talked with them most of the evening. On the next Sunday there was a 'gathering of the clans' at Dongmenwai for the morning service, followed by the baptism of seven men and one woman and an afternoon communion service, after which people dispersed to their villages, taking medicine with them for sick friends.

Torrance was glad of a chance to talk face to face with Gou about the work. Gou had discovered that his letters to Chengdu were being opened if they went by regular mail so he had been sending them registered. Now that he was occupied with his duties as district headman he had employed Xiong to itinerate in his place. Since the Qiangfeng school closure, Xiong had spent several more months with Torrance in Chengdu and was pleased to put his training to good use. Torrance was appreciating Gou's foresight and sound judgment on many issues, not least the decision to build the church in Dongmenwai, which was off the beaten track. A new church building had been erected in Xuecheng under Pastor Mao that summer and between its completion and actual opening the local military official had put a notice up to say that he was going to occupy it.

Saying farewell to Gou and moving on to Miansi they visited the villagers in Qiangfeng and the Glen. Torrance was pleased to hear that five chickens from Irene Hutchinson's Leghorn eggs had survived and were being used for breeding. He had taken new eggs to Dongmenwai this year so they could be bred there too. Unfortunately, one of the calves brought up the previous year had died but the other was doing well. In the Glen the locals told Torrance of the opposition they were experiencing from the Miansi magistrate, who was angry that the villagers of Qiangfeng and the Glen had wanted to keep their school open. He had taken the names of the Christians and told Wang Tingxiu, the oldest Christian member up there, that he should leave China if he wanted to follow a foreign religion. Hostility was also being stirred up in Miansi, making life difficult for Chen Bingling and his wife.

On Friday they went for the first time to the Wasi village of Daping, home of Gou Guanding, who had asked them to come and preach to his fellow tribesmen there. Daping overlooked the Min River about three miles south of Qiangfeng and was accessed by a narrow path 'where every step you take has to be carefully and precisely made'. But it was worth the risk as many turned out to hear them speak. Gou Guanding and his wife were still mourning the loss of their son in the Heishui fighting.

Back in Miansi on Saturday night it rained heavily causing several rockfalls. 'Great pieces three to five feet square came crashing down the steep mountain side making quite a noise in their rush and kept on increasing their velocity until they were bounding from 20 to 30 yards at a time.' On Sunday not many Qiang came to the meeting, fearing the taunts of the local Chinese, but five people were baptised: two Chinese, one Qiang from the Glen, and two Wasi – one the youngest son of Gou Guanding and the other a village headman on Tongling mountain.

Feeling torn between staying longer and needing a rest before returning to work, Torrance set out for Guanxian on August 16 with

Chen Bingling, who was going down to fetch a young bull which two of Gou Guanding's sons were buying. On their way down the Min Valley a man came asking for treatment who had been sentenced by an official in Guanxian to a beating for 'a delinquency of his wife' and had a 'patch of raw flesh three inches in diameter' on the back of each thigh.

Back in a rainy Lingyan the missionaries were being inoculated against cholera and had been advised to delay their return to Chengdu until the end of August due to a serious outbreak in the city. Torrance was staying with the Kitchen family and wrote to Annie that the community had had some remarkably Spirit-filled meetings, the like of which he had never experienced up there before. Deng's officer, Diao, happened to be staying up there and joined the missionaries for some tennis. Ten soldiers had also been sent up from Guanxian to protect the community, due to the presence of a robber band roaming the area.

Torrance and the Kitchens had a ride back to Chengdu with Dr Wilford, one of the few car owners in Chengdu. It was a sobering return after such a rich time. Thousands had fallen victim to cholera and people were still dying. Thankfully the depot staff and the colporteurs were all well and Torrance made sure they were inoculated but some of his local friends were suffering and seven neighbours had died. On September 7 Torrance sent Annie the sad news that Mrs Amos of the CIM, who was pregnant, had died along with her seventeen month old child. Although the outbreak was over its peak, 450 had died in the city the previous week and 750 the week before that. Taking what precautions he could, Torrance was even washing any coins he received and, not for the first time, he was glad Annie and the children were back home.

Although Torrance stayed free of cholera he was slightly unwell after the summer and was hoping he didn't need his other tonsil removed. It was possibly just a touch of malaria. He mentioned this to Annie with an added warning:

> Every time I go to the Tribes I come back with my hair perceptibly thinner. I'll soon be bald I am afraid, and shan't be able to come home unless I have a wig!!![13]

That summer the family had bought an old gypsy-style caravan which was parked in a farmer's field on the coast in North Berwick, opposite

---

13 TT to Annie, Sept 15, 1932.

the Bass Rock. Easily accessible from Edinburgh, Annie could stay there with the younger children whilst the older ones came and went:

> James and David are having a fine time on the farm here. James loves to 'yarn' to the farmers and he knows the selling prices or buying prices of the chickens, ducks etc ... They love the cows.[14]

Grace, now seventeen, had just joined Mary and Tom at Edinburgh University and had also become an Associate of the London College of Music – grateful to Mrs Brace for her first piano lessons in Chengdu. Annie had written earlier in the year that Tom's 'heart is fully in the Theological more than anything else and he is wearying to be in this part of his studies', but for now he was still working towards his MA in Classics.[15]

In the autumn a letter from Lacy brought the good news that Torrance would definitely receive an ABS pension allowance, even though he had been with the ABS less than the twenty-five years stipulated for a full pension. This would continue as a smaller allowance for Annie if she survived him. As part of Lacy's amalgamation plans, Torrance had agreed to take on Franck's British & Foreign Bible Society work when Franck went on furlough the following spring. On his return in 1934 Franck would then take on the ABS work, releasing Torrance to retire. Lacy had also suggested that Torrance let go of the Wushi-tongtang property and move all operations to the smaller place he shared with Franck but the lack of storage space and colporteur accommodation made this impractical and in the end the lease on the Wushi-tongtang property was extended until his final departure.

In early October Torrance was invited to a museum committee meeting with David Graham and others to plan for the coming year. Graham had just moved from Yibin to become the new museum curator, a position now funded through the recently established Harvard-Yenching Institute, and one of the tasks facing him was a more thorough cataloguing of the museum contents.[16] Torrance had to miss the meeting due to a planned trip to Ya'an with Openshaw but on his return he would make several museum visits to help with 'labelling, classifying and registering the numerous articles'.[17]

14 Annie to TT, no date.
15 Annie to TT, 22 April, 1932.
16 Andres Rodriguez. 'Nationalism and Internationalism on the borders: The West China Union University Museum of Archaeology and Ethnology (1914-51)'. *Museum History Journal.* 2016, p4.
17 TT to Annie, Nov 8, 1932.

Torrance and Openshaw were in Ya'an for most of October. The town, where Openshaw had lived for many years, was now part of a large area controlled by Liu Wenhui in southern Sichuan and tensions were on the rise between him and the other Sichuan generals. On October 12 Torrance wrote to Annie describing the unpredictable situation: 'We live a day at a time. Life is like camping on the edge of a volcano.'[18]

Liu Wenhui was fighting on two fronts. On his western flank his troops had been involved in several clashes with Tibetans and Torrance had heard reports of fighting in Nyarong, northwest of Kangding.[19] On his eastern flank he was now facing General Liu Xiang and his allies. Realising that Liu Wenhui would have to divert troops to his eastern front, Torrance made it clear to Annie where his sympathies lay:

> He shan't be able now to go on attacking the Tibetans and this will be a relief to them. Seeing the cold weather is on there they should be able to drive out the Chinese again. It is wicked the way they have been treated, and the Chinese keep publishing that it is the Tibetans who have been attacking them.[20]

The source of this 'publication' seems to have been Liu Wenhui himself, accusing the 'British-backed' Tibetan troops of launching a large-scale offensive in southwestern Sichuan and also accusing the Nationalists of selling off Chinese territory to the Tibetans behind his back.[21] While Torrance was still in Ya'an, Liu signed a truce with Lhasa, freeing his troops to fight against Liu Xiang.

On October 15 Annie wrote to Torrance saying she had dreamt he was in great danger and, as it turned out, Torrance's absence from Chengdu had possibly saved his life. While tensions were brewing south of Chengdu, Tian Songyao had seized the opportunity to try and push Liu Wenhui's troops out of Chengdu, where he, Liu, and Deng were still officially power-sharing. Fighting had broken out in the city and when Torrance arrived home on October 24, he discovered his bedroom at Franck's had eight bullet holes, two

18 TT to Annie, Oct 12, 1932.
19 TT to Annie, Oct 19, 1932. Torrance uses the name 'Chantui', which is today's Nyarong or Xinlong County in Ganzi Tibetan Autonomous Prefecture.
20 Ibid.
21 Lin Hsiao-ting. 'Making Known the Unknown World: Ethnicity, Religion and Political Manipulations in 1930s Southwest China'. *American Journal of Chinese Studies* 13, no. 2. 2006, p217.

broken window panes, and three bullets lodged in the central ceiling beam. A couple of bullets had also hit the Wushi-tongtang property. Although Torrance had little regard for Liu Wenhui, in this instance he saw Tian Songyao as the aggressor, responsible for drawing the conflict into Chengdu.

Despite the unrest, Torrance and Openshaw went ahead with some Great East Street meetings but numbers were less than usual. On November 3 Torrance wrote that soldiers were 'buzzing around everywhere at the moment like flies. Chengtu and the surrounding country is an armed camp.'[22] As the conflict escalated across southern Sichuan, news came in that Liu Xiang's troops had dropped bombs on Liu Wenhui's men in Luzhou, killing twenty and injuring many. Torrance was hopeful that Chengdu would be spared further fighting but wrote to Annie on November 12 that war was threatening them on every side. He and Wilford had been to see Deng Xihou, urging him to prevent further fighting within the city, but Deng had limited influence over Liu Wenhui and Tian. Further pressure on Deng was coming from his own subordinates, General Huang and Diao, who were siding with Tian Songyao against Liu. Diao's troops were out at Pengzhou and Pixian, north and northwest of Chengdu, and Torrance saw it as a bad sign that Mrs Diao was leaving Chengdu with the family.

Sure enough, the fragile peace was shattered four days later. On November 16 fighting between Liu and Tian's men erupted around the densely populated Imperial City area and raged for twenty-four hours, resulting in the death or wounding of several thousand soldiers and civilians, including, as in 1925, some school students who were incidental casualties. Houses were burnt or destroyed by shellfire and the CMS compound of Bishop Mowll, caught between the two sides and with a top floor ideal for snipers, was devastated.[23]

Liu Xiang seems to have come to Tian's aid and on November 19 and 20, aeroplanes flew overhead dropping several bombs which caused death and injury, although some of the casualties were the result of ineffective shellfire from Liu Wenhui's men, aimed at the planes and falling back into the city. The WCMN editor was appalled that the leaders, all Sichuanese, should bring such destruction on the general population for no obvious reason but their own 'lust of

22 TT to Annie, Nov 3, 1932.
23 WCMN, Dec 1932. 'What's it all About?', p1-3; 'The Fighting at P'i Fang Kai, Chengtu', p4-5.

wealth and power'.[24] The military hospitals were full to overflowing and in his ABS report Torrance wrote that,

> The casualties far exceeded those taken during the cholera epidemic. The Mission hospitals grew crowded to the door. Wounded lay groaning on stairways, halls, lobbies, offices as well as in the wards. Beds had to be removed to allow them to lie in greater numbers on the floors. And the war still goes on. Though the two sides in the City fought each other till they were exhausted and agreed on a truce, the carnage goes on in the country to the South. We are not sure that the struggle may not roll back on us.[25]

Torrance visited the Canadian hospital daily, which was caring for some six hundred injured in the fighting. One man showed him a gaping wound in his abdomen and asked for prayer, and an injured brigadier-general told him the casualties would have been worse had Tian Songyao not heeded his mother's entreaty on her knees to avoid heavy shrapnel guns in the city – something Liu Wenhui was using liberally.[26] Despite Tian's apparent restraint, Kapp describes the fighting in Chengdu as 'heavier than at any time since 1911'.[27]

Eventually Tian Songyao's troops withdrew to the northern part of the city and by November 24 he had pulled out of Chengdu. Deng had managed to remain neutral, 'holding the scales for peace', and Liu Wenhui's men were still holding their ground in the city but Liu's overall situation remained precarious as Liu Xiang and his allies kept up their pressure on the rest of his territory.[28] At the end of November Torrance wrote to Annie that Liu Wenhui was refusing to leave Chengdu and another clash seemed inevitable.[29]

By early December the street barriers in Chengdu had largely been removed but fierce fighting was raging between Liu Xiang and Liu Wenhui to the south in Leshan and Renshou. Torrance suspected that the other militarists were hoping Liu Xiang and Liu Wenhui would decimate each other's forces, enabling the others to profit from their losses. Yang Sen and another military leader, Luo Zezhou, had linked up with Liu Xiang's men and taken the lucrative salt

---

24 WCMN, Dec 1932, p2.
25 TT. 1932 ABS report, written Dec 9, 1932.
26 See TT to Annie, Sept 20, 1933.
27 Kapp, *Szechwan and the Chinese Republic*, p87.
28 WCMN, Dec 1932, p2.
29 TT to Annie, Nov 30, 1932.

wells of Zigong from Liu Wenhui. In Chengdu there was concern that, if defeated, Liu Wenhui's men might flood the city and cause havoc. Thankfully, Deng Xihou was still holding the city centre and the northeastern sector where Torrance lived, and Diao had written to Torrance from Pengzhou saying that things to the northwest of Chengdu were quiet.

Torrance had been invited to a 'Scotch night' at the Neaves, which was a pleasant respite amidst all the tensions. In mid-December he was surprised to receive a visit from He Tianyu and his wife, friends from his CIM days whom he had not seen for years. He Tianyu was working for Tian Songyao and told Torrance that one of Tian's colonels had lost over a thousand men and that Tian's total losses probably numbered about fifteen hundred. Liu Wenhui's losses were even greater, perhaps two and a half thousand men. By this time Tian had managed to push Liu Wenhui's men out of Chengdu and they were camped to the southwest of the city at Shuangliu.

On December 20 Torrance was back at the museum helping with the cataloguing. Dr Beech was highly complimentary about all the museum work he had done and in January a WCMN article by David Graham singled out Dye, Torrance, and James Huston Edgar as those who had made 'very large and valuable contributions' to the museum.[30] Graham took the opportunity to impress on his readers the importance of collecting cultural items on their travels:

> Fifty years from now it will be impossible to secure many of the objects now being used by the Chinese, the Tibetans, and the aborigines of West China. By aiding the museum in its work of collecting, preserving and displaying these things, we are rendering a real service to the West China Union University and we hope, to the people of Central Asia.

With Chengdu now quiet, plans could be made for Christmas. Torrance, Franck, Dr Meuser, and Geraldine Hartwell invited the community to an evening of carol singing, solo performances, and refreshments. Torrance spent Christmas Day with the Smalls at the university, followed by a Boxing Day lunch with the Kitchens, and the celebrations were rounded off once again with tennis and a convivial evening meal at the Mulletts' home.

---

30 D. C. Graham. 'The West China Union University Museum'. WCMN, Jan 1933, p12-14.

Chapter 18

The Reds Arrive

January-June 1933

While Torrance and his friends were enjoying their Christmas celebrations and Tian Songyao was preoccupied by the conflict with Liu Wenhui, the Communist Fourth Front Army entered Tian's territory in northeastern Sichuan and captured the town of Tongjiang near the Shaanxi border. Under the leadership of Zhang Guotao and his chief military commander, Xu Xiangqian, these forces had been pushed westwards from the Henan-Hubei-Anhui border region by Chiang Kai-shek's Nationalist troops, who were still trying to suppress the growing influence of the Communists. Conservative estimates put Zhang's forces at around nine thousand when they reached Sichuan, others at around fifteen thousand.[1]

Making Tongjiang the headquarters of their new Sichuan-Shaanxi Soviet, in January they captured the neighbouring districts of Bazhong and Nanjiang, where Tian Songyao's misrule and over-taxation had already given rise to a local resistance movement. One local paper recorded several thousand people in Bazhong welcoming their arrival and it wasn't long before many of them were subjected to the organisation for which the Communists were becoming well-known, with their propaganda units, political education, military training, youth corps, and units for production, laundry, and sewing.[2] Tian had little choice but to divert his troops away from fighting Liu Wenhui and defend his territory against the 'Reds'.

In the eye of this provincial storm, Torrance was trying to complete an article for the Border Research Society, looking at possible connections between the Qiang and other groups in

1   See Kapp, *Szechwan and the Chinese Republic*, p87; Tony Saich and Benjamin Yang. *The Rise to Power of the Chinese Communist Party: Documents and Analysis*. Routledge. 2016, p516.
2   Kapp, *Szechwan and the Chinese Republic*, p88.

southwest China.[3] In his opening paragraph, somewhat tongue-in-cheek, he described the superficiality of some traveller accounts about the peoples of West China who had 'repeatedly been discovered and announced afresh to the world'. Decrying the impersonal nature of some research methods, he also observed with considerable sarcasm:

> The only thing remaining to be done to acquaint us fuller with these folks is to collect a few live specimens from each and cage them into a specially built human menagerie where the scientist at his ease may study all by measuring their skulls, comparing their chatter, studying their habits, recording their diseases and noting their religious tendencies.

Unfortunately the sarcasm was missed by at least one later commentator.[4]

In contrast to this, Torrance, whose approach had always been relational, argued that knowledge of a people's history was essential in gaining an understanding of them. This would later become a key theme in anthropology, as emphasised by Claude Levi-Strauss in his seminal work *Structural Anthropology*:

> The whole question is to know whether ... even the most penetrating analysis of a unique culture – which includes description of its institutions and their functional interrelations, as well as study of the dynamic processes by which culture and the individual interact – can attain full significance without knowledge of the historical development underlying the present patterns.[5]

Torrance pointed out that tribal groups in the western part of Sichuan had historically been beyond Chinese rule and represented ancient civilizations of their own. The researcher should therefore go 'humbly and patiently, learning from all'. Drawing on western and Chinese sources, he also looked at groups within the wider sphere of Sichuan,

---

3   TT. 'Notes on the West China Aboriginal Tribes'. JWCBRS, Vol 5, 1932, pp10-25. Publication of the journal seems to have been delayed to 1933. All quotes in this section are from this article unless otherwise indicated.
4   Alex Cummings used Torrance's 'menagerie' reference in the title of his paper, 'Life in the Menagerie: David Crockett Graham and Missionary-Scientists in West China, 1911-1948'. *American Baptist Quarterly*, 27 (3): 206–227. 2009. Missing Torrance's irony, Cummings stated that 'Torrance's ideal of a 'human menagerie' was essentially an anthropological museum, which allowed viewers to access truth through careful scrutiny of the human object' (p209). This was precisely the opposite of what Torrance was saying.
5   Claude Levi-Strauss. *Structural Anthropology*. Basic Books, Inc. 1963, p9. (First published in French in 1958.)

Guizhou, and Yunnan, whose religious rituals included sacrifice and the worship of some kind of supreme deity.[6] It was a puzzle to him how these various tribes had come to have 'a monotheistic sacrificial faith' and why they shared similar practices. His hope was that a comparative study of their rituals might bring more understanding of their meaning and he made particular mention of research by David Graham on the Yi people of southern Sichuan and by botanist and ethnographer Joseph Rock on the Naxi of the Sichuan-Yunnan border region. In a recent article, 'The Land of the Tebbus', Rock had suggested that the people of Tebbu (Diebu) on the Sichuan-Gansu border were – along with the Xifan, the Jiarong, and the Naxi - descended from 'the great Chiang race who numbered over 250,000 families, and whose kingdom once was in the Koko Nor.'[7] He and Torrance were corresponding and Rock wrote again that spring, wanting further information about the Qiang.[8]

Torrance was already convinced that the Naxi belonged to 'the Ch'iang family of tribes' and also wondered whether the ancient Qiang of southern Sichuan, where Qiang were no longer found, had formed or become part of other people groups, some of which now had a Tibetan Buddhist identity. In the eighth century an invasion into southern Sichuan by the Nanzhao kingdom of northern Yunnan had influenced historically Qiang territory for more than a century and resulted in considerable movement and intermingling of peoples.[9]

Rather than going into detail about the Qiang, Torrance pointed readers to his earlier work but stressed again that the Qiang were 'distinctly of a Western and not of a Mongolian type'. They were clearly 'descendants of a race of foreigners' and 'anyone familiar with their features and characteristics cannot mistake their outside origin.' Added to this, their high towers and flat-roofed stone houses reminded him of 'the long trail of such houses from Asia Minor across North India and Central Asia down through Kansu to West China', the suggestion implicit that the ancient Qiang had travelled this route.

---

6   His sources included Samuel Clarke's *Among the Tribes in South West China* (China Inland Mission, 1911) and Yan Ruyu's *Miao fang bei lan* (Guide to Guarding Against the Miao, 1820), which Torrance mentioned with the caveat that it had been written 'to help the Chinese be on their guard against the tribes'.
7   Joseph Rock. 'The Land of the Tebbus'. *The Geographical Journal*, Vol 81, no.2, Feb 1933, p108-9. 'Koko Nor' was the region around Qinghai Lake in Qinghai Province.
8   Mentioned by TT to Annie, March 30, April 5, and Dec 12, 1933.
9   It is not unusual nowadays to find Chinese scholars connecting several ethnic groups in Sichuan and Yunnan with the early Qiang.

However, although some people had by now assumed that Torrance was claiming a Semitic origin for the Qiang, he was adamant that he had never committed himself that far and acknowledged the need for caution. On the other hand, he was also unwilling to say categorically that they were not originally Semitic and added that he was intending one day to write more fully about 'the various unique features of their monotheistic religion'.

In his final section Torrance gave a brief overview of the peoples of northwestern Sichuan, describing the rather lax Lamaism of the Wasi people, the Jiarong with their white stones and sacrifices, and the culture of the Heishui people, about whom he knew little but who seemed to have a mix of Lamaism and other practices. A Chinese contact, possibly Ong Guangming, had made enquiries about religious customs in the Heishui Valley and found that the people shared some similarities with the Qiang. 'On their house tops they have a white stone and the horns of an ox. Three times a year they have sacrifices and attendant dancing. The people give heed to the priests and fear them.' However, Torrance didn't yet know to whom their sacrifices were offered or what the role of the priests was.[10]

Acknowledging that these notes were 'very scrappy, provocatively incomplete and probably sometimes not perfectly accurate', Torrance's hope was that they would 'stir up the spirit of enquiry', particularly with regard to religious practices and beliefs. Disappearing traditions meant time was of the essence and he mentioned that some of his older Qiang informants had already died. His parting note was to recommend the climate and the scenery in the Qiang highlands, particularly above A'er in the Longxi Valley and above Qiangfeng in the Glen, and to offer a final word of advice: 'Employ a local guide. Show kindness to all and give help wherever you can. Then you'll reap a harvest of kindness and leave endless good-will behind you.'

On January 11 Torrance wrote to Annie that Liu Wenhui's troops were once again approaching Chengdu. Liao had told him that Deng Xihou would be forced to fight if Liu Wenhui tried to take the city and Torrance feared a siege. Deng's soldiers were billeted in Wushi-tongtang Street and all around the Si-sheng-ci quarter, where the Canadian hospital and press were located. The parade ground had been flattened in readiness for planes to land and the soldiers were

---

10 Several Qiang dialects are spoken in the Heishui region, with some groups identifying as Qiang and others as Tibetan Buddhists.

drilling there every morning. Torrance admitted to Annie that it was nerve-wracking living so close by, knowing that Liu Wenhui's men beyond the city wall might suddenly turn their big guns on any aircraft trying to land. On January 19 he wrote to Annie that Chengdu's south gate had just been closed against Liu Wenhui's men.

Deng had told Openshaw that he and Tian Songyao were willing to resume cooperation with Liu Wenhui if he would return peacefully to power-sharing in the city but with Tian now engaged in fierce fighting with the Communists in the northeast, Deng seems to have acceded to a very shaky renewal of power-sharing in Chengdu with Liu and the situation was tense. On February 14 Torrance wrote that Liu Wenhui was planning an attack on Wenjiang, Pixian, and Guanxian, all in Deng's territory northwest of Chengdu, in retaliation for an earlier attack on his troops by Deng's men, Diao and Huang.

In the south, Liu Wenhui and Liu Xiang's men had fought each other to a standstill and Torrance had received a first-hand account of the front line combat from his colporteur, Hou Li-de, who had been seized that winter to serve in Liu Wenhui's army. With no particular political loyalties, the fighting had no meaning for Hou and he was simply cannon fodder. In one battle he had been on the firing line for nearly three weeks in the Leshan region, where people were fleeing and whole towns and villages were deserted. The soldiers were reduced to using anything they could find, including beds and shop shutters, to make fires for cooking. Their opponents, Liu Xiang and his allies, had superior fire-power, including aerial bombing, and out of a company of eighty-two men with five officers, Hou Li-de was one of about ten who survived, and the only one in his unit of twelve.[11] By April he had managed to escape and Torrance helped him to obtain civilian clothes and sent him to itinerate in the north of Sichuan, away from Liu Wenhui's army and from the Communists.

At the hospital there were deaths almost daily among those wounded in the fighting and Torrance had taken to visiting for an hour or two every morning. Out on the street he would sometimes receive a friendly greeting from ex-patients, some of whom began attending the Great East Street meetings. Geraldine Hartwell, the hospital matron, much appreciated his work among the patients, not least because it contributed to good relations with the military. She suggested that he and Openshaw hold some meetings at the hospital after their Chinese

11 TT. 'Free Translation of a Letter from Colporteur Hou Li-Teh who was Caught and Impressed as a Soldier'. Typed manuscript. 1933.

New Year campaign, which resulted in several patients showing interest in their message.

Torrance had been visiting another patient in hospital for some time. Karl Eger, a German businessman and fellow curio-collector with a particular interest in Sichuan shadow puppets, was dying of cancer. Originally quite hostile to Torrance, he had become a Christian two

TORRANCE WITH CHRISTIAN SOLDIERS DISCHARGED
FROM THE HOSPITAL

years ago and they had become firm friends. In March he succumbed to the cancer and Torrance conducted his funeral service in the hospital chapel, followed by a graveside ceremony in the foreigners' graveyard.

Torrance and Eger's friendship had grown in spite of the worsening tensions in Europe. In April, Plewman's radio picked up a broadcast from London saying that the British government was protesting to Germany about its persecution of the Jews. Later in the year Torrance wrote to Annie, 'Hitler is simply another Kaiser in his antics. The German Christians must be lamenting his election and especially his strangling of church liberty. The ill treatment of the Jews presages no good for the country.'[12] Aware of Biblical promises that the Jews would eventually return to the land of Israel, he was wondering if the hostility would lead to increased emigration to Palestine.

Mrs Gao was still being held in Chengdu and Torrance had asked Mrs Pan of the CIM to take some provisions and visit her in prison.

---

12 TT to Annie, Oct 17, 1933.

He had also appealed again to Deng to provide her with better living quarters and he and Openshaw had even asked if she could attend one of the mission schools but Deng astutely said that he would only permit this if they could guarantee she wouldn't go back up to Heishui and stir up trouble – which they couldn't. Writing to Annie in March and asking for prayer for Mrs Gao, Torrance explained: 'Deng and his men are dead set against her. She has not been discreet enough. I am afraid they will put her out of the way by and by. She, I think, suspects her danger and so keeps writing for us to try and help her. She does not seem to have a friend in the world who dare go near her. How foolish she has been in her day, but the mercy of the Lord is for all who will call upon Him.'[13]

One bright spot in all the turmoil was positive news from the Qiang area. As Torrance had hoped, Ong Guangming had come down from Songpan to Dongmenwai in early February to conduct a winter Bible class, assisted by Xiong. Near the end of the month he visited Chengdu to update Torrance and discuss the work. He wanted to visit the Heishui region, which Torrance agreed to as long as he could find an interpreter to accompany him. Gou Pinsan's son, Gou Quangang, had hoped to come down with Ong but in the current climate he was afraid of being seized and enlisted. Chen Bingling and his wife and two children had also come down in February to stay for three months in Guanxian with Leona Thoering so that Mrs Chen could receive some training to work with the Qiang women. Looking ahead to his retirement, Torrance was already putting funds aside to help the work continue after his departure.

On March 8, exactly five years since parting from her on the dock in Southampton, Torrance wrote to Annie that the situation around Chengdu seemed to be settling down and he was hopeful of a good spell of peace. Gou Quangang decided to risk the journey in this quieter period and came down for Bible study and preaching experience, accompanied by a young Chinese Christian from Xuecheng called Mou. They brought news that Xiong was doing well itinerating around the Qiang villages. Torrance was impressed with Gou Quangang, who had trained in Maoxian as a teacher. 'Gou's son is exceptionally bright and sharp. It is a treat to teach such a man. He can catch on and get to the heart of things like a flash.'[14] In a mid-year ABS report he added, 'It is very rarely I have met one so able to understand the deep things of Scripture as he does.'

13 TT to Annie, March 8, 1933. (Pinyin updated.)
14 TT to Annie, May 1, 1933. (Pinyin updated.)

Some weeks later, Mr Yang, Torrance's usual host in Keku, dropped in for a visit and sat in on Torrance's daily lesson with the two young men.

It had now been arranged that Franck would leave on furlough in mid-April and he was beginning to pack, something Torrance found unsettling with at least another year to wait before his own departure. He wrote of this and a stiff knee to Annie with the comment, 'It's time I was home . . . This year has told on me more than the other four.'[15] He wasn't relishing the added burden of Franck's work, with a 'torturous, laborious' accounting system and a colporteur system which required the 'trying useless work' of almost daily reports.[16] Thankfully, Lacy and the B&FBS were persuaded that the more streamlined ABS system was adequate for both.

Although Chengdu was enjoying a quieter spell, news from northeastern Sichuan was worrying. In Bazhong the Communists had seized the CIM compound and made it their military headquarters and many Chinese Christians were among those who had lost homes and possessions. The poorest were the safest and in spite of their aggressive treatment of certain sectors of society, the Communists were still finding fertile soil among some Sichuanese who had lived through so many years of chaos and were impressed by their disciplined approach. They were also winning over Sichuan soldiers with the offer of reliable monthly pay and the assurance that they only viewed officers as the enemy, not the common soldiers.

Tian Songyao was fighting alongside Liu Cunhou and Yang Sen as they all sought to protect their northern territories and regain ground lost to the Communists. One CIM worker had written in early February that the arrival of Yang Sen's troops in the vicinity was a potential menace. 'They are a well-known set of brigands, and it is feared they may declare for the Reds.'[17] Torrance heard from an officer in the hospital that hundreds of soldiers near Bazhong had shot their leader and gone over to the Communists and the WCMN expressed little confidence in Sichuan's ability to withstand them, particularly as they were rumoured to be 'backed up by a vast network of organization throughout the country'.[18]

In mid-March a large force under Tian Songyao, whom the Nationalists had now appointed as 'Sichuan Bandit Suppression Commander', managed to re-take Nanjiang and Bazhong and on April

15 TT to Annie, March 15, 1933.
16 TT to Annie, May 11, 1933.
17 WCMN, March 1933, p10.
18 Ibid., p6.

29 the Communists were forced out of their main base in Tongjiang.[19] In May the CIM missionaries were able to pay a visit to their home in Bazhong and gave a disturbing report. 'In a mulberry grove adjoining the Mission compound, were found 36 pits in which hundreds of dead bodies had been thrown, and other pits are still coming to light in other parts. We were horrified to see a similar pit in our back garden and we were told that 30 to 40 children were buried there. The greatest crime seems to have been to possess grain or land over and above that which was absolutely necessary to sustain the family.'[20]

In April, with the house feeling empty after Franck's departure, Torrance was glad to head south for a week with David Graham, combining literature distribution, archaeology, and some relaxation on the boat trip. Keen to make the most of Torrance's knowledge of the area, Graham was wanting to examine the tomb caves and also to find some ancient pottery for the museum and for his classes. After two good days with various riverside stops they reached a place called Banbiangai in time for market day, where a man told them of a gold image which was being protected in one of the caves downstream near Jiangkou. Torrance assumed this was an idle rumour but it seems to have been intentional mischief.[21] Needing to rearrange lectures prior to the trip, Graham had told some students of his plans and word of them had reached a disgruntled ex-student, who had apparently been turned down for a place on the university's administrative board. He had sent word to the magistrate at Pengshan that Torrance and Graham 'intended digging into their old tombs and extracting image figures of golden value.'[22]

Moving on to Wangjiatou, they visited some farmers from whom Torrance had previously bought pottery fragments and Graham bought a basketful of small figurines and fragments. Back at the boat they were surprised by a visit from some armed militiamen whose leader had believed the rumour and accused them of digging in the ancient tombs. He insisted on escorting them to Jiangkou where they were taken to the militia headquarters in a local temple. At about two o'clock in the morning the local district head arrived and ordered a search of their boxes but nothing of value was found and he soon left, ordering them to visit the Pengshan county magistrate the following day.

19 Kapp, *Szechwan and the Chinese Republic*, p90.
20 WCMN, July-Aug 1933, p39.
21 Torrance related the story to Annie in an 8-page typed letter on April 28, 1933.
22 Ibid.

By morning word had got out about the captive foreigners and their supposed 'gold figure' and various locals came by, some of whom were sympathetic to their plight, stayed to chat, and took away tracts. At 2 p.m. they were taken to Pengshan, where the magistrate was away. His deputy showed little regard for the militia leader, kept the basket of pottery for the magistrate to inspect, and dismissed them. Graham left immediately for Chengdu while Torrance, much relieved that this 'humiliating trying experience' hadn't become a more serious incident, stayed at the CIM station for a rest and took a rickshaw the next day to Xinjin to catch the bus to Chengdu. To his surprise, the rickshaw-puller told Torrance that the militia leader, who had never produced any proof of his authority, had just been arrested after a search of his home revealed an illegal stash of army shells.[23]

Back in Chengdu, Torrance wrote to Annie on May 3 with good and bad news. In northeastern Sichuan the Communists had suffered a defeat but elsewhere fresh fighting was anticipated between Liu Wenhui and the other generals. A few days later, Liu invited Deng to a banquet, intending to seize him and his senior military officers, but Deng had been forewarned and withdrew to Xindu, north of Chengdu. Liu's men promptly took control of the parade ground where Torrance could see their daily drills from his window. Deng's men, forced deeper into the conflict, were erecting defences at Xindu and Tian Songyao had sent troops from the northeast to help Deng. This would prove to be a costly decision. As the soldiers hurried in the direction of Chengdu, the Communists seized the moment and in the next ten days Tian lost all the territory his men had retaken in four months of fighting.[24]

On May 21 Torrance wrote that he could hear the big guns again booming to the north beyond the city and that Deng and his men were holding a line along the Pi River from Guanxian to Xindu. Deng's men had destroyed an upstream dam, making the river unfordable, and they would now face Liu Wenhui's troops on the opposite bank in a kind of stalemate for over a month. Torrance added at the end of his letter that Deng was inflicting heavy losses on Liu and had refused his overtures for peace.

Many in Chengdu were angry with Liu Wenhui for attacking Deng and betraying their power-sharing agreement. Torrance described the people's exasperation:

---

23 TT to Annie, May 3, 1933.
24 Kapp, *Szechwan and the Chinese Republic*, p90.

Yesterday there was a fracas between the city militia and [Liu's] soldiers outside the East Gate. The soldiers went catching men there and the people grew angry. The militia and even women with knives etc attacked them. Four soldiers were killed – quite a number wounded. Served the soldiers right of course. For these men they seize they make them soldiers and push them forward into the front between themselves and the enemy where the slaughter is very heavy. No wonder the people are getting furious.[25]

His colporteur, Hou Li-de, would have been in the thick of this had he not managed to escape. More wounded were being brought in from the fighting between Chengdu and Guanxian and coolies and rickshaws had become scarce, with anyone strong enough for such work being impressed as a soldier.

Surprisingly, in the midst of all this the Great East Street meetings were thriving, sometimes with standing room only, but the conflict was still a challenge for the ABS work. At the end of May, the colporteurs gathered to plan their next itineraries, faced with the challenge that all the main roads beyond the city were blocked by soldiers. It was decided they would take the back roads and stay within the territory of Deng Xihou and Tian Songyao. Deng's men were still holding fast along the river and on May 26 Deng and Liu Xiang agreed to join forces against Liu Wenhui and create a 'Pacifying Sichuan Army'. Torrance saw this as a major shift: 'Other Generals will now likely start operations against Liu Wen-Huei. If so, there is sure to be a lot more heavy fighting and one wonders if there will be a general looting match should Liu be forced out of Chengtu.'[26]

Although under pressure to yield, Liu Wenhui was still holding three towns he had taken from Deng. However, with Deng and Liu Xiang now allies he was once again fighting on two fronts and Torrance could see that the writing was on the wall for him: 'If they press the attack then Liu is doomed. He will need to leave Chengtu for good and retire to Ya'an.'[27]

Torrance was feeling caged in by the fighting and was struggling with a persistent sore throat. With Franck gone, he was also missing company and it was a nice change to go out to the cleaner air and more social environment of the university campus for a tea and sports day. He was

25 TT to Annie, May 24, 1933.
26 TT to Annie, May 31, 1933.
27 TT to Annie, June 7-8, 1933.

still hoping his summer trip to the mountains would go ahead but right now the Guanxian road was blocked by the fighting.

Unexpectedly, the conflict had affected the fortunes of Mrs Gao, whom Torrance went to visit in mid-June, accompanied by Geraldine Hartwell. With Deng Xihou out of Chengdu, Liu Wenhui had intervened and set her free. Torrance was in no doubt about his motives: 'He wants her, of course, to go back home and stir up the tribes against Deng. I told her to look after herself. She has a chance now to get free and if so she should not stir up any trouble.'[28] As part of her release deal Mrs Gao had given her ten-year-old daughter to serve as an attendant to Liu Wenhui's third wife. Torrance was dismayed: 'This means the girl is to be a hostage. What a life for the girl!'

Torrance's assumptions about Liu Wenhui were correct. Liu proceeded to send Mrs Gao back up to the mountains with about eighty soldiers but word had got out and at the Jiarong town of Dawei, southwest of the Qiang region, they were attacked.[29] Mrs Gao managed to escape and Torrance was hopeful that she would find protection with one of the tribal chiefs up there and not cause any further incitement. She eventually managed to extricate her daughter from Liu's service and took her to be educated at the mission school in Ya'an.[30] Later in the year she wrote to Torrance from Ya'an asking for help and he sent some money, in case she was in need of winter clothing.

By late June Torrance had resigned himself to the depressing prospect of a hot Chengdu summer, even though Gou Pinsan and Ong had both sent word that it was quiet in the mountains. By early July the news was dismal. Fighting was continuing between Liu Wenhui and Deng and the road to Guanxian was still blocked. Annie's old CIM station at Guanxian had been looted by Liu Wenhui's soldiers and valuable medical supplies, destined for a CIM station in the Jiarong region, had been carried off. The WCMN also reported that the Communists had made further gains in northeastern Sichuan and Tian Songyao was rumoured to have lost seven thousand men.[31]

---

28 TT to Annie, June 15. (Pinyin updated.)
29 Torrance doesn't say who attacked them.
30 TT to Annie, May 15, 1934.
31 WCMN, July-Aug 1933, pp5, 39.

Chapter 19
Quake
July-December 1933

David Graham had been planning a trip to Kangding in the summer but that was cut off by the fighting so he was now contemplating a trip to the Zagunao Valley, despite Liu Wenhui still holding Guanxian, and suggested that he and Torrance travel together. Wanting to know more about the situation, Torrance managed to get a ride out with Wilford to visit Deng Xihou, who was living in a temple about four miles north of Chengdu. Deng was pleased to see them and full of praise for Dr Lechler who had been treating some of his wounded men in Guanghan. He was expecting reinforcements from Liu Xiang and preparing for a concerted attempt to drive Liu Wenhui out. Reassured that a trip might be possible, Torrance decided to send a load of literature up to the Qiang area. With the fragility of the wider political situation, he didn't want to miss what might be his last opportunity to visit the Qiang. To his delight, he and Graham were able to set out together on July 17, thankful to be leaving a sizzling hot Chengdu.

Morse and Agnew were also going that summer to Zagunao and Songpan and travelled with them as far as Miansi. With their combined equipment and about forty carriers they were quite a caravan. Graham was also accompanied by several students and others to help with his collecting and Torrance was travelling with Tang Si as cook and the mule boy for Billy. As with their trip south in the spring, Graham was wanting to make the most of Torrance's connections and his knowledge of the area before he left China. In return he had offered to pay some of Torrance's expenses and fit his plans around Torrance's itinerary.[1]

By the time they left Chengdu, Deng Xihou's troops had managed to take control of the road to Guanxian so no detours were necessary. In Guanxian Torrance had planned to buy straw sandals for his travels but every last pair had been bought by the military and although he

---

[1] For Graham's account of the trip see 'David Crockett Graham – Diary B, July 16, 1933-December 3, 1933', available at https://transcription.si.edu/project/7176.

had a couple of pairs from the year before, he returned at the end of the summer in mismatched boots, one of each pair having worn out on the trip. From Guanxian they were advised to break into smaller groups and spread out for the next part of the journey because Liu Wenhui's troops had taken up position beyond the town on the far side of the Min River. Torrance was glad he had been warned not to ride Billy. At one point several shots were fired, forcing him to jump down and walk in a roadside trench, but the firing seemed to be just to scare them and once they started the climb up into the mountains all was quiet. It was a huge relief to be away from the 'rumours and dangers of wars and tumults'.[2] Thankfully, due to an exceptionally cold winter, flies and dysentery were not the problem they had been the previous year.

After a night on Niangziling Pass – where it was heaven to actually need a blanket – they reached the village of Xingwenping where the locals had hardly seen a visitor in two months due to the fighting. Catering for such a large group overnight brought them some much needed income. Pressing on, the large party arrived in Miansi on Friday, July 21, where Morse and Agnew stayed just one night but made the most of it, with Agnew providing cocaine-assisted teeth extractions and Morse treating several patients including a woman with a snake bite. Although there was no meeting that night, the mission house was packed all evening, with young King Suo, who had succeeded his deceased father as chief of the Wasi, among the visitors.

Morse and Agnew had wanted Torrance to go with them to Songpan but the delay in leaving Chengdu and not knowing if this was his last trip meant Torrance's priority was now the Qiang area. Even then, Morse tried to persuade him to accompany them to Xuecheng and Zagunao, where he was wanting to continue the anthropological research started during their 1929 trip. Torrance declined but Xiong, who now had many connections in the area, agreed to assist them.

On Sunday there was a good turnout in Miansi for the morning and evening services, attended by Qiang, Wasi, and Chinese, and Torrance discovered that the magistrate had reined in those who had been disruptive in previous years. With the help of a local Christian, Graham bought a variety of Qiang goods for the university museum, including several pairs of men's and women's embroidered shoes, which Torrance described to the children: 'The patterns have each a signification – some kinds are worn only on certain occasions. Holiday, market and every day shoes are different. A bride's shoes like her wedding outfit

---

2   TT to Annie, July 22, 1933.

are never put on again until she is donned in them at death. She thus enters the future life in her marriage attire. . . . It shows their strong belief in immortality.'[3] He also noted that 'Cremation is very common among the Ch'iang people. On the coffin are placed wooden birds to denote that though the body reverts to dust, the spirit flies to the realm above.'

WOODEN BIRD (*Photo by author, courtesy of David W. Torrance*)

Moving on the next day, Torrance and Graham stopped for a couple of hours in Weizhou, where a young man offered to fill Torrance's water bottle from a nearby spring. He had sought refuge with Torrance that winter having deserted from one of the armies and Torrance had helped him change clothes and get back home. Friends and others came to chat and seek medical help and they then continued to Keku where they were guests of Mr Yang, who had visited Torrance in May. Yang was bold about his faith and they had a good evening meeting.

The next day Gou Pinsan took them up to his native village of Mushang, nearly 3,000 feet above Keku, where Torrance had attended the sacrificial ceremony in 1928. Torrance slept on the roof-top of one of Gou's brothers, with a magnificent view of the surrounding mountains. Graham slept the first night in the next house but his group was too big to be easily accommodated in such a small village so they left Torrance and moved to a Chinese temple further up the hillside to collect insects and butterflies. Graham shot a wild goat which he brought back and divided among the guests and their hosts.

In Mushang Torrance was kept busy treating various ailments and they had three evenings of good meetings. There were four Christians in the village and fifteen gave their names as enquirers, some of whom came down to the meeting in Dongmenwai the following Sunday. Despite all Torrance's experience, the journey down from Mushang was

---

3   TT, diary to children, July 22, 1933. All summer trip quotations are from this unless otherwise indicated.

a challenge. 'Travel in these mountains has done much to accustom me to their narrow paths and steep roads but when it comes to crawling down the face of a precipice and hopping from one ledge to another at dizzy heights I feel still a rank outsider.' Billy was led a longer way round.

In Dongmenwai Torrance slept above the church and Graham and his men were hosted in a large Qiang house. On their second evening, they 'dined luxuriously on wild pigeon' shot by Graham.[4] On Sunday morning folk from the various villages gathered for the meeting. Torrance spoke first, followed by Graham, and although Torrance suspected Graham was more 'modernist' than evangelical in his theology, he noted in his diary that one of the 'pithiest' of Graham's words was 'that rejection of Christ left us with confusion of face before God'. At the evening meeting one of the Christians suggested they start having a prayer meeting in a different home each week, which Torrance 'warmly urged' them to pursue.

Morse and Agnew's party returned from Xuecheng and Zagunao on Sunday and Torrance could see them across the river from Dongmenwai. Unable to communicate above the roar of the water, Morse sent a note to Torrance saying that he had measured about one hundred heads and they were now on their way to Songpan.

On Tuesday Torrance went up to Bulan. Graham had gone up the previous day for hunting and collecting and was lodging at another temple above the village. Torrance stayed two nights in the home of Chen Guangming where they had full meetings, with sixty packed into Chen's main room on the first evening. Graham joined them for the meetings and paid a visit to the sacred grove where he took a photo of a flat stone used for the slaying of the sacrifices. The previous year the Qiang priest in Bulan had been baptised and this year he sold his priest's outfit to Graham for display in the museum.[5] He told Torrance with conviction that Jesus had spoken to him in a dream: 'He told me that all should be well. Yes, He told me that.'

From Bulan they walked to Longxi Village, perched precariously on the mountainside, where they held an open air evening meeting. Graham joined them again, hoping to buy Qiang items for the museum, and then returned to Dongmenwai to prepare for a trip up the valley to Aèr. In a list of new museum exhibits later that year, Graham included a

4   TT to Annie, Aug 1, 1933.
5   Qiang artifacts are still on display at the Sichuan University Museum and at the Southwest Minzu University Museum in Chengdu.

'sacred white stone, used for generations in his family, from Mr. Geo P'in Tsang [Gou Pin San], another hereditary chieftain among the Ch'iang people', as well as a large Tibetan prayer wheel from Chief Yang of Jiuzi.[6] The list also included a Ming Dynasty bowl and about twenty-five clay images from the Han and Tang dynasties, all contributed by Torrance.

On Friday Torrance returned to Dongmenwai to prepare for the Sunday gathering. The husband of the woman Torrance had treated up in Kuapo ten years ago had brought a sick friend down for treatment but Torrance was unable to help and thought he probably had advanced cancer. On Saturday people started arriving for the Sunday meetings, giving extra time for conversations, and on Sunday there were seven baptisms. Two or three others who wanted to be baptised were advised to wait until they had a clearer understanding about such a decision.

With the work growing and Torrance's retirement on the horizon, he and Gou Pinsan took some time to discuss future plans. Chen Guangming had offered his home as a regular meeting place in Bulan, where there were now five Christians and about twenty others interested to learn more. It was decided that once the meeting room was plastered, whitewashed, and had some benches, Gou, his son, and Xiong would take turns to go up and lead meetings, saving the villagers the trek down to Dongmenwai. Meeting rooms were also to be established further up the Longxi Valley at A'er and at Taoping, five miles along the Zagunao valley.

Torrance described their visit to Taoping the following day: 'The prosperity of the village is its well-watered plain, its beauty the trees and the gardens that break the monotony of its semi-sterile mountain sides. This afternoon the Christians conducted me through their gardens to let me see their fertility and some fine fruit trees of which their owners are very proud.'[7] Together they sat in the shade and had a long chat. One of the men asked Torrance to take a photo of his elderly parents, which took some time as the mother wanted to be dressed in her finery for it. Torrance's rooftop 'bedroom' in Taoping was reached by two main ladders and two notched tree trunks.

Graham and his team had spent a few days collecting and hunting in the virgin forest region beyond A'er and weren't expected back yet but Graham suddenly turned up at Taoping and Torrance was glad of his company again – and the leg of wild mutton he had brought. Graham had come down to get more supplies sent up to his netters in A'er, including kerosene for the lanterns they used to attract moths in the evenings.

6   WCMN, Nov 1933, p25.
7   Taoping is now one of the main Qiang tourist sites.

From Taoping Graham accompanied Torrance and Gou Pinsan further up the Zagunao valley to Erwa where they received a warm welcome from Chief Yang. Torrance hadn't visited for three years and there was much to catch up on. In the evening they had a meeting in the village school room and found a new openness to their preaching. The next day Yang's wife and sister, both Jiarong Buddhists, came to talk and his wife was very receptive to the idea of a living God being more important than idols. In her native place, she told them, there was much discontent with the lamas.

Yang, who sadly was still smoking opium, gave permission for an empty house to be repaired and used for meetings. Torrance and the local Christians would contribute to the cost of repairs and pay a minimal annual rent. That evening a folk-dance was held in honour of the visitors and Graham commented on the 'perfect innocence in all the proceedings'. The chief's mother and wife led the women's line as they danced opposite the men. Torrance noted in his diary that 'They have several kinds of dances. Different occasions call for these. As yet I have not seen their religious dance which is performed after a sacrifice. The songs then are said to be very fine.'

DAVID C. GRAHAM AND THE BEAR CAUGHT NEAR A'ER

After just one night in Erwa, Graham returned to A'er and, with help from the village headman, left on a hunting trip the next day with two local guides. After five challenging days of heavy rain, stiff climbs, dense underbrush and long grass, they had seen nothing but the tracks of the bear and big-horned mountain goats Graham was hoping to find and came back with only a couple of small mammals, some moths and insects, and a few small birds. However, on reaching A'er they learned

that a black bear had been sighted the day before, raiding the villagers'
corn crop. Some of the villagers managed to flush the bear out of his
hiding place in the forest and Graham's second rifle shot felled him.

Bidding farewell to Chief Yang, Torrance spent the next week-end
in Xuecheng with Pastor Mao and then stopped for a night in Tonghua,
where a young lad directed Torrance and his companions to lodging
at a local temple and asked if they would hold a meeting so that he
could see what it was like. He and his friends gathered a crowd, mostly
women and children, and they proved to be a receptive audience.

Back in Weizhou Torrance happened to meet a Chinese co-worker
of James Edgar, who had been selling literature in Songpan. He had
attempted to enter the neighbouring Boluozi region and been locked
up for fifty days and robbed of his clothes and money. The sorry tale
showed Torrance how wise Ong had been to build up connections with
the Boluozi people in Songpan itself, with the added advantage of Mrs
Zhang being able to speak their language. He gave the man money to
get back to Guanxian.

From Weizhou Torrance rode down to Miansi on Billy, reading a
letter from Annie as he went. From Miansi he went up to Heping and
stayed with Old Gui. Gui's son was an opium smoker, an expensive
habit that made him a lazy worker and was draining the family
resources. Torrance was glad to see Old Su's daughter, who recalled
how eagerly her father had looked forward to their yearly visits. Old Su's
granddaughter described how peaceful he had been on his deathbed.
'Do not grieve over my death,' he had said, 'I am going to a pure land.'

The priest in Heping, who was friendly but not interested in any
Christian message, escorted Torrance down to Qiangfeng where
Torrance was invited to stay in the Qiangfeng priest's house. Two of the
priest's brothers-in-law were Christians and the meeting that evening
proved to be 'the best of our Ch'iang meetings this summer. There was
a moving force present, a conviction and a great impulsion to believe
that Jesus was the Saviour of the world.'

Moving up to the Glen they set their beds up in the old school
house. Torrance had a long talk with the seventy-year-old priest who
had questions about Jesus and whether there really was any connection
between him and their 'Abba Malak'.[8] Torrance explained how Jesus' death
on the cross had fulfilled any need for sacrifice. On his second day in the
Glen Torrance enjoyed a walk on his own further up the valley, stopping
to bathe in the stream and to watch the wildlife – which included a black

---

8   Torrance had previously spelled this 'Abba Malah'.

frog and a water wagtail with a white face. On the way back he sat a while with some locals herding their sheep and goats, who told him there were too many leopards around for the animals roam freely.

Returning to Miansi on August 26, they found Graham had arrived the day before, having been drying out the bear skin, the insects, and his tents in Dongmenwai. To their surprise, the Brown and Hibbard families from the university turned up shortly after, on their way home from a visit to Zagunao. It was their first trip to the region and a lively conversation ensued over lunch with lots of questions for Torrance about things they had seen. On their way up they had been forced to do a detour through the mountains because fighting between Deng and Liu Wenhui was affecting the road where Torrance had sought protection in the roadside trench.

Completely unaware of the disaster about to strike, the Brown party set off in the direction of Guanxian at about 3.15 p.m. while Torrance and the others returned to the Miansi mission house:

> Half-an-hour or so afterwards a two-minute earthquake surprised us all. It was sharp and alarming while it lasted. It felt as if you were in a sieve being shaken back and forth. The house creaked and shook. Thinking it might fall I cried to all to get outside. But no sooner were we out the back door than boulders and stones began bumping down the steep mountain side and in fear that they might crash through the back wall we stepped in again.

Torrance was anxious about the Browns and Hibbards, out on the exposed road with nowhere to hide, but news eventually came through that they had had a narrow escape, even as rocks fell all around them. In Miansi debris was scattered across the town and down by the river a man carrying a load of Sichuan peppers had been crushed by a steep bank collapsing. Large boulders had crashed down near the spring and rocks were still tumbling down and bouncing off the mountainsides. Over the next few days reports began to come in of 'much damage in different places of the Tribes Country, and not a little loss of life'. The epicentre of the 7.3 quake had been up in Diexi and the shaking had been felt by missionaries in Luzhou, more than three hundred miles away.[9]

The next morning, after a night of rippling aftershocks, Torrance had a strong sense he should go up to the Wasi area and together he and Graham paid a visit to young King Suo, where they discovered

---

9   WCMN, Oct 1933, p32.

that a rescue party had gone in search of ten men who had been out digging for medicinal roots. Six of them had been injured in the quake, including one of the two Wasi Christians, who was later brought down to Miansi for Torrance to treat:

> He had a long deep gash in his forehead, a dangerous wound; and a severe cut on his hip. It took me a long time to get the head wound cleaned and dressed. There had been an avalanche. He had been hit, rendered unconscious and buried in it. His brother had to dig him out. The bruises he sustained gave him much pain as well.

Torrance and Graham were afraid infection would set in and offered to take him to Chengdu for further treatment. Torrance was also taking a Qiang lad in the early stages of leprosy to stay at Wushi-tongtang and get injections at the hospital.

The following day was a Sunday and the service in Miansi had to wait until early afternoon due to so many coming for medical help, including another man with a gashed head. After the service, in a secluded spot about a mile up from the town, ten Qiang and four Wasi were baptised in the stream. Torrance was too exhausted to have an evening meeting but it had been a fruitful day amid all the upheaval and he was particularly encouraged that there were now five Qiang church members in Qiangfeng and five in the Glen.

This had been Torrance's best ever summer trip and it was a great wrench to leave everyone the next day not knowing if he would be back. Despite the boulder-strewn road there were no new rockfalls on the way down and Deng had successfully dislodged Liu Wenhui so they didn't have to run the gauntlet of his troops again. Deng had sent a force of men up to Miansi where they crossed the Min River and marched down the other side to launch a surprise attack on Liu's men from behind. Liu had been holding a line along the Min River all the way from Guanxian south to Leshan but he had been soundly beaten and, as Torrance had predicted, he had been forced to retreat to west of Ya'an.

Torrance spent his last night at the CIM church in Guanxian and went by bus the next day back to Chengdu. Graham had set out early that morning riding Billy and accompanied by the carriers with all his specimens. A while later, from the bus, Torrance was puzzled to see the mule-boy trudging towards Chengdu with Billy in tow. As Graham later explained, a few miles after they set out he had let one of his students ride, who rejected the assistance of the mule-boy, and in a flash Billy, with the student hanging on for dear life, had bolted back towards Guanxian to find Torrance, with the mule boy in hot pursuit.

Billy had been an important part of Torrance's summer trips, often prompting conversation with locals because of his fine appearance and earning Torrance the title among some of 'the pastor who rides the black mule'.[10] However, with all the uncertainties ahead, in September Torrance sent him up to live with CIM missionaries in the Jiarong region of Xiaojin. It would prove to be a wise decision but he missed Billy's affectionate greetings from his stable at Wushi-tongtang.

In Scotland it was an anxious time for Annie and the children as they waited for news from Torrance. A few days after the quake the British press had reported a series of earthquakes along the Min River above Maoxian but Annie had no idea where Torrance was at the time. When they first heard the news, David, aged nine, put his arm on Annie's and said, 'Mother, we prayed for Daddy all summer and so he will be alright.'[11] It was six long weeks before a letter arrived from the ABS on October 5 confirming that Torrance was safe, and four days later Annie received a letter from Torrance written the day of the quake, which seems to have been held up by the fighting in Sichuan. Unaware of the true magnitude of the disaster, Torrance had had no idea the quake had become international news and although he had sent a radiogram to the ABS, neither he nor they had thought to send a telegram to the family.

Annie and the children had been on the coast at North Berwick again that summer, where a tent had joined the caravan to enlarge their sleeping quarters. David and James were impatient to be out there the moment school finished and the older ones gradually followed, along with Cousin Jeannie who was visiting from Bromley. Grace had survived a challenging first year at university and Torrance was concerned at the long study hours she, Tom, and Mary were having to put in, but they had still found time to be involved in an Edinburgh mission week earlier in the year and the house was at times quite busy with various people coming and going. Bernard Walker, whose father and stepmother were still in Chongqing, and whose mother had been a good friend of Annie's, had lived with the family for a few months that year while studying medicine, and his brother Bobby would eventually become part of the family through his marriage to Grace. Tom and the two brothers had found a job that summer grouse-raising.

---

10 TT. 'My Work Among the Tribes'. WCMN, Feb 1934, p20.
11 Annie to TT, Oct 9, 1933.

Financially, times were challenging for both Torrance and the family. As the Great Depression cut deeper, the ABS had no longer been able to avoid a drop in salaries, which for Annie meant a difference between one quarterly allowance of £173 and the next of £110. In June Torrance had written to say a month of his salary was being docked 'due to a cut in the New York appropriation'.[12]

In Chengdu a semblance of normality had returned after all the fighting and the various generals convened there in the first week of September – without Liu Wenhui. Openshaw took advantage of this to invite Yang Sen for a game of tennis and a visit to the School for the Blind, to which Yang was accompanied by two of his many wives. 'No. 4, I think, and No. 13 or something', wrote Torrance.[13] Yang told Torrance he was expecting the political discussions to last another two weeks and on September 20 Torrance wrote to Annie that Deng and his allies had attacked Ya'an, forcing Liu to flee south to Hanyuan. Liu was eventually reduced to administering the mountainous territory from Ya'an west to Kangding, leaving Liu Xiang as the dominant force in Sichuan. Torrance had no sympathy for him. 'What a judgement on the man who fired shrapnel shells all over Chengtu last winter and killed so many!'[14] The total number of casualties resulting from the months of conflict was estimated to be about 120,000.[15]

The generals could now turn their full attention to the Communists, whose ranks had swelled to about 60,000, including many Sichuanese, and who now controlled a large part of northeastern Sichuan. Liu Xiang was appointed by the Nationalists to Tian Songyao's position of Bandit Suppression Commander and on October 4 Torrance was invited to a grand ceremony inaugurating Liu as leader of an expedition to retake the territory. Security was tight: 'Only big officials were there and the yamen was heavily guarded. Not a back wall or side corner was neglected. The streets for a long way were cleared and no one allowed to move. Such precautions showed that they knew the danger from communist quarters.'[16] Deng Xihou and a Nationalist representative from Nanjing were among those who gave speeches.

12 TT to Annie, June 15, 1933.
13 TT to Annie, Sept 13, 1933.
14 TT to Annie, Sept 20, 1933.
15 Jerome Ch'en. *Revival: The Highlanders of Central Asia: A History, 1895-1937(1993): A History, 1937-1985.* Routledge. 2017, p138.
16 TT to Annie, Oct 3-4, 1933.

The rapid Communist expansion was causing concern in various quarters and in September the WCMN editorial encouraged missionaries to reflect on how this contrasted with the considerably slower spread of Christianity. The editor attributed some of this to the high enthusiasm of young Communists for the cause and to the Communists' highly effective propaganda and degree of organisation, but he also acknowledged the attractiveness of an economic revolution that promised redistribution of wealth and an education system not limited to the privileged few. On the downside he noted quasi-religious aspects such as the near-deification of leaders like Lenin and the demand for such complete self-surrender. 'It is thought better' he wrote, 'that thousands of men, women and children should perish now to bring in the new day of universal communism than that a weak compassion by sparing lives should delay the longed-for millennium. It combines the relentlessness of the Inquisition with the religious fervour of the Crusades.'[17] Another contributor pointed out that the appeal of the Communists was magnified by the Nationalist government's own failure to deal with poverty in the agricultural sector, unemployment in the cities, inflation, and their own political and military infighting.[18]

On October 17 Torrance received shocking news from the Qiang area: 'To-day I heard that Miansi suffered in the big flood of water when the pent up waters broke loose and came rushing down the Min valley.'[19] This wasn't a matter of the Min River being just a few feet higher. As a result of the quake, severe landslides in Diexi had created huge dams across the river, causing three lakes to form. As the water built up and breached two of the dams, the three lakes became one body of water more than eight miles long. At 7 p.m. on October 9, forty-five days after the quake, the lowest dam restraining this vast lake suddenly gave way, releasing a wall of water over two hundred feet high. By the time it reached Maoxian two hours later this had reduced to about eighty feet. Hitting Weizhou at midnight, it was still forty feet high by the time it reached Guanxian in the early hours of the morning, where residents heard the thundering torrent ten minutes before it arrived. The floodwater swept along everything and everyone in its path,

17 WCMN, Sept 1933, p2.
18 L. Earl Willmott. 'Impressions from the National Christian Council'. WCMN, Sept 1933, pp17-25.
19 TT to Annie, Oct 17, 1933. (Pinyin updated.)

scattering debris of all sorts in its wake as it reached level ground near Guanxian.[20]

Gou Pinsan was in Weizhou at the time and owed his life to a servant girl. He had been asleep in the house of a friend when the girl heard the roar of the approaching wall of water and raised the alarm. Just as Gou got to the door two men with a lamp appeared and he followed them up the hillside to safety. Moments later the house was completely washed away. The Weizhou mission house suffered the same fate.

A later WCMN report recorded the impact on the wider area, including the Zagunao valley: 'In this sector the earthquake has been very severe for several weeks with disastrous intermittent tremors that have taken a heavy toll of lives and property. Letters from Pastors Mao and Ren recently indicate great damage. One Tribe's village on the mountain side, of over forty families, was engulfed and only three families escaped.'[21] The article also reported that over three thousand had been drowned. The estimated number of deaths from the quake and flood combined was between nine and ten thousand.

After months of almost incessant unrest and the tragedy of the quake, the more mundane aspects of life brought some welcome respite during a calmer autumn in Chengdu. In October Torrance and Openshaw were greatly encouraged by a three-week visit to Chengdu by the Bethel Band – three Chinese evangelists in their twenties who were 'of such personalities that they immediately won their way into all hearts'.[22] On October 31 the trio were part of an unforgettable evening at the Great East Street hall. However, in their contact with the wider Christian community in Chengdu they were disappointed to find so many 'modernists' among the Chinese Christian leaders, for whom setting a moral example seemed to be taking precedence over the essential message of salvation.

This was a disappointment also felt by Torrance, whose own passion for the gospel was not always shared by other missionaries, particularly some at the university, and it was refreshing when he encountered those

---

20 Song Ling (©). *Landslide damming in Western Sichuan Province, China, with special reference to the 1786 Dadu River and 1933 Diexi events.* Unpublished MSc thesis, University of Waterloo, 2015, p61. See p43 for photo indicating height of the quake lake.

21 'Open Letter to the Mei Tao Huei Members on Home Mission – Earthquake Sufferers'. WCMN, Dec 1933, p36. (Pinyin updated.)

22 WCMN, Dec 1933, p4.

of a more kindred spirit. One such foreigner was Dr Robert Lawrence, the eldest brother of Thomas Lawrence (better known as Lawrence of Arabia), who was working with Dr Lechler. Aware of Torrance's fluency in Chinese and his local knowledge, Robert and his mother had sought his help in buying a couple of leopard skins. Torrance enjoyed their company and wrote to Annie, 'They are very evangelical . . . It is nice to meet folks so out and out for the Lord. You know where they stand exactly. It is tiring to have to do with so many who have their tongues in their cheeks.'[23]

In late November, Daniel Diao came from Chongqing to discuss ABS matters. The work was going well and Sichuan had achieved the distinction that year of being the only ABS region to record an increase in distribution. Across the province 579 Bibles, 959 New Testaments, and 768,612 single books of Scripture had been distributed, statistics which didn't include the work of the B&FBS colporteurs under Torrance's supervision.

Following Diao's visit, Torrance went to Guanxian for a week with Hou Li-de and another colporteur to help with evangelistic meetings at the CIM church. The first evening meeting was packed and to Torrance's delight twelve people enrolled as enquirers, including four Qiang from places where he knew of no Christians. He had noticed them on the street in the afternoon and simply invited them to come along. The church was full for the whole week of meetings, with about sixty giving their names and wanting to know more.

On his return to Chengdu Torrance was surprised to receive a visit from a tribal chief from Muping, in the foothills north of Ya'an, with an unusual request. He wanted Torrance to come and open up a work among his people, which was something Torrance would have liked to do, but he knew he didn't have enough time. Back in 1911 Torrance had written to Hykes about the Muping tribesmen when they had joined the rebellion against the Qing government, but it wasn't an area he was very familiar with. In ancient times, the area had been inhabited by the Qingyi or 'Dark Clothes' Qiang, a name still used for the Qingyi River that runs through Muping, but Tibetan Buddhism had long since become the dominant religious culture there. The chief came to the Great East Street meeting that evening and was also there a week later. On January 2 he came again and told Torrance he believed in Jesus.

---

23   TT to Annie, Nov 29, 1933.

Although much of Sichuan was now calm, the situation in the northeast of the province was worrying. November's WCMN reported that streams of refugees were fleeing the towns where the Communists had taken control.

> The great armies of Szechuan, which have shown such eagerness to fight each other during the last year, seem to be powerless up to the present to withstand the incoming Reds. . . . Unless some new spirit comes into the leaders and soldiers of these armies to stiffen their morale and enforce their co-operation, there is little hope of any effective resistance and Szechuan may soon become the stronghold of Red Rule in the West.[24]

In mid-November an ex-student of Annie's dropped in to see Torrance and said that of eight hundred Communists recently arrested in Chengdu, three hundred had been executed. Knowing how effective the Communist military commander, Xu Xiangqian, was reputed to be and how fiercely his men fought, Torrance saw this clamp down in Chengdu as an indication of how afraid the officials were. General Liu Xiang had stayed on in Chengdu since the September conference and Torrance could see from his bedroom that two large new barracks had been erected on the parade ground, which was busy every day with soldiers drilling. One of the fears was that the Communists would manage to push south to the Yangtze River at Wanxian and take control of shipping, leaving Sichuan 'bottled up in the West', as Torrance put it.[25] Added to this was the fear that a smaller Communist army led by General He Long in the Hubei-Sichuan border area would manage to connect with Xu Xiangqian's troops and create a larger, more powerful 'soviet' in eastern Sichuan. In early December the province breathed a sigh of relief as the Communists in the northeast were pushed back to the Shaanxi border area and the two Communist armies were kept apart.

---

24 WCMN, Nov 1933, p1.
25 TT to Annie, Dec 6, 1933.

304

Chapter 20
Farewell to the Qiang
1934

With Torrance's retirement in mind, Chen Bingling came down at the end of January to talk about the work. Torrance was hopeful that Chen, Gou, Xiong, and Ong would each develop their own spheres of influence, covering the areas around Miansi, Dongmenwai, Jiuzi, and Songpan, and come together annually for consultation. Ong and Gou were both able to support themselves, which provided them a measure of protection against accusations of being a 'foreign lackey'. Torrance was hoping he would still be able to offer some support through private donations for Chen and Xiong, and possibly for Mou, the Christian from Xuecheng. Xiong had recently sent a message asking for more books and tracts.

Torrance had been working on an article for the WCMN called 'My Work Among the Tribes', giving an overview of the work since its inception in 1919.[1] Perhaps in order to protect them, he avoided naming Chen and Gou Pinsan but noted how effective a particular man had been in his early itinerations among the Qiang – one who 'created no fuss, gave no offence but went quietly and earnestly about his work' – and then mentioned how a 'Ch'iang preacher' had joined him in the work, which had opened far more doors. Seeking to reach the Qiang wherever they were found, as well as some of the Wasi and Jiarong, the two men had criss-crossed the region from Taoguan to Xuecheng, from Weizhou to Maoxian, and westwards from there to the villages of Heihu and Sanzhi. Torrance then described the building of the church in Dongmenwai and more recent developments, including the jeering that the Christians had to endure from some quarters. Ong had also been facing opposition in Songpan and as a result he was spending more time in the outlying villages.

With regard to his own summer trips, Torrance stressed the importance of taking time to chat with people and described how at

---

1 TT. 'My Work Among the Tribes'. WCMN, Feb 1934, pp13-21. Reprinted with minor revisions in *The Chinese Recorder*, Vol 66 (April), 1935, pp227-234.

ease he felt among the Qiang. Reiterating that when they heard about Christ as the Lamb of God who takes away sin it was a 'religious language they readily understand', he gave a brief summary of some essential similarities between their culture and the Old Testament:

> That God is holy, every White Stone on the roof and every sheet of white paper used in His worship openly implies. That He can only be approached in prayer when sin has been expiated, every grove, every altar, every sacrifice, public and private, declares. Interpreted in the Atonement and the free grace of God in Jesus Christ, these time immemorial customs of theirs doubly convince the thoughtful that the preacher is of the same 'lineage' as their own fathers. If not, from whence comes the similarity of belief.[2]

Giving more practical detail than previously, he described the winter visits of the Qiang to Chengdu. 'They lived for 6 weeks or 2 months in our own "Compound" and we provided all with their food. Never will we forget the joy of reading the Scriptures with these apt pupils and expounding their meaning to their thirsty souls. Their daily surprise and delight were marvellous to watch. On one thing they were unanimous: their ancient sacrifices and those of the Hebrews had a common origin.'[3]

In mid-February, Torrance wrote to Annie of his frustration once again at the suggestion that the Qiang worshipped their white stones. 'The Ch'iang do not. It sounds sensational to say that a stone is worshipped and some people dearly like to make a sensation. The Ch'iang almost certainly are of Jewish extraction tho' I have never dared say so owing to lack of exact proof.'[4] This was the closest he had come to such an assertion – and said privately as he let off steam to Annie.

At the beginning of the year the B&FBS had suggested that Torrance stay on until the end of 1935 but he had been apart from the family long enough and besides, for some time now he had had an intuition that 1935 'was likely to see storm and trouble' and he wanted to be in Edinburgh by then.[5] The anticipation of his home-coming was growing for both Torrance and the family, but not without some trepidation.

---

2   Ibid., p15.
3   Ibid.
4   TT to Annie, Feb 14, 1934.
5   TT to Annie, Jan 3, 1934.

Mary had been fifteen and David three when he last saw them and they would be twenty-two and ten when he returned. Annie had become well-established as a speaker and Bible teacher and was accustomed, almost as a single parent, to making day-to-day family decisions on her own.

In February she wrote to say she had been prescribed a kind of medicinal arsenic, to which Torrance replied, 'Stop it immediately!' In her reply she explained that it was a 'white arsenic' rather than the kind she had once been given to ill effect in Chengdu, and then added a humorous word of warning:

> We enjoyed reading your letter – it sounded so quaintly autocratic – yet it is getting fashionable again – as Hitler and Mussolini-ism etc. But perhaps as yet the family here is more democratically inclined now but in respect to your return and taking up the reins of government again we will call it 'A Dominion'. I can imagine you pulling a wry face and hear from afar some of your favourite ejaculations – but it will be alright and like all good stories we shall wind up 'and they lived Happy ever after'.[6]

Annie had recently been grappling with the introduction of stricter regulations in the British tax system.

Word had come that Franck was due back sometime in the autumn so Torrance was already beginning to dispose of some items, knowing it would take time to sort out the Wushi-tongtang house as well as his lodgings at Franck's and wanting to leave time for one last summer trip if possible. A set of carved chairs had gone to the museum and he was still sending items to Annie with anyone travelling to Britain. In March he sent a small blue vase and a rose tea-caddy, both two hundred years old, as well as a Han dynasty spearhead. His Chinese histories and other books he was passing on to Graham, keeping just a few to bring home. When Tom heard about this, the finality of his father's return seemed to hit him and he wrote back somewhat wistfully, asking if Torrance really had no hope of returning to China in the future, even for a trip, and adding that Annie would probably like to go out again.[7] But he was also realistic about the precariousness of things and, like Annie, made a comment about the rise of dictators in Europe.

Openshaw was now living with Torrance at Franck's place and enjoying the milk and butter from Torrance's cows. He was also retiring

6   Annie to TT, April 10, 1934
7   Tom to TT, May 27, 1934.

this year and together with some CIM workers they threw their heart and soul into the Chinese New Year literature distribution across Chengdu. The month of nightly meetings which followed resulted in 15 baptisms and 452 names given by those wanting further contact. Two of the tracts distributed were written by Torrance, one on prayer and one with the title 'Sichuan is a land of evil spirits', a local saying which reflected Sichuan's strong folk religion traditions.[8] Torrance's Chinese name, Tao Ranshi, was always on his tracts and during one hospital visit he was asked by a colonel if the author of the tracts was Chinese or foreign. Whoever it was, said the colonel, they wrote convincingly and the Chinese was good.

As was his custom, Deng Xihou sent Torrance a New Year gift, this year four pomeloes and some select pears. Liu Xiang was still in Chengdu keeping a firm grip on things and also raising taxes. Together the various generals were planning coordinated attacks against the Communists, hoping to drive them out of Sichuan, but Torrance was pessimistic: 'I doubt it. The Reds are too crafty and have capable leaders in the field.'[9] A week later news came that about two thousand men had deserted one of Liu Xiang's generals and gone over to the Communists. In March Deng won a battle in Guangyuan and news came that Bazhong had been recovered but the Communists were still holding Tongjiang.

In Chengdu, the Qiang lad with leprosy who had come down with Torrance last August seemed to be improving. In appreciation of Torrance's hospital visiting, Dr Wilford was treating the boy free of charge with injections of chaulmoogra oil. A young priest from Gou's village of Mushang was also staying with Torrance in a bid to overcome his opium addiction. In early April Torrance reported to Annie that the man had put on weight and was looking better. Torrance had given him a gown and he had bought himself a waistcoat. 'You would not know the fellow . . . He feels he can go home with self-respect and face up to the people in his village and his wife won't be ashamed of him. Yesterday he recited his priest's chants and Dan Dye took them on a dictograph.'[10] Disappointingly, in the summer Torrance discovered that he had returned to his opium habit and had avoided going back to Mushang.

Gou Pinsan came to Chengdu with three other Qiang in early March. Torrance wrote to Annie that Gou had brought with him 'a

8 四川是邪魔之地.
9 TT to Annie, Feb 20, 1934.
10 TT to Annie, April 3, 1934.

priest's rod that is a real curio. It is like the rod of Moses and Aaron.'[11] In a later account he described it as having a serpent coiled round it in life-like fashion. A metal knob was missing from the top of it and it had come from a family where the hereditary priestly role had been discontinued.[12]

THE 'PRIEST'S ROD'[13]

One of the men with Gou, a Christian from Taoping, had a growth on his neck and was hoping for treatment but sadly Morse and Crawford decided it was too deep to operate. Torrance took the men to the Great East Street meeting and also to Plewman's to listen to his radio, which was broadcasting news in Chinese and in English. Two more Qiang came down a couple of days later and he took them to hear the radio too. Nanjing came through clearly and 'They heard Leipsig too very well. Shanghai, Siam, India and Moscow.'[14]

Torrance was encouraged by Gou's news. His son was going to work full-time as an evangelist and Gou had now established meeting places in Keku and A'er and was planning two others, one in Biaduo, just below A'er, and one in Taoping. Xiong was moving to live in Chief Yang's village, where repairs were in progress on the house Yang had offered for their use, assisted by an unexpected donation from Harold

---

11 TT to Annie, March 21, 1934.
12 TT. 'The Story of Isaac Whiteheart'. Ch 21 in *Conversion Stories of Chinese Christians*.
13 TT. *China's First Missionaries*. 1937, opp p98. This rod is longer, more ornate, and more finely carved than is customary among the Qiang today.
14 TT to Annie, March 6, 1934.

Robertson at the university. Robertson was planning to travel up to Songpan with Torrance in the summer.

Later in March Torrance received news of Ong from an unexpected source. A letter had come from Reginald Bazire at the CIM station in Pingwu, east of Songpan, asking for information about the tribes and mentioning that, on a visit to Songpan, he had had a delightful time with Ong. As a later article by Bazire showed, Ong was clearly quite a character:

> While in Songpan I had delightful spiritual fellowship with an extraordinary character – an evangelist privately employed by a Bible Society agent . . . This evangelist dresses in filthy tattered garments, would not appear to have washed since the cold weather set in last year, and has long dishevelled locks surmounted by a mangy old fur hat that at times is promoted to the upper-storey, the lower storey being occupied by an even more dilapidated bowler! In spite of his extraordinary appearance he is a real good fellow and seems to have an earnest desire to carry the Gospel to the tribes. About the time this letter reaches you he hopes to be travelling three days' journey on the back of a yak to the home of a hitherto unvisited tribe.[15]

Not long after this, Ong arrived in Chengdu for a visit. With him were Mr and Mrs Zhang, the Boluo and Tibetan-speaking Chinese couple. Torrance wrote to Annie that Wushi-tongtang was full, with six tribesmen staying plus Ong and the Zhangs.[16] Sadly Mrs Zhang had contracted leprosy and, like the young Qiang lad, she was being treated with chaulmoogra oil and needed to stay longer in Chengdu than expected. As a result Ong stayed on too and helped at the Great East Street meetings.

Torrance was still helping at the museum occasionally and that month Graham asked him to help date some pottery fragments from excavations he was working on in Guanghan. Remarkably, this proved to be the now famous Sanxingdui site, which revealed the existence of an ancient and unfamiliar culture, known today particularly for its large-scale bronze heads and masks, which lay undiscovered until the 1980s. In the spring of 1931, Vyvyan Donnithorne had heard that

---

15 Reginald Bazire. 'A Journey to Songpan'. *China's Millions*, 1934 (July), p126. Reginald and his wife Eileen would later be interned in the same Japanese POW camp as Eric Lidell of *Chariots of Fire* fame.
16 TT to Annie, March 27, 1934.

knives and discs made of jade and stone were being unearthed on the land of a local farmer. Several of these had been presented to the university and in March 1934 Graham and a Chinese colleague, Lin Mingjun, were invited by the local magistrate to excavate the site.

By now, the museum was home to over eleven thousand objects, among which was 'the largest collection of Ch'iang artifacts to be found in any museum', including 'ancient garments, leather armor, embroidered shoes and belts, and pottery ranging in age between five hundred and two thousand years'.[17] In May's WCMN, Graham acknowledged contributions from both foreigners and Chinese, again emphasising that the museum had been built up largely through the efforts of Torrance, Edgar, and Dye.[18]

Graham also mentioned some items from Palestine in the collection, including a shepherd's sling and models of a grain mill and a stove, which had been donated by Lewis Havermale. Several missionaries had visited the Holy Land on their way from Shanghai to Europe, taking advantage of the convenient train connection between Port Said and Jerusalem, and Torrance was thinking to do the same. Annie was strongly supportive of the idea. 'We do hope you will go to Palestine and take your camera and tell us all about it when you return. It will be very helpful when you return in many ways.'[19] The Lawrences had given him the address of friends in Jerusalem with whom he could stay and Openshaw had already given him a hundred dollars towards the trip.

May 5, 1934, was a sad day for Torrance. After forty-one years in China, Harry Openshaw, elder statesman among the missionaries, was leaving for America – and while they would continue to correspond, he and Torrance never saw each other again. Torrance was deeply grateful for their rich friendship and fruitful partnership. 'Truly God threw Openshaw and I together to do this work.'[20] A farewell in the WCMN reminded readers how much things had changed since Openshaw's arrival in Ya'an in 1893, when he and a fellow missionary had 'had their heads shaved and then ventured into the city, clad in Chinese garments and a false queue pinned in their caps.'[21]

17   D. C. Graham. 'The West China Union University Museum'. JWCBRS, Vol 6, 1934, p134.
18   D. C. Graham. 'The West China Union University Museum'. WCMN, Jan 1933, pp12-14.
19   Annie to TT, April 10, 1934.
20   TT to Annie, Oct 3, 1933.
21   WCMN, June 1934, p2.

On the Tuesday after Openshaw's departure Torrance was back at the Great East Street hall, pleased to see some of the city militia in attendance, several of whom gave their names as enquirers. That same day, May 8, the Communist troops under He Long attacked Pengshui to the east of Chongqing and captured a missionary named Howard Smith and his cook-boy, in the hope of receiving a ransom for their release.[22] He Long's army was now heading west and although Liu Xiang's troops were sent after them, Howard and the cook were kept captive for several weeks, constantly on the move, until they managed a daring escape in Guizhou.

Deng Xihou was in town in May and Torrance went to visit him. His troops were trying to re-take territory from the Communists near the Sichuan-Shaanxi border but it was hilly country and they were having difficulties transporting enough rice to their men. With Deng's troops fighting in the northeast and Liu Xiang's men pursuing He Long in the south, Torrance was conscious of Sichuan's vulnerability: 'One way and another all the troops are being drawn off to the fringes of the province. Things are none too secure.'[23] In June, on a visit to northeastern Sichuan, Bishop Holden of the CIM reported that nearly every person they met had lost at least one relative 'murdered by the "Reds" and none of them rich people. It is said that 30,000 have been killed in Bazhong county alone, and the whole countryside is covered with Red propaganda, carved in stone, on rocks and stone monuments.'[24]

There was an ebb and flow of victories and defeats with refugees fleeing in both directions, some preferring to go over to the Communists and others escaping them.[25] *China's Millions* recorded the presence of 'five huge stone buttressed mounds' containing hundreds of victims, next to which a commemoration stone had been erected, apparently by Deng's men.[26] By early summer the Sichuan troops had had a measure of success but the disunity amongst the generals was once again a major issue, as Torrance made clear to Annie:

Sichuan is in a stew again. The Reds are back in East Sichuan. Liu Xiang, on the advice of his Buddhist fortune-telling adviser,

---

22 WCMN, July-Aug 1934, pp13-18. Howard Smith was with the Christian & Missionary Alliance.
23 TT to Annie, May 29, 1934.
24 *Millions*, Sept 1934, p177.
25 Kapp, *Szechwan and the Chinese Republic*, p94.
26 *Millions*, Dec 1934, p227. Seen by H. W. Funnell and Bishop Holden near Zongba on a visit in June-July 1934.

degraded his main General Wang Fangzhou last February. This
caused great disapproval and irritation to his other Generals so
they lay down on their job. Then Liu Xiang would not supply Yang
Sen with ammunition and he refused to attack the Reds or hold
them back when they returned. Nobody could blame him as Liu
Xiang was not playing square. So the Reds got by him.[27]

Liu Xiang's adviser was a Daoist mystic called Liu Congyun,
meaning 'Liu from the clouds', who, despite no military training,
seemed to hold Liu Xiang in thrall and stand between him and his
officers, which was contributing significantly to Sichuan's military
weakness.[28] Torrance had heard about this from his military friends
and was appalled. In his 1933 ABS report he described Liu Congyun
as the virtual head of the province, professing to be a living oracle
who could 'read the stars and forecast events. To refuse his counsel
is to court disaster.' Ten men apparently stood guard outside Cong's
door and he wielded 'the civil and religious authority of a Pope'. This
had increased Deng and Tian Songyao's frustration with Liu Xiang,
who had already taken more than his fair share of the spoils after Liu
Wenhui's defeat in 1932, and they were now holding back from fully
supporting him in the hope that he would be weakened as his troops
bore the brunt of the fighting against the Communists.[29] The disunity
would be costly for all of them.

In Chengdu Torrance had been preparing a lecture for the West
China Border Research Society, published later as 'The Basic Spiritual
Conceptions of the Ch'iang'.[30] This focused solely on the religious
culture of the Qiang and was his most comprehensive work on the
subject. In terms of their origins, he still maintained that they had
reached China from somewhere in Asia Minor and that 'their Old-
Testament pattern of religion represented an early patriarchal type,
known to the Hebrews before their settlement in the holy land.'
Although some assumed an ethnic connection between the Tibetan,
Jiarong, Yi, and Qiang peoples, Torrance had observed significant
differences among the Qiang:

---

27   TT to Annie, August 29, 1934. (Pinyin updated.)
28   Kapp, *Szechwan and the Chinese Republic*, p93.
29   Ibid., p92.
30   TT. 'The Basic Spiritual Conceptions of the Ch'iang'. JWCBRS, Vol 6,
1934, pp31-48. All quotes in this section refer to this article unless otherwise
indicated.

They are finer in physique and frequently show Semitic features of countenance which these races fail to do. Many of their customs, too, indicate a closer affinity to those of the Hebrews. Even if it be asserted that the Tibetans and Jiarong came also from the West – which we believe – yet, because of these facts, caution is needed before sweepingly including them in the same racial stock . . . The Chiang is a sort of a Jew among our West China peoples. You can scarcely hide him even when his blood has been mingled with a strain of Chinese. He has a way with him, an appearance and a religious outlook that marks him out from others around him.

Having asking the question, 'What then is the nature of the Chiang religion?', Torrance explained that 'It is simply that of the olden-time worship in the high places.' In this high place worship he included the practices of both the Canaanites and the early Israelites. Elaborating on this hypothesis, he looked at the instructions given to the Israelites in the book of Deuteronomy, that they get rid of the altars, idols, sacred pillars, and groves on the high places – instructions which they never fully obeyed. This was followed by a description of each aspect of Qiang religious culture, handed down through generations of priests, with the central importance of purity demonstrated by the cleansing rituals performed prior to the paying of vows. These required the participants to cleanse themselves and their clothes three days before and avoid pungent herbs like garlic or onions, after which the sacrificial animal had to be cleansed and led with a new rope to the sacred grove. The white stone was another representation of purity. In his argument against claims that the Qiang practiced litholatry, Torrance pointed to the use of stone markers in the Bible, which stood witness to certain events but were never intended to be objects of worship.

Something which seemed unique to the Qiang was their 'Nee-Dsu' or 'Je-Dsu' – the venerated roll of white paper 'in the form of an ancient book', which played a key role at the main annual sacrificial ceremony and was, according to Torrance, an indication that they had once had their own script and a 'sacred roll of their law'. As Gou had mentioned in his 1925 list of Old Testament similarities, this roll of paper originally had a human figure made of coarse grass at its centre, which had more recently been replaced by the skull of a monkey. Torrance had now learned that the roll of paper was placed on a small pile of seed wheat before the sacrifice and he was struck by the combination of the sacred roll and its name, as well as the skull and grain as symbols of life and death, and saw a resonance with the

The sacred roll before the sacrifice (L) and after (R)
with the added piece of white paper.
To the right is the bowl of blood from the sacrificed goats.
(Qiang New Year, Nov 2, 2013, courtesy of Yu Yongqing)

'messianic message' of Psalm 40: 'Sacrifice and meal offering You have not desired; My ears You have opened; Burnt offering and sin offering You have not required. Then I said, "Behold, I come; In the scroll of the book it is written of me."'[31] A further parallel was the presence of the flatbread and 'wine' or grain alcohol at the sacrifice, placed on the altar next to the sacred roll. Torrance had discovered that in some places the priest would take seed from the small pile beneath the roll and scatter it over the participants, who gathered what they could in the folds of their garments.

In sharp contrast to these purity-related rituals were the 'strange accretions' that some priests had allowed to creep in to their rituals. According to Torrance, these included the monkey-skin cap of the priest, which in some places had replaced the plain, circular-brimmed felt hat, and the bunch of strange objects that priests in a certain area hung from their belts, as well as other practices similar to those of Chinese exorcists, in particular a kind of spiritism whereby young priests at their initiation would enter a trance and be possessed by a spirit. Torrance had been told this was sometimes feigned for the sake of reputation among others who claimed to have authority over occult powers and he saw a need for discernment: 'Patience and caution are often necessary to disentangle the real from the simulation and what constitutes the old true-Chiang religion from its present day admixture of spurious elements.' This admixture had received considerable

31 Psalm 40:6-7.

impetus in the eighteenth century with increased Chinese control over the Qiang area and the imposition of temples and Chinese religious practices.

Torrance had spent many years living amidst the temple worship and folk religion rituals of the Sichuanese, particularly during his rural CIM itinerations, and this had fine-tuned his ability to differentiate. 'He, however, who knows something of the genius of the beautiful old Chiang religion groans within himself at the sight of such things.' He had much respect for the 'better class of priests who despise the use of such fraudulent practices'.

That same issue of the JWCBRS also contained Torrance's 'Free Translation of a Stone Tablet at Lifan', co-translated with his depot manager, Li Youren.[32] The tablet had been issued by the Xuecheng magistrate in 1881, forbidding local men from marrying women who were related to them in any way. In particular, the proclamation addressed 'a bad old custom' which still persisted 'of a man marrying the wife of a deceased elder or younger brother', a practice seen as unvirtuous by the Chinese. This was now to be severely punished without hope of mercy. Torrance would later compare this 'bad old custom' with a similar custom found in the biblical book of Deuteronomy: 'If brothers dwell together, and one of them dies and has no son, the widow of the dead man shall not be married to a stranger outside the family; her husband's brother shall go in to her, take her as his wife, and perform the duty of a husband's brother to her.'[33]

To Torrance's great relief, there seemed to be no obstacles regarding a summer trip and by the end of May he was already getting ready, hoping to visit as many places as possible. Some literature had gone ahead by post, his supply of medicines was organised, and he had bought seventeen rolls of film, although to his deep disappointment many photos of this final trip didn't come out well and he realised too late that the tripod had come loose.[34]

The Lawrences gave Torrance a lift to Guanxian in the comfort of the CMS car, where he stayed at the CIM station and took two meetings and the Sunday morning service. To his delight, the latter was attended by three Qiang, two of whom were Christians he knew. On Tuesday, June 12, he and Harold Robertson left for the mountains with a cook named Ding Si. Three carriers were taking loads straight

32 TT. 'Free Translation of a Stone Tablet at Lifan'. JWCBRS, 1934, pp22-23.
33 Deuteronomy 25:5-6. See TT, *China's First Missionaries*, p43.
34 TT to Annie, Sept 12, 1934.

to Songpan and two others were taking loads to Dongmenwai. Grace Jephson, Ella Bailey, and Leona Thoering – all CIM workers – were due to join Torrance later in the Qiang area.

It took three days to get up to Miansi and it was probably good that Annie knew nothing of the difficulties until they were long past. On June 15 Torrance wrote to her, 'The road, owing to the flood last year, was much more difficult. Where it had been washed out, as instance along the face of precipices or built up from the edge of the river bed, wide detours have to be made high up on the mountain sides which were difficult, tedious and very tiring. Last night the men were all tired out. Robertson and I too were very tired.'[35] Torrance had hired a chair with two carriers for the journey but the bad conditions meant many stretches had to be walked or even climbed and it was quickly obvious that Billy would not have coped.

The devastation wrought by the post-quake flood was shocking. Much of Baisha village, a few miles outside Guanxian, had been wiped out and at Shaping Pass only one house had survived, in which Torrance and Graham happened to have stayed the previous year. Further up, the village of Suoqiao had completely disappeared. 'Everywhere along the route the same story is repeated.'[36] Even the large temple in Miansi, where the Qiangfeng boys had had to attend the public school, had been washed away, with only a few trees remaining nearby.

Chen Bingling was waiting to meet them in Miansi and took Torrance's spare things to Dongmenwai to await his return from Songpan. Moving straight on to Weizhou, Torrance saw the site of the house where Gou had been sleeping on the night of the flood. 'A great hole with a boulder marks it precisely.'[37] The government yamen and the mosque had also been washed away. From Weizhou he and Robertson went up to Luobozhai for the night where they were joined by Chen, Xiong, Mou, and Zhou Lianqing, Torrance's 'oldest and best' colporteur, who was now working with Chen. It was Torrance's third visit to the village and the headman was particularly welcoming. At the close of the Sunday morning meeting he gave his name as a believer. Another man from a village two miles away had become a Christian through a tract he received in Miansi and several of his friends now believed too. Torrance had a chance to visit the sacred grove at their

---

35   TT to Annie, June 15, 1934.
36   Ibid.
37   TT diary to children, June 17, 1934. All summer trip quotations are from this unless otherwise indicated.

village, which had some fine old trees although the central tree had fallen and a young one had been planted in its place.

From Luobozhai Torrance, Robertson, Chen, and Ding Si continued on to Maoxian, passing three destroyed villages on the way. The rest of the journey to Songpan was worse than Torrance could have imagined. Four villages had disappeared above Maoxian and at the pass where he had treated a man's eyes, the man's house and the local temple were in ruins. The man had died the previous year, grieving for his son who had been lost in the quake. Near the ruined village of Dadian they had to descend to the edge of the river bed which was littered with stones, and more were still falling.

DIEXI BEFORE THE QUAKE

Halfway between Dadian and Diexi, they stayed in a new inn at Shimenkan, having been told by a Christian in Maoxian that it was less at risk from falling rocks. The landlord was away but his Qiang wife, whose mother was from Dongmenwai, was pleased to see them. She had lost her son-in-law and her home in the quake. As they pressed on the next morning they saw the ruins of a whole Qiang village where eighty-six people had died. Crossing the last pass before Diexi they stood aghast at the scene. What had been a beautiful elevated plain was now a wilderness of rocks and boulders. Prior to the quake the town had stood at the southern end of this plain surrounded by a strong wall but on that terrible day massive landslides had 'gouged out two thirds of the plain and pushed it two miles obliquely down into the ravine of the river far below', sending two hundred families to their deaths. Survivors from the wider area told how a cloud of dust produced by the earthquake had shrouded everything in a blanket of total darkness.

The usual road from Diexi to Songpan was nowhere to be seen. In its place there was a small lake behind the remains of the soil dam which had burst last October, and further up a lake nearly eight miles long still remained behind a rock-formed dam, on which two boats were ferrying people back and forth. However – and this was the nightmare part – the only way to reach the ferry on the upper lake was by a makeshift path high above the smaller lake, along the edge of the remnant of the Diexi plain. 'It nearly makes the blood curdle to look at it, as it leads high over and along a fearful precipice.'[38] They managed it with fear and trembling. 'Robertson faced it bravely and never said a word till he was up and over it.'

Taking the ferry across the main lake, they disembarked at the northern end and made for the village of Taiping where they met some Qiang folk on the street. 'An old man escorted me, as I left, to the end of the village simply to show his goodwill. It was touching to see him.' Reaching Pingding Pass late afternoon, they visited the Qiang family with whom Torrance and Chen had lodged two years before. The husband was away but the wife urged them to stay. 'See, it is going to rain. The Lord means you to stay here,' she said. Their last night before Songpan was spent in Guihua, where the imam once again invited Torrance to stay at the mosque.

Arriving in Songpan exhausted and immeasurably relieved, Torrance was greeted by the familiar sight of Lanbu, the Boluozi Christian. Other Boluozi came to the meeting that evening, with Mrs Zhang translating. One 73-year-old Boluozi woman 'cried for sheer joy as she listened to the news of pardon and salvation through Jesus Christ' and others were also deeply affected. Another woman told Torrance that after his visit two years ago some of the women told others back home about the gospel and none of them had died or lost homes in the quake, despite the earth splitting open in the Boluozi area and green fire coming up and burning some people to death.[39] At the meeting Lanbu spoke of his salvation. Accustomed to disdain from other people groups, he explained how deeply moved he had been when Ong and Torrance told them that all men are equal in the sight of God.

After several days in Songpan, Robertson left to visit the Bazires in Pingwu and took a different route back to Chengdu, happy to avoid the treacherous precipice path. Torrance was dreading his return journey but in the meantime he was enjoying the cultural

---

38 TT to Annie, June 25, 1934.
39 Ibid.

diversity of Songpan and he and Ong were out on the streets every day, handing out literature and chatting to all sorts of people, encountering friendliness as they went. Various people called at Ong's rented house to talk or get medical help and the evenings were spent mainly preaching to the Boluozi people. On one evening a man stopped to talk with Torrance on the street and before long Torrance found himself preaching to a whole crowd. He also had chats with a few Tibetan lamas and some of the Xifan people, several of whom came for eye treatment. One lama asked Torrance how he knew where he would go when he died. Another, who had been hostile to the Christians, came in desperation to get help for a Tibetan woman who had swallowed opium. Torrance and Ong went together and the woman was treated successfully, after which the lama invited them to his home for tea.

Sunday, July 1, was a big day, with fifteen Boluozi and two Chinese being baptised. To begin the day Ong invited them all for breakfast, as Torrance described: 'The meal consisted of a loaf of barley meal given to each which was washed down with mouthfuls of their peculiar brew of tea. Into a bowl with a large spoonful of parched barley flour and a piece of butter in it hot tea was poured. The flavour of this they seemed to like much. Several times the bowl was filled. Never had I seen Ong so brimful of delight.'

Ong took charge of the evening meeting and turned it into a moving farewell for Torrance. In his diary for the children Torrance wrote, 'Modesty forbids the relating of all that was said. Underneath there was shown undoubted sorrow over my going. They produced an illuminated address in red silk to remind me of their love.' At daybreak Torrance, Chen, and Ding Si set out with the carriers to return to the Qiang area, escorted beyond the city by several of the Boluozi and others, many of whom had slept on the floor of Ong's house overnight. Torrance found it hard to restrain his tears at this final farewell, although his sorrow was eased by Ong's insistence on joining him a few days later in the Qiang area for the rest of the summer.

Steeling themselves for the ordeal of re-crossing the precipice at Diexi, they discovered that four men had been killed the day before by falling rocks, which had dashed them off the high path down into the lower lake. As the boat carrying Torrance and the others reached the southern end of the upper lake, they could see falling stones still creating clouds of dust and had no idea how they would proceed. However, to their immense relief, yesterday's deaths had forced the authorities to act and a small boat was now ferrying people across the lower lake so instead of the terrifying upper path, they were able to scramble the couple of miles down the rocky barrier between the lakes to be ferried across and find lodgings. The next morning a short, sharp quake shook the area, followed by another tremor a day later as they were on their way back to Maoxian. 'For a whole year there have been occasional quakes of this sort and rumblings . . . The natives are building inns on the upper part of the plain which did not slide. But the ground even there has great cracks and crevices in abundance.'[40]

Torrance would later write a detailed article about the impact of the quake and the ensuing flood, based on survivor testimonies and what he had seen for himself.[41] Unbeknown to him, the article was sent by a former Chengdu missionary named Archibald Adams to the geology department at Harvard, from where it was forwarded to the International Seismological Summary in Oxford. Adams later wrote to the WCMN: 'Your readers may be interested in the unexpected service your paper rendered the international earthquake commission.'[42]

At Shida Pass, twenty miles north of Maoxian, Torrance called on the local Qiang chief and was also greeted by a clerk at the local tax office who had attended some Great East Street meetings. By the time they got to Maoxian Torrance felt he could sleep for a week but after two days they set out for the nearly forty mile trek to Dongmenwai, wanting to be there in time for the arrival of the three CIM women. On this stretch of the journey Torrance's heart was warmed by a rekindled romance unfolding in their midst. As they left Maoxian a woman set out with them, walking alongside the oldest of the carriers. It turned out she was his wife but they hadn't seen each other since quarrelling over ten years ago. He hadn't even recognised her at first but she had made herself known and the man was now 'marching along with a new jauntiness in his air'.

It was good to relax at Dongmenwai and Torrance watched with delight as a colony of monkeys moved with breathtaking agility around the rock face above the church. On Sunday, August 15, there was a big turn-out for the morning service, with many other villagers joining the regular worshippers. Torrance spoke from the book of Luke about rejoicing that their names were written in heaven and in the evening he

40 TT to Annie, July 7, 1934.
41 TT. 'The T'ieh-ch'i Earthquake of August 1933 and Afterwards'. WCMN, Nov 1934, pp7-11.
42 Letter from Archibald Adams. WCMN, July-Aug 1935, p63.

spoke plainly and firmly about things that could keep men in bondage and hold them back in their Christian walk. Opium was undoubtedly on his mind and he had discovered, sadly, that Xiong was using it. Addiction had reached crisis proportions in the 1930s with Ralph Hayward of the Canadian Hospital in Chengdu noting that more than half of his hospital patients were opium addicts.[43]

On Monday a group of them set off for Bulan, including Ong, who had just arrived, and Gou Pinsan's son. Torrance found Ong's presence particularly comforting and before each meeting they would find a quiet spot to pray together. Having spent little time in the Qiang area, Ong was surprised by how dangerous some of the steep paths were.

On their first evening in Bulan about eighty villagers crowded into Chen Guangming's house and twenty gave their names as enquirers, encouraged by those who were already Christians. The villagers were insistent that they stay a second night and invited them to a feast. Two women who were unable to make the descent to Dongmenwai wanted to be baptised. One was the wife of the priest, who had already been baptised, and the other was the 77-year-old grandmother of a young man who had become a Christian the previous year and had since died. It was a timely extra day. In the afternoon Torrance was called to treat the wife of one of the Christians, who had eaten something poisonous. She was semi-conscious with a weak pulse but recovered with a strong purgative.

They were quite a crowd as they continued along the mountainside to Longxi Village, in the company of two Bulan Christians as well as some from Dongmenwai. Spirits were high and thirty-two gave their names after the evening meeting. As in Bulan, there were baptisms of two more in Longxi who couldn't easily get down to Dongmenwai – an elderly lady and her daughter-in-law, whose husband was already a Christian. Torrance was taken aback by the level of enthusiasm and he had much to reflect on as he set up his roof-top bed under the stars.

From Longxi Village they made the two-mile descent to where Gou was now living, about six miles below A'er. Gou advised against travelling in the heat of the day so after a meal and a rest they took some time to pray and take communion together. On reaching A'er, Torrance was pleased to see that the room Gou had rented was being plastered and whitewashed – not a Qiang practice but it brightened the dark

43 The United Church of Canada Archives. General Council Archives Guide to Holdings Related to West China Medical Missions (1800–1950), p208.

interior and was something for which Torrance would be remembered. A man who had been baptised the previous year was serving as school teacher in the village and teaching the Christian message too. He had aroused considerable interest and there were already several other believers, with another thirteen giving their names during Torrance's visit. At the village of Biaduo, below A'er, Gou was arranging for the opening of another meeting room.

The next day they went back down to Dongmenwai to prepare for the Sunday meeting, at which Torrance spoke on the story of Abraham in the book of Genesis. After the meeting final decisions were made as to who was ready for baptism. In the end thirty-four were baptised in the stream that afternoon, among whom was a farmer whom Torrance had met not far from Gou's house. He and his wife had taken down their traditional heaven and earth tablet, as had one of the Dongmenwai villagers.

Torrance was disappointed that Ella, Grace, and Leona hadn't arrived in time for the service but they arrived the next day. Once they were settled in, Torrance, Gou, Ong, and Zhou crossed the new bridge at

Bulan village in Longxi Valley

BAPTISM IN THE DONGMENWAI STREAM

Dongmenwai to preach at the villages on the way to Tonghua while Ella and Grace walked along the opposite river bank to Taoping. Leona had been seriously ill the previous year after nursing soldiers wounded in the fighting with Liu Wenhui and needed time to recover from the journey. That evening the men joined Ella and Grace in Taoping for a meeting which went with great gusto, much to Ella and Grace's delight.

From Taoping they went up to visit Chief Yang in Erwa. A Qiang Christian, whom Torrance described as 'the wealthiest man in the district', brought his mule down for Torrance to ride, which Grace rode part of the way. Ella and Grace were hosted by the Yangs while Torrance and the others continued with the Qiang Christian to his village further up the mountainside, where they were treated to lavish hospitality and had a small evening meeting. The man's mother and two brothers were coming with a few others to Dongmenwai on Sunday for baptism.

The next morning Torrance woke to a stunning view of the snow-capped Xuelingbao mountain and four other distant snowy peaks west of Zagunao. The Erwa villagers urged them to stay another day but they had to get back. They spent another night at Taoping where Gou had secured 'the loveliest, self-contained building' to serve as a church, which, unusually, was one large single room in a garden. It still needed plastering, cleaning up, and furnishing with benches but would be ideal. Several of the Taoping villagers were wanting to be baptised at Dongmenwai.

On Saturday the Qiang in Dongmenwai put on a farewell feast for Torrance and in the evening a good number of women attended the meeting, encouraged by the presence of the CIM women. At the Sunday meeting there were more people than ever before, with some having to stand outside the church and people still arriving from the villages. Afterwards Torrance baptised twenty-six people in the nearby stream – nineteen men and seven women – taking the number baptised this time in the Dongmenwai region to seventy-three and, with the seventeen in Songpan, taking the number so far on this whole trip to ninety, far beyond Torrance's expectations. Later in the day, after some had left for home, there was a communion service for about sixty people, followed by a smaller meeting in the evening at which Gou Pinsan presented Torrance with a farewell tribute embroidered on satin whilst others thanked him for bringing them the gospel, assuring him that they would never forget him.

CHRISTIANS GATHERED IN DONGMENWAI

On Monday Grace and Leona left for a visit to Zagunao whilst Ella Bailey stayed in Dongmenwai for meetings with the women. Torrance needed to discuss work matters with the men and it was decided that Gou Pinsan and his son would be appointed as joint preachers in charge of the Dongmenwai church and of the meeting rooms at Keku, Mushang, Bulan, Longxi, A'er, Taoping, and Erwa, with the Huang brothers appointed as elders to assist them. In Bulan, Longxi, A'er, and Taoping, two of the villagers were to look after the meeting rooms and call people to worship on Sundays so that whoever came to preach was free of these tasks. The church was to be self-supporting and self-propagating and Grace Jephson was hoping to visit twice a year from Guanxian to give what help she could. At Chinese New Year Ong was to come down and give Bible classes.

Later that day Torrance was on his way back from visiting one of the villagers when an old man resting by the side of the road asked if he was Mr Torrance and told him, 'Last night I was thinking I should like to meet you . . . I heard you were here and knew that from you I could hear the truth.' Torrance invited him back to the church where several Qiang Christians helped to explain the gospel and the man 'acknowledged his joy in believing'. On Monday evening Torrance's parting talk was about the Good Shepherd in Psalm 23.

On Tuesday they left for Gou's native village of Mushang. There was a fine evening meeting and on Wednesday ten of the villagers were baptised, including Gou's 84-year-old mother, his two daughters and daughter-in-law, and a lad who looked after their sheep. In the midst of all this Torrance was still making a note of any new cultural observations. In Mushang the oldest building had a cross built into its wall, behind the sacred white stone. A common symbol in the wider region, the Boluozi had a cross symbol on their sacrificial altars. The Boluozi altars also had horn-like projections at the corners, something Torrance hadn't seen among the Qiang, although they did place the horns of a sacrificed animal on the altar. From Mushang they walked along the mountainside to visit the villages of Zhouda and Upper Keku before staying the night at Lower Keku. Two men from Keku had been among those baptised at Dongmenwai.

As they approached Weizhou the next day, the time had come for Gou Pinsan and Torrance to part. Having known each other since 1921, and worked closely over much of that time, it was an emotional farewell. They stopped for prayer just outside the town, where Torrance urged Gou to preach to the Qiang 'only the Apostolic gospel…Christ crucified, risen, ascended and coming again', and Gou urged Torrance to tell people back home about the Qiang and raise up prayer for them. Gou's son, Gou Quangang, continued on with Torrance down to Miansi.

In Miansi Torrance was dismayed to find that the suspension bridge over to Qiangfeng and the other villages had been badly damaged, with two pillars washed away, the cables in a tangle, and the foot-boards removed to save them falling in the river. The only alternative was a high sliding cable further downstream, but Torrance was afraid this would damage his back. Undecided, they slept that night in Miansi to the sound of heavy rain. In the morning the river was muddy brown, the rain kept falling, and there was the fearsome spectacle of banks sliding and rocks crashing into the valley.

While waiting in Miansi, they were visited by some Qiang and Wasi who had been courageous enough to cross the river. Eventually orders were issued for the cables to be sorted. The broken cables were removed and the good ones tightened, two of which were then tied together so that anyone willing to risk it could inch across on them while holding on to a side cable. One Chinese Christian told Torrance he was too old and not strong enough but Torrance was determined to visit the villages one last time and risk the 'tight rope walking business' above the torrent. Gou Guanding's son tied his girdle round Torrance's waist and held his arm as he crossed, with someone else following close behind. Gou Quangang 'confessed plainly he did not have the nerve to attempt it' and Torrance could see that he was not strong enough, but Chen, Ong, Zhou, Xiong, and Ding Si all made it safely while Leona, Grace, and Ella watched from the Miansi side. Although Torrance had wanted them to visit the village women, he advised them not to attempt the crossing and they left for Guanxian later that day.

A group of Qiang Christians

It was a good reunion in Qiangfeng and next morning people began calling before Torrance was even up and came and went all day. By the evening his head was swimming with tiredness but they had a good meeting and a number gave their names for baptism. After two nights there they climbed up to Heping where Torrance had long been hoping for more response, but there was still a reticence. The priest showed more interest than usual but didn't come to the Sunday service in the Glen. Old Gui, whom Torrance had stayed with the year before, had died the previous winter.

Coming down from Heping to the Glen, Torrance was saddened to see two men and a woman pulling their own plough, having lost their ploughing cattle to rinderpest. The response in the Glen was in striking contrast to Heping. 'The Glen people let themselves all out in the Friday and Saturday evening meetings. There was no reserve. Happy people in spite of their losses and hardships!' Many wanted to be baptised and they decided to hold the Sunday service right there, where it was quiet and secluded. The day dawned fair and it turned out to be the best Sunday yet. In his diary Torrance wrote, 'With all their wealth of O.T. like customs it was easy to illustrate point after point.' Thirty-four men and twenty-four women were accepted for baptism, including Ding Si the cook and another Chinese, six Wasi, and fifty Qiang. The first one to go under the water was Gou Guanding's son. Gou Guanding was hoping to open a meeting place in his native village of Daping. More would have been baptised but the stream in the Glen was too high for some of them to ford. Two particularly determined baptism candidates, both women over seventy years old, had been carried across the stream by their menfolk that morning.

From the Glen, Torrance had hoped to pay a final visit to young King Suo but with the heavy rain and concerns that the bridge might give way, they decided to cross back to Miansi. From there he wrote to Annie, expressing a mixture of pain at parting, joy at having such a precious time, and relief that he had survived the trip and was almost on the last stretch before Scotland. 'The most of my dangers are over. Farewell to Lochaber! My face is practically turned homewards now. "That old thing" is coming home at last.'[44]

A final blessing was the friendliness of a new magistrate in Miansi, a marked contrast to 'the long spell of anti-foreign feeling issuing from the Yamen'.[45] Torrance and Ong had greeted him on the street not knowing who he was and he had invited them back to the yamen. The following day Torrance returned the invitation and after a stroll together up to the bridge and back, served him coffee and treated a sore on his neck. One of the magistrate's men told Torrance what a

44 TT to Annie, Aug 13, 1934. 'Farewell to Lochaber' is a traditional Scottish song telling of a man parting from his beloved in the Scottish highlands.
45 TT to Annie, Aug 18, 1934.

good name he had in the mountains. After two final days in Miansi, with good meetings and the baptisms of five Chinese, there was just the painful farewell to dear Ong, who was returning to his work in Songpan. Ong's son, who had joined him in the work, had recently gone with a Boluozi chief to open a school among his people. Torrance asked Ong to come down next summer and accompany Grace Jephson to various Qiang villages – unaware of how impossible that would be in 1935.

QIANG AND WASI CHRISTIAN WOMEN FROM THE MIANSI REGION

Grateful for three dry days on the journey back down, Torrance walked all the way to Guanxian. Landslides had worsened the condition of the road but they made good progress and stopped the second night in Yingxiu, where they were invited by a teashop owner to hold a meeting. Climbing the Niangziling Pass for the last time, Torrance reached Lingyan on August 17 and promptly sent a radiogram via Lacy to let Annie and the children know he was safely back. In a longer letter the next day he wrote with a full heart:

> This journey into the mountains has been the longest, most arduous, most dangerous and most full of blessing. The way the Lord led, guarded and blessed us was nothing short of miraculous.

He had lost a lot more hair and it had taken a lot out of him physically but it had also given Torrance 'new and great experiences of the divine power and goodness . . . it is enough to say that a wave of revival swept through the villages as we went along that surprised ourselves and the Christians.'[46]

---

46 Ibid.

Chapter 21
Heading Home
1934-35

Torrance arrived back in Chengdu to news that Franck was expected in mid-October, leaving him free to depart in early November. On September 23 he preached for the last time at the Canadian church on Si-sheng-ci Street, writing afterwards to Annie that some 'modernists' from the university hadn't attended but that the more evangelical missionaries had been encouraged by his sermon.

The widening gulf between the modernists and the more orthodox was addressed by Torrance in a WCMN article about his summer trip:

> A number of years ago a well-placed missionary assured the writer that the evangelistic methods of our fathers had no longer any power to move people. The assertion coming from such a man indicated that he himself believed that men could only be educated into the church. Evangelical preaching was foolishness. Since then others have taken a similar stand. Had any of these men witnessed the work of our band this summer they would have seen that their theory did not at all correspond to reality. The foolishness of preaching was still the divine method of bringing men into the Kingdom of God.[1]

The results of this 'divine method' had particularly impacted one Qiang Christian who, marvelling at all that had happened over the summer, remarked that 'the converts gathered in were not done so by any human power.'[2] The gulf was further illustrated in a report on a religious education conference held at the university in July. Describing the keynote of the conference as 'rational religion working to transform individuals and society', the writer noted that the speakers 'all brought

---

1   TT. 'On An Evangelizing Tour Among the N. W. Tribes'. WCMN, Oct 1934, p15. (A shortened version also appeared under the title 'Fruit on a Farewell Tour' in the BSR, Vol 79, Dec 1934, pp142-144.)
2   Ibid.

a message of a dynamic, re-vitalizing, rational, scientific religion.'[3] One author would later describe this 'sociological Protestantism' of the university as 'very this worldly' and 'geared toward the establishment of the Kingdom of God in Republican Chengdu, a Kingdom imagined to be composed of orderly, literate, hygienic and productive citizens, guided by a strong state.'[4]

At the ABS depot Li was supervising the stocktaking, Diao's accounts were in from Chongqing, and in early October Torrance sent his last annual reports off, commenting to Annie that 'Everything but eternal life comes to an end!'[5] On October 3, after a birthday lunch for Dr Beech, he was invited to the university senate where a resolution of appreciation was read for all the help he had rendered to the museum and for making people aware of the Qiang. The Border Research Society journal also published a tribute to him: 'For fourteen years Mr. Torrance has made numerous visits to the region occupied by the Ch'iang people . . . His published articles and monographs on the Ch'iang have been those of a keen pioneer, earnest researcher, and are therefore of permanent interest and value. He has also made exceedingly valuable contributions to the University Museum of porcelain and ancient coins.'[6] On October 16 Torrance returned to the university for Graham to take a photograph of him to hang in the museum.

Two days later Deng Xihou held a dinner for him and the following day Mrs Neave and Mrs Wilford arranged a social evening with some of his closer friends. Deng later sent him a gold satin embroidered bed cover and the missionaries presented him with a silver tea caddy and strainer. The Dyes also invited Torrance for a dinner with several of his friends, at which Dr Spencer Lewis, who had been in China over fifty years, expressed his concern about the continuation of the Qiang church. Torrance was deeply touched by people's kindness.

On Sunday, October 28, the Chinese CIM Christians invited him to a farewell, to which the Baptists were also invited. This had been

3   L. E. Willmott. 'The Summer Religious Education Institute'. WCMN, Oct 1934, p28.
4   Jeff Kyong-McClain. 'Making Chengdu "The Kingdom of God as Jesus Conceived It": The Urban Work of West China Union University's Sociology Department'. *Social Sciences and Missions* 23, 2010, p185.
5   TT to Annie, Oct 9, 1934.
6   JWCBRS, Vol 6, 1934, p xvi. Torrance's trips actually extended over a sixteen year period but, allowing for his furloughs in 1920 and 1927 and not being able to travel in 1925, he spent thirteen summers among the Qiang.

FAREWELL IN CHENGDU
GOU GUANDING AND HIS WIFE, AND THE HUANGS OF DONGMENWAI

some time in the planning and was a particularly memorable occasion: 'A unique feature of the service was the number of Chiang and other tribespeople who had travelled from over a week's journey away so as to be present at this farewell service to one whom they had learned to love as a real father.'[7] Torrance couldn't help observing wryly to Annie that his final address, during this service, was where he had been prevented from preaching in his early days.[8]

Embroidered tributes were presented to Torrance by the CIM Christians, the Baptist churches, and the Chinese at the Canadian Press. From the hospital staff he received an embroidered scroll with a pine tree representing old age without decay and white cranes for long life. His workers also held a dinner for him and perhaps the most touching tributes of all were from two of his colporteurs: a gold thread silk bag from Zhen and two pieces of gold thread silk from Zhou. 'It cost them something,' he wrote to Annie.[9]

Packing decisions were a challenge but Torrance decided to keep all his correspondence, even though this filled another box for shipping.

7   WCMN, Dec 1934, pp24-25.
8   TT to Annie, Oct 17, 1934.
9   Ibid.

'What a pile of letters to bring home,' he wrote to Annie. 'May be the children one day will want to scan them for information, so I am bringing them.'[10] Tom had written recently, recognising how difficult it would be for Torrance to leave China and especially the Qiang. Mary had also written of 'the wrench it would be to pull up stakes and leave'.[11] Torrance appreciated their thoughtfulness, knowing how painful their own sudden uprooting from Chengdu had been.

One of the cows went to Frank Dickinson at the university and Torrance sold the other one, but no-one wanted any of his large pieces of furniture. In the current climate the foreign community seemed cautious to buy, perhaps fearing another sudden exodus if the Communists made further gains in Sichuan. In need of the newly-harvested grain, the Communists had recently been expanding westwards, pushing the Sichuan armies towards the Jialing River. Tian Songyao was much weakened and Liu Xiang had reportedly lost fifteen thousand men and vast amounts of weaponry, which was now being used against his troops.[12]

On October 1, two CIM missionaries, Alfred Bosshardt and Arnolis Hayman, had been captured by Communist forces in Guizhou, south of Sichuan, and a ransom demanded which, to protect other missionaries from the same fate, the CIM were loath to give.[13] Torrance wrote to Annie on October 24 explaining the background to the situation:

> Ten thousand Reds were let out of Jiangxi. They marched West thro' South Hunan on a 30 miles front into N. E. Guizhou to link up with the notorious He Long, the Red General on the Sichuan and Guizhou border. So these missionaries were taken unawares. The papers here dare not print the news of these Reds coming West. The panic is strong enough already. A few Nanjing troops are coming up river at last for Liu Xiang's men are demoralised.[14]

The Nationalists had been tightening their noose around the main Communist base in Jiangxi Province and the Communist leadership were planning a full-scale move while they could still get out. The ten thousand mentioned by Torrance were an advance army sent west under a young general named Xiao Ke to link up with He Long's army,

---

10 TT to Annie, Oct 2, 1934.
11 TT to Annie, Oct 17, quoting Mary's letter to him.
12 Kapp, *Szechwan and the Chinese Republic*, pp94-95.
13 *Millions*, Nov 1934, p216.
14 TT to Annie, Oct 24, 1934.

and it was Xiao Ke's forces who had captured the missionaries. By the end of October the joint forces of He Long and Xiao Ke had entered southern Sichuan with their captives.

Unbeknown to Torrance, the main army of the Jiangxi Communists, a vast company of 85,000 male and female soldiers along with 15,000 government and party officials, had also broken through Chiang Kai-Shek's Nationalist encirclement and was following Xiao Ke's advance units towards the Sichuan-Guizhou border region.[15] To make matters worse, the number of troops under Zhang Guotao, political leader of the Communists in northeastern Sichuan, had now swelled to about 80,000, thanks in part to those deserting the Sichuan generals. During Torrance's final week in Chengdu, Zhang issued a report boasting of their success and revealing their aspirations:

> How should we estimate our victories? . . . We have merely prepared the ground for greater victories – such as the complete annihilation of enemies like Liu Xiang, Tian Songyao, and Deng Xihou and the routing of Chiang Kai-shek's main forces and all enemies in Gansu, Hubei, and Shaanxi. This will provide the possibility and conditions to turn Sichuan and the northwest into red areas. . . . If it is true that we have the capacity to attack Chengdu as the soldiers of the 271st Regiment claim, we should do so.[16]

The three armies seemed to be creating a perfect storm for Sichuan.

Franck eventually reached Chengdu on November 1, just in time for a brief hand-over. The following day, as Zhang Guotao was writing his sabre-rattling report, Torrance was at a farewell tea with his close friends the Kitchens, and on November 6, his last evening, he led his final Great East Street meeting. His colporteurs had delayed setting off on their travels in order to say farewell and some of the Qiang had stayed in town to see him off. On Wednesday, November 7, he bade farewell to the city he had called home since 1896 and boarded the bus to Chongqing with an array of trunks and boxes. Annie had been instructed to address her next letters to the British & Foreign Bible Society in Port Said and then to 'Mrs Shelley, Chamber of Commerce, Jerusalem'.

Reflecting Torrance's inner turmoil – wanting to go and hating to leave – the bus had only gone a short distance when it developed problems and had to return to the bus garage. The delay meant that

---

15   Hsu, *Rise of Modern China*, pp560-561.
16   Saich & Yang, *Rise to Power*, p568. The report was written on Nov 2, 1934.

Torrance's first night on the road was spent in Jianyang, giving him a chance to say farewell to a Chinese pastor there and hold a meeting with him in the evening. In heavy rain the bus then ploughed laboriously through sticky yellow mud, with the passengers at times disembarking to lighten the load and men hired to push the straining vehicle out of ruts and holes. The 250-mile journey took five days and Torrance had never been so happy to see Daniel Diao, who was waiting to help with his luggage.

It was a pleasant respite to stay with the Walkers, parents of Bernard and Bobby, at the CIM mission, where four young missionaries from Guizhou were also staying, having fled the advancing Communists. Torrance wrote to Annie of the prevailing fear in Sichuan that the whole province would be overrun. That same day, November 13, General Liu Xiang left Sichuan for Nanjing to appeal for Nationalist support against the Communists.[17]

Having survived all the physical challenges of his summer trip to the Qiang, the cold, wet bus journey proved too much for Torrance and he came down with a bout of dysentery but he was in good hands. 'The Walkers have been remarkably kind,' he wrote to Annie. 'I have had every attention, and the best of food and comfort. They have remembered your kindness to their boys in Edinburgh.'[18] Robert Walker had visited Palestine and was able to give Torrance some useful information. At the British Consulate in Chongqing, where Torrance's passport was stamped with permits for Egypt and Palestine, he discovered that the Consul was being transferred to Genoa and would be a fellow passenger on the SS Ranpura.

Much to Torrance's delight, the Chongqing missionaries asked him to give a talk on the Qiang and he also had time to catch up with Mrs McCartney, whose friendship dated back to his early days and whose late husband, Dr James McCartney, had been involved in the decision to send Mary Bryce back to Shanghai in 1899. She sent a present for Annie. Torrance particularly appreciated his final days at the ABS depot with Diao, who presented him with an embroidered scroll and a roll of linen. The final hurdle in Sichuan was the Chongqing customs but thanks to a permit provided by General Liu Xiang, nothing was opened and no taxes levied.

Torrance's final journey down the Yangtze to Shanghai was in complete contrast to the bus journey from Chengdu. The SS Wantung,

---

17   Kapp, *Szechwan and the Chinese Republic*, p96.
18   TT to Annie, Nov 18, 1934.

one of the steamers at the centre of the 1926 confrontation between Yang Sen and the British, was fast and comfortable and the river was high which made for smooth passage through the rapids. Several missionaries boarded along the way and from Yichang to Hankou Torrance enjoyed the company of the Squires, a CIM couple whom Annie had met on her first journey up the Yangtze.

Arriving in Shanghai on Thanksgiving Day, Torrance discovered that the ABS staff weren't expecting him and 'had gone to eat turkey and pumpkin pie.'[19] However, with the help of Walter Milward of the National Bible Society of Scotland, his luggage was dealt with and he made his way to his lodgings. That evening, with missionaries from various parts of China, he sat and listened on the radio to the wedding ceremony of Prince George, Duke of Kent, and Princess Marina of Greece – a far cry from Sichuan and his beloved Qiang villages. The transition had begun and he was truly on his way home.

It was a sociable twelve days in Shanghai, which Torrance had not visited since 1928. He had dinner at the CIM home where he met other missionaries who had fled from northeastern Sichuan. He spoke at the Navy YMCA and was also asked to give talks to some young American students on Sichuan history and on the tribes. On December 6 he gave an open lecture on the Qiang for the Royal Asiatic Society.

He was also invited for lunch by the eminent Shanghai-born Sinologist, Florence Ayscough. They found much to talk about and later went curio shopping together, joined by Milward, who proved to be a good companion in these final few days. Torrance helped Florence to buy a Han sword and bought for himself a Tang plate, a Han vase, and a mirror. Florence gave him a note of introduction to a professor in London who taught Chinese archaeology and asked if he would consider returning to China for further research work, but Torrance knew this was unlikely.

Muriel Ramsay, daughter of Clarence Ramsay, Torrance's friend and predecessor at the ABS, also managed to come by train to see him from where she was now working as a missionary. They spent several hours together and Torrance talked to her almost as a father, writing afterwards to Ramsay that 'She was heart hungry for somebody near to her.'[20]

On December 10 Torrance's boxes went on board the SS *Ranpura* and he spoke at a weekly missionary prayer meeting on the tribes work,

---

19 WCMN, Oct 1935, p23. Reprint of a letter from TT to Daniel and Jane Dye, dated Feb 12, 1935, about his journey home via Palestine.
20 TT to Annie, Dec 10, 1934.

which was followed by 'very fervent prayer'.[21] He then had dinner with
Miss McGill, who had sailed on the same ship as the Torrances when
they left China in 1927. The next morning he led morning prayers in
the mission home, after which Milward accompanied him out to the
ship where he was delighted to run into Kaoroz Doodha, the Postal
Commissioner in Chengdu who had offered refuge to Annie and the
children during the 1917 fighting, when Torrance was attempting
his first trip to the Qiang. Doodha was saying goodbye to some Parsi
friends who were sailing.

It was a remarkable end to Torrance's time in China that so many
strands of his years there should be woven together in these last few
days. At 2 p.m. on December 11, 1934, almost thirty-nine years since
he first set foot on Chinese soil, the SS *Ranpura* moved off from the
wharf as Torrance watched the land where he was forever leaving part
of his heart gradually recede into the distance.

The last two months had been so full that Torrance was only now
beginning to unwind and prepare for home, 'reading and sleeping and
cogitating a lot', and appreciating the excellent food and an upper-deck
cabin where he could keep his port-hole open.[22] It was still strange to
think that his time in China was really over and his mind was much on
the Qiang work and Ong's upcoming winter Bible classes in Dongmenwai
and Miansi. Taking advantage of the time on board, he was working on
a revised, photographic version of 'My Work Among the Tribes', which
had been requested by Frank Rawlinson of *The Chinese Recorder*.[23]

The ship's first port of call was Hong Kong, where news arrived of
the murder of missionaries John and Betty Stam in Anhui Province and
of the continued captivity of Bosshardt and Hayman, compounding
Torrance's very mixed emotions as the distance from China increased.
After further stops in Singapore, Colombo, Bombay, and Aden – where
he was shown round by a friendly British soldier and gave Scriptures
to some Chinese shopkeepers – the *Ranpura* docked in Port Said on
January 6, where a B&FBS missionary was waiting with Torrance's
train ticket for Jerusalem. Leaving two cabin boxes at Port Said and
his main luggage on board to continue to Britain, he boarded the train
with one suitcase, arriving in Jerusalem the next day for one of the
most memorable trips of his life.

21 TT to Annie, Dec 16, 1934.
22 TT to Annie, Dec 24, 1934.
23 TT. 'My Work Among the Tribes'. *The Chinese Recorder*, April 1935,
pp227-234.

His hosts, the Shelleys, treated him royally and were a mine of information, having been in the Middle East for many years. Mrs Shelley showed him around Jerusalem and escorted him by car to the Jordan River and the Dead Sea. At the ancient town of Jericho they called on Professor John Garstang, who took them around the excavations he was working on, giving Torrance an opportunity to discuss dating methods and compare pottery fragments with those he had seen in West China. They arrived back to an evening vista of Jerusalem as they drove over the Mount of Olives.

Mrs Shelley also took him to Jaffa and Tel Aviv and he took a bus to Hebron where he was intrigued to see a whitewash outline of a tree on many of the houses, reminding him of the tree outlines he had seen drawn on the outer wall of Qiang homes after a private sacrifice. His guide couldn't give a detailed explanation for the tree markings but said it was a custom when a marriage had taken place. Torrance came back in one of the ubiquitous shared taxis, stopping at Bethlehem on the way, where he was inspired not only by reflections on the birth of Christ but also by the thought of Jerome completing his painstaking Latin translation of the Old Testament there in the fifth century.

From Jerusalem he travelled by shared taxi to Nazareth. His fellow travellers turned out to be an Arab couple, Mr and Mrs Faris of the Church Missionary Society, who much enhanced his journey by pointing out biblical sites along the way. To Torrance's delight, the driver agreed to make a detour to Jacob's Well, which was a highlight of the trip: 'To sit on the same stone at Jacob's well that Christ sat on and to drink of the water from the same well that He drank from and to live over again in thought the scene of the conversion of the Samaritan woman brought you to one of the greatest moments of life!'[24]

In Nazareth he stayed with William Bathgate, director of the Edinburgh Medical Mission Hospital. An ex-patient kindly served as Torrance's guide and after seeing the town they climbed up a hill from where Torrance could glimpse Mount Hermon away to the north. From Nazareth he travelled to Tiberias with two lady missionaries on their way to Damascus. The hospital in Tiberias, which overlooked the Sea of Galilee, had been established in 1894 by David Watt Torrance, a distant relative, and was now being run by his son Herbert. Herbert refused to let Torrance stay at the guest house. 'He took me home as if I had been his long lost brother. He and Mrs T. couldn't do enough for me.'[25]

---

24 TT to the children, Jan 22, 1935.
25 Ibid.

Herbert took him to Capernaum, Bethsaida, Magdala, and the Mount of Beatitudes, and arranged a boat trip on the lake. On the following day, accompanied by a Miss Radford, he visited an Arab village and a Jewish power plant at the southern end of the lake and then had a walk around Tiberias, where an orthodox Jewish man, touched by their curiosity, invited them home to show them some traditional clothing and other artifacts. Back at the hospital Torrance was asked to give a talk to the staff about China and he gave another at the weekly Church of Scotland mission meeting.

Herbert insisted on driving him back to Nazareth and as they passed an Arab farmer with his plough, Torrance noticed an interesting detail. 'He had a long stick in his hand with a tiny shovel-like end for cleaning the plough. "There" I said, "I have discovered at last, the use of such a rod I have often seen on figures from our West China tombs.''[26] After tea with Dr Bathgate, Herbert returned to Tiberias but a firm friendship had been established and from that time on he would visit the Torrance family on his trips back to Scotland.

Taking a bus to Haifa, which Torrance described as 'a new development and very modern', he stayed at the German mission home on Mount Carmel and paid a visit to Dr William Christie, a fellow Scot and Hebrew and rabbinic scholar at the Mount Carmel Bible School, who lived down in the town. Torrance was happy to have someone who could answer his many questions and they had a long talk. On his last day his guide book helped him to pick out various places of interest as his train from Haifa skirted the Mediterranean on its way south. Nine hours later the train pulled into Kantara, where the passengers were treated to a full eclipse of the moon as they crossed the Suez Canal to wait for the local Port Said train.

Torrance's final night was spent at the Sailors and Soldiers Home in Port Said, where he was asked to lead the Sunday evening meeting. Boarding the SS *Corfu* for the last stretch of the journey, he found himself sharing a cabin with a pleasant young Scotsman from the Orkneys. The company on board proved equally congenial, especially the several other Scots, among whom the 'Johnnie Walker' was flowing liberally. After calls at Malta, Marseilles, Tangier, and Gibraltar, on January 31, 1935, the *Corfu* docked at Tilbury on the River Thames, from where Torrance took the train to London. At 11.15 a.m. he stepped on to the platform at St Pancras to see Annie waiting for him. It was a moment of deep emotion and thanksgiving.

---

26 Ibid.

He was carrying a suitcase, a small bag, an attaché case – and the Qiang priest's rod.

After a night at Jeannie's in Bromley Torrance and Annie moved to the Mildmay conference centre in north London, a short walk from the CIM headquarters where Torrance had done his missionary training forty years earlier. Enjoying a day in the city centre, they visited Westminster Abbey to see the grave of David Livingstone, Torrance's boyhood inspiration, and Torrance put his watch right by Big Ben, whose chimes he had so often heard on Plewman's radio. They also visited the British Museum, where Robert Hobson, the curator with whom Torrance had corresponded, was about to leave for China to select items being loaned by China for the Royal Academy's forthcoming London International Exhibition of Chinese Art. On their last night in London Torrance was suddenly enlisted to talk to a class of trainee evangelists whose speaker had failed to arrive.

Back in Bromley with Jeannie for two nights, he wrote to the children,

> Already your mother has begun drilling me for residence in civilized Edinburgh. Fresh from the backwoods of West China, I am not to do this, that and the other things; particularly I must on no account preach at home with a Chinese accent, or seek to go to bed with my boots on![27]

As their train pulled into Edinburgh Station, Torrance could see all six children waiting eagerly to meet them. Annie took the luggage in a taxi and the children, who had been talking for weeks about Torrance's return, walked the mile home with their Dad. As promised, David and James had the next day off school. 'This will give them their innings', explained Torrance, 'before you older ones on Saturday. Alone with me on Friday they shall have opportunity to talk all they want, unrestricted by their University and philosophical elders.'[28] Mary and Grace were both still at Edinburgh University, soon to be followed by Margaret, and Tom had started his theological studies at New College, having completed his MA in Classics that summer. He was also on the executive committee of the Inter-Varsity Christian Fellowship magazine and serving as a representative for the theological colleges. Graham Brown of the CIM, one of Torrance's first visitors in Edinburgh, told him what

---

27   TT to the children, Feb 6, 1935.
28   Ibid.

a fine impact the children were having at the university. To Torrance's great pleasure, the first church service he attended was led by Tom and a fellow student.

After a few days in his new Edinburgh home, Torrance wrote a long letter to the Dyes in Chengdu, describing his journey and his initial adjustment to life in Scotland, where the family were still working on his acculturation:

> Mrs. T. abjures me to drop my Chinese accent and talk pure English. And the children have informed me that no one is allowed to give away tracts in Princess Street! Since Harry Openshaw is not with me I shan't therefore attempt it.[29]

He had been asked to speak at the annual meeting of the National Bible Society of Scotland and at a Christian campaign in Perth, but the new reality of retirement and the loss of all the activity, the familiar community, and even his status and identity in Chengdu, was a challenge, despite the joy of being with the family again. He unburdened some of this later in the year to Ramsay in America, who sent a heartfelt reply, empathising with his sense of having been laid aside.

---

29 TT to the Dyes, Feb 12, 1935.

PART FIVE

Chapter 22

Accurate Forebodings

1935-36

Torrance's sense of foreboding that 1935 would bring storm and trouble proved well-founded. In Europe, Hitler's intentions were becoming clearer as he began re-arming Germany, in violation of the Treaty of Versailles, and passed the Nuremberg Law, removing German citizenship from Jewish people. In China, the Japanese were aggressively expanding their influence in the north but the most disturbing news for Torrance was coming from the Qiang area, much accentuating his sense of helplessness and redundancy.

In January 1935, after marching hundreds of miles from Jiangxi, the main Communist First Front Army had come to a halt in Guizhou. Here, at a conference in the town of Zunyi, Mao Zedong had become the dominant political leader, both of this First Army and of the Chinese Communist Party, and rumour now had it that he was planning to move north into Sichuan, connect with the Fourth Front Army of Zhang Guotao, and establish a new Soviet base.[1] The disunity of the Sichuan generals and the ongoing antipathy of some to Nationalist interference, together with Sichuan's remoteness, fertility, and mountainous defences, made the province a good potential springboard for Communist expansion across China.[2]

The added pressure from Mao in the south finally forced more cohesion among the Sichuan generals and more cooperation with the Nationalists. On February 2 a new Sichuan government was formed, led by Liu Xiang but with a Nationalist staff corps in Chongqing to oversee military operations. This was followed by the abolition of the autonomous garrison regions previously ruled by Deng Xihou, Tian Songyao, and others, who, with their armies, were now subject to the

---

1   In 1935 the three main Communist armies were known as the First Front Army (led by Mao Zedong and others), the Second Front Army (led by He Long and Xiao Ke), and the Fourth Front Army (under Zhang Guotao and Xu Xiangqian). For brevity 'Front' has generally been omitted.

2   Garavente, Anthony. 'The Long March'. *The China Quarterly*, no. 22, 1965, p112. http://www.jstor.org/stable/651546.

provincial government.³ Robert Walker in Chongqing welcomed the arrival of the Nationalists after the years of provincial in-fighting: 'They are here, I am sure, to stay and many are the people who will be right glad at the turn of events.'⁴

To the relief of many, Mao's advance into Sichuan was blocked and his First Army was forced to turn south again and then west towards Yunnan. Through a combination of combat, desertion, sickness, and the physical challenges of the journey, his troops had by this time been reduced to about 30,000 and in a further blow, Hunanese forces had prevented the Second Army of He Long and Xiao Ke from joining Mao. However, as the WCMN made clear, their high degree of organisation was giving the Communists a strength which could yet make them a menace, and their march from Jiangxi was earning them an awe-inspiring reputation: 'A force of armed men actuated by definite political ideals that has recently completed a march of nearly two thousand miles and is not yet effectually scattered cannot be despised with impunity.'⁵

Although he was now heading towards Yunnan, Mao had not given up on Sichuan, nor on uniting with the Fourth Army. As his First Army marched west, planning now to enter Sichuan from the southwest, Zhang Guotao's Fourth Army was also marching westwards across northern Sichuan, causing mounting apprehension as streams of refugees fled from their advance. Crossing the Jialing River, Zhang's 80,000-strong army 'paused north of Chengtu for nearly a month while their trailing elements caught up and Chengtu waited, terrified, for a Communist invasion.'⁶ By the beginning of April, Zhang's front line troops were nearing Mianyang, about seventy miles north of Chengdu, and Deng Xihou's forces were proving no match for them.

Chengdu was barricaded, with watchtowers erected everywhere, and on April 14 the staff at the West China Union University were ordered either to evacuate completely or move within the city walls.⁷ The next day a message went out to the whole missionary community:

> The situation at the front is very tense; and it is possible that the Red forces may break through and get nearer Chengtu. Nearly all mission stations to the North and West are already evacuated.

3 Kapp, *Szechwan and the Chinese Republic*, pp106-107.
4 *Millions*, April 1935, p67, written Jan 6.
5 'Notes on the Communist Situation', WCMN, March 1935, p14-15.
6 Kapp, *Szechwan and the Chinese Republic*, p103.
7 A. J. Brace. 'Tragedy in West China Home Mission'. WCMN, Nov 1935, pp20-22.

Many Chinese are leaving this city. According to the teachings of these Communists, no parley can be held with the representatives of Religion, more especially the Christian religion. So, if within the next few days, the government forces are driven to retreat from their present positions, prudence will prove to be the better part of valor; and we shall have to withdraw from Chengtu.[8]

In the end, Nationalist attacks from Gansu and Shaanxi diverted Zhang's forces away from Chengdu. Instead, his vast army continued west into the mountains beyond Mianyang, taking it closer to the Qiang area. On May 18, Harold Maxwell of the CMS sent grave news: 'According to today's papers the main body of the Reds is at Beichuan, and from there forces are pushing in the Mianzhu direction . . . and the forces between them and Maoxian are almost negligible.'[9]

Maoxian had actually been captured by units of Zhang's Fourth Army on May 15, after almost a month of fierce fighting at Tumen Pass to the east of the town, with high casualties on both sides.[10] Zhang promptly set up a 'Northwest Special Committee of the Chinese Communist Party' in Maoxian, from where he was planning a takeover of the region.[11]

This victory in Maoxian brought new fears that Zhang's forces would try to push through Weizhou to the Zagunao Valley, link up with Mao, whose army was now moving up through the mountains of western Sichuan, and that together they would make another push for Chengdu via the Min Valley. On May 28, John Sinton of the CIM wrote that the Communists were apparently working their way down the valley from Miansi towards Guanxian.[12]

Sinton's information was half-correct. On the east bank of the Min River the Communist advance had been blocked by government troops, who were positioned all the way up from Guanxian to Banqiao Gully, north of Miansi, where they stayed entrenched opposite Communist forces for two months. However, although Liu Xiang and Deng Xihou's forces in

8   WCMN, May 1935, p35.
9   Harold A. Maxwell (CMS, Mianzhu). 'The April Evacuation and the Present Red Situation'. WCMN, June 1935, pp31-33. P32. (Pinyin updated.) Although Torrance's research didn't extend to Beichuan, its western part, adjacent to Maoxian, was historically Qiang. In 1988, Beichuan Qiang Autonomous County was created, stretching from east of Maoxian to the Chengdu plain.
10   Sun Shuyun. *The Long March*. HarperCollins Publishers. Kindle Edition. This was a major victory for Zhang's units who, according to Sun, numbered 30,000 against 160,000 Nationalist troops.
11   Saich and Yang, *Rise to Power*, p xxvi.
12   *Millions*, 1935, p153.

Weizhou had burned the town as they fled the Communist advance, the bridges were still intact, enabling the Reds to cross to the river and move almost unopposed down the west bank to beyond Yingxiu.[13] This meant that the Communists and provincial forces were facing each other across the Min for some thirty miles but also meant that Qiangfeng and the higher villages like Heping and Gaodongshan had fallen to the Reds.

Zhang's forces were also advancing towards Songpan but were repulsed north of Diexi by forces under the powerful Nationalist leader, Hu Zongnan, who had reinforced Deng's troops in the area. Other Communist units were moving west from Maoxian into the Heishui Valley where they encountered fierce resistance from Su Yonghe, the powerful local chief who had been instrumental in the defeat of Colonel Liu and his troops in 1931. Although Su was no friend of Deng Xihou and the Nationalists, cooperation with them was preferable to having another Chinese army challenge his power in the region, and he had been appointed by Hu Zongnan as 'guerrilla commander' in Heishui and Lifan. Tian Lijun records about eighty battles, large and small, fought in the Heishui Valley between June and September, which resulted in many casualties and made Communist passage through the region extremely difficult.[14] On one occasion the locals requested three thousand guns from the Red Army to fight the Nationalists, which they then turned on the Reds.[15]

Zhang's Fourth Army took Weizhou on May 29 and quickly advanced to Xuecheng and Zagunao, establishing bases in each place and sending military units with political leaders, many only in their twenties, out to the mountain villages where local Party committees were set up to ensure implementation of their ideology. A key element of this, as noted by Alfred Bosshardt, was that 'If a man tills his own soil he's all right; but if others work his land, he's an oppressor.'[16]

On May 30 Zhang extended his authority with the declaration of a 'Northwest Federal Government of the Chinese Soviet Republic', boasting with characteristic bravado that 'From now on, Chengdu and Chongqing in the south, Shaanxi and Gansu in the north, and Qinghai

---

13 T. E. Plewman. 'The Red Terror in the Tribes Country'. WCMN, Jan 1936, p11.

14 Tian Lijun. '1935-1936 nian guogong neizhan yu chuan xibei tusi (guan) de zhenzhi taidu' (The Nationalist-Communist Conflict of 1935-1936 and the Political Attitude of NW Sichuan's Headmen). Xinan minzu daxue xuebao. Renwen shehui kexue ban. 2011, no. 2, pp211-219.

15 Kang & Sutton, *Contesting the Yellow Dragon*, p148.

16 Alfred Bosshardt. *The Guiding Hand*. Hodder and Stoughton. 1973, p85.

and Xinjiang in the west will be better connected with the large forces of the western Central Red Army.'[17] Appealing specifically to ethnic minorities to join the fight against their three enemies – the Nationalists, the Japanese, and foreign imperialism – he issued the battle cry, 'Fight to Chengdu and Chongqing to spread communism throughout Sichuan!'[18]

As Zhang's troops were spreading out through the Qiang region, Mao's First Army was making its way through the mountains west of Ya'an to Luding, where its forces seem to have met little resistance from those of Liu Wenhui.[19] From there they continued on through the mountains to the Jiarong region of Xiaojin, where, on June 12, advance units from both armies met up in the town of Dawei.

It would be three more weeks before Mao and Zhang met in person, but having assessed the situation with the new information from Zhang's troops, on June 16 Mao and his fellow leaders sent a letter to Zhang and his military leaders, outlining a strategy in which the Qiang area played a significant role. The first two points were as follows:

1. In order to place the development of the soviet movement on a stabler and stronger foundation, the general principle for our First and Fourth Front Armies in the future should be to occupy the three provinces of Sichuan, Shaanxi, and Gansu, to establish soviet regimes in the three provinces, and to dispatch, at an appropriate time, an expeditionary force made up of one unit to occupy Xinjiang.

2. The current plan is that the whole of your troops and the main force of our field armies should be placed east of the Min River to deal a resolute blow to the enemy's imminent massive new attack, and expand toward the areas between the Min and Jialing rivers. When such expansion is contained, we will utilize parts of Shaanxi and Gansu as areas of strategic mobility. Therefore, the key to this plan is firmly to consolidate Maoxian, Beichuan, and Weizhou in our hands, and to rout Hu Zongnan's southward advance.[20]

---

17 Saich & Yang, *Rise to Power*, p675.

18 Ibid.

19 Much has been made of the battle of Luding bridge but reports vary as to how tough it really was. Sun Shuyun suggests that the silence regarding the Fourth Army's victory at Tumen, in contrast to the glorification of the First Army's taking of Luding Bridge, reflects Mao's 'monopoly of victories'. (*Long March*, Kindle Edition.)

20 Mao Zedong and Stuart R. Schram. *Mao's Road to Power – Revolutionary Writings, 1912-1949: Toward the Second United Front. January 1935-July 1937.* Vol 5. M. E. Sharpe. 1992, p16.

Essentially, the Qiang area was to serve as the base for a re-launch of operations into northern Sichuan and from there into Gansu and Shaanxi. The next part of the letter revealed the difficulties presented by Mao's current situation. The mountainous Xiaojin region was sparsely populated and finding provisions for his troops was proving difficult, making it unsuitable for a long stay. Added to this, Hu Zongnan's Nationalist forces in the Songpan region were obstructing a northward advance towards Gansu and for now Mao could only see one option: 'Because there is very little food it is impossible to rest, and the whole army may be concentrated around Lifan toward the end of the month, and prepare to cross the Min River.'[21]

This presented the prospect of more than 90,000 troops dominating the main Qiang region between Zagunao and Maoxian, far outnumbering the locals and in need of food and accommodation. Mao's force of 30,000 had by this time been depleted by more than half, with many of his ill-equipped men and women succumbing to the icy, high altitude conditions on their trek over the Jiajin Mountains to Xiaojin – a route which had taken them through the territory of the Muping chief who had become a Christian in the autumn of 1933. However, Zhang's forces still numbered about 80,000 and throughout that summer these joint Communist forces dominated a wide area which included Maoxian, Weizhou, the Zagunao valley, and parts of Heishui, southern Songpan, and the Xiaojin area. The impact on the Qiang villages was huge.

Although Torrance and Annie were receiving general news of the fighting in Sichuan, it was some time before they learned what had happened in the Qiang area. On September 27, having heard that the Communists had moved on, Edgar Plewman travelled to the area on behalf of the Chinese Church Mission Society, with medicine, food, and funds for those suffering in the aftermath of the conflict. On his return to Chengdu, he sent a devastating letter to Torrance.[22] Further detail emerged in two later WCMN reports, also written by Plewman.[23]

Plewman was travelling with Mr Zhao of the Canadian Press and Deng Weihan of Xuecheng, who had managed to flee when the Reds

21 Ibid., p17.
22 Plewman to TT, Oct 19, 1935, reprinted in large part in WCMN, April 1936, pp14-18.
23 T. E. Plewman. 'The Red Terror in the Tribes Country'. WCMN, Jan 1936, pp11-18; 'The Church in the Tribes Country'. WCMN, April 1936, pp5-18. Other accounts may differ but this is Plewman's perspective on the situation.

arrived, walking for nineteen days through the mountains to Guanxian. As the three men made their way up the Min Valley the road was teeming with soldiers and with coolies carrying supplies for the large government forces now stationed in Maoxian, Weizhou, Xuecheng, and Zagunao. The arrival of these troops had been a mixed blessing, as Plewman lamented: 'The lack of discipline of the government troops was everywhere evident. Buildings were torn down to supply them with a little firewood. Wooden partitions, beds, bandengs [benches], tables, floors, were seized and burnt.'[24] Thousands of people were now sick with dysentery and typhus and those who had died on the road were simply heaved off the path, some still lying below on the river bank, others carried away by the turbulent waters.

In Miansi the locals had fled the approaching Reds, terrified by news of the fall of Maoxian. The town was spared in the end, but the mission house had since fallen victim to the government soldiers' hunt for firewood, with flooring ripped up and even basic utensils removed. Chen Bingling and his family had moved to Dongmenwai and the derelict property was now a make-shift teashop run by a soldier. On the road to Weizhou the next day Plewman happened to meet Chen, who was on his way to visit Qiangfeng. Qiangfeng had been stripped by the Reds and Xiong, who had been living there, had also moved to Dongmenwai, knowing that the Qiangfeng villagers had no spare food to support him. Plewman had no time to visit the villages across the river and had little news for Torrance except that Wang, one of the Christians in Qiangfeng, had reportedly been killed by the Reds.

North of Miansi, from Banqiao onwards, villages were in ruins and the road was lined with 'inscriptions, posters and deeply cut slogans on stone', calling on people to rise against their oppressors and join the Red Army.[25] In an attempt to win over the Muslims and Tibetan Buddhists, the Reds had described Deng Xihou in one inscription as the 'executioner of the Hui and Fan people', whilst another encouraged people to 'catch Liu Xiang alive'.[26] Weizhou was a scene of complete desolation and they hastily moved on along the south bank of the

24 Plewman, 'The Red Terror', p16.
25 Plewman, 'The Church in the Tribes Country', p6.
26 Chen Shiying. *Wenchuanxian hongjun changzheng lishi yiji xianzhuang fenxi yu baohu* (Analysis of the Current Situation and Protection of the Historical Remains of the Red Army's Long March in Wenchuan County). Fangzhi Sichuan – zizhi. March, 12, 2021. https://www.sohu.com/a/455281413_120158407

Zagunao River towards Xuecheng, passing Dongmenwai on the opposite bank. On the way they met one of Pastor Ren's sons heading to Chengdu to find his older brother and get help for the family. Ren and his family had tried to escape from Zagunao, taking the same mountain route as Deng Weihan, but had left too late. Having almost reached government lines beyond Yingxiu, Ren and two of his sons had been caught by the Reds while searching for food. Government troops fired towards them and the two boys got away, finding refuge with a Wasi tribesman, but Ren was taken back up the valley to Heping where he was charged with being anti-Communist and executed along with several others. Ren's wife and two daughters, almost destitute, had managed to make their way back to Zagunao.

Despite the violence, not all reports of the Communists were bad. In sharp contrast to life under the Sichuan generals, they had made opium use a crime punishable by death and their message of equality was offering hope to many trapped in interminable cycles of poverty and debt to unscrupulous landlords. They had also continued to maintain their high levels of organisation, with a labour corps which included carpenters, straw sandal-makers, and sock-makers with modern knitting machines, and boy and girl scouts, theatrical troupes, and 'men and women orators, who descanted on the blessings of Communism to the population of the occupied area'.[27]

The Christian manager of an inn near Xuecheng said the Communists usually paid for what they took and were more disciplined than the government troops, who had stripped his inn of all its bedding when they retreated in May. Now that the government soldiers were back they were again helping themselves to anything they wanted. When Reginald Bazire returned to Pingwu after the departure of the Communists, he observed that the locals had been faced with a choice between Reds 'who pay their way and do not molest them so long as they stay, but who burn your city as a parting present, or the military who undercut their business, occupy their homes, steal their furniture, and impress their labour'.[28]

In Xuecheng, which had been a main base for the Communists, Plewman encountered yet more desolation. Pastor Mao's home was a pile of rubble. Mao might have met the same fate as Ren but he had died of pneumonia the previous January. His wife died of disease during the Communist occupation. The town was in such a state that it was

---

27 Plewman, 'The Red Terror', p15.
28 Reginald Bazire. 'Notes from North Szechwan'. WCMN, May 1936, p35.

difficult to recognise where the church had stood, 'so monotonously similar were the half-standing walls and piles of debris'.[29] The Fourth Army had used the church as a Red Guides school until they evacuated and burned the town. One of the few houses still standing was that of a Christian, who was weak with typhus. His home had now been commandeered by a recently arrived Nationalist commander.

One of the Xuecheng church members had escaped the Reds but came back having heard his brother had been taken prisoner and was then himself captured. With six other men they were 'taken to the middle of a bridge, bound hand and foot and thrown into the river'.[30] Neither brother was seen again although one man did escape, having drifted on to some rocks. Altogether, eleven people connected with the churches in Xuecheng and Zagunao had been killed. Others had suffered considerably, including some from the disease that followed, and Plewman was glad he had funds to distribute to those in greatest need.

Ironically, as Plewman pointed out, the tribespeople and their chiefs in the Zagunao Valley had had no particular reason to side with the Chinese against the Communists. Not long before the Communists arrived, Deng Xihou had imposed a military tax on the locals who, in response, told him that they would either pay the taxes or fight for him but not both. However, the Communists failed to capitalise on this discontent and Plewman's report of what followed was a sorry tale:

> . . . when the Reds came many of the native headmen reasoned that the Communists would not concern themselves with them. Their quarrel was with the Chinese government and officialdom. Moreover the Communists had sent messages in advance saying that they had been maligned – they did not slay people wantonly, nor did they destroy property. In fact, the town of Weizhou had not been destroyed by them but by the government troops. The Chinese were not deceived. The entire population of Xuecheng except the very poverty-stricken left before the Reds got there. The native headmen, however, led processions to welcome them, fired firecrackers, and feasted them. Everything went fine for a few days, during which time the Communists were busily engaged finding out who were the men with property, also who had been in any kind of government employ. They sent their forces into every tiny

29 Plewman, 'The Church in the Tribes Country', p11.
30 Ibid., p9.

village in the mountains and then when they had got the needed information they threw off the mask and started making prisoners of the headmen. No-one was in a position to resist. True, in one or two places a few of the tribespeople tried to save their chieftains, but usually in vain.[31]

Chief Yang of Jiuzi had gone to welcome the Communists with one hundred of his local troops and gifts of pigs and sheep, more in a bid for self-preservation than from any sense of allegiance.[32] It was a bid that failed and Plewman broke the sad news to Torrance that Yang, who had welcomed him so warmly at Erwa and stayed so long at Wushi-tongtang in 1929, had been killed. Chief Sang of Ganbao had also been killed, having been found hiding in the Zagunao lamasery. His wife was captured at home and met the same fate.[33]

These deaths provoked fury among the local population and were followed by a major uprising which the Reds only managed to quell after ten days of fighting.[34] Plewman was told that in Zagunao the tribespeople had been willing to do the front-line fighting 'because the Reds had alienated the tribespeople by their wanton slaughter of their headmen'.[35] Nationalist planes had also scattered pamphlets across the region, urging the people to rise up against the Reds and, in some cases, containing graphic descriptions of what the Reds might bring upon them.[36] The devastation witnessed by Plewman was testimony to the price the locals had paid for their resistance.

The destruction was the same all the way along the valley except for a few houses at Weiguan, near Zagunao, where Plewman, Deng, and Zhao stayed a night. In Zagunao they visited the lamasery where many buildings had been destroyed. Some forty monks had either been killed or died of disease and the remainder, perhaps a hundred or so, were 'wandering disconsolate about the ruins'.[37] Just eighteen months before, twenty of the monks had been part of another group visit to

31 Plewman, 'The Red Terror', p12.
32 Tian Lijun, '1935-1936 nian guogong neizhan', p215.
33 Chief Sang Futian's death is well-documented. It is harder to find any proof of Yang Jisheng's death. Information regarding his younger brother, Yang Jizu (1910-1991), is easily available online but apart from references to Yang Jisheng succeeding his father (Yang Anbang) in Jiuzi, there seems to be little trace of him.
34 Tian Lijun, '1935-1936 nian guogong neizhan', p215.
35 Plewman, 'The Red Terror', p17.
36 Tian Lijun, '1935-1936 nian guogong neizhan', p215.
37 Plewman, 'The Church in the Tribes Country', p11.

Chengdu, which had included a banquet organised by the West China Border Research Society, also attended by the now deceased Pastors Mao and Ren.[38] After the banquet the guests had viewed the Tibetan exhibits in the university museum and expressed their pleasure at the care being taken of them. Now the head lamas had apparently lost face having consulted the oracles and predicted that the Reds wouldn't reach Zagunao.

Plewman found Mrs Ren and her children in a tiny shack behind the Zagunao church. Their home had been commandeered by the Reds, at one point even accommodating Xu Xiangqian, the Fourth Army military commander, and was no longer habitable.[39] Giving them some funds, Plewman encouraged them to move to the inn near Xuecheng, where other Christians could help care for them. Mr Zhao's sister lived in Zagunao and he wept as she told him what they had gone through. She was now living with her family in the rear of their burnt house.

The visit to Zagunao was cut short by news that the Communists were still active further along the valley and that the government troops had retreated to Erdao Bridge just ten miles beyond the town, making the front line uncomfortably close. Returning to Weiguan they were joined for prayer by a Jiarong Christian who had been the business manager for the monks' visit to Chengdu. He had been asked several times by Xu Xiangqian for local information and, nervous about his fate, had managed to escape. However, in retribution, at least thirteen members of his household had been killed, including his wife. Taking Plewman and the others up to his village, almost two miles above Ganbao, he showed them the spot outside his house where some of them had died. His two young children had survived by hiding in a cupboard for three days and were now with him.

More shockingly, the man also told Plewman that in Zagunao the heads of some victims had been partially severed, retribution perhaps all the more severe because of the uprising and general resistance. Plewman didn't spare Torrance the detail: 'In some places they left large numbers of their victims with their heads half cut off, so that the poor wretches could sustain their heads under the jaw and even talk and take a little food, but all died in agony. Such devilry is

---

38 WCMN, March 1934, pp49-50. One of the Buddhist temples in Chengdu had invited them to read their sacred texts in the temple to raise funds for the repair of a Buddhist pagoda in Zagunao, damaged in the 1933 earthquake. Liu Xiang and other generals contributed donations.

39 Plewman, 'The Church in the Tribes Country', p12.

incomprehensible.'[40] Plewman heard the same story from others too. One chief from the Heishui valley, whom Plewman knew from earlier trips, told him that fifty to sixty of his people had been treated in this way and when others returned to the village after the Reds had gone 'they found quite a number who were using their hands to support their heads. Some of them could take a little food and talk and actually lived five or six days before death ended their sufferings.'[41] The chief demonstrated how they had had to support their heads.

Among those who had survived the summer, finding enough to eat was a serious problem. For such a large army to stay even a couple of months in this mountainous, thinly populated region had resulted in the same story wherever the Communists went. There just wasn't enough food for all. And although the Reds had usually paid their way, they were consuming crops and livestock upon which the locals depended, and money was no replacement when no other food was available. Plewman was concerned about the coming months:

> The winter is only just beginning and the scanty supplies of food are exhausted. Not till next summer will any new crop be available and who will feed the people in the meantime? The government is too much concerned getting supplies to the soldiers to worry about the civilian population, so it is fairly apparent that a number of people will die of starvation and that seed grain should be sent in to assure a harvest next year.[42]

Returning from Xuecheng along the north bank of the Zagunao River, they called in at Taoping and saw Wu Baobao, the man with the inoperable growth on his neck who had visited Torrance in Chengdu the previous year. His home had been used as a military kitchen with several wok stoves installed and subsequently torn out when the Communists left. His furniture had been stripped, the place was a wreck, and he was out of food. Plewman gave him some funds.

In Dongmenwai, the village and church had been looted but not destroyed. The army's need for accommodation and the fact that the church had been built simply in the local style were probably a factor in this and it seems to have been used for political meetings. The wall around it was now adorned with Communist slogans and some of the benches had been used for fuel. As the Fourth Army had spread out

---

40 Plewman to TT, Oct 19, 1935.
41 Plewman, 'The Red Terror', p14.
42 Ibid.

TWO DONGMENWAI CHRISTIANS BENEATH GRAFFITI ON THE CHURCH WALL. *It reads 'Chiang Kai-Shek and Deng Xihou are evil tyrants who drink the blood and sweat of young people.'*[43]

along the Zagunao Valley, Xu Xiangqian had chosen Dongmenwai as a base, describing it in his memoirs as a good location from which to direct the fighting of his front-line troops.[44] Mid-way between Maoxian and Zagunao, it was slightly off the beaten track and easily defended. Like Torrance, Xu had enjoyed watching the monkeys leaping around the mountainside above the village.

Word of the tragedies in Dongmenwai had already reached Plewman before he arrived there. Gou Pinsan had been a target of the Reds, not just as a Christian but also due to his educated background and his role as a government official. Knowing he was wanted, he had managed to escape but then heard that when someone in a similar official position had escaped, his wife and daughter had been killed. Hoping to spare his own family such a fate, he returned and gave himself up in Weizhou, where he was executed. No-one knew the exact details. As with the two brothers from Xuecheng, the executions were often at night with the bodies thrown in the river. Gou's wife had died of illness not long after.

Of the other Christians in Dongmenwai and the Longxi Valley, another was confirmed killed, six had been taken by the Reds and were

43 Photo: Princeton. Presumably taken by T. Edgar Plewman and sent to Torrance.
44 Xu Xiangqian. *Lishi de Huigu* (A Look Back at History). Jiefangjun chubanshe. 1988, pp303-305, 318.

assumed dead, and seven had died of disease. These included friends of Torrance from the villages of Longxi, Bulan, and Wa-ge, high above Dongmenwai. The villagers also asked Plewman to tell Torrance that the local blacksmiths, father and son, who had no doubt tended to Billy over the years, had been killed. The house of one Dongmenwai church member had been requisitioned for a month for one of the Fourth Army's wireless transmitters. Some of the villagers were now absent having been enlisted by government troops as rice carriers, with Chen Wenbing, one of the Christians, placed in charge of them. Chen's son was among those taken by the Communists.

On October 10, while Plewman was in Dongmenwai, a message came through which struck fresh terror into the locals. Rumour had reached the Nationalists that Communist forces still in the Heishui valley were planning to come south over the mountains to A'er and down the Longxi Valley. In response to this the Nationalist commander had sent word that his troops would only guard the south bank of the Zagunao River, leaving the north side, where Dongmenwai, Keku, and Taoping were situated, unprotected. The villagers there were urged to evacuate all the elderly, women, and children. Plewman wasn't impressed: 'The rotten military are all ready to retreat and putting the native auxiliaries in the front line while they take it easy.'[45] Thankfully, the threat seems to have passed and whilst every house on the south bank was occupied by government troops, the Dongmenwai villagers were spared the nuisance of having soldiers billeted in their homes.

Although no Bibles had been in evidence in Xuecheng and Zagunao, in Dongmenwai some of the Christians had buried theirs and five complete Bibles had survived. This was particularly courageous considering the presence of Red Army leaders in the village. Determined to carry on despite his father's death, Gou Pinsan's son was now preaching in Dongmenwai and Taoping on Sundays and sharing general oversight of the work with one of the Dongmenwai Christians. Another local Christian had taken on preaching in Bulan and A'er. Plewman gave them the remainder of his funds, which was spent on cornmeal for the most needy.

It was a precious time with the Christians, who were 'standing up nobly'. Together they looked at various Bible passages, reading of tribulation, the love of God, the crown of glory that awaited those who had died, and the need to continue to pastor the believers. From his village Gou's son managed to produce potatoes, cornmeal, and a

---

45   Plewman to TT, October 19, 1935.

rooster, the latter as 'scarce as diamonds' and something Plewman hadn't seen since leaving Guanxian.[46]

Plewman's parting shot to Torrance must have tugged at his heart strings: 'Any likelihood of Tom coming out here to take up your work amongst the Ch'iang? They were all asking if you are coming back.'

GOU PINSAN WITH HIS FAMILY

There was a story behind the reappearance of Communist troops in October. At his first encounter with Zhang early in the summer, Mao had realised that Zhang was a challenge to his political power, with better equipped troops who far outnumbered his own. Added to this, many of Zhang's troops were Sichuanese, so the original decision to move into northern Sichuan would have placed Zhang in an even stronger position. Mao immediately revised his plans and it was decided that both armies would unite and move north into Gansu.[47] However, as

46 Ibid.
47 Mao and Schram, *Mao's Road to Power*, p xlii; Garavente, 'The Long March', pp120-121.

a concession to Zhang, some of his troops were to keep control of areas that would facilitate a move further into Sichuan should that still become necessary, hence their presence in the Qiang area until the last of them pulled out at the end of August.[48]

Struggling to win over the local populace during this time, the Communists had announced that their policy towards ethnic minorities was to help them oppose the imperialist Nationalists, stand up against their own exploiting class, and gain their independence.[49] However, the attacks on the headmen and the Communist aversion to anything religious were poor diplomacy among people whose religious and cultural identities were so intertwined. With the additional problem of language barriers and the drain on local provisions, it became clear that gaining support in the area was a losing battle, even though a few locals joined their numbers.[50]

For the move north to Gansu, the combined troops were divided into two columns, with Xu Xiangqian and a large contingent of Zhang's troops joining Mao's right column to make the risky northward trek across the grasslands to Banyou near the Gansu border, thus avoiding Hu Zongnan's Nationalist troops around Songpan. The left column, led by Zhang Guotao and joined by some of Mao's troops and his military commander, Zhu De, were to go northwest and enter Gansu via Aba County, which would avoid the worst of the grassland bogs.[51]

Many of Mao's right column perished on the grasslands, weak from lack of food, easily sucked into the bogs concealed beneath the long grass, and also prey at times to hostile Tibetans. Ever mindful of the threat posed by Zhang, who was now in Aba County, Mao then sent word that Zhang should change course and also cross the grasslands to join Mao in Banyou, a route that would inevitably result in many casualties in Zhang's column. From there the reunited columns would continue into Gansu.

On September 3, Zhang sent word that his troops were blocked by the floodwaters of the Bai River and that to advance would be certain

48 Saich & Yang, *Rise to Power*, p657.
49 Tian Lijun, '1935-1936 nian guogong neizhan', p217.
50 See Kang and Sutton, *Contesting the Yellow Dragon*, pp145-146; A'er *Dang'an* (A'er Archive, compiled by the A'er villagers). Beijing wenhua yichan baohu zhongxin congshu. Beijing: wenwu chubanshe. 2011, p241. Four A'er villagers joined the Red Army and never returned home.
51 Jung Chang and J. Halliday. *Mao: The Unknown Story*. Vintage Publishing. 2007, p195.

death.[52] In defiance of Mao he decided to stay in Sichuan and turn south again, still with Zhu De and some of Mao's troops in his column. This put Mao in a predicament, knowing that many of Zhang's Fourth Army in his own column were still loyal to Zhang. Rather than face a mutiny, he chose to slip away at night with his own remaining troops and cross into Gansu, from where he would continue to northern Shaanxi and develop the power base which led to the Communist takeover of China in 1949.

Xu Xiangqian then led the Fourth Army troops deserted by Mao on the tortuous journey back across the grasslands and down towards Heishui to join up with Zhang. It was the reappearance of these troops in the Heishui Valley which had provoked the sudden fear, witnessed by Plewman in Dongmenwai on October 10, that they might come south over the mountains and down through A'er and Dongmenwai to the Zagunao Valley. The discovery of a cache of weapons and sewing machines in the hills between Xuecheng and Zagunao had already raised fears that the Red Army was planning to return. In the end, however, although some Fourth Army troops did once again pass through Heishui, they seem to have skirted the main Qiang region.

By the time Zhang and Xu Xiangqian were reunited, Zhang had realised there was little prospect of feeding their troops through a bitter winter in the mountains, especially in the face of local hostility, and he decided to move south towards Ya'an. Following part of Mao's earlier route, his forces took Xiaojin, Danba, and Dawei, defeating troops of Yang Sen and Liu Wenhui as they went and taking many prisoners. Still on the offensive, they then took towns to the north and west of Ya'an and a move towards Qionglai brought them within seventy miles of Chengdu, but by now the Nationalists had moved 200,000 troops to the Ya'an region, blocking any further advance.

Zhang's southern expedition was ultimately a disaster. His troops were forced on to the defensive and had difficulty replenishing both food and ammunition. Harrison Salisbury records that in November, during seven days of fighting, Zhang lost more than 10,000 men.[53] In mid-February 1936 his troops, now reduced to 40,000, retreated through the mountains back to Xiaojin. They were unmerciful in defeat and returning missionaries found the wider Ya'an region 'in great confusion and distress', particularly the towns of Lushan and

---

52 Ibid., pp196, 198.
53 Harrison E. Salisbury. *The Long March: The Untold Story*. Pan Books Ltd. 1986, p316.

Tianquan, just west of Ya'an, where 'the Communists had carried carnage and destruction to the limit'.[54]

Perhaps already knowing that he had made an implacable enemy in Mao, Zhang was still determined to stay in Sichuan and from Xiaojin he moved further west into today's Ganzi prefecture. However, despite his troops being reinforced in June 1936 by the arrival of He Long and Xiao Ke's Second Front Army from Guizhou, he eventually had to concede that long-term settlement in Sichuan was untenable. On the pretext that joining Mao to fight the Japanese now took precedence over everything else, he ordered his troops to cross the grasslands to Gansu. Divided this time into three columns, one column again passed through the western end of Heishui County, which was the last the region saw of them until the Communists came to power thirteen years later.

Mao never forgave Zhang the challenge to his authority and made life increasingly difficult for him. In an unexpected twist to the story, in 1938 Zhang seized a sudden opportunity to defect to the Nationalists and in 1949 fled with them to Taiwan. After living quietly in Hong Kong for many years, he moved to Toronto, where he is said to have embraced the Christian faith towards the end of his life.[55] Whatever the truth of this, Zhang Guotao's 1935 sojourn in and around the Qiang area had cost the church dearly and caused untold suffering to thousands, and Plewman's letter would leave a deep scar on Torrance's heart for the rest of his life. In spring 1936 the sad news reached Torrance that Chen Bingling had died of sickness.[56]

There was, however, a glimmer of hope in the midst of all the tragedy. A package arrived in Edinburgh one day, sent through a Christian Chinese general receiving medical treatment in Canada. To Torrance's surprise it contained a Chinese New Testament with an inscription on the front page: 'Because of the Communist persecution, this book was hidden in a cave during the 24th year of the Chinese Republic (1935). In this way the book was saved from destruction. In memory of the Dongmenwai church in Lifan prefecture.' Accompanying it was a note from one of the Qiang Christians saying they were sending it as a pledge that the church would rise again.

---

54 WCMN, April 1936, p39.
55 Chang and Halliday, *Mao: The Unknown Story*, p260.
56 Plewman, 'The Church in the Tribes Country', p18.

Chapter 23

'Ancient Israelites'

1937

Spurred on by the news of Gou's death and mindful of Gou's request that he raise awareness of the Qiang, Torrance had begun working on a photo-illustrated book. Unlike his more academic research, to which Torrance pointed readers in his preface, the book's twelve short chapters were a presentation of Qiang culture designed to appeal to an audience familiar with the Bible and written against the backdrop of a distinct theological framework, that of belief in the dispersion of the tribes of Israel and the promise of their eventual regathering.[1]

Torrance made his hypothesis clear from the outset, both in the main title, *China's First Missionaries – Ancient Israelites*, and in the title of his first chapter, 'Outcasts of Israel', a reference to the promise in the book of Isaiah that those Israelites who had been cast out of the land would one day be brought back from the four corners of the earth.[2] Looking at the history of these outcasts, he cited the apocryphal book of Esdras, which told of the ten tribes of Israel's northern kingdom being exiled to a region beyond the Euphrates called 'Arzareth', thought by some to be associated with Afghanistan. He also made reference to a tradition among the Jews of Bukhara, in present-day Uzbekistan, that some of their number had continued east into China.

Having acknowledged that it would never be determined exactly where these exiled Israelites had settled or where their descendants might be found, Torrance recounted his surprise at discovering in western China 'a colony of ancient immigrants whose religious observances resembled very closely those of the Old Testament'.[3] Describing how his own thinking had developed over the years, he explained that their 'customs, laws, architecture, demeanour and physiognomy' had

1 The four works referred to in his preface were: *The History, Customs and Religion of the Ch'iang* (1920); 'The Religion of the Ch'iang' (1923); 'Notes on the West China Aboriginal Tribes' (1932); and 'The Basic Spiritual Conceptions of the Religion of the Chiang' (1934).
2 Isaiah 11:12.
3 TT. *China's First Missionaries*, p16.

early persuaded him that they hailed from Asia Minor, possibly from Semitic origins which predated the existence of Israel.[4] However, 'with an increased knowledge of their traditions and a better understanding of their religious mysteries, the conclusion was forced on us slowly that they were indeed descendants of ancient Israelite settlers.'[5]

Lending credence to this, in Torrance's view, was the Qiang tradition that they had come from elsewhere and had travelled for 'three years and three months', encountering some difficult river crossings on the way.[6] He followed this with an overview of the Qiang, noting how the remoteness of their location had contributed to the preservation of their culture and recounting their history according to Chinese sources but stressing the difficulty of tracing their very early history because the Chinese term 'Qiang' had been used so broadly in antiquity.

Torrance's use of 'missionaries' in the book's title was explained in the second chapter. Drawing on his 1928 article about religious life in China,[7] he looked briefly at early Chinese history and religious practices and then suggested that, just as later missionaries had brought the Christian gospel to China, so the early Qiang had brought with them an awareness of the God of the Old Testament and a 'higher conception of righteousness', as seen in their sacrificial practices, in their reverence for the 'Giver of all good', and in their social mores.[8]

In support of people having traversed such great distances in those days, he cited a recent lecture given in Edinburgh by Professor Li Ji of the Academica Sinica and entitled 'Ancient China in the Light of Recent Archaeological Discoveries'. Li had pointed out that 'Ancient China was not developed in isolation. The idea that China was all by herself until the time of Marco Polo was absolutely erroneous. She was already hopelessly entangled with all sorts of foreign relations as far back as the prehistorical time.'[9]

Writing for the first time for a wider British readership, Torrance's next nine chapters introduced different aspects of Qiang culture, this time with the inclusion of biblical references regarding the parallels he and Gou had observed, and with references to various books on

---

4   Ibid.
5   Ibid.
6   Ibid., p19.
7   TT. 'Religious Life in China from Ancient to Modern Times'. WCMN, Nov 1928, pp5-24.
8   TT, *China's First Missionaries*, pp25, 22.
9   Ibid., pp26-27. An excerpt from Professor Li Ji's lecture, reported in *The Scotsman*, February 26, 1937. Li Ji (李濟) had a PhD from Harvard in anthropology and was seen by some as the founder of Chinese archaeology,

the Old Testament and the Middle East. Describing his winter Bible study periods with the Qiang in Chengdu, Torrance noted how 'the book of Hebrews became to them a spiritual lexicon to interpret what they and their fathers had so long conserved.'[10] And despite some intermarriage and the layers of syncretism added over the centuries, he stressed the continued existence among the Qiang of the fundamental concept of a holy God and of salvation through sacrifice, which was so different from the traditional Chinese concept of personal merit acquired by 'alms-giving, prostration before idols, incense-burning and pilgrimages to heathen shrines'.[11]

The Qiang lack of idolatry, a practice forbidden in the Mosaic Law of the Israelites, was in stark contrast to this, as was their recognition of a need to be cleansed from sin in order to approach a holy God, and their concept of atonement as a means of restoring fellowship between man and God.[12] Torrance did, however, note that some idolatry was creeping in and also that the Qiang generally had no aversion to eating pork or food containing blood. But he refuted any suggestion that the Qiang were animists who believed in an impersonal spirit world, and declared instead that 'they know whom they worship and they do not worship Him ignorantly.'[13]

As far as he was concerned, 'The whole Bible from Genesis to Revelation and the ritual of the White Religion of the Chiang abound in striking points of similarity.'[14] Among these similarities were the more obvious ones such as the sacrifices themselves. The substitutionary nature of these sacrifices and the cleansing role of the sprinkled blood were key aspects for Torrance and he had found agreement on these among the aged priests he had talked with: both were necessary for the Qiang to have any communion with God.[15] Another clear parallel was the sprinkling of blood on the lintel and doorposts of the home as part of a private sacrifice on the rooftop, something reminiscent of the Jewish Passover ritual. He also pointed out that after a sacrifice the Qiang priest would receive a portion of the lamb, a practice recorded in Leviticus 7:32: 'You shall give the right thigh to the priest as a contribution from the sacrifices of your peace offerings.'[16]

---

10 Ibid., p61.
11 Ibid., p117.
12 Ibid., p91.
13 Ibid., p64.
14 Ibid., p94.
15 Ibid., p72-73.
16 Ibid., p104.

In the Qiang emphasis on white and the need for cleansing before any sacrificial ceremony, Torrance found echoes of God's command to Moses: 'Go to the people and consecrate them today and tomorrow, and let them wash their garments; and let them be ready for the third day, for on the third day the Lord will come down on Mount Sinai in the sight of all the people.'[17] As for the white stone which marked the place where the Qiang met with their 'Abba Chee', Torrance pointed to the biblical use of memorial and covenant stones, such as the one set up by Jacob at Bethel to mark the place of his encounter with God.[18] The priest's rod Torrance likened to the Nehushtan or bronze serpent on a pole used by Moses, which had become an idol by the time of King Hezekiah of Judah.[19] The rod had been another significant factor in Torrance's conclusion that the Qiang were of Semitic origin, as had the Semitic features of some of the Qiang.

Other parallels included the Qiang practice of a younger brother marrying his deceased brother's wife, which Torrance likened to the biblical practice of Levirate marriage in Deuteronomy 25:5-6, and the similarity between the Qiang door lock and the lock described in Song of Solomon 5:4-6.[20] In relation to the Qiang roof parapet he drew attention to an instruction in Deuteronomy 22:8: 'When you build a new house, you shall make a parapet for your roof, so that you will not bring bloodguilt on your house if anyone falls from it.'[21] Another observation was the similarity between the Qiang custom of two chickens accompanying a coffin to its cremation site – one of which was slain and the other kept alive – and a passage in Leviticus 14 regarding the treatment of leprosy, in which one bird was slain and another released. Towards the end of the book he included a list of Qiang rituals taken from Gou's 1925 comparison but omitting Gou's biblical references. Within the list Torrance included the twelve sheets of white paper put on the wall at a private rooftop ceremony, which he understood to represent, 'twelve sons of one man who was the ancestor of the Chiang'.[22]

17 Ibid., p40. Exodus 19:10-11.
18 Ibid., p64. See Genesis 28:18.
19 Ibid., pp96-98, pp35-36. See Numbers 21:9, 2 Kings 18:4.
20 Ibid., pp33-34. More comparative research is needed, but the Qiang lock shares similarities with a lock found in Khorsabad at the palace of Sargon II of Assyria (r. 721-705 BC), who boasted of taking 27,290 inhabitants of the northern kingdom of Israel into exile.
21 Ibid., p32.
22 Ibid., pp114, 105.

There were some Qiang practices for which Torrance could find no precise biblical parallel but in which he saw possible echoes of Old Testament laws, for example the Qiang ceremonial practice of sealing off a forest for fifty years and the Israelite tradition of a fiftieth jubilee year.[23] And although the Qiang didn't practice circumcision, they did have a sacrificial naming ceremony forty days after the birth of a boy, which was followed three years later by another ceremony where a white cord was placed around the boy's neck. The boy would then place his hands on the head of a sacrificial lamb or cockerel, the cord would be cut and placed on the altar, and blood and fat daubed on the boy's forehead.[24]

Although keen to emphasise that the white stone and the sacred tree in the grove were not objects of worship, Torrance devoted a chapter to the sacred groves of the Qiang and their similarity to Canaanite high-place worship, which had been adopted by many ancient Israelites. In the time of Moses the Israelites had been told, 'You shall utterly destroy all the places where the nations whom you shall dispossess serve their gods, on the high mountains and on the hills and under every green tree.'[25] However, centuries later the Israelites were still sacrificing on high places and even after the building of the temple in Jerusalem, the northern kingdom of Israel had chosen to build its own high places rather than attending the Levitical ceremonies in the temple.[26]

Torrance also found resonance between the Qiang use of stones and branches and the biblical use of symbolism, as found, for example, in the book of Zechariah, where the prophet uses the imagery of a branch to represent the one who was destined to rebuild the temple, and the imagery of a stone with seven eyes to represent the cornerstone of the temple and the all-seeing Spirit of God. Torrance was particularly curious about the symbolic nature of the Qiang roll of white paper, renewed with a clean sheet of paper at each major sacrifice. As far as he could ascertain, it was a sacred symbol of one who was yet to come, suggesting that the Qiang were awaiting some kind of Messiah figure, and signified 'the virtual Presence of the Heaven-Sent-One at the altar'.[27] He also saw it as an indication that they had once had their own sacred scroll of the law.

---

23 Ibid., pp45, 54.
24 Ibid., pp105-106. Also mentioned in Torrance's 1923 paper, 'The Religion of the Ch'iang'.
25 Ibid., p62. Deuteronomy 12:2.
26 Ibid., p71.
27 Ibid., p74.

Essentially, within the religious culture of the Qiang Torrance could see reflections of all the key themes of the Old Testament – God's holiness, man's sin, the need for righteousness, gracious atonement provided through sacrifice, and the keeping of laws in a covenant relationship with God. Actually seeing the rituals performed had enabled him to view the Old Testament through fresh eyes and he even wondered if an examination of the age-old practices of the Qiang might shed light on Old Testament high-place worship.

A QIANG FARMER

Conversely, an understanding of the origins of the Israelite practices might help shed light on various cultural practices in the Sino-Tibetan border area which were 'now a subject of debate'.[28]

In relation to this he made some final observations regarding traces of Qiang religious practices found among other groups in the southwestern border region, including the Nosu, the Jiarong, and the Naxi, as well as within the ancient Bon practices of the Tibetans. He was also wondering whether there was any connection between the southernmost ancient Qiang and Myanmar's Karen people and other 'certain hill tribes' on the China-Myanmar border, among whom missionaries had noticed Old Testament-like monotheistic beliefs.

Torrance was well aware that 'certain schools of liberal thought' might take issue with his findings but the book received positive reviews in several Christian publications of the period.[29] An initial review in *The Chinese Recorder* was less positive, appreciating the detailed description of Qiang culture but dismissive of Torrance's Israelite theory.[30] However, a later issue of the *Recorder* contained an

---

28 Ibid., p124.
29 Ibid.
30 *The Chinese Recorder*, Sept 1937, p592.

abbreviated version of a review in the *Times Literary Supplement* which fully accepted Torrance's theory, noting that the descendants of these 'original Israelite settlers' had eventually spread across a large area of Western Sichuan before the arrival of the Chinese. Torrance's choice of photos had clearly had an impact on the reviewer: 'Mr. Torrance's conclusions are confirmed by the illustrations to the text, which show convincingly Jewish types.'[31]

The book also prompted correspondence with various readers, including Professor Charles Seligman, Professor of Ethnology at the London School of Economics, whose students had included noted anthropologists Bronislaw Malinowski and Edward Evans-Pritchard. With his compliments, Seligman sent Torrance his own paper, 'The Roman Orient and the Far East', which included a reference to a 'socketed celt' thought to have reached China around 500-600 BC, possibly from northern or central Europe via the Scythians, and another reference to lapis lazuli reaching ancient Egypt from the lapis mines in Afghanistan.[32] In line with Professor Li Ji's view, Seligman concluded his paper with the prediction that 'early contacts between Europe and the Far East will, as knowledge advances, prove to have been far more numerous than has hitherto been generally accepted.'[33] He was co-authoring another paper on early Chinese glass and wanted to know if Torrance had come across any specimens from the Tang period or earlier.[34]

In 1939 an article by Torrance on 'The Bible in China' was published in the *Bible League Quarterly*. This made no mention of the Qiang by name but described Israelites who had 'trekked their way, after the Dispersion, through Central Asia and Turkestan to the great grazing lands of China's Western frontier' – an allusion to the early presence of the Qiang and their sheep and cattle in Qinghai and Gansu.[35] That same year Torrance was asked to present the Rev. S. Runsie Craig

---

31 *The Chinese Recorder*, March 1938, p136; *Times Literary Supplement*, July 1937.

32 C. G. Seligman. 'The Roman Orient and the Far East'. *Antiquity*, Vol 11, Issue 41, March 1937, pp5-8.

33 Ibid., p30.

34 C. G. Seligman and H. C. Beck. 'Far Eastern Glass: Some Western Origins'. *Bulletin of Museum of Far Eastern Antiquities* 10, pp1-64, Stockholm, 1938.

35 TT. 'The Bible in China'. *Bible League Quarterly*, No. 158, Jan-March 1939, p8. The *Book of Han* (Chapter 69) tells of a Han general, Zhao Chongguo, seizing thousands of horses, cattle, and sheep after a battle in eastern Qinghai against a group called the Xianlian Qiang in the 1st century BC.

Memorial Lecture, which had been established a year earlier to defend the integrity of the Bible in the face of 'philosophies and theories opposed thereto'.[36] His lecture, entitled 'The Survival of Old Testament Religious Customs Among the Chiang People of West China', was selected on the grounds that it embodied 'the results of an original investigation of unique evidential value in confirmation of the Old Testament Scriptures'.[37]

Speaking to a theologically sympathetic audience, Torrance clearly felt free to discuss the spiritual significance he had perceived within Qiang rituals, as well as the Old Testament parallels. Describing these in considerable detail, he concluded that for anyone familiar with the Old Testament, 'at every turn the Chiang religion bristles with allusions to its well-known truths'.[38] The lecture was followed by a discussion chaired by Lieut-Col. F. A. Molony, who referred to a debate then current as to whether biblical sacrifice had been instituted by God or man. He reminded the audience that, as Chief Rabbi Hertz had argued, the prophets had called on the Israelites to abandon their evil ways but not their sacrifices, suggesting that the sacrifices were God-instituted. Molony saw the Qiang sacrificial practices as supportive of this: 'If the Chiang-min were not firmly convinced that their sacrifices were inspired by God, how are we to account for their keeping the essential points of the ritual, unchanged through so many centuries?'[39]

Molony also raised the question of whether the Qiang were descendants of the lost tribes or of some later Jewish dispersion. Following this, one participant cited a verse in the book of Deuteronomy: 'The Lord will scatter you among all peoples, from one end of the earth to the other end of the earth; and there you shall serve other gods, wood and stone, which you or your fathers have not known.'[40] Another asked Torrance if he thought that 'God may have some unrevealed purpose in planting the Chiang where they are found' and suggested that they might 'help one day to fulfil Isaiah's prophecy that Israelites will come from the land of Sinim, which has for centuries been identified as China, to inherit again the

---

36 *Journal of the Transactions of The Victoria Institute or Philosophical Society of Great Britain*, Vol LXXI, 1939, p99.
37 Ibid., pp100-116.
38 Ibid., p110.
39 Ibid., p111.
40 Deuteronomy 28:64.

Holy Land.'[41] Torrance wouldn't be drawn on this but reaffirmed his view that they were 'of the seed of Abraham, Isaac, and Jacob.'[42]

Towards the end of 1939 Torrance presented his final major paper about the Qiang to the Scottish Geographical Society, which was published in the society's magazine in May 1940 as 'The Emigrations of the Jews: Israel in China'.[43] Addressing a more diverse audience this time, he took a different approach. Beginning with a history of the Jews, he described how their dispersion had turned them into a 'great, if unnamed, Geographical Society, able, because of their travels, to provide expert information on all the caravan routes through Africa, Asia, Europe, and to the Far East', and also familiar with 'all the shipping ports in the Red Sea and the Mediterranean'.[44] Looking at the places to which Jews were known to have scattered, including India, Ethiopia, the Mediterranean coast, Arabia, Yemen, Asia Minor, Babylon, and Afghanistan, he again referred to the Jews of Bukhara, noting that the nineteenth century traveller Dr Joseph Wolff had encountered ancient Jewish colonies in Bukhara and in Samarkand and had been told that some of their number had 'pushed on to the very frontier of China'.[45]

Torrance then traced out a possible route for the Qiang along an ancient highway which ran from Persia to Bukhara and Samarkand, east through Tashkent and Talas to the Issyk Kul lake, and then south into the Tarim Basin and northwest China.[46] In support of this he pointed out that Chinese envoy Zhang Qian had taken this route from China to Central Asia in 138 BC, and also that the Qiang were known to have migrated to Sichuan from Gansu in the northwest, where Chinese historians had recorded them living 'in strength during the Han Dynasties, 209 B. C. – A. D. 220'.[47]

---

41 *Journal of the Transactions of The Victoria Institute*, Vol LXXI, p114. See Isaiah 49:12.
42 Ibid.
43 TT. 'The Emigrations of the Jews: Israel in China'. Presented to the Scottish Geographical Society in December 1939 and published in *The Scottish Geographical Magazine*, Vol 56, May 1940, pp59-64.
44 Ibid., pp59-60.
45 Ibid.; Joseph Wolff. *Narrative of a Mission to Bokhara: In the Years 1843-1845, to Ascertain the Fate of Colonel Stoddart and Captain Conolly.* Vol 1. Harper & Brothers. 1845. According to Wolff, 'The tradition is an old one at Bokhara, that some of the Ten Tribes are in China.' (p30)
46 An unlikely alliance of Tibetans and Arabs of the Abbasid Caliphate defeated Chinese troops in Talas in A.D. 751.
47 TT. 'Emigrations', p61.

His research had led Torrance to conclude that the Qiang had been in China since at least around 400 BC, with some in the northwest, another group in the west, and a third group in the southwest. They were led by tribal chiefs and some of their 'subdivisions were known by animal names as in Old Testament days', an apparent reference to Genesis 49 in which several of Jacob's twelve sons were likened to animals, including a wolf, a doe, a snake, a donkey, and a lion.[48] Moving on to a much briefer look at Qiang customs, Torrance then described the general geography of the Qiang territory he was so familiar with. Although he had avoided the more biblical aspects of his Runsie Craig Memorial Lecture, he ended with a reference to the Qiang as 'West China Jews' and quoted the promise in the book of Isaiah that some Israelites would be regathered from the land of Sinim.[49]

In an era when church attendance was common and returning missionaries were often a respected and significant source of geographical and cultural information, it is perhaps not surprising that Torrance's ideas were met with interest, particularly within the more evangelical wing of the church. Back in 1843 a short book entitled *The Jews of China* had been written by James Finn, who subsequently became British Consul in Jerusalem. Although Finn's primary focus had been the remnant of the Chinese Jewish community in the Northern Song capital of Kaifeng, he clearly felt there was more to be discovered in China and noted in his closing reflections that, 'Some students of the unfulfilled prophecies look towards China for the discovery of the ten tribes.'[50] Similar to Torrance's Qiang migration hypothesis, Finn recorded that, according to their own account, the ancestors of the Kaifeng Jews, 'came from the west, probably by way of Khorassan and Samerkand, the main route of ancient commerce in that direction.'[51]

---

48 Ibid., p62. Some of the ancient Qiang tribes went by names such as the White Wolf clan, White Horse clan, Yak clan, Ploughing Ox clan, and Fierce Wolf clan.

49 Isaiah 49:12. The meaning of Sinim has long been debated, the two most common interpretations being China and Aswan (Syene) in Egypt. One argument against the former is that the Qin dynasty, from which 'China' is derived, was only founded in 221 BC, centuries after the book of Isaiah. However, the state of Qin was founded in today's northwest China in the 9th century BC.

50 James Finn. *The Jews in China*. B. Wertheim. 1843, p64.

51 Ibid., p61.

With a general growth in evangelicalism in the years after Finn's book, coinciding with Russian pogroms which accelerated Jewish migration to Palestine, there was curiosity in some Christian circles as to whether the time was near for a fulfilment of various biblical prophecies concerning Israel, not least the return of these Jews from 'Sinim'. Even the CIM, with its focus on China, took an interest in such matters. One book review, published in *China's Millions* when Hudson Taylor was editor, recommended a book called *Israel My Glory*, noting that it was 'the outcome of life-long study of the Scriptures and work amongst the still scattered remnant of Israel'.[52]

Hudson Taylor was undoubtedly influenced by Henry Grattan Guinness, the father of his daughter-in-law Geraldine and founder of Cliff College, where Torrance had studied. In his 1888 study of biblical prophecy entitled *Light for the Last Days*, Guinness had calculated that 1917 would mark a significant shift in Muslim and Gentile power in relation to Palestine and declared that, 'there can be no question that those who live to see this year 1917 will have reached one of the most important, perhaps the most momentous, of these terminal years of crisis.'[53] Guinness died in 1910 but his readers would have noted with interest that 1917 saw the fall of the Ottoman empire, the transfer of Palestine from Ottoman to British rule, and the issuing of the Balfour Declaration which stated that the British government viewed with favour 'the establishment in Palestine of a national home for the Jewish people'. With such developments taking shape, Torrance's book and papers were finding fertile soil amongst some readers.

Back in China, as Plewman had predicted, the Qiang and Jiarong areas were dealing with serious food shortages.[54] Not only had the Red Army troops exhausted local food supplies, but from early autumn 1936 no rain had fallen for about eight months and much of Sichuan had been plunged into famine conditions. In April 1937 a WCMN report from Pengzhou described famine in the foothills extending towards the Qiang area, where the previous year's corn had been eaten and seed corn for the spring planting was scarce.[55] Conditions were severe in all

---

52 *Millions*, 1895, p12; John Wilkinson. *Israel My Glory*. Mildmay Mission to the Jews Book Store. 1894.
53 Henry and Fanny Grattan Guinness. *Light for the Last Days: A Study in Chronological Prophecy*. Hodder and Stoughton. 1888, p224.
54 T. E. Plewman. 'The Red Terror in the Tribes Country'. WCMN, Jan 1936, p16.
55 George Rackham. 'Every Believer A Worker'. WCMN, Oct 1937, p16.

parts of today's Aba Prefecture, particularly in Jinchuan, just west of the Qiang area, where people were reduced to eating edible roots and tree bark, and starved corpses lay on the roads.[56]

In the years immediately after Torrance's departure the WCMN carried few references to the Qiang but interest was developing in other quarters. In May 1937 Torrance sent a copy of his book to Chiang Kai-shek and his wife, Soong Meiling. With the Communists still a major threat and China on the cusp of full-scale war with Japan, it is remarkable that Torrance received any acknowledgement but on June 21 a reply was sent by Soong Meiling's secretary, thanking Torrance on her behalf. Although she hadn't yet read the book, the letter assured Torrance of her concern for the various tribespeople in Sichuan and Guizhou.

Generalissimo's Headquarters of the National Forces

Kuling, Ki., China.

June 21, 1937

Dear Sir,

Madame Chiang Kai-Shek instructs me to acknowledge your letter of May 12 and the copy of "China's First Missionaries: Ancient Israelites." Madame Chiang thanks you very much for sending the book, which she hopes to be able to read shortly.

Madame Chiang also appreciates your mention of the Chiang-Min. While out in Kweichow and Szechwan the Generalissimo and Madame became interested in the hard conditions of life of the tribes people and took steps while there to try and ameliorate their lot. They also took steps to try and raise the standard of living of these people. Madame Chiang and the Generalissimo personally made contributions of live stock and poultry so that the tribes people could improve their conditions. Both the Generalissimo and Madame have also done everything they could to facilitate the work of the missionaries not only in the West but in every other part of China which they have visited, because they appreciate the great contribution which the missionaries make to the betterment of the lot of the people, especially those in the interior.

Because of this recognition of missionary effort Madame and the Generalissimo took steps to secure co-operation between the

56 Aba Tibetan Qiang Autonomous Prefecture Local Annals Office. 'Dashi zhuanshu' (Major Events). April 18, 2019. http://dfzb.abazhou.gov.cn/abzdfsbgs/c104057/201904/36dbd6a0c17d44d3aebe508f8142f577.shtml

missionaries and the Chinese leaders of the New Life Movement in various centers. Both the Generalissimo and Madame are hopeful that missionary effort will become more and more effective as time goes on.

Madame and the Generalissimo wish to express their appreciation to you and so many others who have devoted so much of their lives to work in China.

Yours sincerely,　　D. Z. Koo (Secretary)[57]

It is clear from this how much official attitudes to Christianity had changed in the Nationalist-controlled areas. Many of Chiang's officials were Christians, including his mission school and American-educated brother-in-law, H. H. Kung, who was minister of finance. An article in TIME magazine even reported that the governor of Sichuan was worshipping each Sunday at the West China Union University chapel.[58] (The article also noted that Chiang was counting on American and British support in his fight against the Japanese.)

The New Life Movement mentioned by Koo had been founded by the Nationalists in 1934 in an attempt to unite the Chinese under a viable alternative to the Communist message and to strengthen national solidarity in the face of Japanese aggression. Combining Confucian and Christian values in what was largely a moralistic campaign, it was, according to the WCMN, 'training young people from every part of the country in social services of the most varied kinds' and was 'one of the most extensive and valuable programmes of social engineering the world has ever seen'.[59]

In Sichuan the influence of the movement was strengthened by the Nationalist government's relocation from Nanjing to Chongqing in late 1937 as a result of the conflict with Japan. Similarly, Chengdu had now become the destination for several universities evacuating from regions under threat from the Japanese, and staff and students alike became involved in these New Life projects, some of which would extend to the Qiang and Tibetan areas of Sichuan.

In 1938 Christian students in Chengdu formed a Summer Rural Service Group with the goal of improving conditions among farmers and serving their country 'according to the Christian spirit of service'.[60]

57　Typed letter from D. Z. Koo, secretary to Soong Meiling. Yale University Divinity School Library, Thomas Torrance Papers, box 3, folder 35.
58　'Religion: Christianity in China'. *TIME*, April 28, 1941. (No page nos.) http://content.time.com/time/subscriber/article/0,33009,765521-1,00.html
59　WCMN, Sept 1937, p39.
60　WCMN, Sept 1938, p296.

Aspects of the idealistic message they hoped to convey were not dissimilar to the moralising campaign of the Communists in 1935, with aims and activities including 'abolition of superstitions, smoking, drinking etc, lecture on ethics and morality, religious hymns, moral stories, instruction in Christian living, introducing Jesus' struggle against evil forces and introducing Jesus on Love and doing God's will.'[61]

The following year a more formally established organisation came into being. Faced with a lack of personnel for social projects, the Nationalist government had turned for help to the reliably patriotic Church of Christ in China and out of this collaboration came the Border Services Department (BSD), a joint project aimed at winning the hearts, minds, and political loyalty of the border peoples by means of educational, medical, and economic services, as well as facilitating the church's goal of spreading of the Christian message. Essentially, they were developing on a larger scale what Torrance and others had already been doing.

In the Qiang region medical clinics were set up in Weizhou, Xuecheng, and Zagunao, primary schools were established in the villages of Luobozhai and Jiashan, both with about thirty boys, and an animal husbandry station was opened in Weizhou.[62] For the local Christians, the Christian emphasis in all this activity helped to create a much freer atmosphere for them to meet without fear of repercussions.

In the spring of 1940 two evangelistic BSD workers were sent to the area, with Pastor Geng Duzhai assigned to Zagunao and Shao Yunting to the Weizhou region. Having conducted an initial investigation into local religious beliefs, they concluded that 'it would be comparatively easier to convert the Qiang than converting the Jiarong for the looser religious organization in Qiang society.'[63] A base for evangelistic work among the Qiang was then set up in Weizhou alongside the other BSD projects there, with Shao holding regular Bible studies and Sunday services. At first, these were attended mainly by BSD workers and a few teachers and students from the Weizhou Teachers School but Shao also started visiting various Qiang villages.[64]

---

61 Ibid., p297.
62 Jiashan (佳山寨), a high Qiang village across the Zagunao River from Taoping, was not a village Torrance ever mentioned visiting.
63 Diana Junio. *Patriotic Cooperation: The Border Services of the Church of Christ in China and Chinese Church–State Relations, 1920s–1950s*. Leiden: Brill. 2017, p263.
64 Ibid., p269.

A significant part of the BSD activity was their summer student programmes and that same year seventy-nine BSD students were assigned to various locations in today's Aba Prefecture, including Miansi and Weizhou. Describing his experiences, one student wrote that the Qiang people were 'the most interesting. They are like the Jews in many ways: they worship only one God; a priest offers sacrifices. The sacrifices are offered on a high mountain, upon a rock near a wood.' The student added that he would 'like to find out more of the history, customs and religion of the Ch'iang people. There might be greater historical data here even than that discovered in Sian through the Nestorian Tablet.'[65] Although this seems to suggest he had read some of Torrance's writings, a later Chinese article in the BSD journal, giving an overview of Qiang history and culture, made no mention of Torrance and declared that the first real contact between the Qiang and Christianity had only begun with the advent of the Border Service Department in 1939 and that there were still no 'real Christian converts.'[66]

This was clearly, however, not the case. To the surprise of one group of summer students who were holding morning devotions in the Qiang village to which they had been assigned, they were asked by some of the locals to hold a service for them. The students did so and later that same day others came from further afield wanting to know if there would be a service, so they held another.[67] It seems likely this would have been Dongmenwai and that news of the students' presence had spread to the Christians scattered in the various villages in Longxi Valley. Diana Junio notes that a BSD service station had been set up in Longxi Valley in January 1940 to establish medical and educational work.[68]

Perhaps not wanting previous missionary work to be overlooked in this new wave of Christian activity, Daniel Dye wrote an article for *The Chinese Recorder* that summer called 'The Challenge of the Far Western Border', which included an overview of early missionaries and their remote stations in western Sichuan. Describing the inhabitants

---

65 'Christian Activities in War-Torn China'. *The Chinese Recorder*, March 1941, p154. The Nestorian tablet, discovered in Xi'an and dating to the Tang dynasty, indicates the arrival of Christians in China in the 7th century.

66 Lu Yu. 'Seen and Heard on the Border: Informal Notes on the Ch'iang-Min' (Bianjiang jianwen: xianhua Qiangmin). *Bianjiang Fuwu*, No. 8. July 1945, pp15-19. Translation by David M. Kamen, 1985, p11. (Thomas Torrance Papers (RG 16), Special Collections, Yale Divinity School Library, Box 6, Folder 92.)

67 'The Border Service Team'. *The Chinese Recorder*, March 1941, pp 153-154.

68 Junio, *Patriotic Cooperation*, p133.

of the Lifan region but without specifically naming the Qiang, he mentioned Torrance's discovery of the people there, adding that, 'Their customs, their religion, their prayers, their sacrifices partake of the nature of Old Testament religion. They have been open to the impact of Christianity.'[69]

In 1941 Mabel Nowlin, a leader in Christian educational work in China, visited the region with some friends and was taken up by Shao Yunting to stay in Luobozhai for a few days. Making no reference to Torrance she described life in the village: 'Their way of living reminded us of what the Old Testament records of tribal days of the Israelites. The houses looked Palestinian, too, – flat roofed, square, built of stone and adobe, the ground floor for their sheep and cattle, the next floor for the family, and the roof for threshing and storing their corn, beans and other produce.'[70] Describing their beliefs as 'kind of animistic', she observed that the white stone was 'the symbol of their religion'.[71] As for the role of the religious leaders, they 'exorcised spirits of disease' and conducted marriage and funeral ceremonies but also worked the land like their neighbours. One of the locals told her that their religious book had been eaten by a goat. Intrigued by how the Christian message might be best presented to the Qiang, Nowlin was planning to search for more information in the *Journal of the West China Border Research Society* on her return to Chengdu.

In the spring of 1943 Shao Yunting rented a house in Luobozhai and before long people were gathering for meetings. In July he went on furlough and was replaced by Fan Wenhai, a theological graduate of the WCUU who was to run the primary school and meet regularly with any villagers wanting to study the Bible. In the summer Fan was joined by a small BSD team composed of volunteers with medical, dental, and theological training, who, as Zhang Bohuai, the head of the BSD, described, had come to serve the local people, make a simple survey of the community, and carry out 'an intensive evangelistic program among the Ch'iang people'.[72] To their surprise, when the team started preaching, 'Men, women and children came in great

69 Daniel Sheets Dye. 'The Challenge of the Far Western Border'. *The Chinese Recorder*, July 1940, p440.
70 Mabel Nowlin. 'A Vacation in the Tribes Country'. *The Chinese Recorder*, Nov 1941, p588.
71 Ibid., p589.
72 W. B. Djang (Zhang Bohuai). 'The 1943 Summer Missionary Work of the Border Mission'. WCMN, May to Dec 1943, p90. (This was the final edition of the West China Missionary News.)

numbers', displaying an enthusiasm which was assumed to be because 'the preaching of the Gospel was a new teaching'.[73] Once again, there seemed to be no awareness of Torrance's earlier visits or of the work done by Chen Bingling and Gou Pinsan.

The numbers in Luobozhai eventually became 'too big and unwieldy for effective preaching' and it was suggested that people invite their neighbours to a meeting in their home, which the preachers would attend.[74] Seven families volunteered their homes and the response was so positive that Zhang summed the Luobozhai venture up as the beginning of a new era both for the village and for the Qiang people generally.

---

73 Ibid., p91.
74 Ibid.

Chapter 24

Criticism

In a review of *China's First Missionaries* Daniel Dye wrote of Torrance's 'uncanny sense of seeing the significant' and described the parallels Torrance had found between Qiang and Old Testament practices as 'astonishing to say the least'.[1] However, Dye was clearly surprised by the more direct association Torrance had made between the Qiang and Israel and acknowledged that some would not accept his conclusions.

Among those who rejected Torrance's conclusions was David Graham, who made his objections clear in his own 1942 article describing the customs of the Qiang.[2] The paper stemmed from his participation in a 1941 Border Services Department (BSD) summer programme, an opportunity for which Graham acknowledged his gratitude to Wang Wenxuan, the Nationalist Minister of Education, and Zhang Bohuai, head of the BSD.

In line with the general trend of foreigners taking a back-seat, Graham had by this time relinquished his post as museum curator to Harvard-educated archaeologist Zheng Dekun but he was still teaching at the university and with his collecting expeditions for the Smithsonian Institute, a doctoral thesis on religion in Sichuan from the University of Chicago, and further training from Harvard in archaeology and anthropology, he had much to contribute to the summer programme. In the company of a sociology student he spent several weeks visiting the towns of Miansi, Weizhou, and Maoxian, and the villages of Dongmenwai, Longxi, Qiangfeng, Buwa (on the hillside above Weizhou), and Heping, as well as the Wasi domain of King Suo.

This was Graham's first expedition to the area specifically for cultural research and he described his paper as a preliminary study, expressing the hope, presumably with Torrance's Israelite hypothesis

---

1   WCMN, July-August 1937, p39.
2   David C. Graham. 'The Customs of the Ch'iang'. JWCBRS, Vol 14, 1942, pp95-97.

in mind, that it would encourage further research into a people 'who are so little known and in some places so misunderstood'.[3] There is no indication that Graham had, by this time, personally witnessed the ceremonies he described and although there was no reference to Torrance's works in his footnotes, he listed three of them in the bibliography and it seems likely that these had supplemented his own observations.[4]

Beginning with a general introduction to the Qiang, Graham included a brief history and geography and a description of their daily lives and customs. As with Torrance, the Qiang had clearly made a good impression on him and he described them as 'strong, industrious and generally of good morals'.[5] He made no direct reference in this first part to Torrance's Israelite theory but, having described the Qiang and Chinese as similar in appearance, he did note that Qiang noses were slightly thinner and then added a comment that may have puzzled readers unfamiliar with Torrance's theory: 'There are probably no more convex or "Roman" noses among them than among other eastern Asiatic races.'[6]

Despite his assertion of similarity, one marked difference Graham had found among the Qiang was that the epicanthic fold, so typical of Asian eyes, was frequently absent.[7] In an earlier field diary he had noted that Tibetan eyes often had a 'Mongolian slant', so this lack of epicanthic fold clearly set the Qiang apart from both their Chinese and their Tibetan neighbours and was perhaps one of the reasons why earlier travellers like Isabella Bird and William Haines-Watson had perceived Aryan or European similarities among the Qiang.[8] It had also contributed to Dr Morse's agreement with Torrance that the Qiang were 'of an Aryan or non-Mongolic stock'.[9] In 1937 the JWCBRS had issued a supplement containing Morse's anthropometric measurements, which

3   Ibid.
4   TT: *The History, Customs and Religion of the Ch'iang* (1920); 'The Religion of the Ch'iang' (1923); 'The Basic Spiritual Conceptions of the Religion of the Ch'iang' (1934).
5   Ibid., p98.
6   Ibid., p72.
7   Ibid.
8   David C. Graham. Diary No. 10, August 11, 1930, cited in Hartmut Walravens, *David Crockett Graham (1884–1961) as Zoological Collector and Anthropologist in China*. Wiesbaden, Germany: Harrassowitz Verlag. 2006, p214.
9   TT diary to children, July 26, 1929.

showed 99 out of 111 Qiang lacking the epicanthic fold.[10] Morse also noted that almost half of these same Qiang had wavy hair, unlike the more typical straight hair of many Chinese.

The latter part of Graham's paper focused on Qiang religious customs and it was here that his objections to Torrance's theory became more evident. Stressing that 'The Ch'iang are not monotheists, and there is no certain evidence that they ever have been', he gave clear evidence of polytheism.[11] In some villages he had discovered 'five major gods and twelve minor gods', as well as some Chinese gods.[12] Despite this, Graham was in no doubt that the Qiang had a supreme god whom he described as one who 'is righteous and pure, controls everything everywhere under heaven and on earth, requires righteousness among men, protects men and domestic animals, gives rain and good crops, and helps people secure children and a numerous posterity'.[13]

In Mushang the priest told Graham that he worshipped 'beside the greatest god twelve other gods'.[14] In some places these twelve minor gods were represented by twelve smaller stones surrounding the usual larger white stone. Graham had seen these on several housetops in Longxi Village and Torrance had described them in his 1922 paper on the religion of the Qiang.[15] According to Graham, the role of these lesser twelve gods was protection of the home, the livestock, the grain and the harvest, finances, childbirth and children, men and boys, women and girls, and keeping demons from the home, as well as two of them representing the male and female ancestors of the Qiang.[16]

The remoteness of Mushang and Longxi perhaps indicates that this worship of one supreme god and twelve lesser gods was more typical of traditional Qiang religious beliefs than the wider mix described by Graham above.

In their exploration of biblical parallels, Gou Pinsan and Torrance had both wondered if there might be a connection between the number twelve in Qiang culture – also found in the twelve flags and twelve sheets of paper present at rooftop sacrifices – and the twelve

---

10 W. R. Morse. 'Schedule of physical anthropological measurements and observations on ten ethnic groups of Szechwan Province, West China'. 1937 supplement to JWCBRS, Vol 8, 1936, pp129-134.

11 Graham, 'The Customs of the Ch'iang', p86.

12 Ibid.

13 Ibid., p87.

14 Ibid., p86.

15 TT. 'The Religion of the Ch'iang'. JNCBRAS, Vol 54, 1923, p152.

16 Graham, 'The Customs of the Ch'iang', p89.

sons of Jacob from whom the tribes of Israel were descended, who had perhaps become deified over the centuries.

Deification of people was not unusual in China and was something Graham had referred to in a later work on folk religion in Sichuan.[17] Some human beings with extraordinary abilities were deified after their deaths, thus enabling people to seek help from them, and he had come across a saying about ancestors in general that: 'Living they are people, after their death they are gods.'[18] Like the term 'god' in English, the Chinese term 'shen' (神) has a broad application. It is used for the God of the Bible but it can equally be used for a spirit or even for a man-made idol. Graham had observed that some Chinese priests in Sichuan had a ceremony for transforming a clay figure into a deity. However, it is clear from Graham's description of the supreme god that he differed considerably from the other Qiang 'gods', and it was the centrality and nature of the Qiang supreme god which had provoked Torrance to explore further and wonder if an earlier monotheistic concept of a supreme god had been overlaid with belief in other deities.

Not included in Graham's list of gods but described by him without explanation as 'the second god' was the Abba Mula (Torrance's Abba Malah) – the roll of paper containing a monkey skull and various monkey innards.[19] Gou Pinsan and Torrance had both described the Abba Mula as having a kind of mediatory role between the Qiang people and the spiritual realm and Graham's description also reflects this in some measure: 'No priest is without this god, for without it he would be powerless. It is his patron or guardian deity and instructor . . . Abba Mula has a permanent place in the hearts of the Ch'iang.'[20]

Graham's description of the Abba Mula placed more emphasis on the monkey remains than on the roll itself, even though Gou Pinsan, in his 1925 account, had stated that traditionally the paper was wrapped around the figure of a person made of coarse grass, which had only recently been replaced by the monkey skull. This was confirmed in a later work by Graham containing a translation of a Qiang priest's chant: 'A person makes a straw image and binds it with a cord. The sacred book binds the straw image.'[21] This suggests both that it was

17 David C. Graham. *Folk Religion in Southwest China*. The Smithsonian Institute. 1961, pp175, 200.
18 Ibid., p119.
19 Graham, 'The Customs of the Ch'iang', p87.
20 Ibid., p87-88.
21 Graham, *Customs and Religion of the Ch'iang*, 1958, p84.

customary for a straw figure to be in the centre of the roll of paper and that the Qiang saw the roll of blank paper as representing a book with spiritual significance.

In his 1937 book Torrance had made a connection between this sacred roll of paper and the Qiang tradition of lost scriptures: 'Originally, the Chiang had their own scriptures, or writings. With the loss of the knowledge of letters, what was once a sacred roll of their law is now only a mere cylinder of white paper. But it preserves the form. It represents the reality. This explains their veneration for it.'[22] In contrast, Graham assumed that the lost book tradition was simply a legend, on the basis that several tribes in Burma also had legends about a lost book.

Regarding the sacrifices, Graham took issue with Torrance's use of the word 'lamb' and pointed out that they were, in most places, a full-grown goat. In his book Torrance had deliberately used the term 'lamb' rather than sheep or goat, presumably to emphasise the connection for his Christian readership with Jesus as the Lamb of God. However, as early as 1920 Torrance had noted that the 'animals for the sacrifices are bulls, goats and fowls' and that the 'goats must be full grown young males', and although his use of 'lamb' is perhaps a case of narrative licence, it does not contradict the actual parallel between Qiang sacrificial practices and those of the Israelites.[23] The book of Leviticus stipulates that sacrifices could be bulls, goats, one-year old lambs (i.e. a full-grown animal), or – for the poorer Israelites – turtledoves or pigeons.[24]

Like Torrance, Graham noted that the sacrificial animal 'must be of only one color, and unblemished – that is, its horns, ears, etc, must have no defect'.[25] But he clearly felt Torrance had placed too much emphasis on the atoning role of the sacrifices. In Graham's understanding the sacrifices were 'a gift to the deity' and their primary purpose was 'to make contact with the god in order to secure his favor and help'. He did acknowledge that 'Forgiveness of sins naturally is included in the list of favors sought', but added that this 'is far from the only purpose for the offering of the sacrifice'.[26] With regard to the blood, Graham denied that it had any cleansing power but offered no clear alternative explanation: 'The shedding of blood is a natural part of the sacrifice.

---

22 TT, *China's First Missionaries*, p74.
23 TT, *The History, Customs and Religion of the Ch'iang*, pp29, 31.
24 E.g. Leviticus 5:7, 23:18-19.
25 Graham, 'The Customs of the Ch'iang', p94.
26 Ibid., pp93-94.

The blood is not shed for remission of sins, but is a necessary part of the performance.' As for the sprinkling of the blood after the sacrifice, this was simply 'to show that the sacrifice has been performed'.

A SHEEP BEING PREPARED FOR SACRIFICE BY QIANG VILLAGERS
WITH THE SCROLL OR ABBA MALAH RESTING ON ITS HEAD
(Courtesy of Gordon Ip, 2008)

Torrance had understood the blood to play a central role in Qiang sacrificial rituals, with it being sprinkled at the sacred grove on the white stone, the sacred tree, the paper flags, and the altar.[27] He had also seen it sprinkled on the lintel and doorposts during a rooftop sacrificial ceremony, and on a young male child at his naming ceremony.[28] It was daubed on the child again with melted animal fat at three years old. In these various rituals Torrance had seen echoes of the Mosaic practices in which blood, sometimes called 'the blood of the covenant', was sprinkled on the altar, the priests, the people, and on the mercy seat in the tabernacle.[29] Blood was also used in Israelite rituals to cleanse people and homes from leprous infection.[30] Torrance was in no doubt that the purifying role of the blood was a shared aspect of Israelite and Qiang sacrifices.

At the end of his section on religious customs Graham summed up his main criticisms of Torrance's theory under the heading, 'The

27 TT, *China's First Missionaries*, pp79, 91, opp p95.
28 Ibid., pp105-106, 114.
29 E.g. Exodus 24:8, 29:21; Leviticus 8:15, 16:15.
30 E.g. Leviticus 14.

Tradition of Hebrew Origin'.[31] Describing the theory as most unlikely he reiterated that the Qiang were not monotheists, that their physical characteristics would not persuade an anthropologist of any Hebrew origin, and that forgiveness of sins was a part but not the primary purpose of their sacrifices. To this he added his view that the rod with the snake carved round it which featured in Torrance's book was a pilgrim's walking stick from Mount Emei rather than a Qiang sacred rod – but unfortunately without a photo for comparison. He did, however, acknowledge that Qiang priests very occasionally had a more crude version to assist in exorcising demons.

According to Graham, other parallels perceived by Torrance, such as the flat-roofed houses, watchtowers, and white stones, were found elsewhere in western Sichuan and were not unique to the Qiang. Finally, he questioned why the Qiang had no taboo on eating pork and how it was that neither they nor the Chinese were aware of their Hebrew origins, both questions he would return to in a later work.

Although he acknowledged the sincerity of Torrance's relationship with the Qiang, Graham described his and Gou Pinsan's research as 'seeking for facts to prove a theory' and Torrance's book as the finest example he had seen 'of the results of subjective research in the interpretation of the life and customs of a somewhat primitive people'.[32] As far as Graham was concerned, the key to understanding the Qiang and their culture was precisely 'a knowledge of the psychology of primitive people' and it was obvious to him that the Qiang, with their lack of education and scientific understanding, would tend to see misfortunes and natural disasters as caused by 'the working of mysterious forces that may do good or harm'.[33] And it naturally followed that the 'priests, the gods, the ceremonies and the sacred implements are surcharged with mysterious power' which provide blessing and protection.[34]

A certain irony could be seen here in relation to Graham's own Christian background of religious ceremonies, sacred elements, and belief in an invisible but powerful God. However, Graham was perhaps less inclined to emphasise the supernatural aspects of Christianity and had espoused a more liberal, rational approach than some of his

---

31   Graham, 'The Customs of the Ch'iang', pp95-97.
32   Ibid., p96.
33   Ibid., pp96, 86.
34   Ibid.

fellow missionaries, an approach which, according to authors Charles McKhann and Alan Waxman, included 'a large dose of progressive humanism.'[35]

Gou Pinsan was no longer around to address Graham's charge of primitiveness but it is of note that Gou was probably the most educated and socially accomplished Qiang known to Torrance and Graham and it was his reading of ancient Israelite history and customs in the books of Exodus and Leviticus which had convinced him of their shared origins.

Whether coincidentally or in response to Graham, Zhang Bohuai, writing about the future of the Qiang, took issue with the notion of primitivism: 'It would be a mistake if anyone should draw the conclusion that these simple dwellers of the mountainside are primitive aborigines who have neglected and been neglected by the rest of the world during past centuries. On the contrary, they are the remnants of a race that has had a long and glorious history in China almost from the beginning of Chinese civilization.'[36]

In his 1942 conclusion Graham acknowledged how incomplete his study was and that 'the great variation in language and mores in different localities, and the natural reticence of the people make it extremely difficult to understand and to interpret accurately the life and ideals of these people.'[37] This was perhaps a factor in his emphasis on description rather than analysis, for example in his lack of explanation about the role of the blood and in his dismissal of any historical origin regarding the lost book tradition, rather than questioning why tribes in the same wider region would share a similar legend.

Graham's first paper was followed in 1945 by two further papers, one on Qiang incantations and exorcism of demons and another on their religious chants, and in 1958 he combined all three papers in his book, *The Customs and Religion of the Ch'iang,* published ten years after

35 Charles F. McKhann and Alan Waxman. 'David Crockett Graham: American Missionary and Scientist in Sichuan, 1911-1948'. In D. M. Glover et al. *Explorers and Scientists in China's Borderlands, 1880-1950.* University of Washington Press. 2012, p181.
36 W. B. Djang (Zhang Bohuai). 'The Decline and Possible Future of a Great Race, "The Ch'iang People"'. Unpublished manuscript, c.1948, pp2-3. Yale University Divinity School Library, Border Service Department of the Church of Christ in China Records, Series III, box 3, folder 1.
37 Graham, 'The Customs of the Ch'iang', p97.

his retirement to Colorado.[38] Valuable for its detailed observations, the book included sixteen pages of photographs depicting the Qiang people and various aspects of their culture.

Although Graham chose to omit 'history' from the title of his book, he had added further historical observations and declared at the outset, before any mention of Torrance's theory, that he 'had not found or heard of one reference on the oracle bones or in any Chinese history that would indicate that the ancestors of the Ch'iang of western Szechwan migrated eastward from western Asia, or that they are descendants of the Israelites.'[39]

Instead, Graham assumed a direct connection between the twentieth century Qiang and the people represented by the Qiang character in early oracle bone inscriptions of the Shang period (c.1600-1046 BC). He also asserted that there was 'strong evidence that in ancient times they lived in northeast China' before migrating westward to Gansu and Sichuan.[40] His footnote in relation to this northeastern origin referred to three different works, one of which Graham referred to as 'The conquering of the Ch'iang by the Emperor Hsiao I', although the actual title was, 'On the conquering of Ch'iang Fang by Emperor Hsiao I'.[41] In contrast to the broader term 'Qiang', the term 'Qiang Fang' indicated a more specific Qiang polity located to the northwest of Shang territory, which was frequently attacked by the Shang people. Although the author, Liu Chaoyang, had concluded that these early Qiang had been pushed westwards from this location northwest of Shang, he gave no indication that they were ever in China's northeast.

Another work cited in the same footnote was *The Birth of China* by Sinologist Herrlee Creel which, rather than supporting a northeastern origin and a definite connection between today's Qiang and those recorded on the oracle bones, made it clear that although 'Qiang' was the name used by the Shang for some of their neighbours, the word 'was also used in a wider sense as a general term for at least a part of

---

38 David C. Graham. 'Incantations and the exorcism of demons among the Ch'iang'. JWCBRS, Vol 16a, 1945, pp52-56; 'The "Sacred Books" or religious chants of the Ch'iang'. JWCBRS, Vol 16a, 1945, pp57-71; *The Customs and Religion of the Ch'iang*, Smithsonian Miscellaneous Collections. 1958. 135 (1):1–110.

39 Graham, *The Customs and Religion of the Ch'iang*, p2.

40 Ibid., p4.

41 Liu Chaoyang, 'On the Conquering of Ch'iang Fang by Emperor Hsiao I'. In *Studia Serica*, (Journal of the Chinese Cultural Studies Research Institute, West China Union University), Vol 5, 1946.

the barbarians of the north and west'.[42] Creel was not confident that the Qiang of the Shang period were a distinct people group and viewed any link between them and today's Qiang as 'very hard to determine'.[43] He pointed out that early Chinese books gave the meaning of Qiang as 'western barbarians who raise sheep', a definition found in the first century AD Chinese dictionary, the *Shuowen Jiezi*, which indicates that by the Han period the Qiang were seen as non-Chinese living between the Chinese and Central Asia.

The third work cited in Graham's footnote in support of a northeastern origin and a westward migration to Gansu and Sichuan is the 'Account of the Southwestern Barbarians', in Chapter 116 of Sima Qian's *Historical Records*.[44] The Qiang are not actually mentioned by name in this chapter but it does mention the states of Ran and Mang, whose territory in the Han period included today's Qiang region and whose inhabitants are thought to have included some Qiang. Although the reference indirectly points to these Qiang, it does not support Graham's assertion that they came from northeastern China.

Sima Qian's *Historical Records* does, however, contain chapters which refer specifically to the Qiang. The first chapter includes the Qiang in a list of people to the west of the Chinese in early Chinese history and the sixth chapter, describing the reign of the first emperor of Qin (r.221-210 BC), situates the Qiang to the west of Lintao in Gansu, beyond the western border of Qin territory. As James Edgar had mentioned back in 1920, the *Historical Records* also includes Chinese envoy Zhang Qian's late second century BC account of having to negotiate hostile Qiang territory in the northwest on his return from Central Asia.[45]

Although the Han dynasty was arguably the most significant period of interaction with Qiang tribes in China's history, and Graham included both the *Book of Han* and the *Book of the Later Han* in his bibliography, after two pages of early ancient history Graham's account moved from the eighth century BC to one brief reference to the Han emperor Wudi, and then to the fourth century AD and later history. Admittedly, he noted that with no space for a full historical account he, as author, was only mentioning 'such facts and events as he regards as

42 Herrlee G. Creel. *The Birth of China*. Jonathan Cape Ltd, London. 1936, p215.
43 Ibid., p213.
44 See Watson, *Records of the Grand Historian of China*, Vol II, pp290-296.
45 J. H. Edgar. WCMN, 1920, May pp5-9; June pp23-27.

most important and most interesting',[46] but in so doing he had omitted key factors such as the mention in the 'Account of the Western Qiang', in the *Book of the Later Han*, of a linear history beginning with the first named Qiang ancestor, Wuyi Yuanjian, of the fifth century BC, who is described as of unknown origins. According to this account, Wuyi had been captured by the Qin state but had escaped to the region of eastern Qinghai, west of the Chinese, where the local Qiang appointed him as their chief. His descendants flourished and became powerful Qiang tribal leaders in China's northwest during the Han period.

The earlier *Book of Han*, completed in AD 111, is one of the most reliable historical sources for the Qiang of the early Han period. One of its compilers was Ban Gu whose brother, Ban Chao, was commander of China's northwest during the latter half of the first century AD. This placed Ban Chao in close proximity to the Qiang, who were clearly seen as foreigners with whom the Chinese were frequently in conflict, largely due to China's northwestern expansion which threatened Qiang grazing grounds in Gansu, Qinghai, and Xinjiang.

Unlike other non-Chinese groups of that era such as the Xiongnu or Yuezhi, these Qiang were not a cohesive group but were scattered groups who obviously shared traits similar enough for the Chinese to describe them as 'Qiang'. They were sometimes referred to as the 'various' Qiang, which was not an expression used for other non-Chinese peoples of the period and points to diversity within a wider generic group.[47] Chapter 69 of the *Book of Han*, which recorded major clashes between the Chinese and the Qiang of the Qinghai region, describes 'an alliance with more than 200 of the various Qiang-type chieftains, who resolved their mutual enmity and exchanged hostages, swearing oaths of allegiance'.[48]

The *Book of Han* describes these various Qiang groups as extending from Qinghai and Gansu to the Kunlun foothills south of Xinjiang's Tarim basin. There is even one mention in Chapter 96 of some Qiang 'south of Nandou', which seems to have been west of the Karakoram

---

46 Graham, *The Customs and Religion of the Ch'iang*, p2.

47 诸羌. See for example the *Book of Han*, Chapter 79: 'The Biography of Feng Fengshi'. The Chinese general, Feng Fengshi, feared that the 'various Qiang' in Gansu would unite and easily defeat his troops. This was indeed the case until Emperor Yuan (r. 48-33 BC) sent 60,000 reinforcements and these Qiang, described as living deep in the mountains, were defeated.

48 Rachel Meakin. 'Qiang 羌 References in the Book of Han 汉书, Part 1'. (www.academia.edu)

range in northern Pakistan.[49] According to historian Igor P'iankov, the territory of Nandou extended south across Afghanistan's Wakhan Corridor into Gilgit in Pakistan, which would suggest that these Qiang were possibly to the south of Gilgit.[50] Professor Liu Enlan, a contemporary of Graham who had been evacuated from Nanjing to Chengdu, gave a comprehensive picture of a broad swath of Qiang who 'once occupied the territories all the way from Shensi [Shaanxi] to east of the Pamir and south to Yunnan'.[51]

Although much Qiang historical research has been written from a Sinocentric perspective which tends to embed them in an ancient Chinese past, it seems that some of these westernmost Qiang were more closely associated with a multi-cultural Central Asian-influenced environment. Their locations in Xinjiang were relatively close to territory which had come under the influence of empires further west, for example Bactria and northern India where Persian and Greek influence had been so significant. The ancient Khorasan Highway, mentioned by James Finn in *The Jews of China*, had connected Bactria with western Iran and Mesopotamia and, as Professor Seligman had pointed out, lapis lazuli from mines in Afghanistan had become a prized commodity as far away as Egypt. In the fifth century BC, Herodotus wrote of tribes from today's northeastern Libya being relocated to Bactria by King Darius of Persia, an indication of the distances people and goods were travelling.[52]

In his conclusion Graham again stressed that many references in Chinese histories 'indicate that the Ch'iang migrated westward from their early home in northeast China', also adding that 'Many have said that the Ch'iang have probably come from eastern China.'[53] In this adamance about a northeastern or eastern origin he was in danger of the very thing of which he had accused Torrance, although in this case it seems to have been seeking for facts to disprove a theory.

---

49 *Book of Han*, Chapter 96, 'An Account of the Western Regions'. For a discussion of the location of these Qiang south of Nandou (难兜), see R. Meakin, 'Qiang 羌 References in the Book of Han 汉书, Part 2'. pp26-27, n.127 and n.129. (www.academia.edu)

50 Igor V. P'iankov. 'The Ethnic History of the Sakas'. *Bulletin of the Asia Institute*, Vol 8, 1994, p44.

51 Liu Enlan. 'The Tribes of Li-Fan County in Northwest Szechwan'. JWCBRS, Vol 15, 1944-45, p7.

52 Herodotus. *Histories*. Ed. Tom Griffith. Wordsworth Editions Limited. 1996, p376.

53 Graham, *The Customs and Religion of the Ch'iang*, p100.

By affirming a solidly Chinese history for the Qiang Graham was also conforming to the Nationalist project of a united China and the absorption of the border peoples. In their essay, 'David Crockett Graham in Chinese Intellectual History', Geng Jing and Jeff Kyong-McClain note that the Ministry of Education, to whom Graham was indebted for summer trips in 1941 and 1942, 'exerted increasing pressure on scholars to tell the story of Chinese history as the story of the harmonious integration of various people-groups.'[54] They also point out that the Nationalist state 'became increasingly aggressive in bringing the borderlands and their inhabitants under its control, and it encouraged anthropologists to submit their services to the state.'[55]

In contrast, Torrance's theory of Hebrew origins flew in the face of Nationalist efforts to bring the Qiang more firmly into the Chinese fold and a national sense of identity, something which depended in part on the diminishing of cultural differences. Evidence of this can be seen in a 1945 BSD paper by Lu Yu, who concluded that the main stumbling blocks to this unity were the clothing and language of the Qiang: 'Changing the way they dress will of course be easy ... If we can continue to positively apply education, the Ch'iang-min language will be naturally eliminated in the not-too-distant future. The Ch'iang-min will be completely assimilated and "Ch'iang-min" will become only a historical term.'[56]

In 1959 a brief review of Graham's book appeared in the journal *Man* by anthropologist Maurice Freedman of the London School of Economics, later Professor of Social Anthropology at Oxford University.[57] While appreciating certain aspects, Freedman described the work as reflecting a 'random method of collection' and he seemed somewhat perplexed by Graham's early comment that he had found nothing indicating Israelite descent or an eastward Qiang migration from western Asia. As in his 1942 paper, Graham had only specifically addressed Torrance's Israelite theory at the end of the book, where he reiterated his earlier objections, adding with perhaps a slightly softened stance that, 'While there are parallels in their cultural traits to those of

54 Geng Jing and Jeff Kyong-McClain. 'David Crockett Graham in Chinese Intellectual History'. In D. M. Glover et al, *Explorers and Scientists*, p223.
55 Ibid., p222-223.
56 Lu Yu, 'Seen and Heard on the Border', p12.
57 Maurice Freedman. *Man*, Vol 59 (Sept 1959), p172. Published by the Royal Anthropological Institute of Great Britain and Ireland. https://www.jstor.org/stable/2796790

the Hebrews, there is none that cannot be very satisfactorily explained without reference to Jewish customs.'[58]

Clearly unhappy with Freedman's review, Graham responded in a 1960 issue of *Man* with an explanation that shed new light on his research and some of the motivation behind it: 'I was requested to make a study of the Ch'iang people by some Chinese leaders. In almost every article and the one book published about them in English, they were declared to be monotheists, and one writer asserted that they were descendants of the ancient Israelites. These leaders wanted to know whether or not these things were true.'[59]

Perhaps responding to Freedman's comment regarding a 'random method of collection', Graham acknowledged that he had only been able to travel to the Qiang area in his two-month summer vacations and for shorter trips at other times. This had been further limited during the Second World War when the Chinese government eventually prohibited westerners from making research trips to the tribal areas of West China, after which Graham had hired some Qiang men to come to Chengdu for extended periods to help with his research. As a result, his summer trips had primarily been his Smithsonian collecting trip with Torrance in 1933 and his BSD summer trips of 1941 and 1942, something which illustrates how timely Torrance's own years of association with the Qiang had been, with relative freedom of travel and little pressure to conform to any government narrative.

Ironically, Graham's opposition to Torrance's theory actually served to keep his and Torrance's research in the public eye for longer than might otherwise have been the case and it is not hard to find their names juxtaposed in current discussions of the Qiang, both in Western and Chinese material. Chinese scholar Bian Simei has even coined the term 'the Torrance-Graham debate', although it is not clear that Torrance ever responded to Graham.[60] Owing in part to this interest, several works by Torrance and Graham have been translated

---

58 Graham, *The Customs and Religion of the Ch'iang*, p100.

59 David C. Graham. *Man*, Vol 60, Jan 1960, p10. Published by the Royal Anthropological Institute of Great Britain and Ireland. https://www.jstor.org/stable/2797902.

60 Bian Simei. 'Qiang wei heren: 20 shiji qianqi xifang xuezhe de Qiangmin yanjiu' (Who are the Qiang People: A Study of the Qiang People by Western Scholars in the Early 20th Century). *Yunnan shifan daxue xuebao*, Vol 45, No 3, May 2013, pp9-16.

into Chinese and both men are seen as significant contributors to Qiang research in the first half of the twentieth century.

McKhann and Waxman describe Graham's book as 'a model of dispassionate scholarship' compared to Torrance's work but their comparison overlooks Torrance's earlier writings, which have more equivalence with Graham's work.[61] Instead, they refer only to Torrance's 1937 book, which in style and purpose – and passion – was intended less as an academic work and more as a means of drawing the attention of the wider public to the Old Testament parallels perceived by Torrance and Gou Pinsan. McKhann and Waxman also describe Graham's 'systematic rebuttal of Torrance's arguments' as appearing to be 'wholly justified' but without a critical look at Graham's rebuttal or a detailed examination of Torrance's theory.[62]

One of the key arguments in Graham's rebuttal was that the Qiang had no taboo on eating pork.[63] However, as Margaret Scott points out in her study of the Qiang in early AD, 'Pigs are never mentioned in the records of animals captured from the Ch'iang; they cannot be kept by nomads, and may have been unknown among the Ch'iang.'[64] It seems that the practice of eating pork was only adopted by the Qiang once they had become more sedentary and come under Chinese influence. In a ceremony attended by a Qiang friend of the author, the Qiang priest declared in a chant that it was only with the arrival of the pig that they could present a pork offering to their ancestors – which hints at both these Chinese customs being later additions for the Qiang.

Graham's argument regarding pork rests on the assumption that any Israelites reaching China would have been strictly observant and would have continued to be so down to the present day. However, even before they went into exile, the Israelites of the northern kingdom had abandoned many orthodox biblical practices. Jewish history records that after Israel split into two kingdoms in about 930 BC, King Jeroboam of the northern kingdom rejected the Levitical priesthood in Jerusalem and 'made houses on high places, and made priests from among all the people who were not of the sons of Levi.'[65] He also

---

61   McKhann and Waxman, 'American Missionary and Scientist', p203.
62   Ibid., p205.
63   Graham, *The Customs and Religion of the Ch'iang*, p100.
64   Margaret I. Scott. 'A Study of the Ch'iang with Special Reference to their Settlements in China from the Second to the Fifth Century A. D.' (Unpublished PhD thesis.) Newnham College, Cambridge. 1952, p25.
65   1 Kings 12:31. See also 2 Chronicles 11:14-15.

introduced a new feast in the eighth month, which included burning incense on altars erected for his new order of priests. Abijah, king of Judah in the south, accused these northerners of making priests 'like the people of other lands' to such a degree that 'whoever comes to consecrate himself with a young bull and seven rams, even he may become a priest of what are no gods.'[66] Even in Judah, a later prophet named Zephaniah accused the people of worshipping the host of heaven on their housetops.[67]

In the latter half of the eighth century BC, contemporary with the beginning of China's Eastern Zhou period, various Assyrian attacks resulted in the eastward exile of many from this renegade northern kingdom. The author of 2 Kings 17 lists the sins seen as the cause of this expulsion, which clearly included polytheism: the Israelites had revered other gods, adopted the customs of their neighbours, and 'built for themselves high places in all their towns, from watchtower to fortified city. They set for themselves sacred pillars and Asherim on every high hill and under every green tree, and there they burned incense on all the high places as the nations did.'[68] It is clear from this that any Israelites arriving in China were unlikely to have been adhering strictly to biblical laws.

Scott also refers to the custom recorded in the 'Account of the Western Qiang' in the *Book of the Later Han*, that if a brother dies another brother will marry the widow.[69] The similarity between this and the 1881 stone tablet edict translated by Torrance, which forbade the custom in the Lifan district of 'a man marrying the wife of a deceased elder or younger brother', suggests some cultural continuity from the Qiang of the Han period to today's Qiang. Graham acknowledged that the similar practice in Deuteronomy 25:5-6, to which Torrance had drawn attention, was a 'real parallel'.[70]

With regard to the sacred rod, there is no doubt that the rod pictured in Torrance's book was more elaborate and refined than the average priest's rod. However, although Graham questioned the provenance of that particular rod, he did describe a cruder version in his 1958 book: 'Sometimes on the side of the cane is the imprint of a wild vine that

66   2 Chronicles 13:9.
67   Zephaniah 1:5.
68   2 Kings 17:9-11. Asherim: sacred trees or wooden poles set up near the altars of various gods, or more particularly of the goddess Asherah.
69   Scott, 'A Study of the Ch'iang', p35.
70   Graham, *The Customs and Religion of the Ch'iang*, p97.

grew around the limb . . . and at the top a snake head is carved so that the imprint of the vine and the carved snake head give the appearance of a snake coiled around the cane.' Graham was inclined to think the cane was a ritual item borrowed from the Daoist priests, with the Qiang 'making some adaptations of their own'.[71] Torrance was more inclined to think that, if there was any connection at all, the dragon-carved rods of the Buddhist priests and the *duangongs* were degradations of the Qiang rod,[72] and whereas Graham understood the rod to be used by the Qiang priests solely for exorcism, with the snake increasing their spiritual efficacy, Torrance had also seen it set up in the sacred grove at a sacrificial ceremony.

In the biblical parallel referred to by Torrance, the Israelites were facing a plague of snakes and Moses was commanded by God to set a bronze snake on a pole. Anyone looking at the bronze snake would recover from the snake bites.[73] Centuries later, when the northern kingdom was taken into exile and Hezekiah was king of Judah, this snake on a pole or 'Nehushtan' had become an idol to which people were burning incense.[74] In his desire to return to orthodox temple worship, Hezekiah broke the idol in pieces. Torrance clearly considered it feasible that this Israelite idol, associated with healing and deliverance, may have been copied in some form by the northern kingdom and taken with them into exile.

A century after Hezekiah, King Josiah of Judah ordered repairs to be carried out in the temple in Jerusalem, during which 'the book of the law of the Lord given by Moses' was re-discovered, having lain neglected for some years.[75] Josiah tore his clothes in grief when the book was read to him, distraught that 'our fathers have not observed the word of the Lord, to do according to all that is written in this book'.[76] The northern kingdom would already have lost this book in a sense when they cut themselves off from the temple worship of the south and eventually went into exile, but it is clear that this book or scroll of 'the law of the Lord' had been central to early Israelite society and may well have continued to exist in the folklore of the exiles and their descendants.

---

71 Ibid., p57.
72 TT, *China's First Missionaries,* p101.
73 Numbers 21:8-9.
74 2 Kings 18:4.
75 2 Chronicles 34:14.
76 Ibid., 34:21.

In his 1958 book, Graham again dismissed the lost book as a legend: 'It is well-known that the Ch'iang have no written language. How, then, can they have sacred books?'[77] As far as he was concerned the only 'sacred books' the Qiang had ever had were their oral chants and a pictorial book used by some priests for divination. However, this didn't take into consideration the Qiang people's own certainty, based on their oral history, that they had once had both a script and a sacred book. Nor did it allow for the possibility of a previously settled people becoming nomadic, adopting other spoken languages as they migrated, and gradually losing their own written language.

Although Graham had used the existence of the lost book tradition among tribes in Burma as a basis for dismissing it as legend, he would have read Torrance's 1937 reference to the monotheistic beliefs of the Karen people of Burma, beliefs which had led other missionaries to suggest a link of some kind with the Old Testament, and caused Torrance to wonder about a connection with the Qiang.[78] In a 1922 study of the Karen people, Harry Marshall, who, like Graham, was with the American Baptist Foreign Missionary Society, had noted the Karen lost book tradition as well as the existence of Karen legends with biblical themes such as creation, the fall, the flood, and the building of a high edifice like the tower of Babel.[79] Marshall's understanding was that in ancient times the Karen had probably reached Burma from China's upper Yellow River region via Yunnan, a route which would have taken them through the Sichuan-Tibetan border area. There were clearly reasonable questions to be asked about this shared lost book legend, not least because the Qiang had their own stories of a great flood.[80] Marshall also recorded that in 1917, two years before Torrance's first trip to the Qiang, a local Burmese man named Ba Te

77 Graham, *The Customs and Religion of the Ch'iang*, p64.

78 TT, *China's First Missionaries*, p123.

79 Harry I. Marshall. 'The Karen People of Burma: A Study in Anthropology and Ethnology'. *The Ohio State University* Bulletin, Vol 26. University at Columbus. 1922, pp 10-11.

80 One version of the Qiang flood story is told within the context of defeating their enemies, the Ge people. The god, Aba Mubita, ordered all the Qiang who feared God to get into a cow-skin boat. He then sent a flood, after which he told his third son to go down to earth and check on the situation. He looked here, there, and everywhere, and saw the Re [Qiang] people who feared God sitting in the boat, but the birds, animals and bugs had all drowned, as had the savage Ge people, disappearing without a trace. (See Li Ming et al (eds). *Qiangzu wenxueshi* (A History of Qiang Literature). Sichuan minzu chubanshe. 1994, p84.)

had wondered about a possible link between the Karen and the Qiang, based in part on a linguistic similarity between the two names.[81]

Whatever the origin of the lost book legend, there was no doubt that the discovery of the Bible – another ancient sacred book telling of a sacrificial system, a supreme God, and a people exiled from their own land – had clearly struck a chord with some of the Qiang. Even in his early days among them, Torrance had seen how much the books of Exodus and Leviticus resonated with some of them, in marked contrast to the more common experience of enquirers initially focusing on the New Testament. This resonance perhaps helps to explain why some Qiang had been open to reading the Bible when for centuries they had resisted the encroachment of Tibetan and Chinese religious influence.

Another of Graham's arguments against Torrance's hypothesis was that if any Israelites had reached China and were still in evidence in the twentieth century, they would not have the dark eyes, dark yellow or brown skin, and straight or wavy dark hair of the Qiang.[82] However, by the time Graham's book was published in 1958 the modern state of Israel had been in existence for ten years and had received Jewish immigrants of diverse physical appearance from various countries, including India and Afghanistan – both bordering China, at least some of whom had dark eyes, brown skin, and straight or wavy hair.

In 1957, Itzhak Ben Zvi, the first president of Israel, described some of these Jewish communities in his book, *The Exiled and the Redeemed*.[83] Ben Zvi had also heard from Afghan Jews in Israel about the belief among the Afghan Afridi tribe of the now Muslim Pathans that they were 'descendants of the Israelites, more particularly, the sons of Ephraim'.[84] Like Torrance, Ben Zvi described the tradition found among the Bukharan Jews that some of their number had migrated further east and that 'they are direct descendants of the Ten Tribes'.[85] Ancient links between the Bukhara region and China are well-documented. Bukhara had been a Sogdian city and the Sogdians,

81 Marshall, 'The Karen People of Burma', p6. The text says this correspondence was August, 1914, but a footnote (p6, n.6) dates it as August 14, 1917.
82 Graham, *The Customs and Religion of the Ch'iang*, pp9, 100.
83 Itzhak Ben Zvi. *The Exiled and the Redeemed*. The Jewish Publication Society of America. 1957.
84 Ibid., pp221-222.
85 Ibid., pp79, 67. Ben Zvi suggests that among the Bukharan Jews there are descendants of both the northern and southern kingdoms of Israel.

known in Han period records as the people of Kangju, had extensive trading connections with China.

Graham also argued that it would be 'practically impossible for a large group of Israelites to migrate into China without this being noted in Chinese histories'.[86] However, Torrance had made no assumption that they had arrived in one large group.[87] Instead, he described the Qiang as groups spread out from the northwest to the southwest in a period before China's unification under the first Qin emperor in 221 BC. Rather than migrating into clearly defined Chinese territory, these pastoral nomads had lived to the west of the states of Shu and Qin and it was only as a unified China later pushed westwards and encroached on their grazing lands that references to the Qiang became numerous in Chinese dynastic records.

Tracing the identity of any people group entering China is complicated by the Chinese practice historically of identifying people by cultural difference rather than by ethnicity. Had any groups of Israelites entered territory to the west of China, they may simply have been seen by the Chinese as one of the various Qiang groups with their flocks and herds, and perhaps certain physical attributes, and were therefore documented under this broad generic term rather than with a name that gave any clues to their origin. Torrance had noted that before the Qin-Han period, 'Border races are confused and the term Chiang applied too generally.'[88]

An added difficulty is the lack of clarity regarding what the Israelites of the northern kingdom were known as in the years after their exile. In Assyrian records they were known as the house of Khumri, named after Omri, the first Israelite king to pay tribute to the Assyrians. Regarding personal names, although there was still some evidence of Hebrew names within the Assyrian army in the seventh century BC, there seems to be nothing later than this, which suggests the Israelites had adopted local names.[89] The lack of Qiang written records further complicates the issue, as does the lack of clarity regarding what they were known as by any Central Asian neighbours.

The Qiang people's own awareness of their origins derives nowadays from a mixture of Chinese historiography and their own

---

86 Graham, *The Customs and Religion of the Ch'iang*, p100.
87 TT, *China's First Missionaries*, p7.
88 Ibid., p18.
89 Tudor Parfitt. *The Lost Tribes of Israel: The History of a Myth*. Weidenfeld & Nicolson. 2002, p4.

orally transmitted traditions, which say that they reached their current location after a lengthy migration involving river-crossings, the loss of their sacred scriptures, and the defeat of the previous occupants of their current territory.

Although various Qiang groups over time became more clearly distinguished by their tribal names, such as the Er Qiang and Shaodang Qiang, the transcription of names into the phonetic limitations of Chinese characters makes it difficult to know what any Qiang tribal names might have been in their own language. Wang Mang, who ruled China from AD 9-23 and was a strong opponent of the Qiang, issued an edict that no-one under Chinese rule was to have names with multiple syllables. For example, Nangzhiyasi, the leader of the Xiongnu people, was rewarded for changing his name to Zhi.[90] Another factor adding to the elusiveness of foreign names was the Chinese custom of granting Chinese surnames to foreigners who submitted to them, something which served as a way of grafting them into Chinese ancestral lines.

To some degree, the Chinese can be seen as the authors of the history of the early Qiang, with accounts focusing primarily on times of conflict rather than on identifying cultural, physical, or linguistic traits, and in some cases describing, and perhaps even constructing, events that happened many centuries before the histories were written.[91] Among the few cultural traits mentioned in early records we are told that the customs of the Qiang of the Han period were different to those of the Chinese; that their language was unintelligible; that they had sheep, cattle, horses, sometimes camels and donkeys, and wagons; that they esteemed bravery and strength, used spears, bows, and swords, sometimes had armour, and were skilled at shooting their arrows on horseback.[92] Chapter 107 of the *Book of Wei*, compiled in the mid-6th century AD, describes them as having no script, sacrificing their sheep and cattle to heaven once every three years, and marrying their widows to male relatives. Chapter 19 of the *Book of Song* mentions dances of the Qiang, a kind of Qiang flute or pipe, and the possibility that a kind of animal horn was also used by the Qiang to scare the horses of the Chinese.

---

90 The *Book of Han*, Chapter 94, 'The Account of the Xiongnu'.

91 For example, 'The Account of the Western Qiang' in the *Book of the Later Han*, compiled by Fan Ye in the 5th century AD, begins its history of the Qiang at the end of the 3rd millennium BC, in the time of Emperor Shun.

92 See the *Book of Han*, Chs 69, 79, and 96; the *Book of the Later Han*, Ch 117.

Upper, Middle, and Lower Altars[93]

One aspect of Qiang religious culture not directly referred to by Graham or Torrance perhaps gives some clues regarding earlier and later elements of the culture. Current research describes the division of Qiang priestly rituals into three spheres: the upper, middle, and lower altars, with the term 'altar' denoting not a physical altar but a set of rituals carried out by the priest or *shibi* – as he is commonly called today – who is proficient in that particular sphere. Although some priests are familiar with the chants and rituals of all three altars, some only carry out those of the upper and middle altar, whilst others perform only those of the lower altar. A 2011 study of A'er Village, carried out by the villagers themselves, gives a list of local *shibis* who died between 1962 and 2007, several of whom were only familiar with the lower altar rituals.[94]

The rituals of the upper altar are connected with the supreme god and other deities seen as benevolent in nature, and include sacrificial offerings and the making and paying of vows. Because the authority of the supreme god is above all others, he is worshipped in the highest place, for example in the sacred grove above the village or on the family rooftop, where he is represented by a small tower and a white stone. One A'er villager describes the god of heaven as the highest and most sacred of gods and one who governs all things.[95] In another study of A'er, authors He Siqiang and Jiang Bin use the Chinese transcription *Ah-bi-qie* for the highest god, similar to Torrance's Abba Chee, describing him as the head of all the deities and governing affairs in both the spiritual and the human realm.[96]

Purity is a key element in the preparation of priest, people, and sacrifice for the upper altar ceremonies, which include the autumn Qiang New Year ceremony in the sacred grove and the coming of age ceremony for twelve-year-old boys. Upper altar chants are also used as part of the funeral ceremony when a sheep or goat is slain to release the deceased from guilt. This part of the ceremony is called 'killing the sheep who corrects sins' (杀改罪羊) and the sheep is seen as

---

93 上坛，中坛，下坛。
94 A'er cunren (A'er villagers). *A'er Dang'an* (A'er Archive). Beijing wenhua yichan baohu zhongxin congshu. Beijing: wenwu chubanshe. 2011, pp 241-243.
95 Ibid., p171.
96 He Siqiang and Jiang Bin. *Qiangzu: Sichuan Wenchuanxian A'ercun diaocha* (The Qiang People: A Survey of A'er Village in Wenchuan County, Sichuan). Yunnan daxue chubanshe. 2004, pp349-350.

bearing the guilt of the deceased and dying in his place (替死), a clear indication that there is an element of atonement in the sacrifice.[97]

The middle altar rituals are more to do with human affairs, focusing on village matters such as weddings, house-building, agriculture, and livestock. In some places these rituals are associated with various of the twelve lesser gods.

The lower altar rituals relate to the sphere of evil spirits and include exorcism, particularly where sickness or disaster are seen as caused by such spirits. The emphasis here is more on the efficacy of the *shibi's* magic arts and there seems to be considerable overlap with the rituals of the Sichuan *duangong*, who connects with the spirit world through magic charms, incantations, and in his exorcism rituals.

Although Torrance didn't use the term 'lower altar' he did point out that 'a number of priests, though not all, have copied some of the customs of the Chinese exorcists [*duangongs*]', and that 'spiritism, in some parts with its customary admixture of real phenomena and base trickery, has crept in.'[98] Similarly, among the Qiang priest's ceremonial implements Graham had seen a metal seal with Chinese characters, like those used by Daoist and Buddhist priests and by the Sichuan *duangong*, as well as wooden tablets carved with Chinese characters for printing charms.[99] He also noted that 'special priests or shamans' were required to perform exorcism rituals and he had been told by some of the Qiang priests he encountered that they were of the 'black religion', by which he understood that they had learned their arts from the *duangongs*.[100] This suggests that the Qiang priests of the 'black religion' in Graham's day would now be classed as lower altar practitioners, with many of their rituals originating in Chinese folk religion.

Confirmation of this connection between the lower altar and the 'black religion' is found in a study of Taoping, where researchers were told that the *shibis* could be divided into those of the black religion, which was to do with evil spirits, and those of the red religion, which was to do with the gods.[101] One priest from Zengtou village, above

97 *A'er dang'an*, p71.

98 TT, *China's First Missionaries*, p81.

99 Graham, 'Customs of the Ch'iang', p92.

100 Graham, *The Customs and Religion of the Ch'iang*, p87; *Folk Religion in Southwest China*, p105.

101 Lu Ding. *Qiangzu lishi wenhua yanjiu* (A Study of Qiang Historical Culture). Sichuan renmin chubanshe. 2000, p165.

Taoping, was of the red religion and focused primarily on the upper altar ceremonies. He explained that in the past some priests had been unwilling to carry out rituals involving contact with evil spirits because of the danger involved. Another priest from Zengtou said that such rituals conflicted with the role of the *shibi*, which was to benefit society and help people.

The A'er villagers also warned of the danger of some lower altar rituals, with one villager telling of a *shibi* named Labi, whose wife had died as a result of one of his rituals, after which Labi had decided not to pass such rituals on to future generations of priests.[102] There are also tales of showdowns between Qiang *shibis* and Han *duangongs*, perhaps indicating pressure on the lower altar *shibi* to prove his efficacy in dealing with evil spirits. Nowadays, the lower altar rituals sometimes include visible demonstrations of power such as treading on a hot ploughshare, cheek-piercing, divination using a bowl of water, and breathing out fire, some of which have become part of a more tourist-oriented presentation of supposed Qiang culture. Hill Gates describes similar rituals practised by spirit mediums in Taiwan, including cheek-piercing and walking on hot coals, a strong indication that they are not specifically Qiang practices.[103]

From the above it seems that the lower altar rituals contain much that has been absorbed through contact with Chinese religious practices of various kinds. In contrast, the rituals associated with the upper altar and the 'red religion', such as the sacrifices and paying of vows in the sacred grove, seem to represent more traditional Qiang religious customs and it is within these that Torrance saw most similarity to biblical sacrificial culture.

---

102 *A'er dang'an*, p190-191.
103 Hill Gates. *Chinese Working-Class Lives: Getting By in Taiwan*. Cornell University Press. 1987, p65.

Chapter 25

Epilogue

Not long after Torrance's homecoming the family moved to 12 Chalmers Crescent, a house with a garden where James and David learned the art of beekeeping, and where, as the older children moved on, Torrance and Annie took in student boarders to supplement their missionary pension. Always a preacher at heart, Torrance found himself invited to speak in various parts of Scotland, both in the Church of Scotland and elsewhere, and also continued to write. His book, *Expository Studies in St. John's Miracles*, was published in 1938 and later translated into Chinese. In a WCMN review, Harry Openshaw described the work as 'scholarly, strictly evangelical (need I say that to any of Tom's West China friends?), charmingly devotional, and spiritually refreshing and comforting.'[1]

Just four years after the tragedies in the Qiang area, Britain was plunged into the Second World War and Torrance and Annie watched and prayed as Tom, and later James and David, all served in the armed forces, Tom as a chaplain in the Middle East and Italy, for which he was awarded an MBE, James working in radar, and David serving with the army in India. All three brothers went on to pursue extensive academic studies, with James and David following in Tom's footsteps and being ordained as Church of Scotland ministers. Tom later became Professor of Christian Dogmatics at Edinburgh University and was described in a 2007 obituary as 'one of Scotland's foremost theologians of the last century'.[2] James became Professor of Systematic Theology at the University of Aberdeen whilst David chose to remain in parish ministry but maintained his academic interests, writing and editing a variety of books and articles. David also served for several years as a board member of the National Bible Society of Scotland. In 1947 Torrance had the joy of baptising Tom's first son, also Thomas, using water he had brought from the Jordan River.

---

1   TT. *Expository Studies in St. John's Miracles*. J. Clarke. 1938; WCMN, Sept 1938, p322.
2   'Obituary for The Very Reverend Professor Thomas Torrance'. In *The Daily Telegraph*, Dec 10, 2007. See also: Alister E. McGrath. *T. F. Torrance: An Intellectual Biography*. Edinburgh: T&T Clark. 1999; David W. Torrance. *The Reluctant Minister*. Handsel Press. 2015.

On graduation from Edinburgh University, Mary, Grace, and Margaret became teachers, with Mary the first of the six siblings to marry in 1937. Her husband, Ronald Wallace, was a parish minister and later became Professor of Biblical Theology at Columbia Theological Seminary in the USA. Margaret and her husband, Kenneth Mackenzie, also a minister, worked in Malawi and Zambia, where Kenneth became an influential advocate for African independence and played a significant role in raising awareness of apartheid. Grace's husband, Bobby Walker, trained as a minister and as a medical doctor, and he and Grace spent the early years of their marriage working in Malawi. David's wife Elizabeth

JAMES, TORRANCE, ANNIE, AND TOM, 1945
(Courtesy of David W. Torrance)

had also served as a young missionary doctor in the Middle East and in Botswana, having been encouraged to study medicine by her own local doctor, a former missionary to China named Ernest Cromwell Peake.[3] At the beginning of her studies in Edinburgh Elizabeth had lived in a hostel run by Dr and Mrs Lechler, the missionaries Deng Xihou had praised so highly for treating his wounded soldiers.

After an active retirement, with summers often spent in North Berwick enjoying the company of his various grandchildren, Torrance died on March 11, 1959, a day before his eighty-eighth birthday and a decade after the Communists came to power in China. By 1953 the Communists had expelled all missionaries and in the last few years of Torrance's life he and Annie had to resign themselves to China being closed to the outside world, but they continued to maintain a keen interest in the Far East and hosted a weekly prayer meeting for China and the Qiang.

It is clear from Torrance's correspondence at that time that he had also continued his interest in the origins of the Qiang and in their possible links with other groups. In 1952 the *Bible League Quarterly* published his 'Notes on Monotheistic Beliefs in the Far East', which started with a brief look at early Chinese worship of one God, Shangdi, and at the 'White Lord' or 'King of Heaven' of the Miao people of southwest China, whose ancient stories tell of a flood and of a tower reminiscent of the biblical tower of Babel.[4] However, the main focus of Torrance's attention this time was the Karen people in Burma, with further research having strengthened his view that they were related to the Qiang and had previously lived in southern Sichuan. One of his sources was Ba Te, who had suggested such a connection to Harry Marshall in 1917, and with whom Torrance had been corresponding.

One year after Torrance's death, a film was released in China called *The Song of the Qiang Flute*, which painted a bright picture of events in the Qiang region.[5] Beginning with the first arrival of the Communists in 1935, the film portrayed young Red Army soldiers valiantly trying to liberate Qiang villages from the oppression of Nationalist officials and local landowners and from the 'superstition' of the Qiang priest. As the villagers watched the Communists leave, they were clearly longing for

---

3   D. W. Torrance, *The Reluctant Minister*, p197. Ernest Cromwell Peake was the father of poet, writer, and artist Mervyn Peake.

4   *Bible League Quarterly*, April-June 1952, pp10-11.

5   *Qiang Di Song* (The Song of the Qiang Flute*). 1960. Directed by Zhang Xinshi. Changchun Film Studios. https://www.youtube.com/watch?v=oRFPd-L4ttM

their return and the film ended with the victorious Red Army, having captured Chengdu in December 1949, marching back to the villages and singing their song of Qiang liberation:

> The spring breeze turns the waters of the Min River green,
> And a huge red sun is shining on the Qiang villages,
> The heroic Red Army has returned,
> And all the Qiang villagers break into smiles.
> The mighty eagle spreads its wings and soars to the heights,
> The fish escape their nets and swim to the open sea,
> The thousand-year old shackles are broken,
> From now on the Qiang people will stand tall![6]

There were positives and negatives over the next two decades. Land reforms led to a fairer distribution of land, and infrastructure improvements such as electricity lines and proper roads brought a better standard of living to many villages, but there were also challenges to the traditional Qiang way of life. In a short story, Qiang author Ye Xingguang tells of the friction between Qiang customs and Communist policy during the so-called 'Great Leap Forward' of the late fifties and the Cultural Revolution of 1966–1976, when ethnic cultural practices fell into the category of the old customs and ways of thinking which the Party was trying to eradicate.[7] Reflecting the tensions of that time, the story describes the painful schism that develops between the village priest and his son, who has become Party secretary, when faced with an order to cut down the sacred grove for firewood. As the story draws to a close, China has emerged from the chaos of that era and the son has been able to combine his Party membership with assuming his hereditary priestly role. His own son is planning to replant the sacred grove, and the repentant official who issued the order to cut it down has sent funds to help the replanting – all an indication that Communism could now accommodate a degree of cultural diversity.

Before her death in 1980, aged ninety-six, Annie was able to witness the beginning of China's gradual re-opening to the world following Mao's death in September 1976.[8] Of the generals who had dominated the political scene during Torrance's final years in Sichuan, Liu Xiang had died of suspected poisoning in 1938, Yang

---

6   Author's translation.

7   Ye Xingguang. *Shen shan, shen shu, shen lin* (Sacred Mountain, Sacred Tree, Sacred Grove). Sichuan minzu chubanshe. 1999.

8   Annie lived to see her sixteenth grandchild and spent her last years living with Margaret, whose husband died in 1971.

Sen fled with the Nationalists to Taiwan in 1949, whilst Tian Songyao, Liu Wenhui, and Deng Xihou all managed to negotiate the transition to Communist rule. Deng, ever the survivor, became vice-governor of Sichuan and died in 1964, two years before the excesses of the Cultural Revolution.

By the early 1980s, under the leadership of Deng Xiaoping, foreign visitors were again able to visit China and in 1984, almost six decades after the family's hasty evacuation, Tom was invited to join some old China classmates on a short visit to Chengdu. In October 1986, aged seventy-three, he returned for a longer visit. Hiring a bike and joining the flow of cyclists in Chengdu's broad cycle lanes, he found his way to many familiar places. The family home on Wushi-tongtang Street had given way to modern apartment blocks overlooking a bustling street market, and on the university campus, which was now the West China University of Medical Sciences, his old school had become the Institute of Public Health. Enguang (Gracious Light) Church, the Canadian church on Si-sheng-ci Street where the family had worshipped on Sundays, had been damaged in the Cultural Revolution but was being restored and the site now also housed the Sichuan Theological Seminary. On a visit to the Southwest Institute for Nationalities, Tom was able to meet the principal and also the head of the library, who was interested to see the old photos and articles he had brought with him from his father's time in Chengdu and among the Qiang.

A government-approved travel agent in Chengdu helped Tom to obtain the required Alien's Travel Permit for a visit to the Qiang region and also contacted officials in Wenchuan County to arrange a visit. As he made the five-hour bus journey up the Min Valley to Weizhou, memories of his childhood trips riding behind his father on Billy came flooding back. Although his Chinese language was slowly returning he had lost the fluency of his youth and on arrival in Weizhou, Aba Teachers College kindly provided two staff members to serve as interpreters. The following day he made his first visit to Dongmenwai since 1926, accompanied by the interpreters and three officials, two of whom were Qiang. As word spread that Torrance's son had returned, people came out to greet him. One remembered Tom swimming in the local stream, secured to Torrance by a rope around his waist, and to Tom's delight, members of the Huang family took him up to the rooftop he had slept on as a boy.

Although the church building hadn't survived the turmoil of the preceding years, Tom was pleased to discover that some of the local

Christians had, for some time, continued to meet in one of their homes, although that had now ceased. In his journal he described this Dongmenwai reunion as 'one of the most memorable days of my life' and wrote of how moved he was by 'the love and regard the Chiang people still retained for my father after more than half a century, and by the way they came to show their appreciation.'[9] Tom presented them with the inscribed Chinese New Testament which had been buried by the Dongmenwai Christians in 1935 and sent to his father in Edinburgh. He also gave them Annie's Chinese New Testament and some enlarged photos of Dongmenwai taken by Torrance. In return he was presented with an embroidered Qiang robe for his wife Margaret.

From Dongmenwai Tom was taken further up the valley to see a small hydro-electric power plant and to visit the local school, where about four hundred children were now studying. This was followed by tea with Qiang apples and walnuts at the local government centre, where one of the older men happened to be from A'er. There wasn't time to go up to A'er but Tom told them of his 1926 visit when his father had learned much from the priest there about their sacrifices and the priest had been so impacted by the sacrificial rituals recorded in the book of Leviticus. To Tom's surprise, another man said excitedly that he had been present back then and could remember the occasion.

The next day they visited Keku where Tom had the joy of meeting a grandson of Gou Pinsan, as well as a member of the Yang family who lived higher up in Lesser Keku. In the afternoon they went south to Miansi and over the river to Qiangfeng, crossing the bridge which had been in such disrepair at the end of Torrance's final trip and whose old bamboo structure had now been replaced by steel cables. In Miansi, where Chen Bingling had lived in the small mission house and where Torrance had been called an 'American capitalist', local officials presented Tom with a woven Qiang girdle.

On his fourth and final day, Tom received a visit from Wang Xichun, the official archivist and one of the few Muslims in Weizhou, whose father had been a good friend of Torrance and whose mother still cherished a clock he had given them. He and Tom struck up a warm rapport and Tom promised to send more of his father's material for the archives. That same morning he was invited to speak to some English classes at Aba

---

9   Thomas F. Torrance. 'The Visit of Thomas F. Torrance to Chengdu, the capital of Sichuan, and to Weichow and Chiang Villages in Wenchuan County, the upper Min Valley, Sichuan, 1986 Oct 4-18', p13.

Teachers College, where he received a warm welcome from the staff and students and was impressed by the elegance of the campus. It was hard to leave Weizhou but he was hoping it wouldn't be his last trip.

On the way back to Chengdu Tom stopped in Guanxian where an official guide took him up to the old summer hill resort at Lingyan Temple, which held so many precious childhood memories. In Guanxian, now better known as Dujiangyan, the CIM station where Annie and Torrance had first met in 1908 had become a children's clothing factory but was still recognisable in part. To Tom's surprise, an elderly man on the street suddenly said 'Hallelujah' and told Tom he could remember his father preaching in Guanxian and in the nearby towns of Pixian and Pengzhou.

After one last day in Chengdu Tom returned to Scotland where he set about arranging for his father's papers to be sent to the archives of Yale Divinity School Library, making much of the material publicly available for the first time. The following year, Torrance's 1920 monograph, *The History, Customs and Religion of the Ch'iang*, was translated into Chinese, with a publisher's note added by the Wenchuan County Archives Bureau.[10] A year later, in 1988, Tom arranged for a second English edition of *China's First Missionaries – Ancient Israelites* to be published.[11]

Some time before Tom's 1986 trip, an Israeli rabbi named Eliyahu Avichail had come across the 1937 edition of *China's First Missionaries*. Avichail was the founder of an organisation called Amishav (My People Return) and since the 1960s he had been pursuing research into people groups with possible Jewish links. As he explained in his book, *The Tribes of Israel: The Lost and the Dispersed*, his interest stemmed from his reading of Bible passages suggesting that the tribes of Israel's northern kingdom would one day return from where they had been scattered.[12] Jewish rabbis and sages had been debating such matters for centuries, with some believing that these Israelite descendants were lost forever and others anticipating their restoration. Avichail listed the opinions of various rabbinic authors, including that of Samuel Eliezer ha-Levi Eidels, a sixteenth century Polish rabbi:

---

10 The translator was Chen Sihui (陈斯惠).

11 Thomas Torrance. *China's First Missionaries, Ancient "Israelites"*. Daniel Shaw Co. 1988.

12 Rabbi Eliyahu Avichail. *The Tribes of Israel – the Lost and the Dispersed*. Amishav. 2012, pp13-19. (1st ed. 1990.) E.g. Isaiah 11:11-16; 27:12-13; 49; Jeremiah 30 and 31; Ezekiel 37.

Hosea prophesied that a ruler would rule over the Ten Tribes when they return. You may side with those who say at the end of Helek that the Ten Tribes will not return. But for those who say that the Ten Tribes will return, it is self understood that the ruler over the Ten Tribes when they return will be the Messiah, and may it be in our day, Amen.[13]

Like Torrance, Avichail equated the 'Sinim' of Isaiah 49:12 with China and suggested, based on the biblical locations of the exiles 'in Halah and Habor, on the river of Gozan, and in the cities of the Medes', that the exiles had moved east from Iran and Afghanistan to Pakistan, Kashmir, Tibet, and China.[14] He divided the exiled Jews into three types: those who had retained their Jewishness and had the Torah and the Talmud; those with the written Torah only; and the 'third group, the great majority of the tribes, living as gentiles with signs of Jewishness', which he believed to be 'in the countries of the East'.[15] Among the groups that possibly fell into this third category he included the Pathans, Kashmiris, Karen, the Shinlung of India, and the Qiang.

An indication that a wider interest in such things was growing was the publication in 1987 of *The Thirteenth Gate – Travels Among the Lost Tribes of Israel* by Tudor Parfitt, founding director of the Centre for Jewish Studies at London's School of Oriental and African Studies (SOAS).[16] Although Parfitt made no mention of Torrance or the Qiang, he did refer to the Shinlung of northeast India, who saw themselves as descendants of the tribe of Manasseh, and to the Lemba of Zimbabwe and South Africa, who possibly had Jewish roots.

Sometime after his 1986 trip to China, Tom was contacted by Dr Shalva Weil of the Hebrew University in Jerusalem requesting the loan of some Qiang artifacts for an Israeli exhibition entitled 'Beyond the Sambatyon: the Myth of the Ten Lost Tribes', which was held in 1991 at the Nahum Goldmann Museum of the Jewish Diaspora in Tel Aviv.[17] Dr Weil had carried out extensive research on the Jews of India, in particular the Bene Israel, and her interest would later extend to other groups in Africa and Asia. The Qiang section of the exhibition contained the rod with the snake around it, a sacred scroll (the Je-Dsu

13 Avichail, *The Tribes of Israel*, pp34-35. From the Commentary on Aggadot, Arakhin 33.
14 Avichail, *The Tribes of Israel*, p52; 2 Kings 17:6.
15 Ibid., p59.
16 Tudor Parfitt. *The Thirteenth Gate – Travels Among the Lost Tribes of Israel*. London: Weidenfeld and Nicolson. 1987.
17 Now known as ANU – The Museum of the Jewish People.

or Abba Malah), two woven girdles, various Qiang photographs, some of Torrance's articles, and his 1937 book.

Two years after the exhibition, the first Shinlung people (some of whom are now known as the Bene Menashe) arrived in Israel from northeast India, provoking a flurry of articles about the lost tribes. In September 1993 a magazine called *The Jerusalem Report* carried an article entitled 'Return of the Lost Tribes', which focused primarily on the Bene Menashe but also mentioned the Pathans of Afghanistan and the Qiang.[18] On August 9, 1994, perhaps reflecting the scepticism of some towards such things, a cartoon by Oleg in *The Jerusalem Post* showed a shepherd with his alien sheep-like flock explaining to two men who had just landed on the moon: 'We came here with the ten tribes but now that our brethren in India have returned to Israel we thought we might apply for aliyah too.' Even *The Economist* printed an article about the difficulties faced by some of the Chinese Jewish descendants in Kaifeng in their efforts to be recognised by both China and Israel as Jews.[19]

In May 1994 Tom was able to make one last trip to Sichuan, having been asked to give a series of lectures at Hong Kong's China Graduate School of Theology, as well as a public lecture on 'The Scientific Mind and Christian Thinking'.[20] From there he flew to Chengdu where he renewed friendships and paid another visit to the university and the museum. With the help of two maps, one old and one new, he did his best to track down other places from his childhood. The modernisation of the city made this difficult but he managed to find a pedicab driver who knew San-dao-guai, the site of the old Ramsay house where he was born.

On this visit Tom had allowed plenty of time for a visit to the Qiang region and had a room booked in the new Jiangwei Hotel in Weizhou. At his request, one of the interpreters from his last trip took him to visit the head of Wenchuan County. Tom had been hoping for permission to stay in one or two of the villages but he was now eighty and although he was given a permit enabling him to travel freely, he was advised to make daily trips out from Weizhou.

---

18   Yossi Klein Halevi. 'Return of the Lost Tribes'. *The Jerusalem Report*. Sept 9, 1993, pp12-17.

19   A Jewish Question'. *The Economist*. Dec 3, 1994, p9.

20   In 1978 Tom had received the Templeton Prize, awarded for those whose 'exemplary achievements' served to advance Sir John Templeton's philanthropic vision of 'harnessing the power of the sciences to explore the deepest questions of the universe and humankind's place and purpose within it'. https://www.templetonprize.org/

In Weizhou he met up again with archivist Wang Xichun and with relatives of Gou Pinsan, one of whom drew him a family tree of Gou Pinsan's descendants. In Dongmenwai he met with various villagers and again visited the government offices further up the Longxi Valley, as well as the Longxi school where he enjoyed meeting some rather excited but shy Qiang children.

Back in Weizhou several Qiang came to visit, including a villager from A'er who was now living in the town. On Sunday evening two Weizhou officials came to see him, one of whom was also from A'er. He showed Tom some photos of a trek he and some friends had made over the mountains beyond A'er, similar to that of Torrance, Gou, and Chen in 1921. The man now had aspirations to turn the area into a nature reserve and had published a book to draw attention to Qiang culture and the beauty of the area. To Tom's delight he promised to take him up to A'er.

A few days later they all set out for A'er – Tom, the interpreter, the two Weizhou officials, and, to Tom's surprise, the head of Aba Prefecture, who had decided to join them in a personal capacity. The road became rougher as it wound up the valley and at one point some obliging villagers helped to repair a bridge over the stream so that they could continue. Up in A'er they were hosted by a local family who thought they recognised some people in the photos Tom showed them from his father's book. One of them told Tom his father had shot a bear up there but Torrance had never had a rifle and Tom knew this must have been the bear shot by David Graham in 1933. In Biaduo village, below A'er, they saw the sacred grove and met the 78-year-old priest.

After saying a last farewell to Gou Pinsan's family, Tom left the following day for another visit to Guanxian and Lingyan Temple and a further week in Chengdu. It had been a rewarding visit but there was one disappointment. Remembering the Qiang pledge in 1936 that the church would rise again, Tom had been raising funds prior to his trip to help with the rebuilding of a church in the Qiang area, and in the hope of assisting two or three young Qiang to take courses at the theological seminary in Chengdu, but despite enthusiasm on the part of some of the Qiang and a more open attitude in China towards Christianity, neither of these came to fruition.

In 1998, four years after Tom's final visit, Rabbi Avichail paid a short visit to the Qiang area as part of a longer trip to the Shinlung (Bene Menashe) in northeast India, with whom he had developed close links. Travelling with him was Israeli author Hillel Halkin, who had almost backed out of the

China part of the trip when he discovered that all Avichail knew about the Qiang had come from Torrance. Deciding to do some research of his own, Halkin came across a 1990 article by anthropologist Schuyler Cammann, who had visited the Qiang area in 1938 whilst helping David Graham to catalogue the Tibetan collection in the WCUU museum.[21]

Cammann's article was an expanded version of a response he had written in 1986 to an article in the Hong Kong Jewish Chronicle entitled 'The Lost Tribes – Found in Asia', which had made reference to both Torrance and Avichail.[22] Rejecting Torrance's theory, Cammann drew largely on Graham's work for his conclusions, including Graham's assertion that the Qiang had originated in northeast China. Presumably unaware of the first century *Shuowen Jiezi* dictionary definition of 'Qiang' as a term for western shepherds, he described the term Qiang as 'simply a tribal name in Chinese' that had no association with sheep.[23]

By this time, various research publications were available in Chinese describing the culture and history of the Qiang who, in the 1950s, had been given their own status as one of China's official ethnic minority groups.[24] Despite this, Cammann, who had never returned to the Qiang area, assumed that the Qiang had been 'annihilated or dispersed in recent years' and that, if any were still to be found in their former territory, they would probably not have retained 'any traces of their traditional religion'.[25] In his conclusion he urged that the Qiang 'should continue to live in memory as a sturdy group who managed to retain their distinctive customs and strange religion, in the face of strong external pressures, down to the mid-twentieth century'.[26]

---

21 Schuyler V. R. Cammann, 'The Ch'iang People of Western Szechuan: The Miscalled 'West China Jews'.' In *Faces of the Jewish experience in China*, Dennis A. Leventhal and Mary W. Leventhal (eds), Monographs of the Jewish Historical Society of Hong Kong, Vol 3. Published by The Hong Kong Jewish Chronicle. 1990, pp64-88.

22 S. V. R. Cammann. 'Some Comments on the Origin and Beliefs of the Ch'iang People'. *The Hong Kong Jewish Chronicle*, February 1986, pp 41-44; J. P. Eliav. 'The Lost Tribes – Found in Asia?' *The Hong Kong Jewish Chronicle*, May-June, 1985.

23 Cammann, 'The Ch'iang People of Western Szechuan', p67, n.8.

24 E.g. Sun Hongkai (ed). *Qiangyu jianzhi* (A Brief Description of the Qiang Language). Beijing: minzu chubanshe. 1981; Ren Naiqiang. *Qiangzu yuanliu tansuo* (Exploring the Origin of the Qiang Nationality). Chongqing chubanshe. 1984; Ran Guangrong et al. *Qiangzushi* (The History of the Qiang Nationality). Sichuan minzu chubanshe. 1984.

25 Cammann, 'The Ch'iang People of Western Szechuan', pp64, 81.

26 Ibid., p82.

To Halkin, Cammann's article seemed to demolish Torrance's thesis and he urged Avichail to cancel the China part of their trip. However, Avichail had waited a long time to visit the Qiang and responded with, 'So what? If I believed what every professor wrote, I'd never get past my front door.'[27] And the trip went ahead as planned.

After an unpromising start, Avichail and Halkin found a small elementary teachers college in Weizhou where three Qiang teachers were willing to answer questions about their culture. The teachers said that the Qiang in the more remote villages had still retained their language and their customs. In the rather confusing conversation which followed, the visitors gleaned that the white stone was a symbol of the most powerful god, who had helped the Qiang to victory through a dream showing them to use snow-covered stones against the enemy. Sacrifices were made in front of the white stone and the blood of the sacrifice was poured on the stone. The next day, bearing a letter of introduction from one of the teachers, Avichail and Halkin went south to the village of Qiangfeng, where white stones were visible on the roofs and they were introduced to the local Qiang priest. He showed them a wooden staff with a snake coiled around it and a pair of silver bells used to accompany his chanting to 'Apimala', which Rabbi Avichail saw as an approximation of Torrance's 'Abba malah'. They also saw his monkey-skin headdress and the ceremonial sheep-skin drum.

Halkin's conclusion from their short visit was that Cammann had been mistaken about the disappearance of the Qiang and their customs but was accurate in his rejection of any link between Qiang customs and the Bible. Avichail disagreed. What they had seen concurred with Torrance's descriptions, which showed him to be a reliable witness of Qiang culture in the early twentieth century.[28]

Halkin described this visit to the Qiang in the first chapter of his book, *Across the Sabbath River: In Search of a Lost Tribe of Israel*, which was primarily about the Shinlung but also included a brief visit to the Karen people. Since the trip he had continued his own research into the Shinlung and, although highly doubtful at first, he had been surprised to discover cultural elements indicating possible Israelite connections.

Coincidentally, that same year Tudor Parfitt launched a new course at SOAS on 'The Jews of Africa and Asia' and published a

27 Hillel Halkin. *Across the Sabbath River: In Search of a Lost Tribe of Israel.* Houghton Mifflin Company. 2002, p10.
28 Ibid., p24.

more extensive work than his 1987 book, entitled *The Lost Tribes of Israel: The History of a Myth,* with a chapter on the Karen and the Qiang which contained references to Torrance, Graham, Cammann, and Rabbi Avichail.[29] Despite his obvious interest in the topic, Parfitt was unequivocal regarding his own view: 'The present writer does not believe that the Ten Tribes are still to be found and accepts their disappearance as a historical fact that requires no further proof.'[30] As far as he was concerned, since the loss of Hebrew names in Assyria after the seventh century BC, the story of the tribes had become a myth sustained primarily by various biblical passages, in particular Ezekiel 37, Isaiah 11, Jeremiah 31, and the apocryphal II Esdras 13, pointing to the future restoration of Israel and the reunification of the tribes of the northern and southern kingdoms.[31]

In contrast to Parfitt's scepticism, the premise for a 2003 documentary by Simcha Jacobovici, entitled *Quest for the Lost Tribes,* was a firm belief in these biblical promises. Starting with a look at Assyrian wall reliefs dating to the exile of Israel's northern kingdom, Jacobovici followed a trail east to China via Bukhara and Samarkand, arriving in Kaifeng. He made no mention of the Qiang but the belief among the Bene Menashe that they had reached India via Central Asia, China, and Myanmar caused Jacobovici to ask whether there had been an unknown Israelite exodus across Central Asia and China. His journey also took him to the Pathans in the Afghanistan-Pakistan border regions and to the Bene Israel in India.

Any thought that Qiang culture would gradually disappear amidst the modernity and growing uniformity of Chinese culture was quickly dispelled in 2008. On May 12, at 2.28 in the afternoon, just as students were on their way to class, farmers were in their fields, and shops were quiet in the slow after-lunch period, the whole Qiang area was rocked by a massive earthquake measuring 8.0 on the Richter scale. The number of dead and 'missing presumed dead' exceeded 87,000, with many more injured and left homeless. Casualties in Aba Tibetan and Qiang Autonomous Prefecture numbered more than 20,000. In Luobozhai the clay-built houses collapsed as the ground rippled beneath them and although many working in the fields were

---

29 Tudor Parfitt. *The Lost Tribes of Israel: The History of a Myth.* London: Weidenfeld & Nicolson. 2002.

30 Ibid., p225, n.1.

31 Ibid., p4.

spared, more than forty were killed, many of whom were young and elderly at home. In Longxi Valley, where the houses are made of stone, some homes were destroyed while others stayed standing but were structurally unsound, and the threat of landslides and mud-rock flows was so high that the 5,000 residents of the valley were evacuated to a tent village. Eventually most were able to return home to face the task of rebuilding or repairing, although two villages, Xige and Zhitai, were deemed uninhabitable and the villagers were relocated permanently to the hills west of Qionglai, a 130-mile journey from their old homes.

In the midst of all this tragedy, the spotlight was suddenly on the Qiang people in a way that won the hearts of people across China. Like a phoenix rising out of the ashes, the Qiang sense of identity was renewed as the preservation and promotion of Qiang culture became a key facet of earthquake recovery across the region. The village of Taoping, already a popular tourist destination, became well-known across China for its ancient Qiang towers and unique defensive structure, and in Maoxian a giant Qiang citadel was built overlooking the town, where performances of Qiang music and dancing are now hosted. Tourism development also received a boost in Longxi Valley which, having retained more Qiang language and culture than other less remote areas, had already been designated by Wenchuan County as the 'Qiang People's Valley'. In addition to this, the celebration of Qiang New Year has been recognised by UNESCO as an intangible cultural heritage urgently in need of safeguarding.[32]

This growth of tourism has tended to promote the more visible aspects of Qiang culture like the singing and dancing, the ancient architecture, and the revered white stone, whereas the core religious practices of the priest or *shibi*, such as the sacrifices, have remained less visible to the public. However, as *The A'er Archive* shows, such practices have survived until today, even though most of the remaining priests are elderly, and younger people are often not so interested in such things. In a 2007 rooftop ceremony attended by a Qiang friend of the author, the priest proclaimed in his chanting that

---

32 See Zhang Qiaoyun. 'Heritage making after the earthquake. Safeguarding the intangible heritage of the Qiang people in China'. International Institute for Asian Studies. The Newsletter 80, Summer 2018. Zhang notes that some *shibis* have tried to keep a clear division between authentic Qiang sacrificial rituals and cultural demonstrations detached from their original purpose and aimed solely at tourists.

he was dependent on the god of heaven for his singing and for the performing of the sacrifice. Appealing to God to bless the villagers and their crops, the priest told of their moral ways, assuring God that those coming to pay their vows were clean and had done nothing to displease him. He then knelt before the small sacred tower on the rooftop and his assistants slew a ram and several roosters.

Research is also playing a significant role in preserving knowledge about Qiang culture and whilst some of this assumes a Chinese past for the ancient Qiang, there are those who, like Herrlee Creel in the 1930s, challenge a linear Qiang history dating back to the Shang period and instead see the term Qiang as a broader Chinese term for nomadic sheep-herders historically to the west of the Chinese.[33] Reminiscent of Liu Enlan in the mid-1940s, Wang Mingke describes the Qiang of early AD as 'widely distributed along the mountainous fringes of the northern and eastern Tibetan Plateau, from the Kunlun Mountains in Xinjiang province (East Turkestan), and eastern Qinghai area, to southern Gansu, western Sichuan, and northern Yunnan.'[34]

As Professor Seligman had predicted in 1937, in more recent decades archaeological discoveries in China's northwest have revealed a steady flow of cultural interaction across the region. Referring to archaeological finds in Xinjiang, Nicola di Cosmo notes that,

> The presence of so many different physical types demonstrates the occurrence of various migrations into Eastern Central Asia, coming from west, southwest, north and east, some of which seem to have occurred during the first millennium B.C. These migrations, and the presence of so many racial types, show that Xinjiang had become the meeting point of different cultures before the historical opening of communication between East and West.

In 1994, physical anthropologist Han Kangxin, in his study of skulls in various cemeteries in Xinjiang, concluded that:

---

33   E.g. Wang Mingke. *Qiang zai Han Zang zhijian – Chuanxi Qiangzu de lishi renleixue yanjiu* (The Qiang Between the Han and the Tibetans – a Historical and Anthropological Study of the Qiang of Western Sichuan). Zhonghua shuju. 2008.

34   Wang Ming-ke. 'From the Qiang Barbarians to the Qiang Nationality: the Making of a New Chinese Boundary'. In Shu-min Huang & Cheng-kuang Hsu (eds). *Imagining China: Regional Division and National Unity*. Taipei: Institute of Ethnology. 1999, pp43-80.

Several centuries B.C.E. or a little earlier, other racial elements close to that of the East Mediterranean in physical character entered into the western part of Xinjiang from the Central Asian region of the former USSR. Their movement was from west to east (Xiangbaobao, Tashkurgan, Shanpula-Luopu, Loulan cemeteries).

This west to east route mentioned by Han Kangxin includes the southern edge of the Tarim basin where the *Book of Han* recorded Qiang groups living in the Kunlun foothills.[35]

In Zaghunluq cemetery, along this southern route, a steppe harp dating to the fifth century BC has been found, which is similar to those depicted on Assyrian monuments of 850-650 BC. Bo Lawergren concludes that this and another harp found at Yanghai in eastern Xinjiang 'appear to be the result of an eastward migration' and he surmises that the harps were introduced to Xinjiang by equestrian people such as the Scythians, some of whom, like the Israelites, served in the Assyrian army.[36] Zaghunluq cemetery lies in today's Qiemo County which, in the Han period, was recorded as to the west of a Qiang group known as the Er Qiang (婼羌), who traded with the people of Qiemo for grain, raising the possibility that woollen fabrics found in some of the Zaghunluq tombs were made from Qiang wool used for barter. Chinese records describe the Er Qiang extracting iron from the Kunlun Mountains and using it to make various weapons, a skill which Donald Wagner suggests may also have been brought from further west several centuries earlier through Scythian intermediaries.[37]

A further discovery at Yanghai points to an even firmer connection between China's northwest and Assyria. In 2015 an international team of researchers carried out an examination on the well-preserved remnants of some leather scale body armour and concluded that it 'resembles the scale waistcoats for armoured cavalrymen invented in Assyria in the 9th/8th century BCE and most widely used to equip

---

35 *Book of Han*, Chapter 96, 'Account of the Western Regions'.

36 Bo Lawergren. 'Harps on the Ancient Silk Road'. In *Conservation of Ancient Sites on the Silk Road*. Neville Agnew (ed). Getty Conservation Institute; 2 edition, Aug 3, 2010, pp122-123; Bo Lawergren. 'Angular harps Through the Ages; a Causal History'. In *Studien zur Musikarchäologie* VI, Orient-Archäologie 22. Rahden. 2008, pp 264-265, 276.

37 Donald B. Wagner. 'The Earliest Use of Iron in China'. In Suzanne M. M. Young et al (eds), *Metals in Antiquity*. (BAR international series, 792), Oxford: Archaeopress. 1999, pp.1-9. http://donwagner.dk/EARFE/EARFE.html. See also R. Meakin, 'Qiang 羌 References in the Book of Han 汉书, Part 2', p14.

Neo-Assyrian forces during the 7th century BCE.'[38] Although the researchers acknowledge that the armour may have been made in the later Persian empire or by people bringing this technology further east, they suggest that the place of manufacture was the Neo-Assyrian Empire, which, if true, would make the Yanghai armour 'one of the rare actual proofs of West-East technology transfer across the Eurasian continent during the first half of the first millennium BCE.'[39]

Neither the harps nor armour can necessarily be attributed to the Qiang of that period but the presence of Assyrian-related artifacts in close proximity to the Qiang of China's far northwest does indicate that, geographically and historically, Torrance's hypothesis is not unreasonable. Like the Scythians, the equestrian Israelites of the northern kingdom had served in the Assyrian army and it is feasible that some of their number eventually reached China, where they managed to maintain traces of their original culture – such as the parallels perceived by Torrance – but gradually lost other aspects and absorbed external influences.

Another musical instrument of interest is the Qiang flute. In November 2010, Song Xiping, a professor at the Sichuan Culture and Art Institute in Mianyang, presented a paper at the First Qiang Intangible Heritage Forum, in which he discussed the structural similarities of this traditional double flute and the Middle Eastern zummara, and raised the possibility that the two instruments shared a common origin.[40] Still used today in the Qiang region, the Qiang flute featured in Tang Dynasty poetry as a symbol of China's northwestern frontier region.[41] Another custom which possibly migrated with

---

38   Patrick Wertmann. 'No borders for innovations: A ca. 2700-year-old Assyrian-style leather scale armour in Northwest China'. In *Quaternary International*, https://doi.org/10.1016/j.quaint.2021.11.014, p15.
39   Ibid., p16.
40   Song Xiping's original paper was entitled *Cong Qiang di he Zummara bijiao fenxi shixi Qiang di xilai de kenengxing* (A Comparative Analysis of the Qiang Flute and the Zummara and the Possibility of the Qiang Flute Originating in the West). A revised paper was published as: *Qiang di he Zummara yinyue bijiao* (A Comparison of the Music of the Qiang Flute and the Zummara). In Long Zhenxu, Lin Chuan (eds). *Qingxi Erma: shoujie Zhongguo Qiangzu feiwuzhi wenhua yichang yu zaihou chongjian yanjiuhui lunwenji.* Lanzhou daxue chubanshe. 2011, pp90-99.
41   See for example 'Saishang ting chuidi' (The Sound of the Flute on the Borders) by Gao Shi, and 'Liangzhou ci' (A Song of Liangzhou) by Wang Zhihuan.

the Qiang to their current location is their use on special occasions of long bamboo straws to drink from a common pot of their grain alcohol (*zajiu*), a custom known to have existed amongst the ancient Sumerians of today's Iraq region.

In 2012 David Torrance was finally able to return to Chengdu, aged eighty-seven. Having left China as a two-year-old, his impressions of China had come mainly from family conversations and his father's letters during their years of separation, but the desire to see China again had never left him. Travelling with his daughter Grace, he spent time visiting the university, the church, and Wushi-tongtang Street, where he had been born during a steamy hot Chengdu summer. From there they travelled up to Weizhou and were able to visit Taoping, Luobozhai, and Dongmenwai, where his father had felt so at home. Although it was nearly twenty years since Tom's last visit, there were one or two locals who could still remember Torrance.

Four years later, Grace returned to China and was able to represent the Torrance family at the opening ceremony of an exhibition at the Sichuan University Museum to commemorate Torrance's contribution towards the establishment of the museum, as well as his archaeological, historical, and Qiang research. The exhibition featured many enlarged photos taken by Torrance, and Grace presented the university with an exquisite Chinese embroidery passed down from her grandparents. With all that had happened in China between Torrance's departure in early 1935 and his death in 1959, he could never have envisaged his work being honoured in such a way – and in the presence of a family member.

The determination that had taken Torrance as a teenager from his parents' small dairy farm to the Hamilton drapery, and then to study so diligently at college and leave all that he held dear to go to the mission field, remained with him throughout his life. Persevering and triumphing in the Chinese language, he had pressed on through the sorrow of losing Mary Bryce and the difficulties leading to his departure from the CIM, and then found his place alongside Annie, putting his heart and soul into the work of the American Bible Society, as well as the Great East Street work with Harry Openshaw and his work among the Qiang.

Despite the long hours spent working, travelling, researching, and writing, Torrance was at heart a relational man with a deep love for his family and for those he worked with and met on his travels. His relationships with co-workers like Gou Pinsan and Daniel Diao reveal much about his loyalty and love towards those dear to him, as do his summer trips and his enjoyment of the winter visits of the Qiang. His desire to help improve people's lives was an intrinsic part of his character, whether through offering medical treatment; trying to improve livestock in the Qiang area; fighting the injustice and blight of the opium trade; enabling children to get an education; or helping the missionary community in various ways. In return he received the affection of many.

He was also a man of innate curiosity, something which, despite his lack of formal training, took him into the fields of history, archaeology, and anthropology and earned him the title of Fellow of the Royal Geographic Society. Maintaining his interest in national and international affairs until the end, he had, over the course of his long life, witnessed the demise of imperial China, the impact of the First and Second World Wars, the dissolution of the British Empire, the birth of the modern state of Israel, and the rise of Communist China.

More than anything, Torrance's life was marked by a passion for the Christian message of salvation, a costly passion which had resulted in the seven-year separation from his family, and a passion which ignored denominational differences and made him willing to work with whoever asked, be it the CIM, the Chinese churches, Openshaw and his Baptist mission, or Ernest Hamilton, the 'Episcopalian Tory' in Xindu. It was also a passion for which he was willing to risk his life, staying on in China through the violence of the Yu Manzi and Boxer rebellions and later through the fighting between Sichuan's ever-changing militarists, as well as facing the dangers of his summer trips – as recognised by the Qiang in their tributes to him. This 'pastor who rides the black mule' was equally at home whether at a banquet hosted by Deng Xihou or negotiating landslides and sleeping wherever he found somewhere to lay his head.

It remains to be seen whether further research will shed more light on the origins of today's Qiang people but for as long as the mystery of Israel's lost tribes stirs people's imagination, it seems likely that there will be interest in Torrance's theory of Israelite ancestry for the Qiang, even as there will always be those who are dismissive. Whatever the truth, there is no doubt that some of the Qiang in Torrance's time were sufficiently struck by the biblical parallels in their culture to want to explore them further, with some, like Gou Pinsan, coming to the conclusion that the similarities could not be coincidental.

Perhaps the more important legacy in Torrance's eyes was the founding, with Chen Bingling, Gou Pinsan, and others, of the first Qiang church, as well as the response of all those across Sichuan who, through the ABS literature and the preaching of Torrance and his colporteurs, had received the message of forgiveness and eternal life which so captured Torrance's own heart as a teenager. His final message, to anyone visiting Grange Cemetery in Edinburgh, was from his beloved John's gospel, inscribed on the gravestone he shares with Annie:

(Photo by author, 2018)

Bibliography

A'er Dang'an (A'er Archive, compiled by the A'er villagers). Beijing wenhua yichan baohu zhongxin congshu. Beijing: wenwu chubanshe. 2011.

American Bible Society: One Hundred and Sixth Annual Report. American Bible Society, New York. 1922.

Avichail, Rabbi Eliyahu. *The Tribes of Israel - the Lost and the Dispersed.* Amishav. 2012.

Bagster family (compilers). *Daily Light on the Daily Path.* Samuel Bagster & Sons. 1875.

Ben Zvi, Itzhak. *The Exiled and the Redeemed.* The Jewish Publication Society of America. 1957.

Beresford, Charles. *The Break-Up of China.* Harper and Brothers Publishers. 1899.

Bian Simei. 'Qiang wei heren: 20 shiji qianqi xifang xuezhe de Qiangmin yanjiu' (Who are the Qiang People: A Study of the Qiang People by Western Scholars in the Early 20th Century). *Yunnan shifan daxue xuebao*, Vol 45, No 3, May 2013, pp9-16.

Bickers, Robert. *Out of China.* Penguin Books Ltd. 2017.

Bigham, Clive. *A Year in China: 1899-1900. With some account of Admiral Sir E. Seymour's expedition.* Macmillan and Co., Ltd. 1901.

Bird, Isabella. *The Yangtze Valley and Beyond.* John Murray. 1899.

Bosshardt, Alfred. *The Guiding Hand.* Hodder and Stoughton. 1973.

Broomhall, A. J. *It is not Death to Die!* (Book 7 of *Hudson Taylor & China's Open Century*). Hodder & Stoughton and the Overseas Missionary Fellowship. 1989.

Broomhall, Marshall. *The Jubilee Story of the China Inland Mission with Portraits and Map.* London: Marshall, Morgan & Scott Ltd. 1915.

Cammann, Schuyler, V. R. 'Some Comments on the Origin and Beliefs of the Ch'iang People'. *The Hong Kong Jewish Chronicle*, February 1986, pp 41-44.

'The Ch'iang People of Western Szechuan: The Miscalled "West China Jews."' In *Faces of the Jewish experience in China*, Dennis A. Leventhal and Mary W. Leventhal (eds), Monographs of the Jewish Historical Society of Hong Kong, Vol 3. Published by The Hong Kong Jewish Chronicle. 1990, pp64-88.

Ch'en, Jerome. *Revival: The Highlanders of Central Asia: A History, 1895-1937(1993): A History, 1937-1985.* Routledge. 2017.

Chen Shiying. *Wenchuanxian hongjun changzheng lishi yiji xianzhuang fenxi yu baohu* (Analysis of the Current Situation and Protection of the Historical Remains of the Red Army's Long March in Wenchuan County). Fangzhi Sichuan – zizhi. March, 12, 2021. https://www.sohu.com/a/455281413_120158407

Chen Zhongping. 'The May Fourth Movement and Provincial Warlords: A Reexamination'. In *Modern China*, Vol 37, No.2, March 2011, pp135-169.

Creel, Herrlee G. *The Birth of China*. Jonathan Cape Ltd, London. 1936.

Cummings, Alex. 'Life in the Menagerie: David Crockett Graham and Missionary-Scientists in West China, 1911-1948'. *American Baptist Quarterly*, 27 (3), 2009, pp206–227.

Eliav, J. P. 'The Lost Tribes – Found in Asia?' *The Hong Kong Jewish Chronicle*, May-June, 1985.

Fergusson, William. *Adventure, Sport and Travel on the Tibetan Steppes*. Charles Scribner's Sons. 1911.

Finn, James. *The Jews in China*. B. Wertheim. 1843.

Garavente, Anthony. 'The Long March'. *The China Quarterly*, no. 22, 1965, pp. 89–124. *JSTOR*, http://www.jstor.org/stable/651546.

Gates, Hill. *Chinese Working-Class Lives: Getting By in Taiwan*. Cornell University Press. 1987.

Geng Jing and Jeff Kyong-McClain. 'David Crockett Graham in Chinese Intellectual History'. In D. M. Glover et al. *Explorers and Scientists in China's Borderlands, 1880-1950*. University of Washington Press. 2012, pp211-237.

Gill, W. J. *The River of Golden Sand: Being the Narrative of a Journey Through China and Eastern Tibet to Burmah*. London: John Murray. 1883.

Glover, Archibald. *1000 Miles of Miracle*. Christian Focus. 2001.

Glover, Denise. M., Stevan Harrell, Charles F. McKhann, Margaret Byrne Swain. *Explorers and Scientists in China's Borderlands, 1880-1950*. University of Washington Press. 2012.

Gottschall, Terrence D. *By Order of the Kaiser: Otto Von Diederichs and the Rise of the Imperial German Navy, 1865-1902*. Naval Institute Press. 2003.

Graham, David Crockett. *The Customs and Religion of the Ch'iang*. Smithsonian Miscellaneous Collections. 135 (1):1-110. 1958.

    Folk Religion in Southwest China. The Smithsonian Institute. 1961.

Grattan Guinness, Henry and Fanny. *Light for the Last Days: A Study in Chronological Prophecy*. Hodder & Stoughton. 1888.

Haines-Watson, W. C. 'Journey to Sungp'an'. *Journal of the North-China Branch of the Royal Asiatic Society*, Vol 36, 1905, pp51-102.

Halkin, Hillel. *Across the Sabbath River: In Search of a Lost Tribe of Israel*. Houghton Mifflin Company. 2002.

Han Suyin. *The Crippled Tree*. Triad/Panther Books. 1984.

He Siqiang and Jiang Bin. *Qiangzu: Sichuan Wenchuanxian A'ercun diaocha* (The Qiang People: A Survey of A'er Village in Wenchuan County, Sichuan). Yunnan daxue chubanshe. 2004.

He Yimin. 'Sichuan Province Reforms under Governor-General Xiliang, 1903-1907'. *Chinese Studies in History*, 28:3-4, pp136-156. In Douglas R. Reynolds. *China, 1895-1912: State-sponsored Reforms and China's Late-Qing Revolution: Selected Essays from Zhongguo Jindai Shi (Modern Chinese History, 1840-1919)*. M. E. Sharpe. 1995.

Headland, Isaac T. *Court Life In China: The Capital Its Officials And People*. Revell, New York. 1909.

Herodotus. *Histories*. (Ed. Tom Griffith.) Wordsworth Editions Limited. 1996.

Hesselink, John I. 'A Pilgrimage in the School of Christ - An Interview With T. F. Torrance'. *Reformed Review 38*, 1984.

Hsu, Immanuel. *The Rise of Modern China*. Oxford University Press. 1983.

Huang Peiqiao (compiler). *Xizang tukao* (An Illustrated Research Report on Tibet). 1885-86.

Hutchings, Graham. *Modern China: A Guide to a Century of Change*. Harvard University Press. 2003.

Jordan, Donald. A. *The Northern Expedition: China's National Revolution of 1926-1928*. University of Hawaii Press. 1976.

Judge, Joan. *Print and Politics: 'Shibao' and the Culture of Reform in Late Qing China*. Stanford University Press. 1997.

Jung Chang. *Empress Dowager Cixi: The Concubine Who Launched Modern China*. Vintage Publishing. Kindle Edition.

Jung Chang and J. Halliday. *Mao: The Unknown Story*. Vintage Publishing. 2007.

Junio, Diana. *Patriotic Cooperation: The Border Services of the Church of Christ in China and Chinese Church–State Relations, 1920s–1950s*. Leiden: Brill. 2017.

Kang Xiaofei and Donald S. Sutton. *Contesting the Yellow Dragon: Ethnicity, Religion, and the State in the Sino-Tibetan Borderland*. Brill. 2016.

Kapp, Robert A. *Szechwan and the Chinese Republic: Provincial Militarism and Central Power, 1911–1938*. Yale University Press. 1973.

Knightley, Phillip. 'Reverse Discrimination'. *London Review of Books*. Vol 10, No 10, May 19, 1988.

Kyong-McClain, Jeff. 'Making Chengdu "The Kingdom of God as Jesus Conceived It": The Urban Work of West China Union University's Sociology Department'. *Social Sciences and Missions* 23, 2010, pp162–186.

Lawergren, Bo. 'Angular harps Through the Ages; a Causal History'. In *Studien zur Musikarchäologie* VI, Orient-Archäologie 22. Rahden, 2008, pp261-281.

'Harps on the Ancient Silk Road'. In *Conservation of Ancient Sites on the Silk Road*. Neville Agnew (ed). Getty Conservation Institute; 2 edition, Aug 3, 2010, pp117-124.

Levi-Strauss, Claude. *Structural Anthropology*, 1963. Basic Books, Inc.

Li Jieren. 'Weicheng zhuiyi' (Memoirs of an Endangered City). Originally published in *Xin Zhonghua* 5, nos. 1-6 (1937). Reprinted in Vol 5 of *Li Jieren Xuanji* (Selected Works), pp96-148. Chengdu: Sichuan Renmin Chubanshe, 1986b.

    Ripples Across Stagnant Water. Panda Books. 1990.

Lin Hsiao-ting. 'Making Known the Unknown World: Ethnicity, Religion and Political Manipulations in 1930s Southwest China'. *American Journal of Chinese Studies* 13, no. 2, 2006.

Liu Biyun. 'From Kinship to State and Back Again'. In J. Wilkerson and R. Parkin (eds), *Modalities of Change: The Interface of Tradition and Modernity in East Asia*. Berghahn Books. 2013.

Liu Chaoyang, 'On the Conquering of Ch'iang Fang by Emperor Hsiao I'. In *Studia Serica*, (Journal of the Chinese Cultural Studies Research Institute, West China Union University), Vol 5, 1946.

Lu Ding. *Qiangzu lishi wenhua yanjiu* (A Study of Qiang Historical Culture). Sichuan renmin chubanshe. 2000.

Ma Xuanwei and Xiao Bo. *Yang Sen*. Chengdu: Sichuan renmin chubanshe. 1989.

Mao Zedong and Stuart R. Schram. *Mao's Road to Power - Revolutionary Writings, 1912-1949: Toward the Second United Front. January 1935-July 1937*. Vol 5. M. E. Sharpe. 1992.

Marshall, Harry I. 'The Karen People of Burma: A Study in Anthropology and Ethnology'. *The Ohio State University Bulletin*, Vol 26. University at Columbus. 1922.

Matthews, James J. *The Union Jack on the Upper Yangzi: The Treaty Port of Chongqing, 1891-1943*. Unpublished PhD thesis. York University, Toronto, Ontario. 1999.

McGrath, Alister E. *T. F. Torrance: An Intellectual Biography*. Edinburgh: T&T Clark. 1999.

McKhann, Charles F. and Alan Waxman. 'David Crockett Graham: American Missionary and Scientist in Sichuan, 1911-1948'. In D. M. Glover et al. *Explorers and Scientists in China's Borderlands, 1880-1950*. University of Washington Press. 2012.

Meakin, Rachel E. 'Qiang 羌 References in the Book of Han 汉书, Part 1.' (www.academia.edu)

    'Qiang 羌 References in the Book of Han 汉书, Part 2.' (www.academia.edu)

James Neave. 'The Hill Tribes of China'. Chapter 9 in *Our Share in China* by George J. Bond. Toronto: Missionary Society of the Methodist Church, Young People's Forward Movement Dept. 1909.

Ng, Kenny Kwok-kwan. *The Lost Geopoetic Horizon of Li Jieren: The Crisis of Writing Chengdu in Revolutionary China*. Leiden: Brill. 2015.

Parfitt, Tudor. *The Thirteenth Gate - Travels Among the Lost Tribes of Israel*. London: Weidenfeld and Nicolson. 1987.

      The Lost Tribes of Israel: The History of a Myth. Weidenfeld & Nicolson. 2002.

P'iankov, Igor V. 'The Ethnic History of the Sakas'. *Bulletin of the Asia Institute*, Vol 8, 1994, pp37-46.

Pruen, Kate. *The Provinces of Western China*. Alfred Holness, London; R. L. Allan & Son, Glasgow. 1906.

Ran Guangrong et al. *Qiangzushi* (The History of the Qiang Nationality). Sichuan minzu chubanshe. 1984.

Ren Naiqiang. *Qiangzu yuanliu tansuo* (Exploring the Origin of the Qiang Nationality). Chongqing chubanshe. 1984.

Rock, Joseph. 'The Land of the Tebbus'. *The Geographical Journal*, Vol 81, no.2, Feb 1933, pp 108-127.

Rodriguez, Andres. 'Nationalism and Internationalism on the borders: The West China Union University Museum of Archaeology and Ethnology (1914-51)'. *Museum History Journal*. 2016.

Ross, John. *The Original Religion of China*. Oliphant, Anderson & Ferrier. 1909.

Saich, Tony and Benjamin Yang. *The Rise to Power of the Chinese Communist Party: Documents and Analysis*. Routledge. 2016.

Salisbury, Harrison E. *The Long March: The Untold Story*. Pan Books Ltd. 1986.

Scott, Margaret I. 'A Study of the Ch'iang with Special Reference to their Settlements in China from the Second to the Fifth Century A. D.' (Unpublished PhD thesis.) Newnham College, Cambridge. 1952.

Seligman, C. G. 'The Roman Orient and the Far East'. *Antiquity*, Volume 11, Issue 41, March 1937, pp5-30.

Seligman, C. G. and H. C. Beck. 'Far Eastern Glass: Some Western Origins'. *Bulletin of Museum of Far Eastern Antiquities* 10, pp1-64, Stockholm, 1938.

Song Ling (©). *Landslide damming in Western Sichuan Province, China, with special reference to the 1786 Dadu River and 1933 Diexi events*. Unpublished MSc thesis, University of Waterloo. 2015.

Song Xiping. 'Qiang di he Zummara yinyue bijiao' (A Comparison of the Music of the Qiang Flute and the Zummara). In Long Zhenxu, Lin Chuan (eds). *Qingxi Erma: shoujie Zhongguo Qiangzu feiwuzhi wenhua yichang yu zaihou chongjian yanjiuhui lunwenji*. Lanzhou daxue chubanshe. 2011, pp90-99.

Stapleton, Kristin. *Civilizing Chengdu*. Harvard University Asia Center. 2000.

Fact in Fiction: 1920s China and Ba Jin's Family. Stanford University Press. 2016. Kindle Edition.

Sun Hongkai (ed). *Qiangyu jianzhi* (A Brief Description of the Qiang Language). Beijing: minzu chubanshe. 1981.

Sun Shuyun. *The Long March*. HarperCollins Publishers. Kindle Edition.

Tian Lijun. '1935-1936 nian guogong neizhan yu chuan xibei tusi (guan) de zhenzhi taidu' (The Nationalist-Communist Conflict of 1935-1936 and the Political Attitude of NW Sichuan's Headmen). *Xinan minzu daxue xuebao*. Renwen shehui kexue ban. 2011, no. 2, pp211-219.

Torrance, Annie, E. *Memoirs*. Unpublished, c.1977-79.

Torrance, David W. *The Reluctant Minister*. Handsel Press. 2015.

Torrance, Thomas. *The Early History of Chengtu: from the Chou to the close of the Shuh Han Dynasty*. Canadian Methodist Mission Press. 1916.

   Conversion Stories of Chinese Christians, (unpublished). https://tftorrance.org/tt-1935-1

   The History, Customs and Religion of the Ch'iang. The Shanghai Mercury. 1920.

   The Beatitudes and the Decalogue. Skeffington & Son, Paternoster House, London. 1921.

   China's First Missionaries: Ancient Israelites. Thynne & Co. Ltd. 1937.

   'The Survival of Old Testament Religious Customs Among the Chiang People of West China'. *Journal of the Transactions of The Victoria Institute or Philosophical Society of Great Britain*, Vol LXXI, 1939, pp100-116.

   'The Emigrations of the Jews: Israel in China'. *The Scottish Geographical Magazine*, Vol 56, May 1940, pp59-64.

   Expository Studies in St. John's Miracles. J. Clarke. 1938.

   China's First Missionaries, Ancient "Israelites". Daniel Shaw Co. 1988.

Tyzack, Charles. *Nearly a Chinese: A Life of Clifford Stubbs*. Book Guild Publishing. 2013. Kindle Edition.

Wagner, Donald B. 'The Earliest Use of Iron in China'. In Suzanne M. M. Young et al (eds), *Metals in Antiquity*. (BAR international series, 792), Oxford: Archaeopress. 1999, pp.1-9.

Walravens, H. (ed). *David Crockett Graham (1884-1961) as Zoological Collector and Anthropologist in China*. Opera Sinologica documenta 1. Weisbaden: Harrassowitz Verlag. 2006.

Wang Mingke. *Qiang zai Han Zang zhijian – Chuanxi Qiangzu de lishi renleixue yanjiu* (The Qiang Between the Han and the Tibetans - a Historical and Anthropological Study of the Qiang of Western Sichuan). Zhonghua shuju. 2008.

'From the Qiang Barbarians to the Qiang Nationality: the Making of a New Chinese Boundary'. In Shu-min Huang & Cheng-kuang Hsu (eds). *Imagining China: Regional Division and National Unity*. Taipei: Institute of Ethnology. 1999, pp43-80.

Watson, Burton. *Records of the Grand Historian of China. Translated from the Shiji of Sima Qian*. Vol II. Columbia University Press. 1961.

Wertmann, Patrick. 'No borders for innovations: A ca. 2700-year-old Assyrian-style leather scale armour in Northwest China'. In *Quaternary International*, https://doi.org/10.1016/j.quaint.2021.11.014.

Westad, Odd Arne. *Restless Empire: China and the World since 1750*. The Bodley Head. 2012.

Wilson, Ernest. H. *A Naturalist in Western China*, Vol 1. London: Methuen & Co. 1913.

Wolff, Joseph. *Narrative of a Mission to Bokhara: In the Years 1843-1845, to Ascertain the Fate of Colonel Stoddart and Captain Conolly*. Vol 1. Harper & Brothers. 1845.

Xu Guoqi. *China and the Great War: China's Pursuit of a New National Identity and Internationalization*. Cambridge University Press. 2005.

Xu Xiangqian. *Lishi de Huigu* (A Look Back at History). Jiefangjun chubanshe. 1988.

Yamamoto, T. and S. 'The Anti-Christian Movement in China, 1922-1927'. *The Far Eastern Quarterly*, Vol 12, No 2, Feb 1953, pp133-147.

Yan Lu. *Re-understanding Japan: Chinese Perspectives, 1895-1945*. University of Hawaii Press. 2004.

Ye Xingguang. *Shen shan, shen shu, shen lin* (Sacred Mountain, Sacred Tree, Sacred Grove). Sichuan minzu chubanshe. 1999.

Zhang Qiaoyun. 'Heritage making after the earthquake. Safeguarding the intangible heritage of the Qiang people in China'. International Institute for Asian Studies. The Newsletter 80, Summer 2018.

Other publications cited in the footnotes:

Bianjiang Fuwu. Journal of the Border Services Department.

Bible Society Record. Published by the American Bible Society.

China's Millions. Published by the China Inland Mission.

The China Press.

The Chinese Recorder and Missionary Journal. Published by the American Presbyterian Mission Press.

Journal of the North-China Branch of the Royal Asiatic Society.

Journal of the West China Border Research Society.

Man. Published by the Royal Anthropological Institute of Great Britain and Ireland.

The North China Daily News.

West China Missionary News. Published by the West China Missions Advisory Board.

Index

Confucianism 16-18, 41, 56, 98, 206
Creel, Herrlee G. 384-385, 414
Cuqiao 238

D

Dai Kan 84, 88-91
Danling 19, 29, 33, 41, 95, 100
Daoism 113, 164, 205-206
Daping 270, 327
Datong 27
Dayi 82
Deng Juezhang 258
Deng Weihan 346
Deng Xiaoping 404
Deng Xihou 183, 194-195, 206, 211, 215, 217, 221-222, 224-225, 226-227, 244-245, 253, 258, 262, 280-281, 297, 307, 311-312, 330, 333, 341-342, 347, 349, 404, 418
Depression, Great 259-260, 299
Dewey, John 135
Di people 137, 141, 149
Diao, Daniel 194, 226, 260, 274, 302, 330, 334, 417
Diaohua 130, 131
Dickinson, Frank 246, 332
Diebu 279
Diexi 250-251, 265, 296, 300, 317-318, 344
Ding Si 315, 317, 319
Dongmenwai 132, 158, 164-165, 180, 200, 212, 213, 231-232, 244, 269, 291-293, 304-309, 320-323, 376, 404-405, 409, 417
Donnithorne, Vyvyan and Gladys 238-240, 309
Doodha, Kaoroz 90, 336
Duan Qirui 89, 171
duangong 175, 392, 398-399
Dujiangyan. *See* Guanxian

Dye, Daniel Sheets 192, 196, 222, 262-263, 340, 373, 376
dysentery 53, 79, 158, 233, 245, 247, 254, 334, 347

E

earthquake 58, 78, 92, 199, 320
1933 Diexi 296-298, 300-301, 316-319
2008 Wenchuan v, 412-413
Edgar, James Huston 102, 106-108, 127, 138, 140-141, 152, 156, 163, 225, 276, 295, 385
Edinburgh 56, 57, 259, 339-340, 419
Eger, Karl 282
Erwa 112-113, 164, 217, 233, 294, 323-324, 350
Esdras, book of 359, 412
Evans-Pritchard, Edward 365
extraterritorial (privileges, rights) 5, 170, 178, 260, 262

F

Fan Wenhai 374
feng shui 24, 56
Feng Yuxiang 191
Fergusson, William 42, 105-106, 112
Finn, James 368, 387
Fitch, Robert 108
Fleming, William 19
folk religion 113, 307, 315, 379, 398
footbinding 37, 160, 249
Foster, Arnold 22
France 5, 8-9, 15, 22, 97
Franck, George 38, 41, 43, 48, 55, 179, 196, 202, 209, 243, 262, 284, 306, 329, 333
Freedman, Maurice 388-389
Fu Anlan 162
Fujian 69